A Select History of

# MATHEWS COUNTY VIRGINIA

17th, 18th, & 19th Centuries and

the Family of Robert and Ann Hall

CONRAD MERCER HALL

2020

This is a work of history and original research. Every effort has been made to record original historical facts accurately and to fully provide sources.

Library of Congress Control Number: 2019911956

Art direction by Katherine Jordan and graphic design by Anthony Nesossis

Published by Dementi Milestone Publishing, Richmond, VA

Endpapers: From the US Register of Vessels. The image shows, from left, a schooner, a ship, a sloop, a brig, and a lighthouse. Courtesy of the National Archives, Washington, DC.

ISBN: 978-1-7330268-3-3

Manufactured in the United States of America

10 9 8 7 6 5 4 3 2 1

In memory of

my dear wife of nearly fifty years,

Margaret Moore Hall,

and in memory of my mother and father,

Elsie Mercer and Otey Williams Hall,

and to the people of Mathews County, Virginia,

generations past, present, and future

# Contents

# Illustrations

# Tables

*Figure* 1 A section of Mathews Courthouse, known as Westville prior to the mid-1800s, in an 1894 photograph. The view is looking east from Church Hill and includes the courthouse (left of center), the old debtors' jail (right), and the Mathews jail (far right). Courtesy of the Mathews Memorial Library.

# PREFACE

This book is the result of my efforts to learn about the Hall family's history, an inquiry that began in 1970. Over a period of almost fifty years and many hours spent in the courthouses of Middlesex, Gloucester, and Mathews Counties in Virginia and in the invaluable depositories of historical records in libraries, the history of my family gradually unfolded. As the basic research involving census records, land transfers, marriages, births, and deaths proceeded, entirely new topics became points of interest, such as military service; occupations; significant events including wars, natural disasters, and economic dislocations; farming methods and crops; trade practices; and many more. Exploring these topics, as they affected each generation of ancestors, created an understanding of certain aspects and periods of the life and times of my family, information that goes far beyond basic genealogical fact gathering.

And thus it became a personal goal that the research conducted over many years and the resulting findings and analysis needed to be shared. Originally, family members now and new ones yet to be born were foremost in mind in planning this book. But as my research expanded, my intended audience became also those who share an interest in the history, especially that of Mathews County, of the years following the settlement at Jamestown and concluding with the eve of the American Civil War, a span of some 250 years.

What follows is a selected history of the seventeenth, eighteenth, and nineteenth centuries centered in what is now known as Mathews County, Virginia, which was created by an act of Virginia's General Assembly in 1790, which became effective on May 1, 1791. The area was previously part of Gloucester County and known as Kingston Parish, Gloucester County, Virginia. The story, for the most part, is centered on a small geographical area south of the Mathews courthouse on the east side of the East River, an important neighborhood in the development of the county and in the life of the Hall family for many generations. The principal focus of the genealogical history is on my great-great-great-great-great-grandfather Robert Hall, born circa 1730, and his descendants.

# INTRODUCTION

Mathews County suffered the tragic loss of its court records in 1865 when a large area of Richmond, Virginia, approximately thirty-five city blocks, was burned by Confederate forces as the Union army advanced to capture the city. The records had been moved to Richmond for safekeeping, as was the case for a number of other Virginia counties. Duplicates did not exist for the vast majority of the records, and thus historians attempting to research Mathews County before 1865 have only a very small number of land records, court proceedings, and most of the other records typically kept by the county court. Further adding to the challenge of finding original source documents was a devastating fire in the Gloucester County Courthouse in 1820, which destroyed most of the documents of Abingdon, Petsworth, Ware, and Kingston Parishes since March 21, 1651. Surviving parish documents, in some instances, are often in poor condition with fading ink and missing and torn pages. Thus it is remarkable that researchers have sufficient surviving records to achieve an understanding of the history of early Gloucester and Mathews Counties. Research in a county such as Middlesex where the surviving records extend to the very beginning offers a smoother path.

Fortunately, a number of census records for Mathews County survive in Washington, D.C. Also in Washington are Revolutionary War pension applications and bounty land warrants, as well as ship certifications made by the port captains of the East River. The Kingston Parish register and the vestry book survive as well as a number of court fee books, merchant ledger books, and family papers, especially those of the Billups, Tomkins, and Patterson families. For the earliest years, those during which the county was first settled, remarkably the original land patents, or copies, survive. Their value is enormous in any attempt to describe the county in the seventeenth century. Beginning in 1736, newspaper reports and advertisements offer additional understanding. I had wonderful good luck in finding Revolutionary War pension applications of members of my family, copies of land survey boundary descriptions, and ship certifications as well as numerous mentions in the Kingston and Petsworth Parish registers.

In an effort to provide the reader with an understanding of Virginia history, the book begins with a look at the earliest days beginning in Jamestown, followed by early settlement patterns and the reasons young immigrants ventured across the Atlantic Ocean and risked their future in an unknown land as well as the motivations for the merchants, land patentees, ship captains, and others. In particular is an analysis of the settlement of Kingston Parish, numbers of settlers, land acquired, and demographics of the first immigrants. Life, the economy, farming, and the work of the church follow through the second half of the seventeenth century and through the eighteenth century.

The emergence of the earliest members of the Hall family began in the seventeenth century, and the book follows their progress until the Civil War. Men and women of Kingston Parish during the Revolutionary War were in proximity to enemy activity, and men of the parish served in the local militia and in the Virginia State Navy. The book explores their activity and the ever-present British navy off the coast of Cape Henry to the upper reaches of the Chesapeake Bay.

The lives and activities of members of the Hall family are woven into the historical record, including shipbuilding, land transactions, the slave trade, and military service. As the years progressed, some members of the family moved to other parts of the country including Salem, Massachusetts; Middlesex County, Virginia; and Portsmouth, Virginia. But even today many of them continue to make Mathews their home.

# ACKNOWLEDGMENTS

I am indebted to the courthouse clerks of long ago who recorded land patents, deeds, tax collections, fines, fees, and proceedings of the courts; to the clerks of colonial churches and vestries for recording births, marriages, deaths, and the activities of the vestry; and to the surveyors who left behind invaluable information on land ownership, boundaries, and the locations of structures. The officers of the decks of British warships during the American Revolutionary War stationed in the Chesapeake Bay and off the Virginia capes recorded eyewitness accounts of significant events in Virginia waters in their logbooks. The reporters and advertisers of Virginia's early eighteenth-century newspapers, who wrote with remarkable accuracy and clarity, added immeasurably to the narrative. This book is the result of the written record they left behind, a priceless legacy.

This book would never have been completed in its current form without the invaluable assistance and partnership of Sandra Hall Diggs, my cousin and a native and resident of Mathews County. Her remarkable research skills and her dedication to meticulously recording original records, honed by years of experience in the legal profession, enabled the discovery and interpretation of invaluable facts from long ago. Her familiarity with the historical archives in Virginia's libraries and the National Archives and her established friendships with local county clerks added a rigor and efficiency to the essential task of research. Her efforts to explore every possible record before making a factual determination added immeasurably to the historical accuracy and usefulness of the book as a source for others. She and I spent many hours searching courthouse and library records, walking over fields and along hedgerows and ditch banks, studying ancient surveys and deeds, and participating in digging and sifting soil in archaeological surveys. We exchanged hundreds of messages over a period of five years. I am most grateful that she shared a similar interest with me in making what we discovered available to others.

The many people encountered in this project were remarkable in their helpfulness, and I am grateful for their assistance. I especially appreciate the time and guidance of Angela D. Shoe, clerk of the Court of Mathews County; Frances S. Pollard, former vice president for Research Services, now retired, and John Mark McClure, director of Library and Research, of the Virginia Historical Society; and Katie McKinney, assistant curator of prints and maps at the Colonial Williamsburg Foundation. The staffs at the Earl Gregg Swem Library at the College of William & Mary, Williamsburg, Virginia; the Slover Library in

Norfolk, Virginia; the Massachusetts Archives in Boston; and the John D. Rockefeller Jr. Library of the Colonial Williamsburg Foundation were unfailingly helpful. The staff at the National Archives were remarkably responsive regarding numerous requests for record retrievals submitted over several years.

This book would never have been published without the extraordinary talents of my editor, Amy Watson. She had the special patience required to work with a first-time book author and applied the extra scrutiny required for a manuscript dense with historical facts and statistical analysis. Her extensive experience in editing historical works and numerous suggestions and creative ideas added immeasurably to the finished manuscript. It was a pleasure and wonderful learning experience to have worked with her. I am also grateful to Margaret B. Pritchard, deputy chief curator of the Colonial Williamsburg Foundation, for her encouragement, for her advice on historic maps, and for introducing Amy Watson to my project.

Lastly, my family encouraged me: They excused my many absences while writing, visiting centers of research, and exploring the countrysides of Mathews, Gloucester, and Middlesex Counties of Virginia; they tolerated my lengthy preoccupation towards writing this book; and without their support the project would have been abandoned long ago. My wife, Peggy, was especially supportive, and my sons, Cosby and Mercer, reviewed early drafts and offered invaluable edits and suggestions.

# CHAPTER 1

# Events prior *to the* Establishment *of* Gloucester County, Virginia

As the ebb tide commenced at Jamestown Island, Virginia, on the second day of June 1608, John Smith, a member of the London Company, and his crew of fourteen men cast off in a shallop* to voyage down the James River to begin exploration of the Chesapeake Bay. His mission was to map the bay, identify Indian tribes, assess their strength in number of warriors, determine their inventories of corn, learn their language, and develop a dictionary for translation to English. His crew included a medical doctor, a tailor, a blacksmith, a fisherman, a fish merchant for identifying edible fish, a carpenter, six gentlemen, and three soldiers/seamen. This was a large crew for the size of his vessel and an ambitious undertaking, challenged by summer weather conditions, occasional hostile actions by the natives, the discomfort of living in an open boat, and the complexity of the mission itself.

June 2, 1608, equates to June 14 on the modern calendar,† a day in 1608 that had a new moon and thus stronger tidal currents than average. On the same day, the supply ship *Phoenix* sailed for England, and it is thought that the ship towed the shallop down the James River. In any case they made good time because they arrived off Lynnhaven Roads, just west of Cape Henry, that night having covered a distance of approximately forty-eight miles. The next day Smith turned northward along the west coast of the Eastern Shore—the start of a remarkable voyage of exploration of the Chesapeake Bay.

* The Jamestown shallop was an open boat, believed to have been approximately thirty feet in length, and propelled by oars and sail. An awning provided protection from the elements. The shallop was brought from England in sections and assembled after making landfall in Virginia.

† The English adopted the Gregorian calendar on Wednesday, September 2, 1752. The next day was Thursday, September 14, 1752. January 1, 1753, became the first day of the year replacing "Lady Day," March 25. Dates referenced in this book follow this convention.

The *Phoenix* was part of the first supply mission to Jamestown and had departed Gravesend, England, on October 18, 1607, under the command of Francis Nelson. Included in the fleet was the *John & Francis*, commanded by Christopher Newport, who was also the fleet captain. The *John & Francis* arrived in Jamestown on January 12, 1608; however, the *Phoenix* was blown off course, failed to find the Chesapeake Bay entrance, and spent January through March in the West Indies. She finally arrived at Jamestown on April 20, 1608.

On July 21 Smith's expedition, after forty-nine days, returned to Jamestown having explored a large territory, including parts of the Eastern Shore, Calvert Cliffs to the Patapsco River, and the Potomac River as far inland as present-day Washington, D.C. He had sailed and rowed the barge approximately 1,079 miles and had walked and traveled by canoe another 244 miles. He identified approximately fifteen Indian tribes and collected data sufficient to begin the creation of a map.

Smith's surveying and navigation instruments and his methods of recording measurements and determining distances are not known, but he likely had the standard instruments of the day: a compass for determining direction, a quadrant and/or backstaff for measuring the altitude of the sun and the North Star (for calculating latitude), an almanac, and a thirty-second (or similar) hourglass, which he would have used to estimate his speed for calculating east-west distances. He or someone else in his crew was obviously proficient in coastal navigation and the science of mapmaking.

Smith would have been able to calculate north-south distances with some accuracy when he had the right conditions for determining latitude. However, dead reckoning, using elapsed time and average speed, would have been the only means of estimating east-west distances. He likely began sketching a map, probably in a blank bound book, by drawing lines of latitude, as latitude was what he could measure with the greatest degree of accuracy. He also must have maintained a detailed diary of his day-to-day progress and observations.

On his return southward on the west side of the bay, on the morning of July 17, the shallop ran aground on sandbars at a point of land separating the mouths of the Piankatank and Rappahannock Rivers near the time of low tide. While waiting for the tide to rise, the crew fished with their swords in the shallow waters. It was here that a cow-nose ray stung Smith. The poison nearly killed him, and Smith memorialized the incident by naming the place Stingray Point.

On April 21, 1846, 237 years after Smith's encounter with the stingray, the author's great-great-grandfather Thomas Spencer Hall acquired Stingray Point Farm from John J. Burke for five hundred dollars and sold it the next year, on July 31, 1847, to Anthony D. Hudgins for seven hundred dollars.[1] The farm contained 105 acres, with its southeastern boundary being the Chesapeake Bay and the entrance to the Piankatank River—the approximate location of the event that would have drastically changed the outcome of Jamestown, and Virginia, if Smith had died. Shore erosion has reduced the eastward extension of the point, and thus the original location of the landing by Smith and his crew is believed to have been lost to the elements.

After resting at Jamestown for just three days, he set out again on July 24 to explore certain parts of the bay in more detail, particularly the upper reaches of the Rappahannock River. On this second voyage, he was accompanied by twelve men. On his return down the western shore, he explored the Rappahannock River to present-day Fredericksburg and then the Piankatank River as far inland as the Dragon Run, a swampy stream.

Opposite Stingray Point, on the south side of the Piankatank, lies Gwynn's Island, now part of Mathews County. Smith would continue his passage on September 3 by sailing

*Figure* 2 John Smith's map of the Chesapeake Bay, first published in 1612, depicts the territory under the control of Powhatan with a warrior/hunter to the right and Powhatan's court in the upper left. The northern direction is to the right, presenting the coastline as ships would see it. The map shown was published in 1636 and is from the author's collection.

southward, passing the island and the present-day Mathews County shoreline. His map shows a crude representation of present-day Mobjack Bay and a suggestion of the East River but not the Ware, Severn, and North Rivers. He probably sailed a few miles into the bay because his map indicates deep water at the entrance and thus he took soundings to determine depth.

In addition to naming Stingray Point, which is in Middlesex County, he gave names to three features in Gloucester County: "Tindals Poynt," now known as Gloucester Point; "Wiffins Poynt," which is the east end of Guinea Neck with Hog Island at its southeastern end; and "Poynt Warde," which is present-day New Point Comfort. The area between New Point Comfort and the Poquoson River to the south was given the name "Gosnolds Baye," named for Bartholomew Gosnold, second-in-command of the first fleet to Jamestown and one whom Smith admired.

*Figure* 3 An enlarged section of John Smith's map of the Chesapeake Bay showing present-day Mathews County. Arrows (added) indicate the Piankatank, York, and James Rivers, Gloucester Point, Stingray Point, Gwynn's Island, East River, Mobjack Bay, Guinea Neck, New Point Comfort, and Old Point Comfort. From the author's collection.

Smith seems to have been remarkably observant in identifying important landmarks that would become constants for future navigation and, in the case of Tindals Point, a deepwater location that would become important for trade and the site of Gloucester Town. In a sense, Mathews County, as a landmass, was discovered on that day in that his survey was the first recording of its existence and partial configuration by the English. Smith and his crew returned to Jamestown on September 7 having logged approximately 1,143 miles by barge, by canoe, and on foot.

After having traveled for a total of ninety-four days over 2,466 miles on the bay in two voyages, Smith and his crew must have become keenly aware of the enormous economic potential of the Chesapeake Bay region and its unusual advantages for settlement. He was most certainly aware of the vast expanse of land available, the remarkable network of rivers for the efficient transportation of cargo, and the temperate climate, one most conducive to crops and husbandry.

At the age of twenty-eight, Capt. John Smith was elected president of the Jamestown governing council in September 1608 but would return to England the following year to recover from a severe burn. While he later returned to North America, to the coasts of Massachusetts and Maine, in 1614, he was never again to visit Virginia. However, his interest in the colony continued, and in 1612 he published *A Map of Virginia* and *The Proceedings of the English Colony in Virginia*, which included the now famous Smith map of the territory he had explored. The map was useful to subsequent immigrants and would not be significantly improved on until the publication in 1673 of the Augustine Herrman map of Virginia.

The challenges and setbacks of the London Company in establishing a secure settlement in Virginia are well-known, especially the high rate of mortality. For example, between 1619 and 1621, some 3,570 people were sent to the colony to join the 700 who had survived disease and other hardships for a total of 4,270, but death and persons returning to England had reduced the population to approximately 1,240 by 1621.

The Indians were observant of the large increase in immigrants, the expansion of their landholdings, and the beginnings of a successful crop, tobacco. At the same time, they were certainly aware of the distress in the settlements, primarily due to a lack of food and essential supplies. In an attempt to regain their dominance and to discourage further settlement, they decided to destroy as much of the English presence as possible. On the morning of March 22, 1621, in a well-coordinated and executed attack, warriors of Opechancanough massacred, 347 of the 1,240 settlers, including women and children, as well as large numbers of cattle. Opechancanough was the brother of Powhatan, who was the chief of approximately thirty tribes of Indians who occupied Tidewater Virginia.

The news of the massacre and lingering discord among the administrators and shareholders of the London Company prompted a review by the king's Privy Council of the event and the lack of progress in developing a strong English presence in Virginia. England was also concerned about Spanish and French intentions for expanding their holdings in the New World. In short order the Privy Council recommended to King James I that the London Company's charter be withdrawn and that all of its holdings in Virginia be transferred into the newly created royal colony of Virginia. The courts approved the decision on June 26, 1624.

King James ordered a head count, which was compiled during January and February 1625. The total of 1,220 people included 487 servants, most of whom had been born in England, and 23 Africans, whose initial legal status may have been more akin to indentured servants than to slaves. These were all that remained from the approximately 7,200 people who had immigrated to Virginia between 1607 and 1624. The loss of settlers was staggering, numbering 5,980 in just seventeen years, 83 percent of the original immigrants. Most died in Virginia with some having returned to England.

In spite of this tragic setback, a period of increased immigration followed. The expansion was the result of greater public awareness of the availability of land, incentives to immigrate, and an aggressive strategy to destroy the Indian presence in the area bounded by the James River to the south, the York River to the north, and on the west by the fall line, the transition from the tidewater to the piedmont.

The London Company had developed a creative strategy for encouraging immigration to the New World, and the Privy Council reaffirmed it when the royal colony was created. "Planters," immigrants who went on to be dwellers, and "adventurers" those who did not necessarily travel to Virginia but who paid the passage of those who did, were entitled to land under what became known as the land patent system.

It was simple, easy to understand, and effective. It provided a grant for each person transported, the "headright," of fifty acres of land to anyone who paid ocean passage for himself and/or others, without limit to the number, provided that the land be "seated," the requirement being the erection of a dwelling and the planting of a crop or establishment of livestock. The requirement specified that the seating had to occur within three years of the award of the land patent in order to obtain a title; otherwise the land grant would become available to others.

Once the county clerk had proof that the cost of the passage had been paid, the patentee received the headright in the form of a certificate of importation. The patentee could sell the headright or choose a parcel of land and engage the county surveyor to ascertain that the parcel had not previously been patented and then measure the metes and bounds (compass bearings and distances) and prepare a survey. With the survey completed, together with the headright, the patentee submitted his claim to the royal governor or, more often, a county court for approval.

Surveyors in the colonial period used English methods and units of measurement. The basic unit of length was a pole, which was 16½ feet long, and at times a surveyor would actually use a wooden pole as a more efficient way of measuring lengths in dense overgrowth compared to a Gunter's chain, which equaled 4 poles, a length of 66 feet. A mile was equal to 320 poles. A furlong was equal to 40 poles, or 660 feet, this being the standard length of a furrow that a team of oxen could plow before being rested and turned around to plow in the opposite direction. The basic headright of 50 acres, for example, was equivalent to a rectangle measuring 320 poles, or one mile in length, and 25 poles, 412½ feet, in width. This helps to illustrate the size of even a modest patent of 300 acres: if one mile in length, it would have been 2,475 feet wide, equivalent to 150 poles or 46.9 percent of a mile. In England, in general terms, it was thought that 1.6 acres were required to support a cow or horse and 120 acres for a family.

For the ten years following the dissolution of the London Company in 1624, there was not much patent activity because of the uncertainty over the permanence of title in land. But in July 1634, the king's Privy Council granted rules that established the equivalent of fee simple title to lands granted and properly seated. As a result, a backlog of three hundred patents were awarded between the spring of 1635 and the end of 1636, representing more than two thousand headrights, equivalent to one hundred thousand acres.

Land patents were obtained by people with the financial means of mounting an expensive expedition that included the cost of ocean passage, typically between five and six pounds sterling, and food and clothing that would add an additional five to six pounds. The all-in cost was approximately equivalent to 2,400–2,880 pounds of tobacco, which was comparable to almost two years of labor for one person producing tobacco.

"Planters" often sponsored members of their families, friends, or indentured servants. "Adventurers" sponsored primarily indentured servants. An indentured servant sponsored by a planter might remain with the planter during his or her term of service, or the planter might sell the indentured servant's contract to another planter. Adventurers typically sold all of the servant contracts they sponsored. The procurement and trade in servants was diversified, with mariners accounting for 35 percent of all servant contracts, merchants 21 percent, and planters 9 percent. Over thirty-eight different trades made up the remaining 35 percent. The newly arrived servant most often had little or no control over where he or she would be employed after arrival in Virginia or by whom unless terms had been negotiated prior to departure from England.

The successful patentee could choose to seat his land, sell or lease a portion, or sell all of the acreage. The marketability of land and contracts for indentured servants were important parts of the economy, and the flexibility of such transactions greatly facilitated the expansion of the colony, allowing for unforeseen changes in the demand for exports, crop yields, labor, and the availability of land.

Most of the immigrants between 1635 and 1680, an estimated 70–85 percent, were white, English, indentured servants. Most were young, in their late teens and early twenties, and approximately 75 percent were male. There were also a few African indentured servants. Enslavement did not become common practice until after 1660. In the early years, most of the servants went into agricultural and husbandry occupations. However, many other trades were required, especially during the last thirty to forty years of the century, including blacksmiths, wheelwrights, carpenters, brickmakers, brick masons, shoemakers, shipwrights, millwrights, millers, clerks, surgeons, coopers, soap boilers, and others. The record of indentured servants departing from Bristol, England, lists sixty-six different trades.

Approximately half of the immigrants from London were from London and the immediate surrounding area, and the remainder were from all over England and Wales. Servants emigrating from Bristol were mostly from the surrounding region, with 87 percent coming from the West Country, South Wales, and the Severn Valley. Sixty percent came from within a radius of forty miles of the port. Half were from villages, 25 percent had lived in market towns, and the rest were from county towns or provincial capitals. There was no clustering of servants from any one particular community. But, as farmers and skilled workers, they primarily came from the productive segments of England, as Virginia planters needed people who could quickly contribute to the efficient running of their plantations. It seems that the primary motivation for a person to become an indentured servant bound for Virginia was the lack of employment opportunities at home and for many the hope of one day owning land, an achievement almost impossible in England unless by inheritance.

A young person without funds who wished to go to Virginia typically went to a merchant or planter's agent. Providing transportation and related items to immigrants was a lucrative business for merchants in Bristol, London, Liverpool, and the other ports trading with Virginia. An individual could also go directly to a ship's captain headed to the colonies, one having extra space for passengers, and negotiate terms. The merchant, planter's agent, or ship's captain typically provided the cost of passage and food and clothing before and during the voyage in return for an indenture, a contract for labor for a certain number of years, the standard being from four to seven.

The volume of servants from different ports in England was somewhat proportional to the number of ships sailing from them to Virginia for cargoes, especially for tobacco. An estimated 80 percent of servants sailed from London before 1640, but London's share dropped to about 60 percent by midcentury with Bristol's rise in the tobacco trade.

Another factor thought to have influenced the decision to immigrate to Virginia was the yield of English crops. During the 1630s, there was just one good harvest instead of the four typically realized in a decade. The year 1646 was the start of five years of poor harvests, and then another five years of disappointing harvests from 1657 to 1661. Poor harvests would have reduced the demand for farm labor as well as nonagricultural employment opportunities for the young people in the rural areas of England.

Only in very special cases did a planter travel to England to recruit a servant although it was not uncommon for an agent of the planter, located in an English port city, to supply a servant. On arrival, those servants who had been specifically recruited by a planter were taken to that planter's plantation while the indentures of all those remaining were sold on the deck of the ship or at dockside to the highest bidder. The new master as well as the servant each kept a copy of the indenture, and with that the newly arrived young person walked or was transported by small boat to his or her new home and place of employment. Those who arrived without an indenture tended to be younger, illiterate, and from more impoverished backgrounds. They comprised approximately 40 percent of total immigrant servants transported to Maryland during 1658–1705; Virginia probably had a similar percentage.

Indentured servants were subject to English common law and its protections, and male servants were expected to serve in the militia. On completing their term of service, they were free to go and to do whatever they wished. The opportunities for freed servants varied considerably, with more opportunity to acquire land in the early years of the colony but much reduced after 1655–1665 because by then most of the land in the settled counties was in the hands of the founding patentees. The choices in the Tidewater region after 1655 typically included moving west into the piedmont, at that time the frontier; renting land, working for wages, or becoming a sharecropper; or, with good fortune, marrying into the master's household.

Trade in indentured servants was an important component of the economies of the port cities of England and an absolute necessity to the Virginia planters. Merchants bargained to make a profit in selling indentures, and in some cases the headright would be part of the consideration, and it too could be sold.

A surprising number of immigrants were literate, as shown by a petition signed in support of the Commonwealth of England in Northumberland County, Virginia, in 1652. Of the one hundred men who signed, fifty-three signed their names in full and forty-seven signed with their mark. At the time probably less than 30 percent of the population in England in the rural north and west were literate and perhaps 40 percent near London. Clearly the immigrants held some educational advantages. Based on this petition and assuming that all of Virginia's planters could read and write, accounting for 30 percent of the population, then the remaining 70 percent, comprised of servants, had a literacy rate of 33 percent.

The term "indentured servant" described a condition of service similar to an apprenticeship, which was the primary way a young person learned a trade, a tradition that had been utilized in England for centuries. As used in colonial America, it further denoted a method of financing immigration. The term of service under the contract or indenture was usually between four and seven years in Virginia. A servant was not free to marry without the permission of the master but enjoyed most other rights under English law and custom. Former servants went on to become landowners, especially before 1660; others were often tenants, or sharecroppers. Some married into the master's family. On the termination of the indenture, many moved to newly opened counties to the west and north. Some returned to England. A detailed analysis of land patents granted in Kingston Parish, Gloucester County, Virginia, follows in chapter 2.

Following the increased awareness of the headright system and the rapid expansion of tobacco cultivation, the colony expanded from 1,220 persons in 1625 to an estimated 2,600 in 1629 to approximately 8,000 in 1640. However, civil wars in England during the first half of the 1640s reduced immigration considerably.

The population was further impacted during the 1640s by a second Indian massacre on April 16, 1644, which resulted in the deaths of 500 men, women, and children, reducing the population to approximately 7,500. Outlying settlements, especially south of the James River, were most affected. What followed was a two-year "war" that ended with the peace treaty of October 1646. Among other provisions, no Indian could enter any part of the peninsula lying below the falls of the York and James Rivers.

After the treaty of 1646, the Indian populations continued to dwindle in even greater numbers due to disease brought by the English and by Indians being forced to resettle from time to time to the west. The problem of safety from the Indians in Tidewater Virginia was no longer a chief concern, and by 1649 the population, with increased immigration, was estimated to be 15,000, mostly English and 300 Africans.

*A Perfect Description of Virginia*, a promotion piece perhaps somewhat exaggerated, published in 1649, offers a sense of the progress of the colony during the forty-two years following the first settlement at Jamestown. The subjects selected for mention give a sense of what potential immigrants would be most interested in:

> 1 That there are in *Virginia* about fifteene thousand *English*, and of *Negroes* brought thither, three hundred good servants.
>
> 2 That of *Kine, Oxen, Bulls, Calves,* twenty thousand, large and good, and they make plenty of Butter and very good Cheese.
>
> 3 That there are of an excellent raise, about two hundred *Horse* and *Mares.*
>
> 4 That of *Asses* for burthen and use, there is fifty but daily increase.
>
> 5 That for *Sheepe* they have about three thousand, good wooll.
>
> 6 That for *Goates* there number is five thousand, thrive well.
>
> 7 That for *Swine* both tame and wilde (in the Woods) innumerable; the flesh pure and good, and Bacon none better.
>
> 8 That for Poultry, *Hens, Turkies, Ducks, Geese,* without number.

The list of resources continues, including "*Six publike Brewhouses*," "thirty several sorts of *Fish,* River and Sea," "five and twenty sundry sorts of *Birds* and *Fowles*," "twenty kinde of Beasts," "fifteene kinds of *Fruits*," "five and twenty sorts of *Trees*, large, good and fit for Shipping, Housing, and other uses," and "4 Wind-mills, and *5* Water-mills to grind their Corn; besides many Horse-mills of several kinds, and Hand-mills for several uses."[2]

About maritime activities, the piece says, "There comes yearly to trade with them above 30 saile of ships, and in these not so little as seven or eight hundred Mariners employed, (some say above a thousand, this is a considerable thing) and they return laden home in *March.*" "Most of the Masters of ships and chief Mariners have also there Plantations, and houses, and servants, &c. in *Virginia*; and so are every way great gainers by Freight, by Merchandize, and by Plantation and Pipe-staves, Clap-board, choice Walnut-tree-wood, Ceadar-tree-timber and the like, is transported by them if Tobacco is not their full lading." "They have in their Colony Pinnaces, Barkes, great and small Boats many hundreds, for most of their Plantations stand upon the Rivers sides or up little Creeks, and but a small way into the Land so that for transportation and fishing they use many Boates."[3]

Where health and welfare were concerned:

> 38 That they have health very well, and fewer die in a year there, according to the proportion, then in any place of *England*; since that men are provided with all necessaries, have plenty of victual, bread, and good beer, and houseing, all which the Englishmen loves full dearly.
>
> 39 That the Passengers also come safe and well: the seamen of late years having found a way, that now in 5, 6, and 7 weeks they saile to *Virginia* free from all Rocks, Sands, and Pirats; and that they return home again in 20 dayes sometimes, and 30 at most: the Winds commonly serving more constantly, being Westerly homeward, the Easterly outward bound. . . .
>
> 43 That since the Massacree, the *Savages* have been driven far away, many destroyed of them, their Towns and houses ruinated, their cleer grounds possessed by the English to sow Wheat in: and their great King *Opechaukenow* (that bloody Monster upon 100 years old) was taken by *Sir William Berkely* the Governour.
>
> 44 All kinds of Trades-men may live well there, and do gaine much by their labours and arts, as Turners, Potters, Coopers; to make all kind of earthen and wooden Vessels, Sawyers, Carpenters, Tyle-makers, Boatwrights, Taylors, Shoemakers, Tanners, Fishermen, and the like.
>
> 45 Young youths from 16 yeers and upward, for Apprentises and Servants for some yeers, then to have Land given them, and Cattel to set them up. Thousands of these kinds of young boyes and maydens wanting.[4]

And the land:

> 52 The Countrey is with plesant rising small Ascents and Descents, Valleys, Hills, Meadowes, and some levell Upland: Its Woody all over, but where labour hath cleared the ground from Trees, and this truely is the great

> labour in *Virginia*, to fell Trees, and to get up the Roots, and so make cleare ground for the Plow. . . .

> We have many thousand of Acres of cleer Land, I mean where the wood is all off it (for you must know all *Virginia* is full of trees) and we have now going neer upon a hundred and fifty Plowers, with many brave yoak of Oxen, and we sowe excellent Wheat, Barley, Rye, Beans, Pease, Oates; and our increase is wonderful, and better Grain not in the world.[5]

The accounting continues with information concerning religion, laws, vineyards, orchards, and lists of beasts, birds, fish, trees, and other items that would be of interest to potential immigrants.[6]

By 1660, the population had reached 25,000, and in 1671 Sir William Berkeley, royal governor of Virginia, reported:

> We suppose, and I am very sure we do not much miscount, that there is in Virginia above forty thousand persons, men, women and children, and of which there are two thousand *black slaves*, six thousand *christian servants*, for a short time, the rest are born in the country or have come in to settle and seat, in bettering their condition in a growing country. . . .

> Yearly, we suppose there comes in, of servants, about fifteen hundred, of which, most are English, few Scotch and fewer Irish, and not above two or three ships of negroes in seven years.[7]

In 1669, there were no more than an estimated 528 warriors from approximately nineteen tribes, and the total Indian population in Tidewater had declined from an estimated 9,000 in 1607 to 2,000 in 1699.

## CHAPTER 2

# Immigration *and* Settlement *of* Kingston Parish

In 1683, Edward Harrison, clerk of the court at Jamestown, copied the original land patents into books that are now located in the Library of Virginia. In 1934 Nell Marion Nugent, using these documents, published volume 1 of *Cavaliers and Pioneers: Abstracts of Virginia Land Patents and Grants*. Nugent published two more volumes, covering the years up to 1732. The remaining volumes, through 1774, were edited by Dennis Ray Hudgins in collaboration with the Virginia Genealogical Society.

The abstracts represent an enormous achievement in research that has made a valuable contribution to the study of early Virginia. The work includes an exhaustive index of names of individuals, natural features, waterways, counties, and other classifications and make possible the study of early settlement patterns, demographics, family formation, and other projects that had been nearly impossible except for narrowly focused studies. Not included is survey information concerning metes and bounds; however, these can be found in many of the original patents.

Appendix 1 is a listing by date, sponsoring adventurer or planter, number of individuals on which the headright claims were made, number of acres, and neighborhood for almost every individual land patent granted between 1635 and 1678 for Kingston Parish, Gloucester County, Virginia, from *Cavaliers and Pioneers*. The analysis in the text of settlement patterns and other information for Mathews County (Kingston Parish, Gloucester County, prior to 1792) is based on information in the appendix.

The expanding population between the James and York Rivers and increasing demand for land, because of the growing popularity of tobacco in Europe, resulted in opening new territories north of the York River for large-scale settlements. During the thirty-seven-year period 1642–1679, 136 patents were awarded for land in what is now Mathews County in the names of 112 patentees, representing 907 persons imported, or headrights, for a land area of 56,332 acres. The one patent awarded prior to 1642, to Hugh Gwynn, is not included in the analysis of how the parish was populated because it predated the official opening of the area to settlement. It was granted by a court order, and thus headrights were not necessary. The property was in what became Kingston Parish and was described as, "Beginning at Gwins Pond lying in a bay short of the mouth of _________ [Piankatank?] River parallel and due West to an island called _________ [Gwynn's Island]."[1] The reference to "Gwins Pond" suggests that Hugh Gwynn had previously occupied or used the land, probably for trading and farming purposes. Trading would have involved provisioning ships passing on the Chesapeake Bay. His patent fronted Hills Bay, at the mouth of the Piankatank River, which was known as a convenient anchorage. Gwynn may have provided water, wood, and fresh provisions, especially hogs.

Virtually all of the names listed in the patents are English; however, no records exist of where the settlers in Gloucester County came from in England or, with the exception of a few isolated instances, the names of the ships that transported them. The problem of origin is a result of sporadic record keeping of outbound immigrants principally from the ports of London and Bristol and the loss of records over time due to fire and neglect. An analysis of outbound servants from Bristol, England, 1654–1662, and from London, 1683–1684, shows that servants came predominately from the classes of people typically engaged in farming, skilled trades, and menial and other physical labor, the people of critical importance to the economy of the time. Occupation classifications show 47 percent engaged in agriculture, 19 percent laborers, 15 percent textile and clothing, and the remaining from a broad array of trades, some sixty-six in number including clerks and accountants. The typical ages of servants were between fifteen and twenty-four years with the predominant cluster at twenty to twenty-one years.

While the land patents do not provide information about origins and occupations, they provide a highly informative record of the names of the early settlers and the land they claimed. The record for Kingston Parish is remarkably complete showing the name of the patentee, names of persons whose passage was sponsored, acres of land granted, and approximate location of each patent. Table 2.1 shows the number of patents awarded by year and by size for the years 1640–1679, the years covering all of the original patents except Hugh Gwynn's in 1635.

The table shows that the period of greatest patent activity was from 1650 through 1654. During that five-year period, fifty-eight grants were made totaling 23,074 acres, representing

**TABLE 2.1**

***Kingston Parish Land Grants, 1640–1679***

Number of Patents by Years and Acres

| | 0–150 | 151–300 | 301–450 | 451–600 | 601–750 | 751–900 | 901–1,050 | >1,050 | Total |
|---|---|---|---|---|---|---|---|---|---|
| 1640–1644 | 4 | 3 | 5 | 1 | - | - | 2 | 3+1* | 18 |
| 1645–1649 | - | - | - | - | - | 1 | - | 1 | 2 |
| 1650–1654 | 12 | 18 | 15+1* | 4 | 4 | 1+1* | 2 | 2+1* | 58 |
| 1655–1659 | 4 | 4 | 1 | 2 | 1 | - | - | - | 12 |
| 1660–1664 | - | 1 | 1 | 1 | - | - | - | 1* | 3 |
| 1665–1669 | 2 | 12 | 2 | - | - | - | - | - | 16 |
| 1670–1674 | 9 | 6 | 2 | 2 | - | - | - | - | 19 |
| 1675–1679 | - | 1 | - | - | 1 | - | - | - | 2 |
| Total | 31 | 45 | 26 | 10 | 6 | 2 | 4 | 6 | 130 |

* patents awarded by court order

45 percent of all original patents and 46 percent of the total land area of the parish. The vast majority of the individual patents, forty-five of them, were for parcels less than 451 acres. Patents awarded over 450 acres numbered thirteen, with two being for land greater than 1,000 acres. The surge in patent activity during this period is thought to have been to some degree the result of the uncertainty caused by the English Civil War. The war lasted from 1642 until 1651, followed by the period known as the Commonwealth of England and the protectorate under Oliver Cromwell followed by Richard Cromwell. Instability continued until the monarchy was restored under King Charles II, who was crowned on April 23, 1661. Presumably at least half of the fifty-eight patents awarded between 1650 and 1654 were for land staked out by patentees in the 1640s, and it is possible that settlement occurred during that time subject to eventual patents.

In the following years, almost all of the patents were for parcels less than 451 acres. Over half, 58 percent, of all patents over all years were for holdings less than 300 acres, and 78 percent were less than 450 acres. Total patents by years, in the far-right column, show that by the end of 1659, ninety patents, or 80 percent, of the total acres had been awarded and that it had occurred in just twenty years. Very large holdings, greater than 750 acres, numbered twelve patents, and they were all awarded before 1655.

In just thirty-nine years, all of Kingston Parish had been claimed with virtually all of the patents settled by English planters and their indentured servants. The vast majority of the land had been claimed by 1659. The transformation from mostly wilderness in 1640 to more than 125 farms by 1679 was a remarkable achievement. The amount of labor, the challenging working conditions, the temporary nature of the dwellings, and the great risk in growing a crop for a foreign market must have resulted in only the fittest surviving. But nothing is left—no personal letter, no observation in the parish vestry book—to give some understanding of what life was like in the early years of Kingston Parish in the seventeenth century.

By comparison, Petsworth, the westernmost parish in Gloucester County, lagged behind the settlement of Kingston Parish by approximately ten years, primarily because it was not as desirable due to the limited shoreline on navigable waterways. It was bound on the south by the York River, and adjacent patents were awarded in the early years, as they were in Kingston, as were lands adjoining the first few navigable miles of the Poropotank River. However, the remaining and vast majority of the parish did not have adjacent deepwater access and thus lacked a degree of competitiveness where freight from tobacco barns to ships was concerned. On the other hand, Petsworth had numerous freshwater springs and streams; its elevation was significantly higher than Kingston, thus providing good drainage and protection from tidal flooding, especially during hurricanes; it had better soil; and there were a number of desirable water mill sites.

By the end of 1679, all of the original patents, 136, had been awarded in Kingston Parish. By the same year, 84 patents had been claimed in Petsworth, just 72 percent out of the total 117 that would be claimed by 1714. By the end of 1649, 20 patents had been granted in Kingston compared to 3 in Petsworth; by the end of 1664, 93 versus 48 had been granted. The period of greatest patent activity in Kingston was during 1650–1654, when 58 patents were granted. By contrast, the period of greatest activity in Petsworth was during 1665–1669, when 20 patents were awarded.

The distributions of patents by size were similar, with both parishes having 58 percent of total patents of 300 acres or less. Patents of between 301 and 750 acres accounted for 29 percent of the grants in Petsworth and 32 percent in Kingston. Petsworth had a slightly higher number of large patents, those greater than 750 acres, with 13 percent of all patents granted compared to 9 percent in Kingston.

Table 2.2 shows the demographic profile of persons for whom a headright was claimed for the purpose of obtaining land in Kingston Parish. However, not all of these individuals can be assumed to have actually settled in the parish. Likewise, some servants employed in the parish came from outside the parish. The total number of persons claimed for headrights closely approximates the award of acres. Men comprised 701 of the total, 166 were women, and there were 30 Africans. The percentage of women

## TABLE 2.2

***Kingston Parish Land Grants, 1640–1679***

Demographic Profile

| Years | Grants | Total Acres | Total Persons | Men | Women | Families | Africans | Other Servants | Percent Women |
|---|---|---|---|---|---|---|---|---|---|
| 1640–1644 | 18 | 10,200 | 191 | 154 | 20 | 25 | 1 | 19 | 10.5 |
| 1645–1649 | 2 | 2,900 | 48 | 38 | 10 | 4 | 1 | 0 | 20.8 |
| 1650–1654 | 58 | 23,074 | 395 | 306 | 87 | 31 | 8 | 2 | 22.0 |
| 1655–1659 | 12 | 3,704 | 65 | 58 | 7 | 2 | 5 | 0 | 10.8 |
| 1660–1664 | 3 | 1,180 | 23 | 19 | 4 | 0 | 9 | 0 | 17.4 |
| 1665–1669 | 16 | 3,973 | 79 | 63 | 16 | 5 | 1 | 0 | 20.3 |
| 1670–1674 | 19 | 3,922 | 79 | 63 | 16 | 0 | 5 | 0 | 20.3 |
| 1675–1679 | 2 | 849 | 17 | 11 | 6 | 0 | 0 | 0 | 35.3 |
| Total | 130 | 49,802 | 897 | 712 | 166 | 67 | 30 | 21 | 18.9 |

to the total varied considerably over time: 11 percent in 1640–1644, 22 percent during 1650–1654, and 11 percent during 1655–1659, with the percentage for all years being 19 percent.

By the end of 1654, 634 persons had been claimed for headrights, 72 percent of the total of the 879 attained by the end of 1679. If all of these persons settled in Kingston Parish, or if most did, there would have been 117 women, 19 percent of the total immigrants by the end of 1654. By 1654, just 10 of the 634 immigrants were listed as "Negroes," with 21 "Other Servants." If those too were Africans, then the total would have been 31, or 5 percent of all immigrants. At the time, it is believed that Africans were in a similar status as white indentured servants.

The number of indentured servants can be estimated by first calculating the number of headrights claimed, by dividing the total acres awarded, 49,802, by 50 acres per headright, which equals 966 people. Of these 966, 67 were listed as family members, and there were

130 patentees. Subtracting patentees and family members yields 769 potential indentured servants, 80 percent of the total, a percentage consistent with other estimates. It should be noted that claiming a headright to obtain land did not necessarily mean that the servant was employed by the patentee.

The thirty Africans identified in the patents represent 3 percent of the total and are counted in the above estimate as indentured servants. While some of these individuals may have been slaves or might have become slaves, slavery did not become a common practice until the last two or three decades of the century as the availability of indentured servants and their economic attractiveness declined.

Table 2.3 is an analysis of patents by year and neighborhood. These data show an interesting pattern with the earliest grants for parcels in the Milford Haven, North River, and Piankatank areas followed by strong demand for property in East River during the years 1650 through 1659, with grants also made for Garden Creek, Horn Harbor, Mobjack Bay, Pepper Creek, Queens Creek, Blackwater Creek, and Winter Harbor. Piankatank and North River would have been attractive areas for settlement. Grants along the southern shore of the Piankatank River would have been considered choice land, fronting on a wide, deep river

**TABLE 2.3**

***Kingston Parish Land Grants, 1640–1679***

Patents by Neighborhood Defined by Waterways

| | Pre-1640 | 1640–1644 | 1645–1649 | 1650–1654 | 1655–1659 | 1660–1664 | 1665–1669 | 1670–1674 | 1675–1679 |
|---|---|---|---|---|---|---|---|---|---|
| Milford Haven | 1 | 6 | 1 | 5 | 3 | 0 | 1 | 3 | 0 |
| Piankatank | 1 | 5 | 1 | 4 | 1 | 2 | 0 | 1 | 1 |
| North River | 0 | 4 | 0 | 6 | 1 | 0 | 4 | 2 | 0 |
| East River | 0 | 1 | 0 | 18 | 3 | 0 | 4 | 5 | 1 |
| Garden Creek | 0 | 0 | 0 | 1 | 3 | 2 | 0 | 1 | 0 |
| Horn Harbor | 0 | 0 | 0 | 9 | 2 | 0 | 1 | 1 | 0 |
| Mobjack Bay | 0 | 0 | 0 | 3 | 0 | 0 | 0 | 1 | 0 |
| Pepper Creek | 0 | 0 | 0 | 6 | 0 | 0 | 0 | 0 | 0 |
| Queens Creek | 0 | 0 | 0 | 3 | 0 | 0 | 3 | 3 | 0 |
| Blackwater Creek | 0 | 1 | 0 | 1 | 0 | 0 | 1 | 1 | 0 |
| Winter Harbor | 0 | 0 | 0 | 4 | 4 | 0 | 0 | 0 | 0 |

with high land elevations, especially to the west. Patents on the North River, especially at the headwaters, which offered the only location in the parish for water-powered mills other than tidal mills, were desirable. Reasons for the early settlement in Milford Haven are less obvious and perhaps were based on the protected characteristics of the Haven, the number of convenient creeks flowing into it, and its proximity to the Chesapeake Bay. East River, with the protected approach of Mobjack Bay, Mobjack's convienient anchorage and direct access to the Atlantic Ocean, and the river's deep channel and numerous creeks, was an attractive area for settlement, with eighteen patents awarded 1650–1654.

Milford Haven, formed by Gwynn's Island and the mainland of Kingston Parish, was named at an early date by someone who likely settled in the northeast part of the parish, which includes Gwynn's Island, and probably was from or familiar with Milford Haven in Pembrokeshire at the southwest end of Wales.

In table 2.4, the average number of acres awarded by years and by neighborhood further illustrates land grant activity and land availability. The majority of all patents had some degree of water access, a necessary feature for transportation especially for the export of crops and the importation of manufactured and other goods from England and elsewhere. Of the eighteen patents awarded for one thousand or more acres, ten were located on the Piankatank River, four on the North River, and one each on the East River, Queens Creek, Blackwater Creek, and Milford Haven. Of the eighteen patents, fourteen of them were granted before 1654.

The four tables can be summarized as follows: The land area of Kingston Parish, highly desirable to early English immigrants, had been 80 percent claimed in the twenty-year period ending in 1659, and rivers and creeks were a distinguishing feature of most of the land patents. Men accounted for 80 percent of the first wave of settlers, and approximately 80 percent of all the men and women were indentured servants. The population was almost all white and English with Africans comprising 3 percent.

What happened to the first settlers? While early court records of land transfers no longer exist, the land patents give some indications of changes in ownership due to land being unseated, abandoned, sold, and inherited. The patent records show the following activity for the years 1640 through 1675: There were 130 original patents awarded to 122 families, 6 patents were granted by court order, and 19 were other grants. Re-patents totaled 50 and included 15 for escheat or abandoned land, 8 based on resales, 9 inheritances, and 18 assignments, and there were 2 resurveys.

A comparison of the names of the patentees with the first rent roll, or land tax, taken in 1704, an elapse of sixty-four years from 1640, a period of immense change for Virginia

**TABLE 2.4**

***Kingston Parish Land Grants, 1640–1679***

Average Number of Acres per Patent by Neighborhood

| | Pre-1640 | 1640–1644 | 1645–1649 | 1650–1654 | 1655–1659 | 1660–1664 | 1665–1669 | 1670–1674 | 1675–1679 |
|---|---|---|---|---|---|---|---|---|---|
| Milford Haven | 1 | 525 | 900 | 230 | 355 | 0 | 400 | 97 | 0 |
| Piankatank | 1,000 | 722 | 2,000 | 1,300 | 740 | 895 | 0 | 150 | 229 |
| North River | 0 | 550 | 0 | 717 | 299 | 0 | 223 | 2,200 | 0 |
| East River | 0 | 0 | 0 | 412 | 317 | 0 | 206 | 214 | 620 |
| Garden Creek | 0 | 0 | 0 | 50 | 200 | 310 | 0 | 500 | 0 |
| Horn Harbor | 0 | 0 | 0 | 206 | 149 | 0 | 0 | 120 | 0 |
| Mobjack Bay | 0 | 0 | 0 | 450 | 0 | 0 | 0 | 230 | 0 |
| Pepper Creek | 0 | 0 | 0 | 317 | 0 | 0 | 0 | 0 | 0 |
| Queens Creek | 0 | 0 | 0 | 753 | 0 | 0 | 280 | 250 | 0 |
| Blackwater Creek | 0 | 1 | 0 | 450 | 0 | 0 | 400 | 230 | 0 |
| Winter Harbor | 0 | 0 | 0 | 313 | 0 | 0 | 0 | 0 | 0 |

and all of colonial America, provides another perspective on the first settlers. Of the 122 original families obtaining land grants during the years 1642–1679, only 50 were listed in the 1704 rent roll. In the tax list of 1791, 42 of the original families are recorded, and 35 are on both the 1704 and 1791 lists. Records for several families were probably lost, or some families were no longer landowners in 1704 but reacquired land before 1791.

Changing family compositions and related land transactions resulted in changes in the profile of land ownership as measured by size of acreage held. For example, over half, 58.4 percent, of the original patents were for parcels smaller than 301 acres. In 1704 the percentage was essentially the same, at 58.2 percent, but there was a larger percentage, 30.4 percent compared to 23.8 percent, owning smaller parcels of less than 151 acres. However, over this brief period, the concentration among the larger owners increased: 13.8 percent of the original patentees held parcels over 600 acres, but by 1704, 20 percent held parcels greater than 600 acres. This is a useful indicator of the above-average success of a few planters in creating wealth invested in land. It also illustrates the difficulty a poor person would have had in obtaining land of his own.

The profile of land ownership changed dramatically during the eighty-seven years following 1704 as land was divided among mostly male heirs over a span of approximately three generations. The Mathews County tax list for 1791 identifies approximately 260 owners, an exact count being difficult to determine because some of the parcels were in estates yet to be settled; 186 parcels, 71.5 percent of the total, were for acreages less than 151 acres, compared to 22.8 percent during 1640 through 1679 and 30.4 percent in 1704. Just 15 parcels, 5.8 percent, were larger than 450 acres, and only five owners held more than 1,050 acres. By comparison, in 1704, 37 owners, 32.2 percent, owned parcels larger than 450 acres, and 10 owners, 8.7 percent, had acreages greater than 1,000.

Many of the family names that survived from the first patents until 1791 continued their presence in the parish until recent times, including Armistead, Billups, Bohannan, Bromley, Callis, Degge (Diggs), Forrest, Foster, Gayle, Hunley, Lilly, Morgan, Rigby, Singleton, Smith, Tompkins, White, and Williams.

Several names long associated with Kingston Parish were not among the first landowners. They may have been tenants or family members of landowners, or they may have moved into the county at later dates and acquired land. A few of these include Fitchet, Hall, Hodges, Hudgins, Hurst, Miller, Patterson, Weston, Saunders, Respass, and Sadler.

The rent roll for 1704–1705 in Petsworth Parish lists 104 families. Of these, 33 had received original land patents. There were 20 families who were listed in both the 1704–1705 and the 1771–1772 tax lists. Of these, just eight families were also among the original patentees: Callone, Grymes, Hall, Jones, Lee, Lewis, Royston, and Stubs.

Up until the 1950s, a telephone book of Mathews County contained a large number of the names of families that go back to these early patents. Significant dilution began in the second half of the twentieth century as people moved to Mathews County from all parts of the country in their retirement years and as people from nearby metropolitan areas acquired second homes in the country.

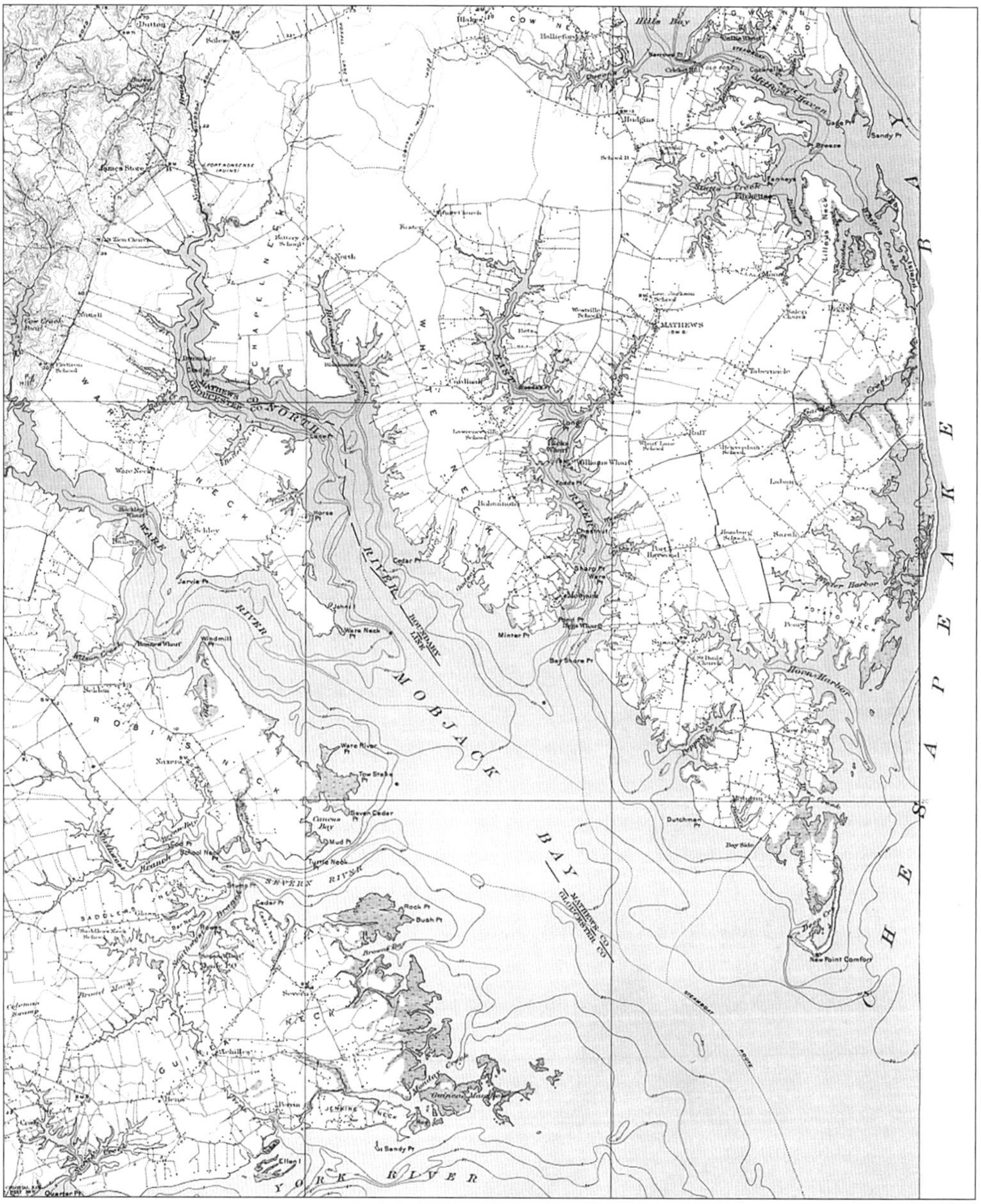


*Figure* 4 Mathews County, excluding the northern portion bound by the Piankatank River, is shown divided from Gloucester County by the North River. The 1916 map illustrates the level topography of Mathews County and the importance of the East River by its central location and deepwater access to Mobjack Bay. The extensive network of bays, rivers, and creeks were fundamental in establishing the commercial nature of the area. This was the first topographical map of the county published by the US Department of War, Corps of Engineers, US Army, later renamed US Geological Survey.

# CHAPTER 3

# The Development *of* Kingston Parish *in the* Seventeenth Century

By 1675, 879 persons had been claimed for headrights for the acquisition of land in Kingston Parish. However, it is not likely that all of the 879 persons actually resided in the parish because the larger patents for which the headrights were claimed were for acreages far greater than would have been initially practical to clear, plant, cultivate, and harvest. Small patents probably absorbed the labor transported equal to the number of headrights used to obtain the land, but landowners in other counties probably purchased the indentures that immigrated on headrights for the larger patents. Thus, the actual population would have been a function of how many servants were needed from year to year, a number determined by the number of acres in cultivation.

Of the 122 original patents awarded 1642–1679, excluding additional patents under the same name, a few were owned by speculators who never lived in the parish or for only a short time and investors from neighboring counties. Most patentees in Gloucester, however, arrived directly from England, with some subsequently moving on to other counties, some dying during the years prior to 1680, and some returning to England.

By 1675, 166 women had been claimed for headrights, and it seems reasonable that a significant percentage of them did live in the parish, and thus there would have been a natural, native-born component of the population that would have enjoyed a gradual increase as the century progressed and especially so in the last quarter of the century. The only data point available for making an estimate of population is the quitrent roll of 1704 in which 116 families are listed owning a total of 46,537 acres.[1]

In addition to households occupied by owners, there were a significant number of households on rented land or on the land of family members. For example, in Surry County there were 422 households in 1703, of which owners occupied 266, or approximately 1.6

households for each owner-occupied household. The ratio in 1720, in Christ Church Parish, Lancaster County, was 1.7:1. If a similar ratio, 1.6:1, were applied to the 116 Kingston Parish owner-occupied households, the resulting total would be 186 owner and nonowner households. Assuming, for example, that the average household consisted of five family members and two servants, the resulting population would have been approximately 1,300. The number of men able to work might be calculated as the head of household plus an assumed average number of four workers per household, a combination of servants and sons, for a total of 930 able-bodied laborers. Though this is an assumed estimate, the number is an order of magnitude.

On first arriving on their newly acquired land, planters, aided in some cases by family members, friends, and indentured servants, were confronted by formidable tasks such as clearing land, digging a well, digging ditches, cutting timber and firewood, constructing basic shelter, erecting fencing, securing initial provisions and tools, beginning a garden, acquiring hogs and other livestock, and planting tobacco. The water table for most of the parish was typically less than fifteen feet from the surface, and shallow wells provided adequate water supplies, except during periods of extreme drought. Springs provided water in several places in Kingston, although they were not as numerous, due to the flat topography, as in nearby Petsworth Parish with its hills, ravines, and streams.

Because the land of Kingston Parish is remarkably flat, except to the north bounded by the Piankatank River, and rarely more that ten feet above sea level, ditches were necessary to improve drainage of fields that would otherwise retain excessive moisture, especially after heavy rainfall. The ditches were often referenced in surveys to indicate the location of property lines. Adjoining landowners typically maintained their own ditches, often resulting in parallel ditches separated by a mound of soil, generally three to five feet wide, on which would grow a hedge row and/or a line of trees, the centerline of which would be the actual property line. In early surveys, they were named "ditch banks" as opposed to a single "ditch." Their construction required major investments in labor, and they were very much a part of the rural landscape. Many of them have survived to present-day.

The land patents suggest that there were a few Indian fields, presumably mostly cleared. These would have been highly desirable for initial settlement as planting could begin without the enormous labor and time required to clear forests.

A newly arrived planter from England together with his servants and family, if any, would typically rent space on an established plantation or stay with family or friends while beginning the search for land to patent. He might also have rented a small plot of land to begin a crop for subsidence and/or a tobacco crop to begin establishing credit. In the mid-seventeenth century, the tools and equipment planters needed for a new plantation included broad and narrow hoes, axes, saws, hammers, spades, augers and gimlets (for drilling holds), hatchets, bills (for cutting), frows (a cleaving tool), pickaxes, and grindstones. The estimated cost for these items was eleven pounds. A fowling piece, shot, and gunpowder were also necessary and would cost from two to three pounds. An iron pot, a frying pan, wooden platters, dishes, and porringers would cost one pound. Recommended clothing and other textiles included a Monmouth cap (a round, close-fitting cap made of wool), shirts, shoes, stockings, canvas for making sheets, blankets, and a rug.

The new planter might also acquire a cow, an ox or two, perhaps a goat or two, and two sows. Until he produced a crop of his own, he would need to have taken with him from England or acquired locally such food as biscuits, peas, oatmeal, malt, pork, beef, salted fish, root vegetables, butter, liquor, and wheat. These items would cost from ten to twelve pounds. The total initial cost for provisions, equipment, and tools would thus be in the range of twenty-four to twenty-seven pounds. In addition, the cost of transportation, freight, finding a desirable tract of land to patent, obtaining a patent, surveying the land, and erecting a simple dwelling all added to what was a significant investment, an amount that required a degree of wealth for a would-be planter.

The dependence in the early years on tobacco is well-known, and it was cultivated in Kingston Parish beginning with the earliest settlers. The chief motivation for acquiring land at that time was to expand the production of tobacco. Gloucester County was ideally suited to its cultivation. In particular Kingston Parish, while not having ideal soil and drainage conditions, had the highly desirable attribute of numerous rivers and creeks that greatly facilitated the transportation of hogsheads of tobacco. The proximity to water gave planters a cost advantage in labor and reduced damage to the leaf due to shorter distances for rolling hogsheads along roads to convenient points for loading ships.

While farm productivity varied depending on soil conditions and prevailing local weather patterns, a planter could produce on average 1,500 pounds of tobacco per year on three or four acres of land during the 1640s. This quantity would gradually increase as better cultivation, curing, and transportation techniques were developed until the mid-1680s, thereafter remaining virtually unchanged during the colonial period. Approximately ten thousand plants yielded that tonnage and, after being pressed, would fill approximately two and a half hogsheads, the size of which varied in the early years from 400–800 pounds. The most standard size of a cask of tobacco in 1686 was 500 pounds.

The price for tobacco realized by the planter is difficult to determine. There did not exist a central market for the crop, and planters had access to several methods to sell their tobacco based primarily on the size of the crop and the sophistication of the planter. Large plantations typically sold to English, and at intervals to Dutch merchants, on consignment, though others sold to local merchants or ship captains at a negotiated price, and small planters most often sold to larger planters. The price varied depending on quality, the success of the crop year, the degree of difficulty a merchant might have in filling a ship to capacity, and many other factors. There were also two different varieties: a strong leaf, oronoco, popular in Europe, and sweet-scented, especially sought in England. Sweet-scented tobacco grew especially well in Tidewater and had a market price up to 50 percent higher than oronoco. A large number of planters grew both varieties in different proportions from year to year as their estimate of market demand evolved, adding to the complexity of determining the historical price level.

The value of tobacco dropped over the second half of the seventeenth century. The fall in price from the mid-1660s to the end of the century was approximately 35 percent, a substantial change that helped usher in the use of slave labor to replace the more costly indentured servant.*

During the seventeenth century, most transactions were done with tobacco. In *A Frenchman in Virginia*, written in 1686, the author observed:

> There is little money in circulation, except among the people of quality. They do business with their tobacco as if it were money. With tobacco they buy lands, hire and buy cattle; and as they can secure all they want with this commodity they become so lazy that they even import from England their linen and their hats, their women's clothes and their shoes, their iron, their nails, nay, even their wooden furniture, although they have the best and a superfluity of wood which could be made into tables and chairs and boxes and wardrobes and generally all kinds of furniture necessary for house or kitchen.[2]

During the colonial period, four farthings equaled one pence (d.), twelve pence equaled one shilling (s.), five shillings made a crown, and four crowns equaled one pound sterling (£). Thus 240d. equaled £1, or 205 pounds of oronoco tobacco, at a price of 1.17d. per pound, in the 1665–1675 period. The average output of one man per year was approximately 1,500 pounds of tobacco, equal to £7.32 assuming a price per pound of 1.17d. If the crop was half oronoco and half sweet-scented, the value of the output of one man would have been approximately £9 since sweet-scented sold for approximately 40–50 percent more than oronoco. By

* The most authoritative analysis of available data using values of tobacco in estate inventories for Maryland, closely related to Virginia prices, shows an average price per pound from 1659 to 1664 of 1.53d., from 1665 to 1675 of 1.17d., and thereafter until 1685 of 1.09d. In the years following, the price dropped to 0.75d. until 1695 and was back to 1d. in 1700. (Russell R. Menard, "A Note on Chesapeake Tobacco Prices, 1618–1660," *Virginia Magazine of History and Biography* 84, no. 4 [Oct. 1976] : 401–410.)

this accounting, a household with four farm workers could produce 6,000 pounds of tobacco per year for an annual income of £36 assuming half oronoca and half sweet-scented.

Assuming that 70 percent of the able-bodied laborers in Kingston Parish worked in the cultivation of tobacco during the 1670s, the total output for the parish would have been 781,200 pounds, having a value of approximately £3,800 if oronoco and £4,670 if half oronoco and half sweet-scented.

Planters grew other crops as well to provide food for the household and servants. *A Frenchman in Virginia* offers this example:

> It is a country so good and fertile that when a man has fifty acres of land, two men servants and a maid, and some cattle, neither he nor his wife have ever anything to do except to make visits to their neighbours. The greater number of them do not even take the trouble to watch their slaves at work, for there is no house so ill provided which has not an overseer, as they call him, who usually is an indenture man recently enfranchised. To him they give (say) two servants in charge. The overseer feeds, directs and himself works with, these servants. He receives a third of the tobacco and grain or whatever else they put in the ground, and so the master has nothing to do except take his share of the crop. . . .[3]
>
> My landlord had only two boys to work his land. For a maid he bought one of the trollops who came in the ship with me. With this force he usually harvested six bushels of wheat and 200 bushels of indian corn, after sowing one bushel of each; fifteen bushels of beans, of yams what would perhaps amount to fifty bushels if they had been measured, and, finally, twelve casks of tobacco, weighing 6,000 pounds.[4]

The author of *A Frenchman in Virginia* wrote extensively about domestic subjects, customs, agriculture, living conditions, and so forth with a large portion of his writings based on his time spent in Gloucester County. He first landed in the North River and was well acquainted with New Point Comfort and the nearby neighborhood.

In observing that they lived on corn bread, he noted:

> This corn bread is as white as paper, and good to the taste, but rather heavy on the stomach to those unaccustomed to it. It cannot be rolled into pastry. They make it by mixing salt and water with the meal, and secure a crust by greasing the dough with a bacon rind while it is in the oven. After it is baked this "pone" cuts like any other bread.[5]

Tobacco, however, was the cash crop, and its cultivation in Virginia and Maryland grew at a very high rate, from sixty thousand pounds in 1622, to five hundred thousand pounds in 1628, and to twenty million pounds in 1700. The average annual compound growth rate 1628–1700 was 5.25 percent, which implies, assuming no change in productivity, the same growth rate of plantation labor and increase of land under cultivation. By 1775, the colonial export to England was one hundred million pounds, by far the largest exported crop in the world at that time and of enormous economic importance to the royal treasury.

The relative value of tobacco in the 1650s is indicated by the following cost estimates:

- A headright, fifty acres of land, was worth forty to fifty pounds of tobacco or 6s. 4½d. Forty to fifty pounds of tobacco could purchase a cow or a half barrel of Indian corn.
- One pound sterling was equal to approximately 205 pounds of tobacco, but this varied greatly as the market value of tobacco fluctuated.
- One seasoned but unskilled servant with three years or more of remaining service was worth 1,500–2,000 pounds of tobacco or in sterling £7.32–9.76.

The value of tobacco, as mentioned, varied, with overproduction being a large problem during 1639–1640, during the mid-1660s, and during 1682–1683. The number of ships arriving each year from England, principally from London and Bristol, varied as the demand for tobacco fluctuated. During good years, the tobacco fleet was often eighty or more ships. The average ship had a capacity of 300–320 hogsheads of tobacco, and with an average weight of 600 pounds per hogshead, the typical ship would have had a cargo of 90–96 tons of tobacco. An eighty-vessel fleet would have carried 7,440 tons of tobacco with an export value to the planters of £94,860 or more depending on the mix in the quantities of oronoco and sweet-scented.

The typical schedule for transatlantic sailing was a departure from England in September with the passage taking the southern route. Beginning in the English Channel, ships would sail southward to take advantage of favorable wind directions off the coast of Portugal and continue in a south-southwesterly direction to the Madeira or Canary Islands off the coast of Africa. From there they would sail southwest to approximate latitude 25° north; then they would change course to due west to enjoy the trade winds blowing dependably out of the east. At approximate longitude 65° west, the course would change to north-northwest and continue until reaching latitude 37° north, at which point the course would change to directly west and hopefully into the mouth of the Chesapeake Bay. Following this schedule and route, ships arrived in the Chesapeake Bay in late fall or early winter, minimizing the risk of hurricanes in the August through October months and the damage from hull-destroying worms prevalent in the warm bay waters during the summer.

Ships would discharge cargoes and winter over in the rivers of the Chesapeake Bay until late winter, during which time they would move from landing to landing to take on the prior year's crop of tobacco. The tobacco fleet would sail for England in March by way of the northern route, generally along the course of the Gulf Stream flowing to the northeast. The passage would last from three to four weeks if wind conditions were highly favorable or as many as five weeks under less-than-ideal conditions. During March and April, the prevailing winds are strong and blow from the west-northwest, and then in the mid-Atlantic above latitude 45° north, their direction is from the west. While the southern passage in the fall most often was in relatively mild sea conditions, the northern course, while faster, was characterized by stronger winds and larger wave formations.

In Kingston Parish, as with other parishes and counties, tobacco, unless loaded at a landing or dock, would have been placed on flats (small barges) and rowed to an anchored ship for loading. Several deepwater locations close to shore, however, allowed for landings for the loading and unloading of cargoes in Kingston Parish, including Williams Wharf and Hicks Wharf, both on the East River, and numerous other locations on the North River and the Piankatank.

Besides raising tobacco, related occupations became common, especially during the last third of the century, including shipwrights for the repair of vessels and the construction of the small boats used for everyday transportation. Coopers were needed for the annual manufacturing of hogsheads needed for the transportation of tobacco. Other occupations included carpenters, brickmakers and masons, mariners, shoemakers, merchants, clerks, physicians, and clergy.

Between the years of greatest land patent activity, 1650–1654, and about 1675, life in Kingston Parish became more settled and structured. Hard work had resulted in established homes and farms, and the Church of England and the authority of the parish vestry had gained influence. The vestry book of Kingston Parish, one of the few surviving records, gives insights into life in the parish. The first book entry recorded is dated November 15, 1679, and concerns timber for the reconstruction of the North River chapel. Apparently Thomas Tabb had contributed more building materials than the other parishioners, and the vestry was working to obtain relief from others. On October 14, 1680, it was reported that a church Bible and two large Common Prayer books had been purchased from James Ranson for use in the chapel. Thomas Clapp was awarded 500 pounds of tobacco "for keepin[ ] Cleane ye Chappell & ye Chappell Yard" and again in November 1681 "for ye paines he taketh upon ye Chappell & Chappell-Yard but partly out of Charity to ye Said Clapp."[6] On October 11, 1687, the vestry ordered the collection of funds to build a new chapel, the cost set at 22,356 pounds of tobacco, a value of £93.15. On October 9, 1690, funds necessary for continuing the "new Brick Chappell"[7] were ordered to be collected. Also discussed was payment to Daniel Hunter for building a bridge at the head of the North River. Collection of funds for the new chapel was still underway in 1692, with the last payment discussed on October 9.

The most burdensome business of the vestry pertained to collecting a tax, paid in pounds of tobacco, for the payment of parish expenses. The taxable unit was a "tithable," a person subject to a tax. Tithables were defined as white males age sixteen and over and African, mulatto, and Indian males and females age sixteen and over. White women were taxed only if they were heads of household. The number of tithables was well-known in the parishes and often noted in the vestry book for calculating the amount of tax that could be raised. In November 1700, 262 tithables were recorded for the North River chapel with an unexplained reduction by October 1701 to 149. (This could possibly have been the beginning of administration by the East Church, although no records support this suggestion. The "Eastermost River Church," as it was known, first appeared in the record on September 29, 1715.[8])

Other tax laws, pertaining to county and colonial governments, changed over time. In 1748, the law pertaining to tithables was amended to exclude mariners and constables. In 1782, in an effort to retire Revolutionary War debts, further revisions were made including changing the tithable age for white males from sixteen to twenty-one years. At the same time, a tax was enacted on personal property to include cattle, horses, and vehicles other than farm wagons and carts. The tax on cattle was discontinued in 1787. Unfortunately, the tax records for Gloucester County prior to 1782 are mostly lost; however, the annual land tax that began in 1782 together with personal property records have survived and are invaluable sources of information on individuals, many of whom left no other record of their existence.

In 1702 the number of tithables in the North River chapel was 180, and on November 1, 1704, 172 tithables were recorded. The number of tithables suggests a small number of households at that time, perhaps no more than forty-five assuming an average of four taxable persons per household. The November 1704 entry provides an example of the activities administered by the vestry. There was an order to collect funds for the repair of the chapel, including 1,650 pounds of tobacco for shingles and 385 pounds for nails. The shingles were shown to cost 15s. per thousand, which equated to the value of tobacco per pound at the time of 1.2d., a data point that confirms other estimates of the farm price of tobacco. William Creedle was paid 1,300 pounds of tobacco for "Covering ye sd Chaple,"[9] equal to £6.5, which would have included labor and materials for the chapel's roof.

Everyday life gradually changed as farms provided an increasing variety of what was consumed. Archaeological evidence indicates that during the first half of the seventeenth century, the everyday diet changed with the seasons and included wild game, fish, and fowl. Eastern Virginia had an abundance of ducks, geese, turkeys, opossums, deer, raccoons, and squirrels. Fish and shellfish were plentiful in the waters of Kingston Parish with black drum, red drum, striped bass, sturgeon, shad, oysters, and blue crabs as well as turtles being in abundance. In regards to farm topics, *A Frenchman in Virginia* observed:

> They do not know what it is to work the land with cattle. Everything is hoed, although it would be easy enough for a single horse to plow the land, for it does not contain a single stone. Some of the people have as many as 100 cows or cattle, and thirty horses. The latter they use only to ride, except at some few plantations, far from the sea or a river, where they are used to draw carts. Their firing wood is so conveniently at hand that the slaves bring it in on their backs. . . .
>
> The quantity of wood available makes it possible for them to fence cheaply their cultivated fields. A man who has fifty acres of land leaves twenty-five in woods. Of the remaining twenty-five, he cultivates half and the other half he reserves as a pasture and paddock for his cattle. Every four years he transfers his fences to this second half, which has thus had a period of rest and of fertilization, and this is all the rotation they use.[10]

Hogs were an important source of protein during most of the century because they grew fast, and they could eat almost anything and thus could survive and flourish in the wilderness. In four months a single pig can birth a litter of as many as fifteen; the litter matures in six months, at which time those sows can become pregnant. Pigs were important in the early colonial period also because they could eat vegetation and thus assist in clearing land. They were independent, self-sufficient, and highly adaptable. They were an important food source for the poor and rich alike, and pork was well-suited to be preserved in salt, which made it versatile for year-round consumption and for provisioning ships.

During the second half of the century, domesticated animals, mainly cattle and chickens, were more prevalent in the diet, as well as the continued consumption of hogs. Sheep were rare until the 1680s. *A Frenchman in Virginia* provides these observations:

> The domestic animals are in all respects similar to those of Europe. They raise numbers of horses, cattle, sheep, swine, turkeys, geese, ducks and chickens, all without expense either for feed or care. They do not know what it is to save hay, for all their animals pasture in the woods or else in that part of the plantation which has been turned out to rest. Thither the cattle come in every night, rather by instinct than by any care the planters take of them.[11]

The colonial diet provided a significant amount of protein, more than in England. Interestingly, it was observed that British soldiers of colonial wars in the 1700s were shorter than the colonists by several inches.

Corn and beans are frequently mentioned in estate inventories, and it appears that European vegetables, including cabbage, onions, and carrots, were grown in kitchen gardens. In addition, vegetable gardens included potatoes, asparagus, turnips, and artichokes. Orchards were common on most plantations, especially apple and peach trees but also pear, plum, apricot, quince, and cherry. Blueberries, blackberries, and grapes grew wild and were rarely cultivated before 1700. Most households produced milk, cheese, and uncured butter, which were typically used with cornmeal.

Interestingly, in the seventeenth century and continuing until the early nineteenth century, self-sufficient animals, especially cattle and hogs, were free to roam the forests, and they had legal access to any land not protected by a barrier. Since they did not consume tobacco, they did not bother the cash crop. In 1631, the first fence law was passed: "Every man shall enclose his ground with sufficient fences uppon theire owne perill."[12] A field without a fence was not a legal field, and planters could not claim damage to their crops by wondering hogs, goats, or cattle.

In 1646 a sufficient fence was specified to be at least four and a half feet high and "substantiall close downe to the bottome."[13] In 1748 the height was increased to five feet, and alternatives were offered, including live hedges and ditch/fence combinations. Most often used was likely "worm" fencing, made of split lengths of timber that derived strength by being constructed in a zigzag pattern. The fence law influenced the landscape, as most fields under cultivation were enclosed as well as kitchen gardens and the area immediately around a house.

The archaeological record of seventeenth-century Virginia, including Mathews, shows that the earliest structures—dwellings, barns, sheds, warehouses, and others—were earthfast: columns of wood were secured by being placed in holes in the ground. Flooring in some cases was the earth, with floor joists to support wooden planking added at later dates as time and resources permitted. Siding was typically riven clapboard, and roofing was made of either clapboards or shingles. In the early years, fireplaces and chimneys were often made of clay covering a wooden frame. None of these crudely built structures have survived, as their useful service was typically less than twenty years. Additional information on construction was recorded by *A Frenchman in Virginia*:

> There are some very good houses in this country. Those of the peasants are all of wood. They are sheathed with chestnut plank and sealed inside with the same. As they get ahead in the world they refinish the interior with plaster, for

> which they use oyster shell lime, making it as white as snow; so that although these houses seem poor enough on the outside because one sees only the weathered sheathing, within they are most agreeable. Most of the houses are amply pierced with glazed windows. They make quantities of brick in Virginia and I saw a number of houses built entirely of brick.
>
> Whatever their estates, for what reason I do not know, they build their houses consisting only of two ground floor rooms, with some closets and one or two prophet's chambers above. According to his means, each planter provides as many of such houses as he needs. They build also a separate kitchen, a house for the Christian slaves, another for negro slaves, and several tobacco barns, so that in arriving at the plantation of a person of importance you think you are entering a considerable village. They provide no stables at all for they never house their cattle. More than that, few of their house doors are ever locked for robbery is here unknown. You could travel 200 leagues through the country with your hat full of money without fear that any of it would be taken from you by violence.[14]

After a planter cleared land, acquired livestock, established a kitchen garden, and produced several years of profitable crops, he might then be in a position to improve the original dwelling, most often built to be temporary, or he could build a more permanent structure.

In the early years of settlement, houses for the less well-off families were typically small, with one room and a fireplace on the first floor and a loft above. More prosperous planters had two rooms on the first floor and one or two on the second with two to four fireplaces. After the early years, especially after the middle of the eighteenth century, well into the second half of the eighteenth century for Mathews County, more substantial homes were built, mostly of wood with brick used for foundations, fireplaces, and chimneys.

During the last quarter of the seventeenth century, as fields became depleted of the nutrients necessary for the cultivation of tobacco, and as cleared land enabled plowing and harrowing, acreages were converted to field crops, especially grains. Abandoned tobacco fields were also fenced for pasture, which reduced the practice of cattle roaming in the forests. Pastureland could be rotated from time to time for crops, utilizing the natural fertilizers from the animals. An important result of cattle enclosed in fenced pastures was the need for more feed corn, and land devoted to this crop increased significantly in the early years of the eighteenth century.

The change in land usage began to change the economy and society. Farmers now needed plows for cultivation and carts and wagons for transporting the harvest. New implements were needed including cart bodies, wheels, and traces for animals to pull carts and plows. These requirements necessitated new trades including blacksmiths and skilled woodworkers. When tobacco prices declined from time to time, imports of English manufactured goods declined as well, creating a market for locally produced everyday items, including furniture, shoes, pottery, and cloth for making garments. As trade expanded with England, the number of ships required to export crops, lumber, and naval stores created an increasing need for provisioning outbound ships with pork, beef, bread, and other items necessary for the voyage back to England and other destinations. Trade with the West Indies and with New England colonies further increased exports of corn, wheat, flour, lumber, and pork. As the ratio of women to men increased and with the resulting increase in family units, home occupations expanded to include spinning yarn, knitting, and home production of butter, cheese, cider, beer, and salted meat and fish. Self-sufficiency fostered larger families, and by the end of the seventeenth century, a growing native-born population was the majority in Gloucester County.

In addition to the multiple challenges of establishing households and cultivating crops, the second half of the seventeenth century brought other hardships. The year 1667 was especially tragic, and the damage to the colony was devastating.

The Dutch Wars during 1664 through 1667, and again in 1672 through 1674, brought periods of disruption to Virginia's economy, including the capture of twenty English merchant ships in the James River in June 1667. In that same year, unusual weather events created extreme losses to the economy and infrastructure. In April, a severe hailstorm destroyed large areas of newly planted crops and killed young hogs and cattle. During the late spring, a period of rain lasted with little relief for forty days, resulting in great damage to the tobacco crop.

On August 27, 1667, the colony was devastated by a powerful hurricane accompanied by high tides and violent wind, which resulted in the extensive loss of crops and cattle. Fallen trees blocked most roads and bridges, and river landings were destroyed. The result of these natural disasters in 1667 reduced the tobacco crop significantly, and only thirty shiploads sailed for England with the year's harvest. An estimated ten thousand houses, barns, sheds, and other buildings as well as wharves, bridges, and millraces were destroyed. The following account is from a letter written on November 4, 1667, by Thomas Ludwell, the secretary of state of the colony of Virginia, to Lord Berkeley:

> This poore country is now reduced to a very miserable condition by a continental course of misfortune. . . . On the 27th of August followed the most dreadful Hurry Cane that ever the Colony groaned under. It lasted 24 hours, began at

> North East and went around northerly till it came to west and so it came to Southeast where it ceased. It was accompanied with a most violent rain but no thunder. The night of it was the most dismal time I ever knew or heard of, for the wind and rain raised so confused a noise, mixed with the continued cracks of falling houses. . . . The waves were impetuously beaten against the shores and by that violence forced and as it were crowded into all creeks, rivers and bays to that prodigious height that it hazarded the drowning of many people who lived not in sight of the rivers, yet were then forced to climb to the top of their houses to keep themselves above water. The waves carried all the foundations of the Fort at Point Comfort into the river. . . . but then morning came and the sun risen it would have comforted us after such a night, had it not lighted to us the ruins of our plantations, of which I think not one escaped. The nearest computation is at least 10,000 houses blown down, all the Indian grain laid flat on the ground, all the tobacco in the fields torn to pieces and most of that which was in the houses perished with them. The fences about the corn fields were either blown down or beaten to the ground by trees which fell upon them.[15]

This hurricane is believed to have passed inland east of Jamestown, which would have placed it close to Gloucester County. It then proceeded to the north and resulted in a severe storm in Manhattan on August 28. The hurricane was followed by twelve days and nights of rain, the result of a second hurricane or tropical depression that apparently passed just off the coast of Virginia.

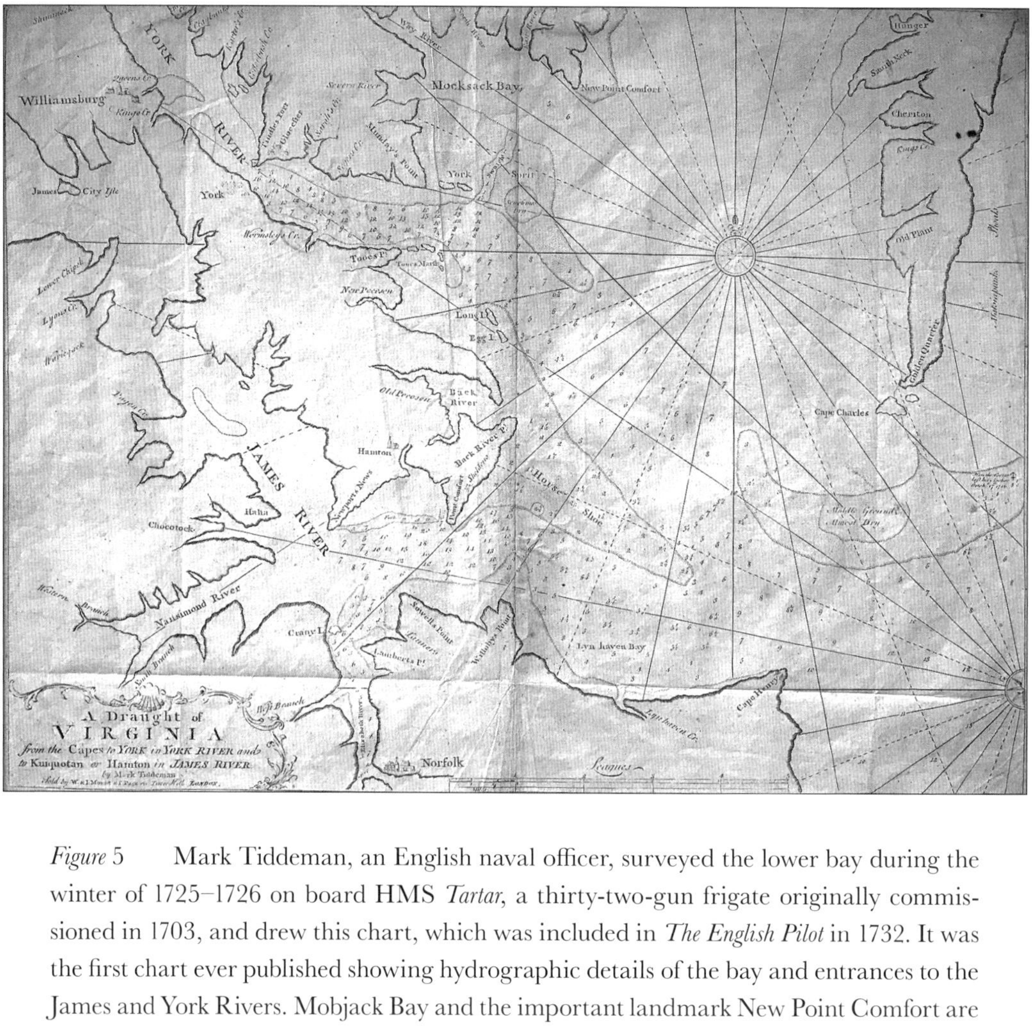


*Figure* 5 Mark Tiddeman, an English naval officer, surveyed the lower bay during the winter of 1725–1726 on board HMS *Tartar*, a thirty-two-gun frigate originally commissioned in 1703, and drew this chart, which was included in *The English Pilot* in 1732. It was the first chart ever published showing hydrographic details of the bay and entrances to the James and York Rivers. Mobjack Bay and the important landmark New Point Comfort are shown at the top of the chart. From the author's collection.

## CHAPTER 4

# Kingston Parish *in the* Eighteenth Century

Hugh Jones, a professor of mathematics for two years at the College of William and Mary, wrote one of the few surviving observations about Virginia society in the early eighteenth century. In 1724 he described the manner of speaking in Virginia as being the speech of London. In his *Present State of Virginia* he wrote:

> The *Habits, Life, Customs, Computations,* etc. of the *Virginians* are much the same as about *London,* which they esteem their *Home*; and for the most Part have contemptible Notions of *England,* and wrong Sentiments of *Bristol,* and the other *OutPorts,* which they entertain from seeing and hearing the common Dealers, Sailors, and Servants that come from those Towns, and the Country Places in *England* and *Scotland,* whose Language and Manners are strange to them; for the *Planters,* and even the *Native Negroes* generally talk good *English* without *Idiom* or *Tone.*[1]

These observations were likely based on his familiarity with Williamsburg and may not have been as applicable in rural districts. Given the "urban" nature of the colonial capital, it is surprising that by the early years of the eighteenth century the people of Virginia no longer had a familiarity with everyday life in England, though the white colonial population was by this time predominantly native born, the period of great immigration in eastern Virginia having been concluded approximately two generations past. On the other hand, separation from England had not been long enough for speech patterns to have changed, nor a shared sense of values and culture.

The last two decades of the seventeenth century were a time of increasing stability in daily life especially for those who owned land. The high mortality rate, in the years before 1650, had declined significantly; the great dependence on tobacco had begun to lessen; there was a gradual movement towards more diversity in crops, especially the cultivation of wheat; and there was a rapidly growing white native population.

Robert Beverley, in his book *The History and Present State of Virginia*, published in 1705, included a population table broken down into the twenty-five counties that comprised the colony. It showed for the year 1702 a total population of 60,606, of which 35,583 were women and children. There were 9,522 men in the militia. The total acreage in the twenty-five counties was 2,164,232, and there were 25,023 tithables.

Gloucester's population of 5,834 was 44 percent larger than the next largest county, which was Prince George, and accounted for 9.6 percent of the total population of colonial Virginia. The number of women and children was 3,206, and there were 594 men in the militia. The number of tithables was 2,628. Populations in nearby counties were 2,357 in York, 1,632 in Middlesex, New Kent had 3,374, and King and Queen had 2,842. Gloucester had 142,450 acres and ranked fifth among all counties in size. The largest county was Accomack with 200,923 acres.

In addition to Beverley's account of Virginia's population, the 1705 Gloucester County rent roll contains the first comprehensive listing of land by owner categorized by the four parishes. The rent roll lists 381 landowners holding a total of 147,698 acres: Kingston had 46,537 acres owned by 115, Petsworth had 41,132 acres owned by 104, Abingdon had 28,426 acres owned by 76, and Ware with 31,603 acres and 86 owners. The average acres per owner were 405 in Kingston, 396 in Petsworth, 374 in Abingdon, and 367 in Ware. Petsworth had the smallest percentage of owners with 100 or fewer acres, 20.2 percent, followed by Kingston with 23.5 percent, Ware with 24.4 percent, and Abingdon with a significantly higher proportion of small holdings representing 38.2 percent of the total. The average for owners having 1,000 or more acres was 8.7 percent with only slight deviations among the four parishes.

The total number of landowners recorded by the rent roll for all counties in Virginia was 5,431, and together they controlled approximately 2.2 million acres. Of these owners, 438, 8 percent of the total, had plantations greater than 1,000 acres. There were extremes among the counties with Accomack having just 9.4 percent of owners with 100 acres or fewer, and Elizabeth City with the highest at 44 percent. Appendix 2 contains a table of ownership by size of holdings for all of the counties in the 1704–1705 rent roll, and appendix 3 shows landowners by average acres.

Kingston Parish had 31.5 percent of the total acreage of Gloucester County. Assuming that the population of the parish was proportional to its share of acreage, then Kingston would have had a population of 1,838, with tithables numbering 828 and women and children at 1,010.

Other significant change was underway, in particular to the labor supply. As the farm price of tobacco gradually fell during the second half of the seventeenth century, the high cost of indentured servants became uneconomical. At the same time, fewer young people in England were motivated to become indentured servants in Virginia. Planters resorted to slave labor at a rapid rate, a trend that continued through the first half of the eighteenth century until slaves provided virtually all of the unskilled labor.

In 1649 there were only about 300 blacks out of the total population of 15,000, or 2 percent; in 1671 the number had crept up to an estimated 2,000, approximately 3 percent of the population. By 1700 the number had increased to 6,000, to 12,000 in 1708, and 30,000 by 1730, equivalent to 23 percent of the total population of 130,000. This dramatic change to the demographic mix of the colony changed not only the economics of producing crops but also in a profound way the social fabric, with consequences still unfolding in present times.

The number of slaves and free blacks in Kingston Parish at the beginning of the century is not known but is assumed to have been small. Applying an estimate of the colonywide percentage of slaves of the total population, 6,000 slaves in 1700 and a total population of 60,606 in 1702, 10 percent, to the estimated population in Kingston in 1704 of 1,838, the resulting number of blacks is 182 in 1704. However, the number of slaves grew rapidly during the eighteenth century and reached over the 1,121 recorded in the 1791 tax list. The actual number of slaves was substantially larger because the 1791 count excluded children under the age of twelve, and, while the count included slaves above the age of sixteen, elderly slaves who could no longer work were often excluded from the tax rolls. Thus the actual slave population in the parish was perhaps as much as 15–20 percent higher.

The year 1791 was the first time a land tax and a separate tax on personal property were implemented, and thus the two lists, when combined by name of head of household, provide an opportunity for a more detailed analysis of the social and economic well-being of the people of Mathews County. The land tax was calculated using the number of acres owned and tax rates that reflected the economic utility of the land. For example, there would have been separate rates for land under cultivation, timberland, swamps, and land with very poor soil conditions. The personal property tax was based on the number of tithables, horses, and expensive vehicles, ones not used in farming or timbering operations, such as riding chairs and phaetons. Cattle, sheep, goats, hogs, and other farm animals were not considered personal property in 1791 for tax purposes.

An analysis of the 1791 tax records for Kingston Parish yields the results in the following tables. The first, table 4.1, shows a summary of the land and personal property taxes organized by the number of acres owned by heads of household. What is initially striking in the data is the large number of households without land ownership. Out of a total of 566 households, there were 303, 54 percent, without land. Seventeen of these were widows or women who had never married, but the status of the remaining 286 cannot be verified. No doubt adult sons and daughters living in separate houses on family land account for a significant number. Other possibilities include households on leased land, sharecroppers, and the use of land as compensation for labor.

Of the 46 percent of households that did own land, the majority, 166, or 63 percent, owned 100 or fewer acres. Households owning 101–300 acres numbered 65, 25 percent of all landowners. Kingston Parish in 1791 was thus characterized by small farms with only 11 households owning more than 500 acres and just 3 with more than 1,000 acres.

**TABLE 4.1**

***1791 Land and Personal Property Tax, Kingston Parish, Virginia***

| | No. of Households | No. of Acres | No. of >16 Tithables | No. of Slaves >16 and >12 | No. of Horses |
|---|---|---|---|---|---|
| No Land | 303 | 0 | 289 | 294 | 193 |
| 1–25 acres | 47 | 678 | 45 | 34 | 27 |
| 26–50 | 57 | 2,262 | 61 | 68 | 40 |
| 51–100 | 62 | 4,872 | 66 | 118 | 63 |
| 101–150 | 21 | 2,551 | 25 | 74 | 31 |
| 151–200 | 17 | 3,109 | 21 | 77 | 39 |
| 201–250 | 15 | 3,358 | 15 | 85 | 25 |
| 251–300 | 12 | 3,426 | 14 | 62 | 34 |
| 301–350 | 9 | 2,945 | 13 | 61 | 24 |
| 351–400 | 7 | 2,665 | 7 | 32 | 11 |
| 401–500 | 5 | 2,219 | 6 | 43 | 18 |
| 501–600 | 5 | 2,711 | 6 | 43 | 14 |
| 601–999 | 3 | 1,928 | 5 | 38 | 11 |
| Over 1,000 | 3 | 3,738 | 3 | 92 | 30 |
| Total | 566 | 36,462 | 576 | 1,121 | 560 |
| Other Owners | | | | | |
| Unsettled Estates | | 8,992 | | | |
| Nonresidents | | 11,739 | | | |
| Total Acres | | 57,193 | | | |

Table 4.2 shows that 100 of the households without land, 33 percent of the 303, owned a total of 294 slaves: 33 had one slave, 22 had two slaves, 18 had three slaves, 8 had five slaves, 5 had five, 5 had seven, 5 had eight, 3 had six, and 1 had ten slaves. These slaves were for the most part employed in agriculture or domestic work with some hired out as contract labor on a daily or weekly basis to those requiring extra or seasonal help; some were employed in manufacture such as shipbuilding, house carpentry, blacksmithing, and cooperage.

The small landowners, holding from one to one hundred acres, show a similar distribution of slaves per household: 95 of 166 households owned 220 slaves for an average of 2.3 slaves per household, compared to 2.9 per household for households owning no land. Of the total number of 469 households owning no land up to one hundred acres, 42.6 percent owned one slave, 22.6 percent owned two, 12.8 percent owned three, 8.2 percent owned four, 3.6 percent owned five, and 10.3 percent owned six or more with one household owning ten slaves.

**TABLE 4.2**

***1791 Land and Personal Property Tax, Kingston Parish, Virginia***

| | No. of Households | No. of Households with Slaves | Percent of Households with Slaves | No. of Slaves | Slaves per Household |
|---|---|---|---|---|---|
| No Land | 303 | 100 | 33.0 | 294 | 2.9 |
| 1–25 acres | 47 | 16 | 34.0 | 34 | 2.1 |
| 26–50 | 57 | 38 | 66.7 | 68 | 1.8 |
| 51–100 | 62 | 41 | 66.1 | 118 | 2.9 |
| 101–150 | 21 | 20 | 95.2 | 74 | 3.7 |
| 151–200 | 17 | 16 | 94.1 | 77 | 4.8 |
| 201–250 | 15 | 14 | 93.3 | 85 | 6.1 |
| 251 300 | 12 | 11 | 91.7 | 62 | 5.6 |
| 301–350 | 9 | 7 | 77.8 | 61 | 8.7 |
| 351–400 | 7 | 3 | 42.9 | 32 | 10.7 |
| 401–500 | 5 | 4 | 80.0 | 43 | 10.8 |
| 501–600 | 5 | 5 | 100.0 | 43 | 8.6 |
| 601–999 | 3 | 3 | 100.0 | 38 | 12.7 |
| Over 1,000 | 3 | 3 | 100.0 | 92 | 30.7 |
| Total | 566 | 281 | 49.6 | 1,121 | 4.0 |

The data also show a significant increase in number of households that owned slaves as acreage increases. The households with no land to 25 acres who owned slaves was 33–34 percent. In the 26- to 100-acre categories, the percentage doubled to 66.1–66.7. Above 100 acres, households owning slaves was more than 90 percent except for the 301- to 500-acre categories.

Starting at 51 acres, the number of slaves per household increased in an almost unbroken rate from 2.9 per household to 30.7 for those owning more than 1,000 acres. This steady increase reflects the economic reality of the times in that owning land was a liability unless there was adequate labor to make it productive. For a large acreage, labor was essential to cultivation, harvesting, fencing, ditching, and all the other tasks essential to a well-managed farm. In the late eighteenth century, the least expensive form of labor was from owning or renting slaves.

Table 4.3 shows the number of horses per household: a total of 560 horses, averaging 2.1 horses per household. This relatively small number compared to the number of acres

**TABLE 4.3**

***1791 Land and Personal Property Tax, Kingston Parish, Virginia***

| | No. of Households | No. of Households with Horses | Percent of Households with Horses | No. of Horses | Horses per Household |
|---|---|---|---|---|---|
| No Land | 303 | 103 | 34.0 | 193 | 1.9 |
| 1–25 acres | 47 | 18 | 38.3 | 27 | 1.5 |
| 26–50 | 57 | 25 | 43.9 | 40 | 1.6 |
| 51–100 | 62 | 36 | 58.1 | 63 | 1.8 |
| 101–150 | 21 | 16 | 76.2 | 31 | 1.9 |
| 151–200 | 17 | 15 | 88.2 | 39 | 2.6 |
| 201–250 | 15 | 13 | 86.7 | 25 | 1.9 |
| 251–300 | 12 | 10 | 83.3 | 34 | 3.4 |
| 301–350 | 9 | 8 | 88.9 | 24 | 3.0 |
| 351–400 | 7 | 4 | 57.1 | 11 | 2.8 |
| 401–500 | 5 | 4 | 80.0 | 18 | 4.5 |
| 501–600 | 5 | 4 | 80.0 | 14 | 3.5 |
| 601–999 | 3 | 2 | 66.7 | 11 | 5.5 |
| Over 1,000 | 3 | 3 | 100.0 | 30 | 10.0 |
| Total | 566 | 261 | 46.1 | 560 | 2.1 |

suggests that they were used primarily to pull carts and other vehicles used in transportation and for saddle riding. Oxen performed the heavy work required in farming and hauling heavy loads. Of the 303 households without land ownership, 103, or 34 percent, owned 193 horses; households with just one horse numbered 58.

Over half of the tax-paying heads of household in Kingston Parish owned no land, but almost half of them owned slaves and/or horses. Table 4.4 shows that, of the 303 households without land, 166, 55 percent, did not own any slaves or horses. These men, and a very few women, would have included young adults, with or without a wife or children, living on land owned by relatives or others and employed as farmers, shipbuilders, mariners, and other trades. Also included in this group were the county's very poor white males and free blacks who earned their living as laborers or trademen. Others were those who could not work due to age or physical limitation.

**TABLE 4.4**

***1791 Land and Personal Property Tax, Kingston Parish, Virginia***

| | No. of Households | No. of Households with Slaves | No. of Households with Horses | No. of Households with Slaves and Horses | No. of Households with No Slaves or Horses |
|---|---|---|---|---|---|
| No Land | 303 | 100 | 103 | 69 | 166 |
| 1–25 acres | 47 | 16 | 18 | 7 | 21 |
| 26–50 | 57 | 38 | 25 | 19 | 13 |
| 51–100 | 62 | 41 | 36 | 27 | 11 |
| 101–150 | 21 | 20 | 16 | 16 | 1 |
| 151–200 | 17 | 16 | 15 | 14 | 0 |
| 201–250 | 15 | 14 | 13 | 13 | 1 |
| 251–300 | 12 | 11 | 10 | 9 | 0 |
| 301–350 | 9 | 7 | 8 | 7 | 0 |
| 351–400 | 7 | 3 | 4 | 2 | 2 |
| 401–500 | 5 | 4 | 4 | 4 | 1 |
| 501–600 | 5 | 5 | 4 | 4 | 0 |
| 601–999 | 3 | 3 | 2 | 2 | 0 |
| Over 1,000 | 3 | 3 | 3 | 3 | 0 |
| Total | 566 | 281 | 261 | 196 | 216 |

Overall, of the 566 households, just 97, or 17 percent, had land ownership over 100 acres. Only 32, or 6 percent, had land in excess of 300 acres. The owners having 100 or more acres owned 28,650 acres, or 50 percent of the total land that was taxed in 1791. Unsettled estates accounted for another 8,992 acres, 11 percent of the total, and 11,739 acres were owned by nonresidents, 21 percent of all land taxed, a significant portion of the county's land area.

**TABLE 4.5**

***1791 Land and Personal Property Tax, Kingston Parish, Virginia***

| | No. of Households | Percent of Households with Slaves | Percent of Households with Horses | Percent of Households with Slaves and Horses | Percent of Households with No Slaves or Horses |
|---|---|---|---|---|---|
| No Land | 303 | 33.0 | 34.0 | 22.8 | 54.8 |
| 1–25 acres | 47 | 34.0 | 38.3 | 14.9 | 44.7 |
| 26–50 | 57 | 66.7 | 43.9 | 33.3 | 22.8 |
| 51–100 | 62 | 66.1 | 58.1 | 43.6 | 17.7 |
| 101–150 | 21 | 95.2 | 76.2 | 76.2 | 4.8 |
| 151–200 | 17 | 94.1 | 88.2 | 82.4 | 0 |
| 201–250 | 15 | 93.3 | 86.7 | 86.7 | 6.7 |
| 251–300 | 12 | 91.7 | 83.3 | 75.0 | 0 |
| 301–350 | 9 | 77.8 | 88.9 | 77.8 | 0 |
| 351–400 | 7 | 42.9 | 57.1 | 28.6 | 28.6 |
| 401–500 | 5 | 80.0 | 80.0 | 80.0 | 20.0 |
| 501–600 | 5 | 100.0 | 80.0 | 80.0 | 0 |
| 601–999 | 3 | 100.0 | 66.7 | 66.7 | 0 |
| Over 1,000 | 3 | 100.0 | 100.0 | 100.0 | 0 |
| Total | 566 | 49.7 | 46.1 | 34.6 | 38.2 |

During the eighteenth century, slaves were a significant asset for a family. Not only did slaves provide labor, but also they were often rented to others who needed extra or temporary laborers, they could be sold to realize capital for other purposes and to pay debts, and they could be exchanged for land. Widows could rent slaves to others, the payments being a form of pension income. Slaves and land comprised the vast majority of planters' assets and were the most important items listed in wills and estate inventories, with cattle, a favorite horse, and selected items of furniture being also of importance.

The average cost to a planter for a slave in the first half of the eighteenth century was from twenty-eight to thirty-five pounds. The cost to the slave trader on the coast of Africa was four to five pounds. The profit potential for the slave trader was thus large even after allowances for the sometimes high mortality rates during the Atlantic crossing. The African tribes that controlled the capture of other tribes also realized large sums for their effort. English merchants, especially those based in Bristol, and New England traders made vast fortunes in the slave trade with great numbers of slaves sold in the West Indies and South America. Trade to the mid-Atlantic colonies was the least lucrative market because less labor was needed to produce tobacco than to produce sugarcane and sugar. In addition, living and working conditions in the mid-Atlantic were conducive to longer life spans, and thus the slave population increased naturally. This dynamic reduced the need for importation of slaves and increased the profitability of owning slaves in Virginia. In the eighteenth century, Virginia became an exporter of slaves to other southern states.

The average annual output per laborer in the first decade of the eighteenth century, productivity that would change little during the next fifty years, was 1,700 pounds of tobacco. A slave would be capable of producing tobacco having a value of £7.1 per year, at a farm price of 1d., based on all oronoco. The planter would thus recoup the investment in a slave in four to five years and thereafter realize a continuing profit for the working years of the slave's life. The planter's investment would be recouped at a faster rate if sweet-scented were grown as it sold at an average of 1.35d. One laborer growing all sweet-scented would yield £9.56 per year of income. Slave labor was a much more profitable system than the earlier dependence on indentured servants, who had to be replaced when their contracts terminated after four to seven years.

As the eighteenth century progressed, those with capital to acquire more land and slaves built large estates and created concentrations of wealth and political influence that changed many aspects of life in Virginia. These generalities were evident in Gloucester County, which was among the larger tobacco-producing areas in the Tidewater region.

With the rapid introduction of slaves in the early years of the 1700s, indentured servants virtually ceased to exist except in skilled trades. The former servants, unable to acquire land of their own in Kingston Parish, lease land, sharecrop, or work for wages, gradually moved to other counties to the west in the Piedmont and southward into the Carolinas. This movement resulted in a significant change in the demography of the county: the number of single white males diminished rapidly after 1670 while the number of Africans increased substantially.

Colonial tax records, vestry records, surveys and deeds, and other original source documents help to illuminate life in those times. Unfortunately, very little that was written about other aspects of life in eighteenth-century Virginia has survived. Fortunately, Robert Beverley's *History and Present State of Virginia,* published in 1705, survives. It provides the first significant account of developments and life in Virginia since the early writings of John Smith and others during the years immediately following the settlement of Jamestown.

Robert Beverley was in a unique position to observe Virginia. He was born in Virginia and educated in England, worked in the office of the colony's secretary of state, and held various clerkships. In 1699, he was elected to the House of Burgesses. He inherited a large plantation, Beverley Park, in Gloucester County and married one of William Byrd's daughters. Among his works was the publication in 1722 of a summary of the laws of Virginia, *An Abridgement of the Publick Laws of Virginia.*

Beverley provides the only comprehensive report on Virginia at the beginning of the eighteenth century, at a time in the development of the colony that would usher in enormous change. His *History and Present State of Virginia* reviewed the history of Virginia, the native Indians, and the government and included an extensive section titled "The Natural Productions and Conveniencies of the Country, Suited to Trade and Improvement." Here are selected passages that would have resonated with Virginians in the early eighteenth century:

> *Of the Bounds and Coast of* Virginia. . . .
>
> The Entrance into *Virginia* for Shipping, is by the Mouth of *Chesapeak* Bay, which is indeed more like a River, than a Bay: For it runs up into the Land about Two Hundred Miles, being every where near as wide, as it is at the Mouth, and in many Places much wider. The Mouth thereof is about Seven Leagues over, through which all Ships must pass to go to *Maryland.*
>
> The Coast is a bold and even Coast, with regular Soundings, and is open all the Year round: So that having the Latitude, which also can hardly be wanted, upon a Coast where so much clear Weather is, any Ship may go in by Soundings alone, by Day or Night, in Summer or in Winter; and need not fear any Disaster, if the Mariners understand any thing; for, let the Wind blow how it will, and chop about as suddenly as it pleases, any Master, tho' his Ship be never so dull,

> has Opportunity (by the Evenness of the Coast) either of standing off, and clearing the Shore; or else of running into safe Harbour within the Capes. A bolder and safer Coast is not known in the Universe; to which Conveniencies, there's the Addition of good Anchorage all along upon it, without the Capes.[2]

Beverley's description of the Virginia coastline is accurate and written for landsmen and mariners alike. Determining latitude was practiced by all ocean navigators, and his reference to "Soundings alone" reflects the very gradual decrease in ocean depth as a vessel approached land once over the continental shelf. His reference to good anchorage "without the Capes" describes a practice that is no longer used, anchoring in the ocean, which was common in the age of sail on the Virginia coast, especially if the prevailing wind was out of the west. Vessels would remain at anchor until the wind became favorable for sailing into the bay. In adverse weather conditions, vessels would weigh anchor and sail away from the coastline until conditions improved.

> *Of the Waters. . . .*
>
> Besides this Bay, the Country is water'd with Four great Rivers. . . . There are also abundance of lesser Rivers. . . .
>
> These Rivers are of such Convenience, that, for almost every Half Dozen Miles of their Extent, there's a commodious and safe Road for a whole Fleet; which gives Opportunity to the Masters of Ships, to lie up and down straggling, according as they have made their Acquaintance, riding before that Gentleman's Door where they find the best Reception, or where 'tis most suitable to their Business.
>
> These Rivers are made up, by the Conflux of an infinite Number of Chrystal Springs of cool and pleasant Water, issuing every-where out of the Banks, and Sides of the Valleys.[3]

Beverley is referring to the James, York, Rappahannock, and Potomac Rivers. Dozens of ships and smaller vessels sailed on them and were a common sight, especially in the early months of the year when ships would move down the rivers taking on cargoes and in late fall with the return of the tobacco ships from England.

> *Of the Earths, and Soil. . . .*
>
> The Land towards the Mouth of the Rivers is generally of a low, moist and fat Mould, such as the heavier sort of Grain delight in, as Rice, Hemp, *Indian* Corn, &c. This also is varied here and there with Veins of a cold, hungry, sandy

> Soil, of the same Moisture, and very often lying under Water. But this also has its Advantages; for on such Land, generally grow the Huckle-berries, Cran-berries, Chincapins, &c. These low Lands are for the most part, well stor'd with Oaks, Poplars, Pines, Cedars, Cypress, and Sweet-Gums; the Trunks of which are often Thirty, Forty, Fifty, some Sixty or Seventy Foot high, without a Branch or Limb. They likewise produce great Variety of Evergreens, unknown to me by Name, besides the beauteous Holly, Sweet-Myrtle, Cedar, and the Live Oak, which for Three Quarters of the Year is continually dropping its Acorns, and at the same time budding, and bearing others in their Stead.[4]

Beverley did not comment on soil conditions most suitable for growing tobacco. However, his descriptions of soils, varieties of trees, and types of clay reveal a time when nature was relied on to supply the greater part of everyday necessities.

> There is likewise found great Variety of Earths for Physick, Cleansing, Scouring, and making all Sorts of Potters-Ware; such as Antimony, Talk, yellow and red Oker, Fullers-Earth, Pipe-Clay, and other fat and fine Clays, Marle, &c. In a Word, there are all kinds of Earth fit for Use.
>
> . . . For tho' generally the lower Parts are flat, and so free from Stones, that People seldom Shoe their Horses; yet in many Places, and particularly near the Falls of the Rivers, are found vast Quantities of Stone, fit for all kind of Uses. However, as yet there is seldom any Use made of them, because commonly Wood is to be had at much less Trouble. And as for Coals, it is not likely they should ever be used there in any thing, but Forges and great Towns, if ever they happen to have any; for, in their Country Plantations, the Wood grows at every Man's Door so fast, that after it has been cut down, it will in Seven Years time, grow up again from Seed, to substantial Fire-Wood; and in Eighteen or Twenty Years 'twill come to be very good Board-Timber.[5]

Beverley continues with comprehensive lists and detailed characteristics of minerals, topography, wild fruits, berries, nuts, wild grapes, myrtle for making candles, flowers, creeping vines, melons, four types on Indian corn, extensive commentary on fish and fishing methods, wild fowl, and numerous related topics. In addition, he addresses climate, clothing, the militia, and government.

Unfortunately, Beverley's comments on housing are limited and disproportionately focused on that occupied by the wealthy:

> The Private Buildings are of late very much improved; several Gentlemen there, having built themselves large Brick Houses of many Rooms on a Floor, and several Stories high, as also some Stone-Houses: but they don't covet to make them lofty, having extent enough of Ground to build upon; and now and then they are visited by high Winds, which wou'd incommode a towering Fabrick. They always contrive to have large Rooms, that they may be cool in Summer. Of late they have made their Stories much higher than formerly, and their Windows large, and shasht with Cristal Glass; and within they adorn their Apartments with rich Furniture.
>
> All their Drudgeries of Cookery, Washing, Daries, &c. are perform'd in Offices detacht from the Dwelling-Houses, which by this means are kept more cool and Sweet.
>
> There Tobacco-Houses are all built of Wood, as open and airy as is consistent with keeping out Rain; which sort of Building, is most convenient for the curing of their Tobacco.
>
> Their common covering for Dwelling-Houses is Shingle, which is an Oblong Square of Cypress or Pine-wood; but they cover their Tobacco-Houses with thin Clap-board; and tho' they have Slate enough in some particular parts of the Country, and as strong Clay as can be desired for making Tile, yet they have very few tiled Houses; neither has any one yet thought it worth his while, to dig up the Slate, which will hardly be made use of, till the Carriage there becomes cheaper, and more common.[6]

Beverley's reference to "Private Buildings" is thought to refer to the homes of the wealthiest families while "Dwelling-Houses" refers to the middling planter. Regrettably, the topic lacks descriptions of foundations, framing, numbers of rooms and fireplaces, chimney construction, and use of brick.

During the first half of the eighteenth century, the local economy became more diversified. Former tobacco fields, often called "old fields," were utilized for the production of grains and other crops, and an active market in trade developed with other colonies, especially New England and sugar plantations in the West Indies. Exports included corn, wheat, flour, tobacco, pig iron, pork, lard, tallow, beans, peas, rye, potatoes, flaxseed, walnut and hickory planks, hemp, sails, cordage, tar, turpentine, deer and other skins, and wax. Imports included codfish, mackerel, cheese, resins, cranberries, apples, hops, rum, beer, cider, chocolate, coffee, and Madeira wine. Trade with England continued to be significant with manufactured goods being imported on the strength of the value of the exported tobacco, which grew to one hundred million pounds on the eve of the Revolution in 1775 including crops from Virginia and Maryland.

Trade within the Chesapeake was also an important factor and created the need for large numbers of small vessels suited for transporting crops and other cargoes in the bay and on its rivers and creeks. Merchants and factors became professions in their own right as the need for arranging freight, negotiating freight rates, knowing tariff schedules, securing cargoes, superintending loading, collecting debts, accounting, and so forth became specialized skills.

Intercolonial trade and local Chesapeake Bay commerce created an increasing need for shipwrights, ship carpenters, shipyards, and providers of victuals. And the shipbuilding industry supported the manufacture of tar, turpentine, sailcloth, cordage, iron, and lumber. As the century progressed, Chesapeake shipyards built an increasing number of seagoing vessels for colonial owners and English merchants. Most popular were sloops for the bay, coastal trading, and trade with Bermuda and the West Indies. Brigs and schooners were used for larger cargoes for these same destinations and transatlantic voyages as well. Three-masted,

*Figure* 6 A typical 1760 schooner. The two-masted schooner was widely used in the eighteenth century because of its ability to sail at an angle into the wind more efficiently than a square-rigged ship and because it did not require a large crew. Schooners were used in the Chesapeake Bay, on coastal voyages to other east coast colonies, and in transatlantic trade. From Howard I. Chapelle, *The History of American Sailing Ships* (New York: W. W. Norton, 1935), 12.

ship-rigged vessels were also built but in smaller numbers than sloops, brigs, and schooners due to the greater investment required and the expense of larger crews.

The 1704 rent roll in Kingston Parish listed 116 landowners. Owners with less than 350 acres numbered 73, or 63 percent. Less than 10 percent, 11, had 1,000 acres or more. By 1791 the number of owners had increased from 116 to 379 as larger holdings were subdivided. Holdings less than 350 acres increased to 346, 91 percent of the total of all landowners. The number of very large estates of 1,000 acres or more declined to 4. These statistics present a parish consisting of almost all family farms, most of which were small, below 350 acres, but large enough to produce a crop or more, pasture for cattle, woodlots, and kitchen gardens. The society was close-knit, with a high degree of self-sufficiency.

In Kingston Parish the vast majority of white families were Anglicans, members of the Church of England. Slaves could also attend church services, and many did. Other than on court days, on which mostly men assembled, the Sunday gathering at church was one of the few opportunities for the women, men, and children of the neighborhood to socialize,

*Figure 7* A typical 1760 frigate. Frigates had three masts with square sails on each with a spanker on the mizzen mast and jibs forward. Large merchant ships and man-of-war naval ships were similarly rigged. From Howard I. Chapelle, *The History of American Sailing Ships* (New York: W. W. Norton, 1935), 14.

exchange news, conduct business, and discuss the outlook for crops, politics, and all things of common interest to the community. A crowd would typically gather an hour before the church service and would linger afterwards, and then often families would dine with neighbors in the early afternoon.

The Church of England was an important factor in colonial Virginia and performed some of the functions that the government would do in future years, such as welfare for the needy. Kingston Parish, from an early date, had an organized congregation and maintained a vestry book from 1679 to 1796 although there is a gap in the record of fourteen years from the end of 1726 to 1740. In addition, the Kingston Parish register covers 1749–1827. Unfortunately, eighty-five pages have been lost.

A board of vestrymen, typically twelve in number, most often from the more prominent men of the parish, presided over the work of the church and set policy. They had total control over the selection of the minister, whose term of service was set by an annual contract and so could be ended in a relatively short time. A minister would thus be especially attentive to the wishes of the vestry. In the late 1750s, approximately one-third of ministers in Virginia were native-born with the remaining two-third from England and Scotland.

The governance structure placed the vestry in a position of considerable power and influence in the parish. The vestry selected its own new members, a practice known as "cooptation," and thus family connections, political influence, and wealth had a determining influence on who would become new members. Since wealth and influence were typically a function of how much land and how many slaves a family owned, members of the vestry tended to be from the ranks of the largest landowners. Vestrymen were typically among the most well-informed citizens concerning parish affairs and were thus the most logical candidates to serve in colonial government. Each parish had two or more church wardens who carried out the instructions of the vestry.

There were three classifications of colonial taxes: The first was determined by the General Assembly to pay for the militia, public officials, expenses of the meeting house, and burgesses. The second was county levies determined by the justices that were necessary for the building and repair of public buildings and bridges, the expenses of running the courthouse and jail, and the payment of legal and other services. Parish levies, the third, were determined by the vestry and were known as a "tithe," an amount that would vary but that tended to average twenty pounds of tobacco annually, an amount equal to approximately two and a half shillings. The tithe, collected by men appointed by the verstry, would be determined based on the expected expenses of the parish including the compensation of the minister, sexton, and clerk of the parish; maintenance of church buildings and the glebe house; and numerous charity cases.

In addition, the vestry was responsible for organizing and overseeing processioning, an ancient custom of adjoining neighbors walking the common property lines together each year to determine that the agreed boundaries were intact. Disputes would require a review of the deeds and perhaps a new survey. The Kingston vestry book does not contain instructions and boundary definitions of precincts for processioning, as compared to the Petsworth vestry book, which has relatively detailed information. Kingston's rivers and creeks may have lessened the importance of regular inspection of property lines.

Other responsibilities of the vestry included maintaining records of vital statistics including marriages, births, baptisms, and deaths. The clerk of the church was responsible for these record-keeping duties as well as the minutes of vestry meetings, the account books, ledgers of parish transactions, fees collected, and all expenditures. The clerk often read from the Book of Common Prayer during the morning prayer section of a church service and in some cases conducted burials when the minister was unavailable.

During the colonial period, marriage ceremonies were most often conducted in the home of the bride. Baptisms, which took place shortly after birth, were performed at church and home. The minister would travel the parish in the performance of his duties. Burial of the dead typically occurred shortly after death, within a day or two, except in cold weather with frozen ground conditions, and would be done by family members and friends. The funeral would be held a few weeks afterward, typically in the home of the deceased, and would be a celebration of a well-lived life.

Other than descriptions of houses in newspaper advertisements and sketches of structures on surveys, the vestry book of Kingston Parish is the only known source of information concerning construction and architecture of buildings in Mathews County in the eighteenth century. For example, on October 22, 1753, the vestry authorized the construction of "two Vestry Houses 12 x 16 Fram'd & plaister'd and floored a Chimney & one window with Eight lights Robt parot to build one @ £7."[7] On November 26, 1754, the vestry authorized an additional £1 to Robert Parret for the vestry house at the new church, the "Eastermost River Church." The payment in tobacco was 160 pounds, indicating a farm price of 0.67d. per pound, a dramatic decline from the early years of the century.

By November 1755, the number of tithables was 1,426. Construction materials listed by the vestry in 1757 mention five hundred feet of paling at 3d. each or 892 pounds of tobacco. This indicates that the farm price of tobacco had increased dramatically and now was 1.68d. An entry in October 1758 gives the value of tobacco at 2d. This is a very useful example of the variability in the farm price of tobacco and the resulting challenges to the planter in managing his affairs.

According to the vestry book of Kingston Parish, on November 5, 1759, for construction of buildings at the glebe, the Reverend Mr. Dixon was given an allowance of 1,500 pounds of tobacco for "a well built Quarter Twenty Feet long & sixteen Feet wide; and a corn House Sixteen Feet long & twelve Feet wide."[8] The price of tobacco at the time appears to have been 2d., so these two structures were estimated to cost £12.5, or £2.44 per one hundred square feet or 5.86d. per foot. The dimensions are typical of similar structures at that time. A few years earlier, in neighboring Petsworth Parish, an advertisement in the *Virginia Gazette*, a newspaper published in Williamsburg, on July 31, 1746, read:

> By Order of the Vestry of *Petsworth* Parish in *Gloucester* County, there is to be a Dwelling-house built on the Glebe Land in the said Parish, 52 Feet long and 20 Feet wide. Any Person inclinable to undertake the same, is desired to meet the Vestry at the said Parish Church, on the first *Wednesday* in *August* next.

On November 9, 1761, the Kingston Parish vestry authorized the church wardens to have the glebe house repaired and the building of a sixteen-by-twenty-foot room made with brick with a brick chimney. The estimated cost was five thousand pounds of tobacco, or £31.25.

The first known survey of the glebe is dated 1689 and is thought to be the oldest survey to have survived from Kingston Parish. It is also quite possibly the oldest piece of paper from Kingston's history other than land patents and the vestry book of Kingston Parish.

A second survey of the glebe made by Thomas Cooke on October 22, 1712, has a sketch of a glebe house on the church-owned glebe lands. It appears to have been a one-and-a-half-story structure with a chimney at each end. The survey is remarkably accurate and drawn to scale. This was a larger than average tract, measuring 455 acres. The line running from B to C was 320 poles long, the length of a mile.

The description of the survey also survives:

> A Survey according to Coll. Dudley Pollard, Gleeb
>
> Beging at the west Side of Pudding Creek & Extending NW along the Eastermost River 180 poles to a marked white oake that Stands in the Mouth of the Creek that divides this Land and the Land of Robt Lendall thence NNE: 320 poles into the woods: thence South East 190 poles thence NE: 28 poles thence SE: 110 poles along the Land of Philp. Hunleys to a marked white oake that stands on the head of Pudding Creek [illegible] : down this Creek 345 poles to the first specified place,
>
> in all by the Pattent 455 Acres.

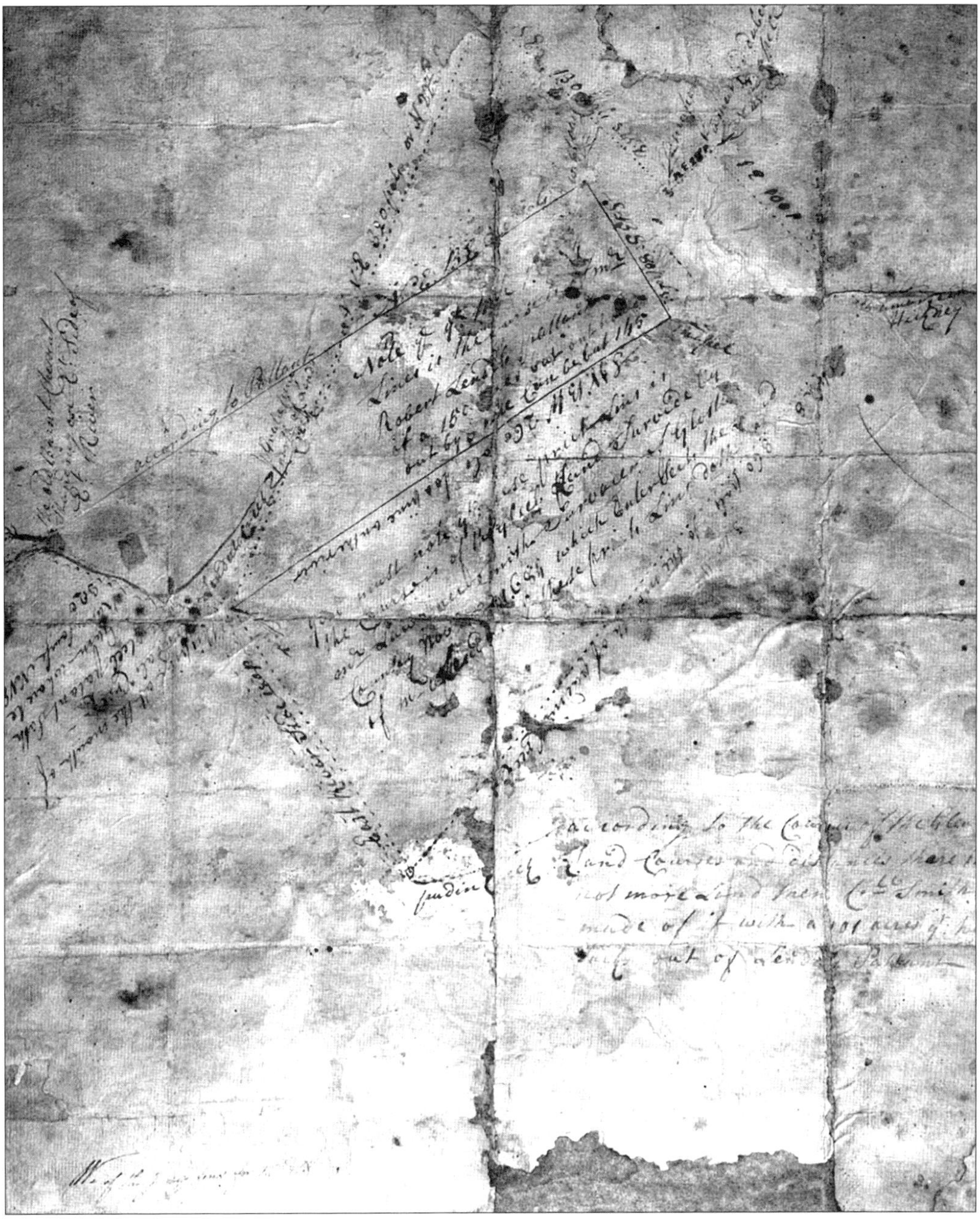

*Figure* 8 The glebe survey is thought to be the oldest surviving survey of a tract of land within Kingston Parish. The date, 1689, can be seen in almost the exact middle of the image. The southwest boundary is the East River. Pudding Creek is on the southeast, and Woodas Creek is to the northwest. Courtesy of Earl Gregg Swem Library, College of William & Mary, Williamsburg, VA.

*Figure* 9 The glebe was surveyed again in 1712 and included a simple sketch of the glebe house. It appears to have had two chimneys and a central entrance. Surveyors often included a sketch of the principal structure, and the sketches were typically fact based with respect to the number of floors, chimneys, and shape of the roof. Sketches on the survey approximate the actual locations, and thus the glebe house of 1712 was about two thousand feet northeast of the mouth of Pudding Creek on its western shore. Courtesy of Earl Gregg Swem Library, College of William & Mary, Williamsburg, VA.

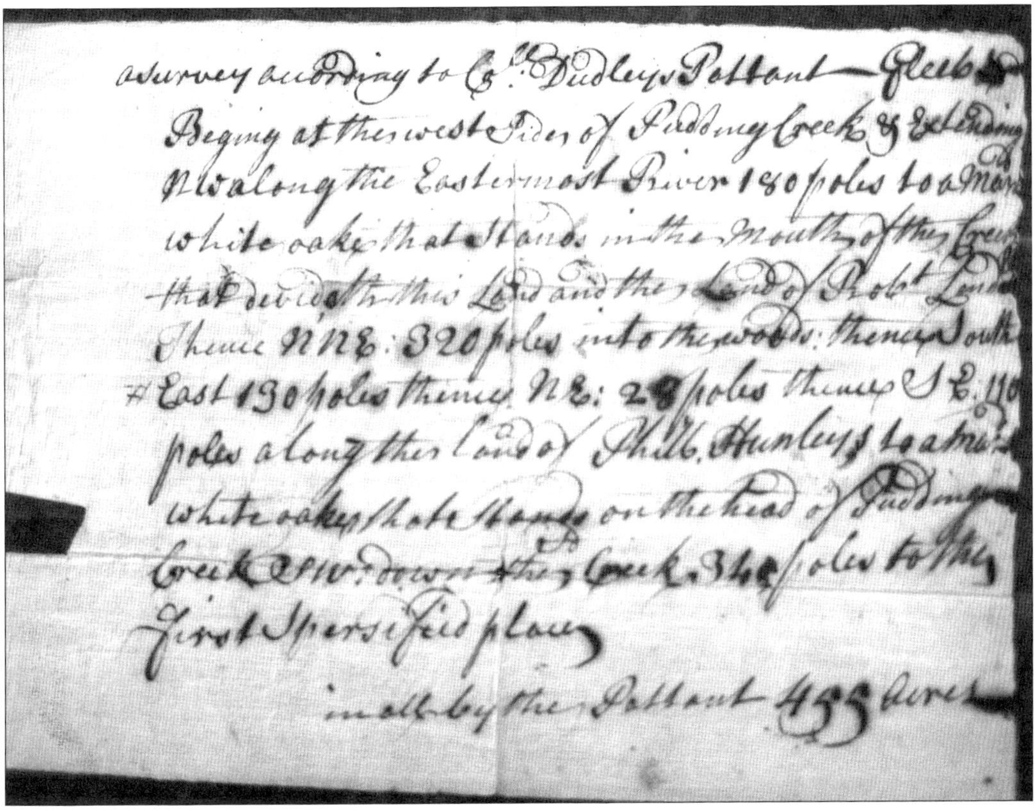

a survey according to Col. Dudley Pollard — Gleeb
Beging at the west side of Pudding Creek & Extending
N W along the Eastermost River 180 poles to a Mark'd
white oake that stands in the Mouth of the Creek
that devideth this Land and the Land of Robt [illegible]
Thence N N E: 320 poles into the woods: thence South
East 190 poles thence N E: 28 poles thence S E 110
poles along the Land of Phill. Hunleys to a mark'd
white oake that stands on the head of Pudding
Creek & S W: down the Creek 340 poles to the
First Sperssified place
in all by the Pollant 455 acres

*Figure* 10 The description of the glebe house survey as measured and recorded by Col. Dudley Pollard. Courtesy of Earl Gregg Swem Library, College of William & Mary, Williamsburg, VA.

The Kingston Parish vestry book does not include a description of the glebe house; however, it might have resembled the one in nearby Petsworth Parish. The vestry there ordered the following specifications in a meeting held on June 28, 1701, 1702, or 1703 (the year is illegible but the context suggests this range). The house described would have been similar to those of wealthy landowners in Gloucester County:

> It is ordr by This p'sent Vestry that William Bernard Church Wardn Doe forthwith Agree with Some Workmen for ye Building & Ereckting of a Gleeb house upon ye Gleeb plantation; Six & thirty foot Long & twenty foot wide with two Outside Chemneys two 8 foot Square Clossetts planckt above & below, with two Chambers above Staires and ye Staires to Goe up in ye midst of ye house with 3 Large Glass windows Below Stair [ ] Each to have 3 Double Lights in ye with a Glass window in Each Chamber above Staires Each to have 3 Lights in ye & Each Clossett to have a window in it and Each window to have 3 Lights.[9]

Nothing was accomplished until November 12, 1704, when the vestry ordered the church wardens:

> Draw Conditions wth Ezra Cotten for ye building of a gleeb-house & kitchen ye Sd house to be of ye Same Dementions as Mr Robt Pourtees. & to be framed on Good white oak Sills and to Stand upon blocks & to be lathd. wth Goo[d] oak lathes and Shingled wth Good Siprus Shingles The Sd house to be 36 foot in Length & 20 foot wide, ye Roof to be 18 Inches Jet and to have two outSide Chimnies and two Closets adjoyning to them, and all things Ells pertaining according to ye Dementions of ye above Sd Robt Pourtees house, Viz, ye above Sd Kitchin to be foot Long & foot wide.[10]

By the October 3, 1705, meeting of the vestry, progress on the new glebe house was complete or nearly so because the vestry authorized payments to Capt. Thomas Buckner for "Carting timber for ye Gleeb-house" in the amount of 450 pounds of tobacco and to Ezra Cottle 3,000 pounds of tobacco for "building ye Gleebhouse" and a second payment to Cottle of 1,000 pounds tobacco "for Extraordinary Service."[11]

The description indicates that the house was constructed of wood, possibly including the chimneys as was common at the time. The foundation consisted of wooden blocks spaced according to even weight distribution. By November 1710, repairs were needed to mend the "Chamber Chimbley of the Gleib-house and build an outside Chimbley to the Citching & playster the Same."[12] In 1714 the vestry ordered the employment of workmen to repair the glebe house. More repairs were needed in 1717, 1718, 1719, 1731, and 1737. At a meeting on May 28, 1746, the vestry ordered a new glebe house:

> Ordered this Present Vestry, have thought it Better to Build a New Glebe house rather then to Repair the old one, therefore tis ordered by the sd. Vestry that there be a New Dwelling house Fifty two feet Long and twenty feet wide from out to out Built on the said glebe, and that the Vestry meet on the first Wednesday in August Next to agree with Workmen accordingly.[13]

The new glebe house lasted until sometime in late 1784 or early 1785 because on April 23, 1785, the vestry made this decision:

> It is ordered by a Majority of the whole Vestry to wit the Seven Members present that the Church Wardens do Sell the whole of the Bricks of the late Glebe House that was burnt in this Parish provided they can find a purchaser or purchasers that will take them on their being Valued by Three Honest reputable residents of Sd Parish giving twelve months Credit &

> taking bond with good Security for the Same & make return of their proceedings.[14]

The Kingston vestry record of November 29, 1760, is complete with the typical business of the church, church expenses, and allowances to parishioners for taking care of orphans and other charity cases. The number of tithables stood at 1,481, and the estimated farm price of tobacco, as used by the church, was 2d. The number of tithables during the years 1760 through 1770 varied from a low of 1,421 in 1769 to a high of 1,552 in 1763. The average for the ten-year period was 1,466, and the number at the end of the period was 1,425 in 1770. The only year for which an accurate record has survived for the number of tithables following 1770 was in 1773 when the number stood at 1,421. The tax per tithable varied from a low of 22 pounds of tobacco in 1766 to a high of 34¼ pounds in 1772. The average tax for the ten-year period 1760 through 1770 was 25 pounds of tobacco per tithable.

The vestry record of October 26, 1773, listed payments to the new clerk, Thomas Hall, in the amount of 1,200 pounds of tobacco and 48 pounds "for cask," an allowance for barrels to contain the tobacco. The minister, the Reverend Thomas Field, was paid 16,000 pounds of tobacco plus 1,280 for shrinkage and cask. Additional payments were authorized for widows, keeping children, and making fires in the vestry house for a total vestry expense of 39,358 pounds of tobacco. There were 1,421 tithables on the list, each taxed at the rate of 28 pounds of tobacco for a total revenue of 39,788 pounds of tobacco, approximately equivalent to £259 16s. 2d., assuming a price per pound of tobacco of 1.567d.

The *Virginia Gazette* offers advertisements and news items that give further understanding of Gloucester, especially during the years preceding the Revolutionary War. For example, the importance of shipbuilding in Kingston Parish is captured in the following two advertisements, two of many published during the late eighteenth century and continuing until the 1820s in the *Virginia Gazette* and other publications. The March 26, 1767, Purdie and Dixon* *Virginia Gazette* advertisement for a ship built on speculation is a good example. This advertisement also gives the terms of payment:

> *To be* SOLD, A NEW SHIP, of about 236 tuns, well calculated for the TOBACCO trade, built of the best seasoned plank and timber, and can be launched in a little time, if required. Twelve months credit will be allowed for two thirds or three fourths of the value. Any person inclinable to purchase may be shown the vessel by applying to the subscriber, living in *Kingston* parish, *Gloucester* county. THOMAS SMITH.

* There were two competing *Virginia Gazettes* in Williamsburg from 1766 to 1773, one published by Rind and one by Purdie and Dixon. From 1774 to 1776, there were three, and through 1780 there were two again.

An example of the sale of a used schooner and a new sloop in Purdie and Dixon's *Virginia Gazette*, July 28, 1768:

> *To be SOLD on reasonable terms, for cash or good bills of exchange,* A SEA SCHOONER, of about eighty tuns burthen, two years old, and now fit to take a cargo in. Also a SLOOP, of fifty tuns burthen, now on the stocks, and may be launched in three weeks. Any person inclinable to purchase may know the terms by applying to the subscriber in *Kingston* parish, *Gloucester* county. ROBERT BILLUPS.

Advertisements for the sale of land and slaves were numerous, with the following example from Purdie and Dixon's *Virginia Gazette*, July 23, 1767:

> *To be* SOLD *at* PUBLICK AUCTION, *on* Thursday *the 3d of* September *next, pursuant to a decree of* GLOUCESTER county court, ONE hundred and fifty acres of very valuable LAND, lying on *Slut's* creek, in *Gloucester* county; also about 15 valuable SLAVES. The terms will be agreed on at the day of sale. LEWIS BURWELL, Jun. Sheriff.

Advertisements for land, including structures, offer insights into the size and construction of the housing stock for the years immediately preceding the Revolutionary War, as in the following two advertisements from the *Virginia Gazette*, November 13, 1766:

> *To be* SOLD, *the 3d of* December, *at* East *warehouse, in* Gloucester *county*, A Parcel of LAND, containing about 40 acres, part lying within 60 yards of the warehouse, is a beautiful place for a merchant, as there is at this time two sea vessels building thereon, and is clear and level. Also 251 acres of wood land, lying adjacent thereto, very rich and well timbered, will be sold at the same time. . . ROBERT TOMPKINS.

The tract described above adjoins or is in the immediate vicinity of what is now known as Williams Wharf. Tompkins was a significant landowner in the neighborhood and was a frequent buyer and seller of land. Another owner in the same neighborhood was Joseph Gayle. Proximity to the east warehouse was a decided advantage and probably commanded a premium in land valuations:

> *To be* SOLD, *on the premises, the 10th of* December *next*, 337 ACRES of GOOD LAND, whereon is a good dwelling-house, with 4 fireplaces below, and 2 brick chimnies, a kitchen with a brick chimney, and two fire-places below, all other necessary houses, and two orchards. Also a quarter of a

> mile from thence, on the said plantation, stands a house 20 by 16, with a brick chimney, and a Negro quarter by it. About 100 acres of the said land is well timbered, the rest very clear and level, and lies within half a mile of *East* warehouse, in *Gloucester* county. The time of payment will be agreed on at the day of sale. JOSEPH GAYLE

The following two advertisements offer good examples of domestic architecture in the years just before the Revolution. House dimensions and construction details help to envision what they looked like as none of them have survived in Mathews County.

> . . . There is on it a very good dwelling house, 45 by 20, underpinned, and gable ends of brick, with two rooms on a floor, and a large passage; likewise a kitchen, quarter, dairy, meat house, a good new barn, 40 by 20, and several other convenient houses, a varity of fruit trees, and as pleasant a situation, and as plentiful a place for fish and oysters, as any in the colony. . . . (Purdie and Dixon's *Virginia Gazette*, September 10, 1767)

> *To be* SOLD, *on* Monday *the 29th instant, on the premises, if fair, otherwise next fair day.* ABOUT 500 acres of good LAND in *Kingston* parish, *Gloucester* county, extending at least 2 miles on *East* river. On it is a very good dwelling-house, with 2 brick chimnies, and all convienient out-houses, also a store-house underpinned with brick, which has a brick chimney, and a good cellar, with an apple orchard that produces 3000 gallons of cyder, and a quarter with 2 brick chimnies. It is a remarkable fine place for fish and oysters, there are several fine springs on the land, and it is well calculated for public business, being in the middle of the parish, the warehouses upon it, and navigable water to them. There are four other houses at the warehouse, and the whole rent for upwards of 40£ a year. Also a tract adjoining the above, containing about 170 acres, more than one half of which is wood land. An undoubted title will be made to the purchaser, by applying to CALEB HUNLEY, and RANSONE HUNLEY. (Rind's *Virginia Gazette*, October 11, 1770)

The plantation advertised by Caleb and Ransome Hunley was probably the land that ancestor Philip Hunley acquired in a patent granted for six hundred acres on June 29, 1651, along the east side of the East River. The Hunley family was long associated with the neighborhood, and the creek now known as Weston Creek was identified in early surveys as Hunley Creek.

Additional advertisements for land:

*To be* SOLD *to the highest bidder, on* Thursday *the 20th of* December, *if fair, otherwise next fair day, on the premises,* A TRACT of LAND pleasantly situated on *Sarah's Creek*, in *Gloucester* county, containing about 205 acres, whereon is a dwelling-house, with brick chimnies and cellar, a kitchen, and all other convenient out houses, mostly new. Also another house 20 by 16, just built; the land is good, and convenient to fish and oysters, with a good landing, where a sea vessel that draws 8 or 10 feet water, may come within 40 yards of the house. The time of payment will be agreed on at the sale. JAMES MUDIE. *At the same time and place will be* SOLD, *for ready money, or short credit,* PART, or the whole, of the sloop *Polly & Fanny*, a new vessel, well fitted, and a prime sailor, has made but one voyage to the *West-Indies*, burthen about 3000 bushels, now lying in *Sarah's Creek*. For terms apply to JAMES MUDIE. (Rind's *Virginia Gazette*, November 29, 1770)

As I find I shall be obliged to make up a large Sum of Money, on Account of my being Security for *Gwyn Reade*, late High Sheriff, I propose disposing of two Tracts of LAND, namely, one lying on the Head of *Slut's* Creek, containing a Hundred and nine Acres, convienient to Fish and Oysters, small Peach and Apple Orchards thereon, a good Tobacco House but one Year old, two Dwellinghouses, with several Outhouses, and every Acre tenable; the other Tract, whereon I now live, on *Queen's* Creek, contains two Hundred and fifty Acres, with a Dwellinghouse thirty two by sixteen, with two Dormers on a Side, a Quarter and large Cornhouse each but a Year old, a new Workhouse forty Feet by twenty, a new Smith's Shop, and several convenient Outhouses, a large young Peach and Apple Orchard, and lies about Middle of the *Kingston* Parish, very pleasantly situated, with a fine Landing for a Ship Carpenter, or a Merchant, where Vessels may lie close ashore; the Land is well timbered, and very convenient to Fish and Oysters. Also a Schooner, and Schooner Boat; the Schooner is thirty one Feet Keel, thirteen Beam, six in the Hold, and eighteen Months old; the Boat is twenty eight Feet Keel, twelve Feet Beam, and five Feet in the Hold, about four Years old. I have likewise a Boat upon the stocks, which I shall be glad to dispose of; it is twenty nine Feet Keel, twelve Feet Beam, and five Feet Hold, and will be finished by the 1st of *December*. Whoever inclines to purchase may have good Bargains for Cash, by applying to the Subscriber. ROBERT BILLUPS. (Purdie and Dixon's *Virginia Gazette*, November 7, 1771)

*To be* SOLD, *by Virture of a Deed of Trust to* Lucas *and* Dixon, *and* John Dixon, *on* Monday *the 18th of* April, *if fair, otherwise next fair Day,* A VERY valuable TRACT of LAND on *Milford Haven*, in *Kingston* Parish, being on the Main

> opposite to *Gwyn's* Island, in *Gloucester* County, containing about 500 Acres. This fine Plantation is remarkable for many Advantages and Conveniencies; for, besides the Land being very good, there is a Brick Dwelling-House with three Rooms on a Floor and a large Passage, a Kitchen, Barn, and all other necessary Houses, in the best Repair; there is likewise a Brick Windmill open to the Bay, which gets upwards of 100 Barrels of Corn a Year, besides an excellent Orchard. And for great Plenty and Variety of Sea and River Fish, and the finest Oysters, it yields to no Place in *Virginia*. (Purdie and Dixon's *Virginia Gazette*, March 17, 1774)

> To be SOLD, on the premises, the 25th of this instant, April, pursuant to a deed of trust conveyed by John Gayle to William Smith, A TRACT of LAND situated on East river, in Gloucester county, and convienient to fish and oysters. The land is in good order for cropping, and produces as good corn and tobacco as any in the said county, if taken proper care of. There are 297 acres; which may be purchased reasonably for ready money. WILLIAM SMITH (Rind's *Virginia Gazette*, April 14, 1774)

> *To be* SOLD, *on* Friday *the 27th Instant* (May) *before the* Raleigh *Tavern*, EIGHT Hundred Acres of very valuable LAND lying in *Kingston* Parish, *Gloucester* County, near *New Point Comfort*, which is well timbered with Pine and White Oak. Upon it there is a Dwelling House with two Brick Chimnies, all convenient Houses, one Peach, and three Apple Orchards.—At the same Time will be sold thirty likely *Virginia* born SLAVES. GEORGE W. PLUMMER. (Purdie and Dixon's *Virginia Gazette*, May 5, 1774)

Most of the advertisements originating from Kingston Parish during the second half of the 1700s were for runaway slaves, slaves auctions, land and houses, and ships. Other parishes were not active in shipbuilding, and listings from these areas pertained mostly to slaves and land. Examples of slave auctions follow:

> *To be SOLD, at Publick AUCTION, at the Subscriber's Plantation, in* Gloucester *County, on the last* Thursday *in* March, TWO Hundred Acres of Land, on *Queen's* Creek, in the said County, 20 *Virginia*-born Slaves, Men, Women and Children, and a Quantity of Stock. Three Month's Credit will be allowed, the Purchaser giving good Security, as usual, to *Robert Reade*. (*Virginia Gazette*, March 2, 1753)

> *By virtue of a deed of trust will be* SOLD *to the highest bidder, at* Gloucester *courthouse, on* Wednesday *the 3d of* February *next*, Forty valuable Slaves, among whom

> are some good CARPENTERS, and a very good COOK. Credit will be allowed until the 25th of next *October*, the purchasers giving bond and security to The TRUSTEES. N. B. Large discount will be allowed for ready money. (Purdie and Dixon's *Virginia Gazette*, January 21, 1768)
>
> A large parcel of very fine SLAVES, *Virginia* born, belonging to the estate of Mr. *John Armistead*, deceased, will be sold on *Thursday* the 24th of *January*, if fair, otherwise next fair day, at the battery, in *Kingston* parish, *Gloucester* county, for ready money, by the executors. At the same time will be sold 25 very fine SLAVES, for ready money only. (Rind's *Virginia Gazette*, January 10, 1771)

News accounts frequently mentioned maritime activities and misfortunes, such as in Purdie and Dixon's *Virginia Gazette* on September 21, 1769:

> The snow [a vessel rigged similarly to a ship] Fortune, Rowntree, from London, bound to Maryland, in going up the bay, in the late hurricane, was obliged to cut away her masts and come to anchor, one of which she lost; and last Tuesday, in weighing, the windlass broke, which made it necessary to cut the cable, and she drove ashore to the northward of New Point Comfort, in Gloucester county, and is entirely lost. There were 59 passengers on board, many of them trademen, labourers, &c. who propose following their several occupations in this colony, unless compelled to go to Maryland, to be there sold to pay for their passages.

There is a surprising absence of commentary concerning the extraordinary circumstances Kingston Parish must have experienced during the Revolutionary War. Family members were in the Continental army, state militia, and Virginia State Navy. They suffered economically as trade, both imports and exports, was severely restricted. The general fear of nearby enemy activity, the safety of family members in military service, and the worry of the outcome all must have taken a toll on the life of the community.

*Figure* 11 John Senex published *A New Map of Virginia, Maryland and the Improved Parts of Pennsylvania & New Jersey* in 1719. Shown here is the southeast portion of his map including the entrance to the Chesapeake Bay and extending northward to the Rappahannock River. Virginia place names had become well established by this time, and his map was considered the most accurate available. The four rivers flowing into Mobjack Bay—the East, North, Ware, and Severn—New Point Comfort, Milford Harbor (instead of Milford Haven), and the primary creeks are shown in detail. He accurately depicted the most significant underwater features in the lower bay, which are still present today. From the author's collection.

# CHAPTER 5

# The Hall Family *of* Kingston *and* Petsworth Parishes

Ships arriving from England carrying passengers—planters, indentured servants, clergy, clerks, craftsmen, merchants, and so forth—and cargoes, including a wide variety of manufactured goods, especially fabrics and clothing, farm implements and carpentry tools, guns and powder, and better grades of utensils and cooking and serving ware, would typically visit the landings or deepwater anchorages of the large planters. In some cases, these planters were also merchants serving the smaller planters in their neighborhoods. In several locations, warehouses were established for the convenience of storing tobacco for shipment and receiving imported goods. Tyndall's Point, now Gloucester Point, on the York River; several locations on the East River with deep water near the shoreline, including present-day Williams Wharf and a dock on the west side of the East River known as Hicks Wharf; similar locations on the North River; and a large anchorage, Hills Bay, in the Piankatank River off Gwynn's Island were all used for loading and unloading cargoes and receiving and discharging passengers.

Ships having Gloucester County as their first port of arrival frequently anchored in Mobjack Bay after making landfall off Cape Henry. The area in Mobjack Bay to the west and just inside of New Point Comfort was a natural harbor that offered good protection from strong winds out of the northeast, and it was just twenty-three nautical miles from the entrance to the Chesapeake Bay. It was a more convenient anchorage than Norfolk, also twenty-three miles sailing distance from the entrance to the bay, especially because, unlike the passage to Norfolk Harbor, the course to New Point Comfort was a straight line. In addition, the course benefited from favorable prevailing winds, except at certain times during fall and winter when seasonal weather patterns frequently brought winds out of the northwest.

The sight of their final destination after weeks at sea would have been a welcomed event even with the prospect of several years of serving out an indenture. Arrival times were typically in the late fall and early winter to avoid the hurricane season, and thus the weather during the final days before arrival would have been significantly cooler than the much warmer Gulf Stream–influenced ocean waters south of Cape Henry from where they were sailing.

The typical passage from England to Virginia would have been by way of the Azores, Madeira, and/or the Canary Islands to replenish provisions. If by way of Madeira, the passage from, for example, Plymouth, England, would have taken from 13 to 17 days assuming average speeds of three to four knots; Madeira to somewhere in the West Indies, perhaps Antigua, would have taken from 30 to 40 days; and the final course to the Chesapeake Bay would have taken 17 to 23 days. The total passage from Plymouth to the Chesapeake would have typically taken 60 to 80 days of sailing plus the time spent reprovisoning, perhaps as long as two to three weeks in total. The passage would thus take approximately 74 to 101 days and in many cases much longer, especially if winds were unfavorable for departure in the English Channel. Assuming a sailing date from England of October 1, arrival in the Chesapeake would have typically occurred from mid-December to mid-January.

Mary Hall was the first of six persons with the Hall family name to appear in the records of the four original parishes of Gloucester County: Kingston, Petsworth (Petsoe), Abingdon, and Ware. She was listed among five headrights in a patent awarded to Philip Hunley, Kingston Parish, on June 29, 1651, for 613 acres: "lyeing on the Ewd. side of the Eastermost river in Mockjack Bay; beg. at a small creek within Budden Cr."[1]

Philip Hunley may have paid the passage of the five immigrants to gain the headrights, or he may have purchased the headrights from another planter and/or adventurer. Each headright entitled him to fifty acres of land. Interestingly, the Hunley patent was close to the eighteenth-century Hall home site. However, nothing else is known about Mary Hall, and thus where she lived and for whom she was employed cannot be determined. Mary was probably an indentured servant, and her contract may have been purchased by Philip Hunley, but it may just as well have been purchased by another planter in Kingston Parish or elsewhere in the county or adjoining county. Given the pattern of how servants came into Tidewater Virginia, though, Kingston Parish, but not necessarily on Hunley property, would have been her most likely new home.

The most common name in the Virginia Colony during the years 1623 through 1666 was "Jones," which significantly exceeded "Smith," followed by, in descending order, Williams, Johnson, Davis, Brown, White, Hill, Thomas, Harris, Green, Powell, Evans, Morgan, Price, Allen, Clarke, Baker, Lee, Parker, Phillips, James, Cooke, Bennett, Jackson, Andrews, Carter, and finally Hall.* The family name "Hall" was one of the least frequently appearing names in

* In the number of times listed in *Cavaliers and Pioneers*.

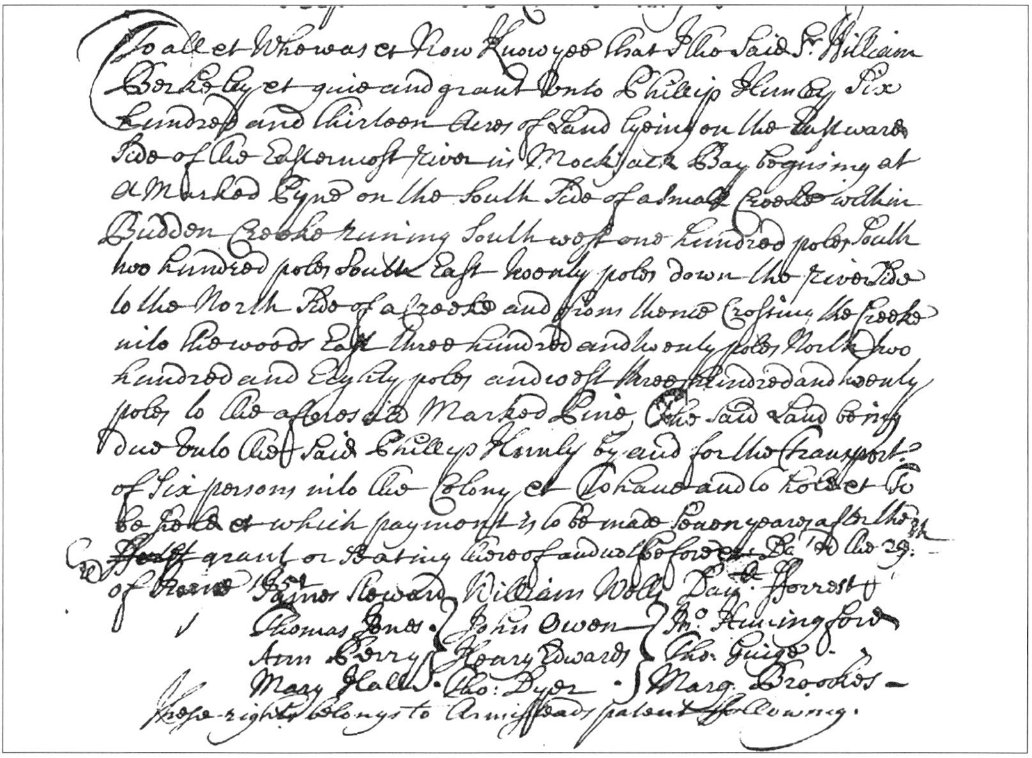

*Figure* 12 The original land patent for 613 acres on the east side of the East River was awarded to Philip Hunley of Kingston Parish on June 29, 1651. Courtesy of the Library of Virginia, Richmond.

Gloucester County and elsewhere in seventeenth-century Virginia.

There was a reference to "Mr. Halls Land" in the patent books, dated November 25, 1653, in conjunction with a patent for 350 acres on the south side of Horn Harbor in Kingston Parish.[2] Unfortunately, nothing more is known about Mr. Hall's identity, what became of him, or how he obtained his land. He may have been a merchant or mariner engaged in land speculation and probably never lived in the parish. The absence of a patent suggests that he acquired his land by purchase.

The next Hall to arrive was Alexander Hall, who was listed in the headrights of Henry Forrest in a patent awarded on September 15, 1658, for seven hundred acres: "Upon Milford Haven Cr., N.E. upon the land of John Lylly, down Garden Cr. to land of Mr. Edward Cheeseman."[3]

Among the headrights listed were Edward Forrest, Henry Forrest, and his wife, Elizabeth

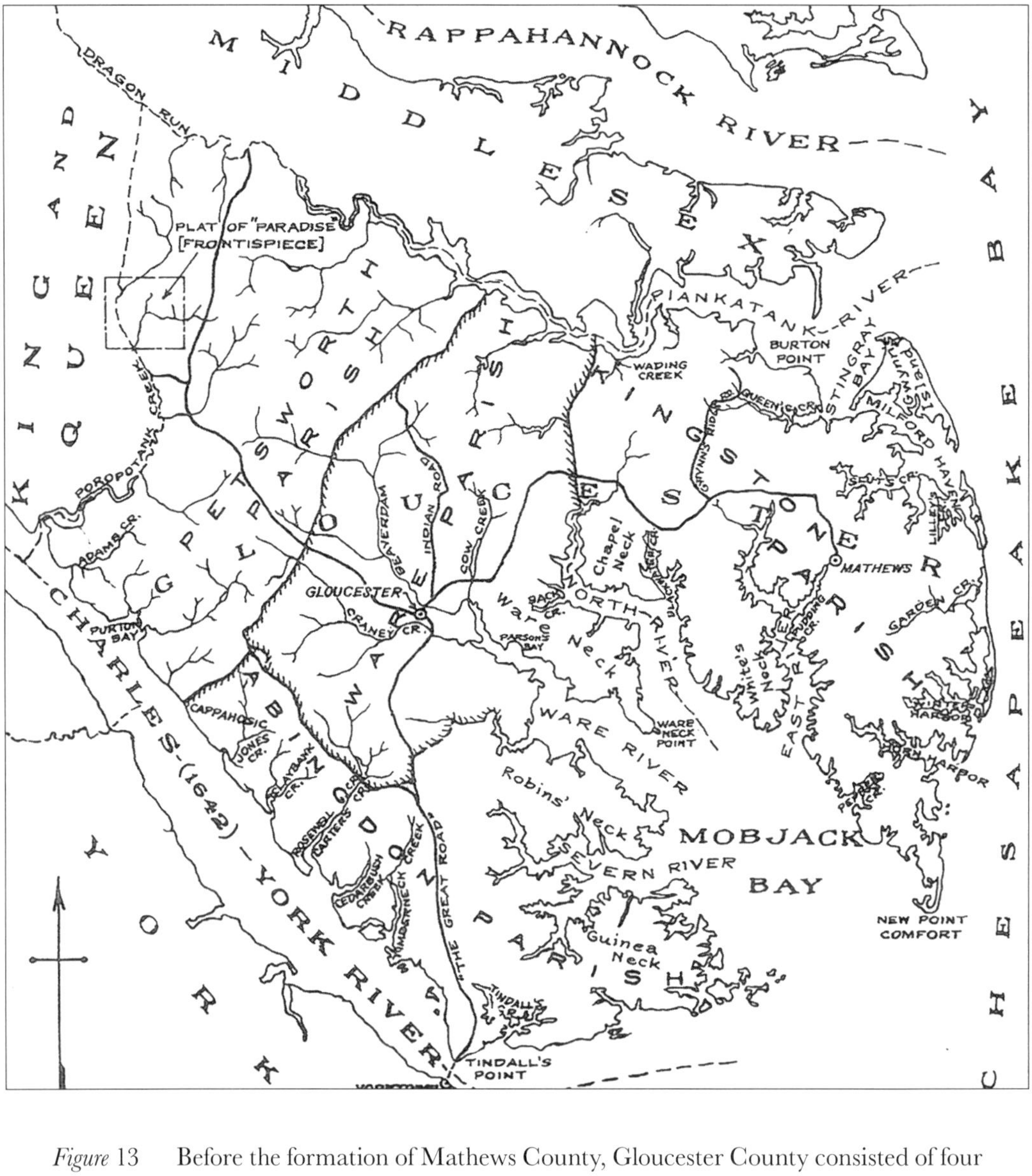


*Figure* 13 Before the formation of Mathews County, Gloucester County consisted of four parishes: Abingdon, along the York River including the Severn River to Mobjack Bay; Ware Parish, which extended from Abingdon to the Piankatank River and to the Ware River on to Mobjack Bay to the east; Petsworth Parish, bound by the Poropotank River to the west and running from the York River to the Piankatank River; and Kingston Parish to the east, bounded by the Piankatank River to the north, the Chesapeake Bay to the east, and Mobjack Bay to the south. Map by G. C. Mason in Polly Cary Mason, comp., *Records of Colonial Gloucester County, Virginia: A Collection of Abstracts from Original Documents Concerning the Lands and People of Colonial Gloucester County* (Baltimore, MD: Clearfield, 2003; originally published 1946), 2:v.

Forrest. In this case Henry sponsored himself and two members of his family. He may have sponsored the ocean passage of Alexander and the others, or he may have purchased these headrights. He may have owned Alexander's indenture and employed him on his new acreage, or someone else may have purchased Alexander's indenture in Kingston Parish or elsewhere. Nothing further has been found concerning Alexander Hall and what became of him.

A patent was awarded to William Ironmonger on June 3, 1664, for 350 acres in Gloucester County at the head of the Ware River. Seven headrights were used to acquire the land and among them was John Hall.[4] Nothing else is known about John, and the rent rolls for 1704–1705 do not list a Hall in Ware Parish.

The last Hall to appear in the patent books for Kingston Parish was Robert Hall, who was listed in the headrights of the patent awarded to John Collis (Callis) for 620 acres on September 26, 1678: "KINGSTON P. At the head of 'the Beaver Damms adjoining Matthew Gayle'. HR: An. Roberts,* Mary Seayres,* Jno. Spragg,* Ja: Grencill, Robt. Hall,* Jno.

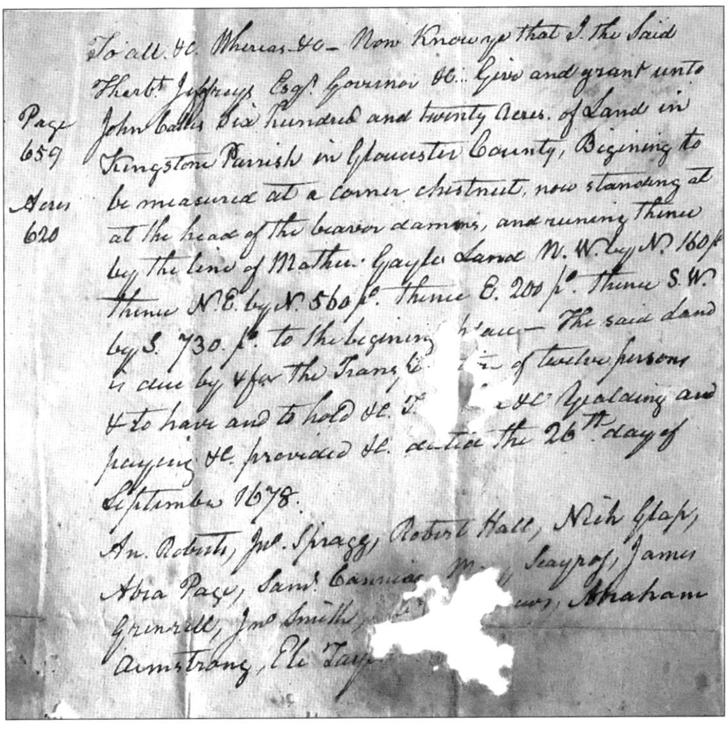
To all &c. Whereas &c. Now Know ye that I the Said
Herbt. Jeffreys Esqr. Governor &c. Give and grant unto
Page 659 John Callis Six hundred and twenty Acres. of Land in
Kingstone Parish in Gloucester County, Begining to
Acres 620 be measured at a corner chestnut, now standing at
at the head of the beaver damms, and running thence
by the line of Mathew Gayle Land N. W. by N. 160 p.
thence N.E. by N. 560 p. thence E. 200 p. thence S.W.
by S. 730 p. to the begining place. The said land
is due by & for the Trans of twelve persons
& to have and to hold &c. &c. Yealding and
paying &c. provided &c. dated the 26th. day of
September 1678.
An. Roberts, Jno. Spragg, Robert Hall, Nich
Abia Page, Saml. Seayres, James
Jno Smith, Abraham
Armstrong

*Figure* 14 A land patent was awarded to John Collis of Kingston Parish on September 26, 1678, for 620 acres in proximity to the "Beaver Damms." This one is thought to be a copy of the original: the cursive style is more akin to late eighteenth- and early nineteenth-century penmanship. Courtesy of the Library of Virginia, Richmond.

Smith, Nich. Glasbe (?),* Edward Andrews, Abra. Page,* Samll. Carriage, Jas. Grencill, Adam Armstrong, Samll. Carriage, Eliz. Taylor."[5]

This patent was located on the eastern side of the East River, to the northeast of present-day Beaverlette and just two miles from the Hall family's dwelling house of the eighteenth century. Six of the names used in the Collis patent, including Robert Hall, were also used in a patent dated the same month awarded to William Grymes (Crimes or Grimes) for 450 acres in Petsworth Parish, Gloucester County, June 5, 1678: "On Poropotank adjoining Capt. Richard Dudley, Geo. Haynes, Spencers land in Dancing Valley along Curtis Path, Richland Swamp & adjoining Majr Richard Lee. Formerly granted Mr. Jas. Stubbins, 1674, and deserted. HR: John Hill, John Dyer, Joan Homes, Ann Roberts,* Jno. Wragg,* Robt. Hall,* Nich. Glass,* Abra. Page,* Mary Seayres.*"[6]

The earlier James Stubbins patent of September 21, 1674, was for the same 450 acres and had the following description, which further helps to determine the location of the acreage. Stubbins "deserted" his patent, meaning he failed to seat it within the required three years, or he may have died without heirs: "At Poropotank in Danseing Valley adjoining Capt. Dudley, George Haynes, & Spencys Land 'by Curles path & branch† . . . & Rich Land Swamp . . . to Mr. Richd. Lee his line.' "[7]

The description on William Grymes's patent placed his acreage in Gloucester County's most western parish, one having high elevations and a rolling topography with numerous springs. Petsworth Parish is separated from King and Queen County by the Poropotank River, which flows southward for approximately twelve and a half miles into the York River. Its beginning is near the headwaters of the Piankatank River, an area known as the Dragon Run, which is a significant swamp that drains into the Piankatank.

Four principal branches of the Poropotank River, beginning near its headwaters, include Coles Branch; Spring Branch, also known as Bridge Branch; Woods Mill Swamp; and Poplar Spring Branch, located approximately three miles upstream from the York River. These four branches range in length from four miles in the case of Poplar Spring Branch to the approximately one-and-a-half-mile Coles Branch. Numerous lesser branches flow into the four main branches and also directly into the river.

Unlike for Kingston Parish, with its remarkably flat topography, where patent boundaries were typically established as straight lines, Petsworth patents were often delineated by river branches because they were at the bases of steep ravines, which made natural barriers or

---

* Asterisks, added by author, indicate names used in both Collis and Grymes patents.

† This could be the Coles Branch.

lines of property divisions. Adding to their attractiveness for settlement was the benefit of fresh water, as they were largely beyond the tidal effect of the York River and were spring-fed. The Grymes property was on one of the lesser branches, the "Curles path & branch," which was likely the Coles Branch, which is near and to the north of the Spring Branch and adjoining Paradise, the Lee family plantation.

It will probably never be known for certain what caused the double entry of headrights in Robert Hall's name, who was most probably an indentured servant. It could have been a clerical mistake, as can be found in other patents. Although unlikely, especially because of the short time interval of just twenty-one days between patents, there may have been two men by the same name. There is also the possibility that the double usage was deliberate and unlawful, although the fact that it occurred in the same county makes this unlikely. Another practice, one that was occasionally utilized, consisted of one indenture purchased in shares by two patentees, in which case a headright for the same person would be granted twice.

The most probable explanation was that it was a mistake made by the clerk, especially since six names were the same in both patents and they were listed in the same order in both. There is a very remote chance that it was a joint purchase of Robert's indenture by Grymes and Collis, which would suggest that Robert Hall was not an agricultural laborer but a more specialized craftsman, one of particular value. Unfortunately, there is insufficient information to determine where Robert worked. He may have worked for Collis in Kingston, with Grymes in Petsworth, in a shared capacity between the two, somewhere else in Gloucester County, or even in another county.

The last Hall to be listed in the patents for Gloucester County was William Hall in Petsworth Parish. He acquired 220 acres in 1691; 278 acres in 1695; two patents in 1698, for 140 acres and 149 acres; and a re-patent of the 149 acres in 1714. His holdings indicate a relatively high degree of wealth. He likely did not arrive in Virginia as an indentured servant. William Hall's parcels of land were all in the northwestern section of the parish. For example, the October 20, 1691, patent for 220 acres was described as: "PETSOE P. Adjoining Mr. Haines, Rich. Lee, Esq., Mr. Brookin, Dudleys line and to the Main Road."[8] This parcel was located on the east side of present-day US Route 17 in the vicinity of Dutton. The adjoining Richard Lee plantation was known as Paradise and was the first patent granted to the Lee family, ancestors of Robert E. Lee.

The parcel of 278 acres, patented on April 21, 1695, can be located with some precision as the references in the patent are known: "PETSOE P. Beginning on Coles Branch of the Poropotank near fork and to Coll: Lees corner 'along the Main road that leads to Dragon Bridge' and to Mr. Wm. Brookins land. Formerly granted Charles Roane 1691, deserted."[9] The same tract was patented earlier to Charles Roane on October 20, 1691: "PETTSOE P.

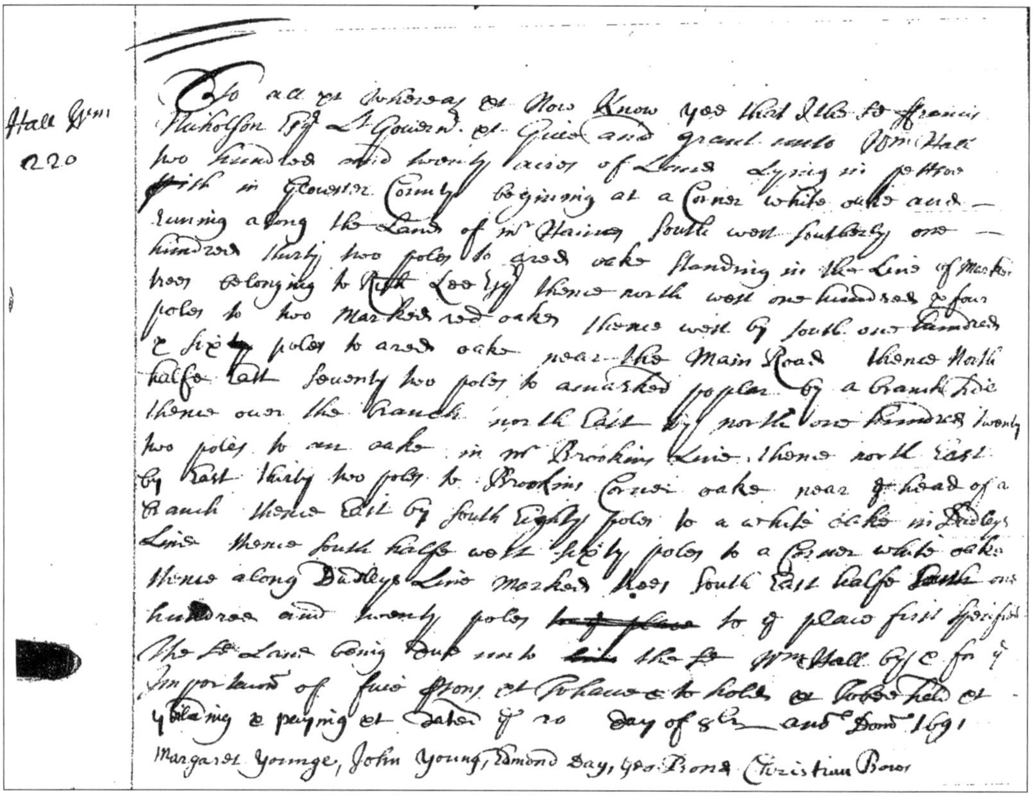

*Figure* 15 William Hall received a land patent on October 20, 1691, for 220 acres in Petsworth Parish adjoining Paradise, the plantation of Richard Lee. Courtesy of the Library of Virginia, Richmond.

On the N side and near the head of Coles Branch of the Poropotank Crk. at Coll: Richard Lees corner NE to the Maine Road that leads to Dragon bridge & along the road to Wm. Brookins Land."[10] The parcel was approximately bound on the east by present-day US Route 17 and on the south by Coles Branch, which divided Hall's property from the Lees'. Brookin's patent was on Hall's north boundary and consisted of 787 acres. Present-day US Route 17 was constructed in 1941, and while the new highway generally follows the main road of colonial times, it occupies right-of-ways in some sections that are as much as a half mile different from the original. This was done to straighten the highway, to better locate new bridges, and to incorporate curves into the roadway suitable for automobile traffic.

William Hall's patent for 140 acres, dated April 26, 1698, was approximately two miles further north: "PETSO P. At a marsh on Peanketank adjoining Mr. Thomas Buckner, Mr. John Grimes and along the road."[11] The John Grymes mentioned may have been the son or brother of William Grymes of the 1678 patent, which claimed Robert Hall as a headright in

Petsworth Parish. John is absent from the record as a patentee and thus probably inherited and/or purchased his holdings. He must have had considerable wealth as he was listed as owning 1,400 acres in the rent roll of 1704–1705. At that time, he was the third largest landowner in the parish, exceeded only by Conquest Wyatt with 2,200 acres and Thomas Read with 2,000 acres. Richard Lee owned 1,140 acres, and John Pate had 1,100 acres.

One of the tracts owned by William Hall adjoined John Grymes's property in the vicinity of the Piankatank River. The 1678 William Grymes patent was in proximity to the 1691 William Hall patent to the south, and they both adjoined the Haynes, Dudley, and Richard Lee plantations. The Halls and Grymeses probably had family connections given that they lived in the same neighborhood.

On the same date in 1698, when the patent for the 140 acres was granted, William Hall patented an additional 149 acres. It was re-patented on December 23, 1714, and included a description of the tract as being in the vicinity of the 220 acres patented in 1691: "PETSOE P. Escheat land formerly in the possession of Owen Caley, dece'd. Beginning at the Brookings corner near Bakers Bridge & adjoining Dawkins, Thomas Dudley and Baker. Part of a former grant to Thomas Hanks, 1663. John Lewis, Esq., Escheator, Thos. Cook, Surveyor. Price: 2 pounds of tobacco per acre."[12] Thomas Hanks received patents in Petsworth Parish in 1667 and 1673, with the first referencing "branches of Peanketanke Swamp & Poropotank adjoining his own land & Coll: Lee, S to the Rappa Path & to Poropotank swamp" and the second "On Poropotank Swamp adjoining his own land & Charles Roane, Tho. Dawkins, Lambert Moore & Huckstep."[13]

If William Hall owned all 787 acres from his patents at the same time, he would have been among the larger landowners in the parish.

The vestry book of Petsworth Parish recorded an order by the Gloucester County Court, dated September 6, 1694, to divide the parish into eight precincts for the purpose of processioning, which was the walking of the boundaries of each landowner each year to verify the integrity of the precinct's borders and the boundaries of the landowners within the precinct. Men selected for this task were typically respected and trustworthy landowners within the precincts they were asked to procession. Processioning continued for many years and proved to be an efficient method of identifying disagreements among landowners concerning boundaries, especially before original patents were resurveyed in succeeding generations, typically to subdivide parcels among family members or upon the sale of land.

The boundaries of precinct no. 6 included all of William Hall's patents and were defined as follows: "from paradice bridg swamp. Along ye Rode on ye left hand to ye Draggon brige."[14] Figure 16 shows most of the precinct, bounded by Spring Valley to the south of the Lee

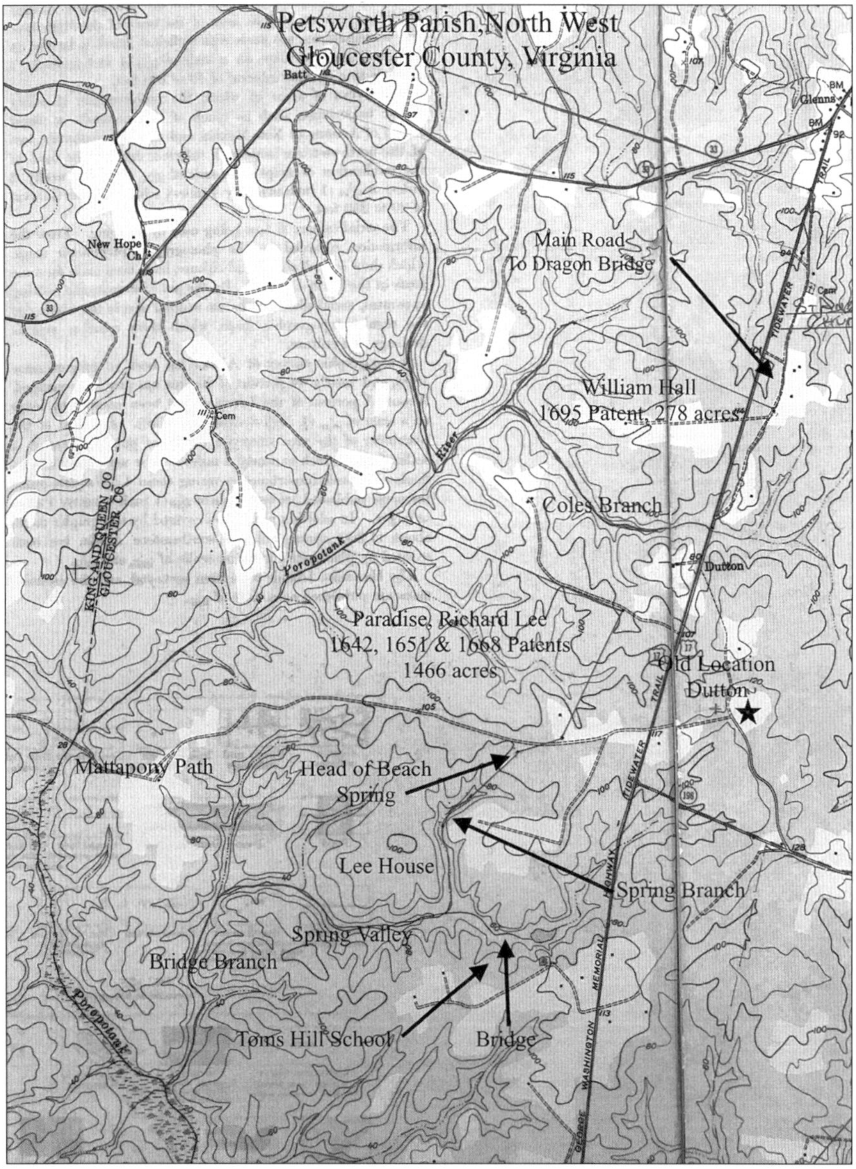


*Figure* 16 A small northwest section of a topographical map of Gloucester County published in 1949 shows the border between Gloucester and King and Queen Counties and the upper reaches of the Poropotank River and its significant branches. Arrows and text (added) mark the principal features, described in several land patents, including William Hall's 1695 patent for land located on the north side of Coles Branch. Richard Lee's house is shown with Spring Branch, Spring Valley, and Bridge Branch. The Mattapony path is seen crossing the Poropotank River and extending to the east to the head of Beach Spring. Published by the US Department of Commerce, US Coast and Geodetic Survey.

house, by the boundary between Gloucester and King and Queen Counties on the west, by the highway to the east, and continuing northward to the Piankatank River and Dragon Swamp.

The Gloucester County Court, fourteen years later, ordered the vestry on March 16, 1708, to again divide the parish into precincts. Ten precincts were established, and while some changed considerably from the 1694 boundaries, precinct no. 6 remained essentially unchanged and was described as "And from Doctr Baker on the Left hand The Dragon Road To The Dragon bridge for the Sixth Precinct."[15]

A second mention of a Robert Hall in Petsworth, probably not the same person listed in the 1678 patent, occurred in the 1704–1705 rent rolls, where he was listed twice, owning a parcel containing 100 acres and a second parcel of 250 acres.[16] This was most likely one individual with two separate parcels rather than two people such as a father and son.

The vestry on April 6, 1709, ordered:

> mr. William Roan & mr. Robt. Hall doe begin on the 13th: Day of this instant aprill and see the lands with the sixth precinct of the said parish processioned and make a return of their procedings to the Church-warden of the said parish by the last day of June next. beginning at Doctr. Beakers to procession & from thence all on the left hand of the Draggon road to Draggon bridg. . . .
>
> And it is allsoe ordered that the minister of the said parish give pubblick notice of this at the Church on Sunday next that all the freeholders may have notice thereof. . . .
>
> and mr. William Roan & mr. Robt. Hall is appoynted to see the Lands within the sixth precinct of this parish processioned.*[17]

It is highly likely that the Robert Hall of Petsworth Parish listed in the 1704–1705 rent roll and in the processioning of 1709 was related to William, probably as a son or perhaps a

---

* The next recorded processioning was ordered at a vestry held on September 26, 1711. The processioners were William Upshaw and William Roan. According to the minutes of the vestry meeting on September 14, 1715, Roan and Upshaw were replaced by James Amis and William Brookin. (C. G. Chamberlayne, trans., *The Vestry Book of Petsworth Parish, Gloucester County, Virginia, 1677–1793* [Richmond, VA: Library Board, 1933], 111, 130.) Brookin owned land bordering William Hall on Hall's northern boundary. William Brookin was involved again in 1719 and 1723, and in 1723, Alexander Rone participated in the processioning of precinct no. 6.

brother. Robert lived in the precinct he was ordered to procession, and all of the William Hall patents were in that precinct. Robert probably inherited his holdings, and they were probably parts of the original William Hall patents. The indentured servant Robert Hall, mentioned in the 1678 Collis patent in Kingston Parish, was in all probability not the same Robert owning the Petsworth tracts, although that possibility cannot be totally eliminated from consideration. He left no further existing record.

The name Robert Hall does not appear again in Kingston Parish for seventy-eight years, until September 19, 1756, the date of the birth of his daughter Ann.[18] This listing marks the beginning of the historical record that can be traced to current times of the line of descent of the Robert and Ann Hall family of Kingston Parish, the first documented ancestors of the Hall family of Mathews County. Robert the father of Ann may have been the descendant of either the Robert Hall in the Collis patent or Robert and William Hall of Petsworth Parish.

The Robert Hall in the Collis patent might present a stronger case because the Collis patent was already in Kingston Parish, and a reasonable assessment of the Collis property places it in proximity to what later is identified as the land of the Hall family.* Also, the Hall family was closely connected to the descendants of Matthew Gayle, referenced in the Collis patent, through marriages and other connections. It is therefore tempting to assume that the Robert Hall in the Collis patent, most likely an indentured servant, was employed in the neighborhood of the Gayle and Collis families, perhaps by one of them specifically.

Alternatively, the name "Spencer" was a frequently used name in the Hall family of Kingston Parish, and the Spencers were neighbors of William Hall and Robert Hall of Petsworth Parish, arguing for a possible family connection. In this case William of Petsworth or his son Robert is assumed to have moved to Kingston Parish.

If Robert Hall in the Collis patent was the immigrant Hall from England, his date of arrival would have been sometime during late 1677 to early 1678, as there was typically a delay between the arrival of a person and the person's name appearing in a patent. The delay was a result of the process the planter had to follow in obtaining his patent: acquiring the necessary number of headrights, proving them in the county court, finding the desired property, having the survey made, and then waiting for final approval and award of the patent.

As the typical age of indentured servants at the time was between nineteen and twenty-two years, the immigrant Robert Hall might have been twenty years old, indicating his birth in 1658. He may have come from Gloucestershire in the West Country because during these

* In Kingston Parish, John Callis (Collis) continued to own land, and he was listed in the 1704–1705 rent rolls with 1,000 acres, an increase of 380 acres from his original patent.

years Bristol had become the leading port for transporting servants to Virginia. If his ship followed the custom of the time, he would have departed an English port, probably Bristol, in the fall of 1677, to avoid the hurricane season in the Caribbean and on the Atlantic coast, and arrived three months or so later in Gloucester County.

Outbound port records for vessels embarking from London, Liverpool, and Bristol were not maintained in a consistent manner, and those that were made have large gaps, due to fire, neglect, and other problems with document storage. Not a trace can be found of a Robert Hall bound for Virginia in the relevant time period.

However, of the few surviving English port records of emigrants, the most complete list was compiled for the port of Bristol during the years 1654–1685, a thirty-one-year period during which Bristol became the largest trading market with Virginia and a period of significant English settlement in Virginia.* Of the eighteen immigrants with the Hall family name, out of a total of approximately ten thousand immigrants bound to Virginia, there is only one to consider: William Hall of Liverpool, who sailed from Bristol on August 27, 1684, on board the *Samuel* bound for Virginia.[19]

Given the infrequent appearance of the family name Hall in eastern Virginia, there is the possibility that the William Hall outbound from Bristol in August 1684, on board the *Samuel*, was the same William Hall who acquired the first Hall patent in Petsworth Parish for 220 acres in 1691. While the *Samuel* may have transported mostly indentured servants, it seems unlikely that William would have been one as it would have been difficult to have discharged his term of service and acquired capital sufficient to patent a significant tract of land in that length of time. However, the seven-year interval from landing in Virginia, probably in the fall of 1684, and the patent awarded in 1691 represents a reasonable time frame for William to have found and patented land in Petsworth Parish, perhaps also to have married and fathered a son named Robert. The odds of this connection to the *Samuel* are maybe one in four; the odds of ever verifying this possibility are very remote.

If Robert Hall of Kingston Parish, given his name, was the firstborn, circa 1730, and if he was descended from Robert the immigrant, he might have been named for him, his great-grandfather. The years between a twenty-year-old immigrant in 1678 and 1730 might have passed as follows: Robert the indentured servant would have been prohibited from marriage until the term of his indenture ended, unless he had received permission to marry

---

* The Bristol list was established according to an ordinance enacted by the Bristol Common Council, dated September 29, 1654, and was primarily intended for those individuals having indentures of service and apprenticeships (*Bristol and America: A Record of the First Settlers in the Colonies of North America, 1654–1685* [London: R. Sydney Glover, n.d.], 4).

from his master. Assuming a five-year indenture beginning in 1678, Robert in 1683, at age twenty-five, would have discharged his term of service and been free to become a laborer, craftsman, or sharecropper or lease land, perhaps eventually acquiring a small parcel of land, or with good luck marry into his master's or another landowning family. By 1683, the opportunity to acquire land in Kingston Parish by a freeman, one no longer bound by an indenture, was extremely limited. All of the parish was by this time owned by first or second generations of settlers, and thus Robert and those in similar situations would have needed sufficient capital to have purchased land, a difficult challenge at the time.

If Robert was married by 1684, at age twenty-six, he probably would have had a child born by 1685, and several more over the following ten to twelve years. A son born 1685–1687 would have probably been married by 1706–1708, with his first child born in 1707–1709, and this child would have been the grandson of the immigrant Hall. His son could have been the father of the known Robert, born circa 1730.

The search for early Hall immigrants was not confined to Gloucester County, Virginia. Every headright in Virginia until 1699 was reviewed. The earliest mention of the family name Hall was on December 1, 1624, for a patent of 150 acres. The patent was awarded to Pharoah Flinton: "An Ancient Planter of Kiccoughton, . . . of Eliz. City, Dec. 1, 1624, p. 22. Bet. Newport News & Blunt Point, adj. John Salford & Lt Giles Allington. Due for his personal right and for trans. out of England of Hugh Hall, who came in the Margarett and John in 1623."[20]

By the end of 1699, the name Hall had been mentioned 208 times in the Virginia patent records: 70 were repeated references to the same person, resulting in approximately 138 unique mentions. Of these, 23 Halls acquired patents, or in some cases an individual acquired several tracts. Thus, of the 138 unique mentions, most, perhaps all, of the remaining 115 were indentured servants. Interestingly, the percentage of Hall-named headrights of the total was 83 percent, similar to the ratio for all headrights during that time.

William Hall was the only Hall to have acquired land by a patent in Gloucester County. Hall land ownership in all of Gloucester County consisted of just three parcels according to the 1704–1705 rent rolls. One John Hall owned 125 acres in Abingdon Parish, and Robert Hall owned two parcels in Petsworth Parish, 100 acres and 250 acres. Robert was most probably the son of William and inherited his land.

# CHAPTER 6

# Robert *and* Ann Hall *of* Kingston Parish, 1730–1791

Robert Hall and his wife, Ann, first appear in the historical record together in the Kingston Parish register on the occasion of the birth of a daughter, Ann, called Nanny, on September 19, 1756. She was baptized on November 14 of the same year. Nanny was probably the younger sister of Elizabeth (Betsey) Jordan Hall, whose birth date is unknown but assumed to have been circa 1755.*

Robert and Ann are the earliest positively identified ancestors of the Hall family of Kingston Parish, and the entry of the birth of Ann establishes their residency and their marriage and provides an estimate of their ages. As outlined in chapter 5, Robert was likely the descendant of the immigrant Robert Hall or of William and Robert Hall of Petsworth Parish and thus was of a well-established and long-standing family of Gloucester County. Successive generations of this family are well-documented in an unbroken line to the present.

Based on the birth dates of their children, Robert was born circa 1730, and Ann circa 1734. Ann's last name is unknown, but based on English naming traditions, her father may have had the first name of Spencer, as that name was frequently used in the family. If born in Kingston Parish, there is a strong likelihood that she was a Hunley, Callis (Collis), Diggs (Degge), or Gayle because of the proximity to these families and their many generations in the same neighborhood. It is reasonable to assume that Robert and Ann were married about 1754, at ages twenty-four and twenty respectively, and they were probably born and married in Kingston Parish. However, it is possible that Robert was born in Petsworth Parish, considering that he may be descended from the Halls of Petsworth Parish, and moved to Kingston for employment or because of his marriage to Ann or because his parents moved

* The Kingston Parish register has survived for 1749–1827. Unfortunately, eighty-five pages are missing and others are illegible.

from Petsworth to Kingston Parish. Likewise, Ann may have been born in Petsworth in the Spencer family, the only family in Gloucester County having that name. The distance from the estimated locations of Robert Hall's land in Petsworth to the Hall-owned property in Kingston is twenty-one miles by road, less than a day's travel by horseback at a walk.

Two years to the day, following the birth of Nanny, on September 19, 1758, Robert Jr. was born to Ann and Robert. He had a distinguished record of service in the Revolutionary War. Chapter 10 is devoted to him.

A son, Spencer, most frequently appearing as Spence, was born on November 28, 1760. He had an interesting but tragic life. Chapter 11 is devoted to his career and family.

The last record in the Kingston Parish register of a child of Robert and Ann's was a daughter, Joyce (Joicey), born on February 17, 1763, who was baptized on March 14 of the same year.

A third son, Thomas, who was born in about 1764, is not recorded, or the record has been lost. Chapter 12 is an accounting of his many accomplishments, activities, and long life in Kingston Parish. The Hall family line of descent continues through Thomas.

By the time their last known child, Thomas, was born, Robert was thirty-four years old and Ann was thirty. Both were young enough to have had more children, but the Kingston Parish register makes no further reference to any.

The brothers Robert, Spencer, and Thomas each left a considerable historical record, including participation in the life of the Kingston Parish church, shipbuilding and ship ownership, real estate transactions, slave ownership, large families, and significant participation in the Revolutionary War. The surviving record is remarkable given that the Mathews County court records prior to 1791 were destroyed by a fire in the clerk's office of Gloucester County in 1820, and the Mathews County records after that date were destroyed by fire in Richmond, Virginia, following its capture by federal forces in April 1865.

Daughters Betsey, Nanny, and Joicey likewise had large families with each of their husbands also participating in the Revolutionary War. Their histories are presented in chapter 13. Regrettably, women during the colonial period did not typically own real estate or other taxable property or engage in matters that would have generated written records, and thus it is impossible to know much about them other than their marriages, children, births, and deaths.

On November 5, 1759, Robert the father appeared in the vestry book of Kingston Parish. The occasion was the annual meeting of the vestry to make decisions on the expenses of the parish and to authorize their payment. The Reverend John Dixon, churchwardens Capt.

William Plummer and Capt. John Peyton, and several members of the vestry were present. The business of the day included the authorization of payment to the minister for one year of service in the amount of 16,000 pounds of tobacco, having a value of £44.44s.* Not included in this amount was the benefit of living in the glebe house furnished by the parish; the value of crops, gardens, and cattle, if any, on glebe land; and the earnings from fees charged for presiding over funerals and marriages.

The clerk of the church, Thomas Dawson, was paid 1,200 pounds of tobacco, and the clerk of the vestry, John Davis, received 1,700 pounds. There were numerous payments for charity cases, including payments to widows; a payment to "Wm Hayes for boarding John Bolton & Curing his Sore foot"; payment for a coffin; sundry lawyers' fees; payments for "taring and painting the Vestry House and making fires therein During the Winter season"; and for "Burying Dorothy Jarrett"; and a large number of payments for taking care of orphans and the indigent.

On that day, Robert Hall received six hundred pounds of tobacco, having a value of £1.67, for "Keeping Hugh Brooks." The following year, Robert Hall received the same payment for keeping Hugh Brooks and was paid another six hundred pounds of tobacco for "taking Hugh Brookes off the Parish." At the November 28, 1763, annual meeting, Robert Hall was paid five hundred pounds of tobacco to "take Thos Thurstons Child off the Parish." This is the last entry mentioning Robert Hall in the vestry book. Hugh Brooks and Thomas Thurston's child were under the care of and probably living in the Hall household. The two boys may well have been orphans of friends of Ann and Robert. At this time the Hall household also included their children Elizabeth, age eight; Ann, seven; Robert, five; Spence, three; and Joyce, nine months. Thomas would be born in the following year.

The vestry book makes clear that its members were responsible for the less fortunate, and the cost of their welfare was shared equally by the rate charged per tithe. The number of welfare beneficiaries during the 1760s was remarkably small, averaging seventeen or eighteen recipients per year, or approximately 1 percent of the tithable households.

Robert Hall probably had at least one sibling, a brother named Thomas. While there is no record to confirm the relationship and even though common at the time, the name Thomas appears often in succeeding generations, and both Robert and Thomas were members of the same church. Three other Halls were recorded in the Kingston Parish register of marriages:

* The value of one pound of tobacco at this time was 1.50d. For many of the years reported in the vestry book, the value per pound is shown in farthings at the end of the accounting ledger where it was used to compute the payment for collecting the tithes. Also recorded was the rate per tithe with the number of tithables.

Edmond Hall married Elizabeth Hill on February 12, 1753; Susannah Hall married William Owen on February 17, 1762; and Jenny (Jane) Hall married William Anderton on July 8, 1764. The marriage dates suggest birth date estimates of Edmond circa 1732, Susannah circa 1741, and Jenny circa 1744. These three Halls were likely related in some way to Robert and/or Thomas, possibly even siblings.

Although little has been found in the record, especially land records and Revolutionary War records, about these three Halls, it can be said that the Hall family was well-represented in Kingston Parish from the early years of the eighteenth century. The Kingston Parish register lists six children of William and Susannah Hall Owen: Sarah, December 11, 1761; John, February 24, 1764; William, June 27, 1766; Joyce, June 19, 1769; Susanna, 1773; and Mary, date not recorded. William and Jane Hall Anderton had five children: Thomas, July 8, 1766; Mildred, July 3, 1767; Joseph, January 25, 1769; Benjamin, July 2, 1773; and Isaac, May 18, 1775. There is no record of children of Edmond and Elizabeth Hill Hall. It is possible that they moved away from Kingston Parish.

Thomas Hall is not mentioned in the register but is prominent in the vestry book of Kingston Parish, being listed as "Clerk of the New Church" on October 26, 1773; November 9, 1774; March 11, 1776; April 28, 1777; and February 6, 1778. Though the record is incomplete for a meeting of the vestry on August 14, 1775, Thomas likely served as clerk that year as well. His compensation in 1777 was 1,200 pounds of tobacco plus 48 pounds of tobacco for cask. During this period, the price of tobacco was erratic due to the Revolutionary War, but for parish compensation purposes the value of one pound of tobacco tended to be 1.5d. Thus Thomas's compensation was equal to £7.16s. The 1778 meeting was the first time tobacco was not used for the accounting of expenses, having been replaced by pounds, shillings, and pennies. Thomas received £7.16s for his service that year.

The vestry meeting records for 1779, 1781, and 1782 are missing, and Thomas Hall was not mentioned in the 1780 meeting.

The years during which Thomas Hall served as clerk of the church include the period of increasing hostilities between Britain and Virginia, preparation for war in Virginia during 1775, and open conflict beginning in 1776. Yet neither the war nor anything even remotely connected with it was ever mentioned in the vestry book.

The vestry book of Petsworth Parish, Gloucester County, Virginia, recorded a Thomas Hall serving as clerk of the church from January 22, 1781, through January 31, 1785, and from March 2, 1792, through July 11, 1793. This was probably the same Thomas Hall who served in Kingston Parish. His birth date is unknown, but given his clerkship continuing during the war years, he was probably young enough to have good health and adequate eyesight but too old to serve in the Revolutionary War.

There is no evidence that Thomas ever married or had real estate holdings of any kind. Given his role as clerk of the church, and the necessary reading and computational skills necessary for that office, he must have been reasonably well-educated. And, he was likely a resident of Kingston or Petsworth Parish and probably resided in the general neighborhood of a church. He is listed in the 1774 and 1775 Kingston Parish register of tithables; however, the record does not list a payment of a quit rent for land, so Thomas was likely not a landowner.[1] No one else was listed with Thomas, suggesting that he was not living in the same household with Robert. There is the possibility that he spent his earlier years as a mariner, and if so, he would have probably been a master or mate given his intellectual abilities.

Thomas did not appear in the tax records for 1770 but was listed in the 1782 Petsworth record, which showed one male, no slaves, two horses, and ten cattle. He was probably living on leased land. He was listed again in 1783 with two horses and nine cattle, in 1784 with three horses and thirteen cattle, and in 1786 with three slaves, three horses, and twelve cattle. The parish stopped recording tax records in 1787, and while a Thomas Hall continued to appear in the Gloucester County lists, with personal property as in earlier years, it is not possible to positively identify him beyond 1786.

Robert Hall left no record after November 1763 at age thirty-three when he took a child off the parish. He was dead eighteen years later, by 1781, at the age of approximately fifty-one. Robert's widow, Ann Hall, age approximately forty-eight in 1782, was taxed 17s.1d. for a forty-one-and-a-half-acre parcel of land. This is the first year for which land tax records are available. The next land tax record, for 1788, showed her having forty-five and a half acres. This change in land area was probably a result of a land purchase or inheritance and not the result of resurveys. In 1790, Ann's holdings decreased by one acre to forty-four and a half acres and would remain at that level until 1800 when a second parcel for seven acres was added and taxed as a separate parcel. In 1806 the tax record shows a combined parcel of fifty-one and a half acres. In the following years, until Robert and Ann's son Thomas's death in 1840, the Hall family lived on and owned those fifty-one and a half acres plus the increase of one acre in 1815.

In 1782 Ann's son Spencer was living in Salem, Massachusetts; her son Robert had completed his service in the Virginia State Navy and was probably a mariner; and her three daughters, Elizabeth, Ann, and Joyce, were married and were no longer living in Ann's household.

Ann's son Thomas, now a veteran of the Revolutionary War, would have been eighteen years of age and probably was the man of the house, with the responsibilities of everyday work associated with managing a small farm. Those responsibilities would have included tending a small herd of cattle and perhaps a horse or a team of oxen; planting and harvesting crops, most likely wheat and corn for market and fodder for feed; maintaining a kitchen garden; tending small animals, hogs and chickens for family consumption and probably a couple of goats for controlling underbrush; cutting timber for firewood and fencing rails; maintaining ditches and hedgerows; repairing the house and barn; directing the work of a few slaves; and countless other activities.

A farm of approximately 50 acres or less was the most typical size in Mathews County during the 1780s. The record for 1791 shows a total of 345 parcels of land identified for tax purposes. Of these, 138, or 40 percent, were for parcels of 50 acres or less. There were 108 parcels between 51 and 150 acres, or 31.3 percent of the total. The remaining parcels included 52 parcels between 151 and 300 acres, 27 parcels between 301 and 450 acres, 9 parcels between 451 and 600 acres, and 11 parcels over 600 acres, with 4 of these having more than 1,050 acres. Thus, slightly more than 71 percent of all parcels in Mathews County were 150 acres or less. It was a county of mostly small family farms with the majority of them utilizing slave labor in addition to work by family members.

In the 1787 personal property list, Ann Hall was recorded as having one unnamed male over the age of twenty-one for whom she was charged with a tax. This must have been Thomas, who was twenty-three at the time. Ann had seven cattle and three slaves, one over the age of sixteen and two under sixteen. She was shown as not owning horses or mules.[2]

An extensive search of land surveys, land transactions, and deeds enabled finding the most probable tract of land owned by Ann Hall. The location was on the east side of the main road, 2.6 miles south of the courthouse. An additional family property, Sutherland, as it is now known, was acquired by Thomas Hall in late 1834 or early 1835 and was located four hundred yards to the southwest of Ann Hall's land. Sutherland faces Weston Creek, which flows into the East River. Weston Creek was previously known as Hunley Creek, named at a time when the Hunley family owned significant acreages in the neighborhood.

An archaeological survey conducted during 2016–2018 on the likely tract of land owned by Ann Hall found evidence of continuous occupation from approximately 1720 to 1830 by families of above-average material condition as measured by the quantity and quality of the artifacts discovered. Thus, it is highly probable that Thomas Hall's grandfather built the first Hall house on the property, around 1720–1730, and that it may have been the birthplace of his father, Robert Hall.

The site is noteworthy for a very large variety of ceramics dominated by delft and followed by creamware, pearl ware, whiteware, redware, and white salt-glazed stoneware. Somewhat expensive commodities at the time, the ceramics suggest a relatively high standard of living among the inhabitants. A large number of hand-wrought nails indicates usage before 1800. A majority of the glass, green wine-bottle glass, was produced in the eighteenth century. Fragments of handmade bricks, pipe stems, and pipe bowls have been found in large quantities, including several pipe bowl fragments with maker's marks from Europe.

Of particular interest are two half coins, both parts of two Spanish half real coins, one dated 1733 and the other from approximately 1724. The 1733 coin is especially significant because it was pierced, a common practice to permit it to be worn around the neck on a string as a token of endearment or to commemorate a significant date. Appendix 9 has additional information on the archaeological survey.

In 1784 there were two "white souls" living in Ann Hall's house, and there were three additional buildings. One of these was probably a barn, the second may have been a kitchen with a washroom and slave quarters in a loft, and perhaps the third building was for storage. The enumeration* for Kingston Parish was not in alphabetical order and may have been done by neighborhood, in which case Ann Hall was in proximity to John Tabb, Hannah Tompkins, Peter Foster, Edward White, William Tompkins, Caleb Hunley, and Peter Smith.

At the time of the 1784 enumeration, there were 243 heads of households in Kingston Parish, and of these 22 did not own a dwelling. Of the remaining 221 households, 14.9 percent owned a dwelling but no additional buidings, 34.8 percent owned one or two additional buildings, and 20.8 percent owned three additional buildings. Farms having four or more accounted for 29.5 percent of the remaining properties. The largest number of buildings, thirty-three, were in the estate of William Armistead. Thomas Smith owned the next largest, nineteen.

* The original 1790 schedules of the first US Census for Gloucester County, VA, were lost. However, state enumerations were made in many counties in 1782, 1783, 1784, and 1785. The enumeration for 1783 counted white and black residents while the enumeration for 1784 recorded all white members of a household and the number of dwellings and other buildings. The count of dwellings equals in most cases the numbers of heads of households, and thus dwellings for other family members, tenants, and slaves are in the other buildings classification. The 1783 and 1784 enumerations are complete for the four parishes of Gloucester County; however, Gloucester was not in the enumerations for 1782 and 1785. Of the seventy-eight Virginia counties in the 1790 census together with enumerations made during the 1780s, Gloucester, with a total population of 13,498, was the sixteenth largest and had the seventh largest enslaved population, 7,063, who represented 52.3 percent of the total county population.

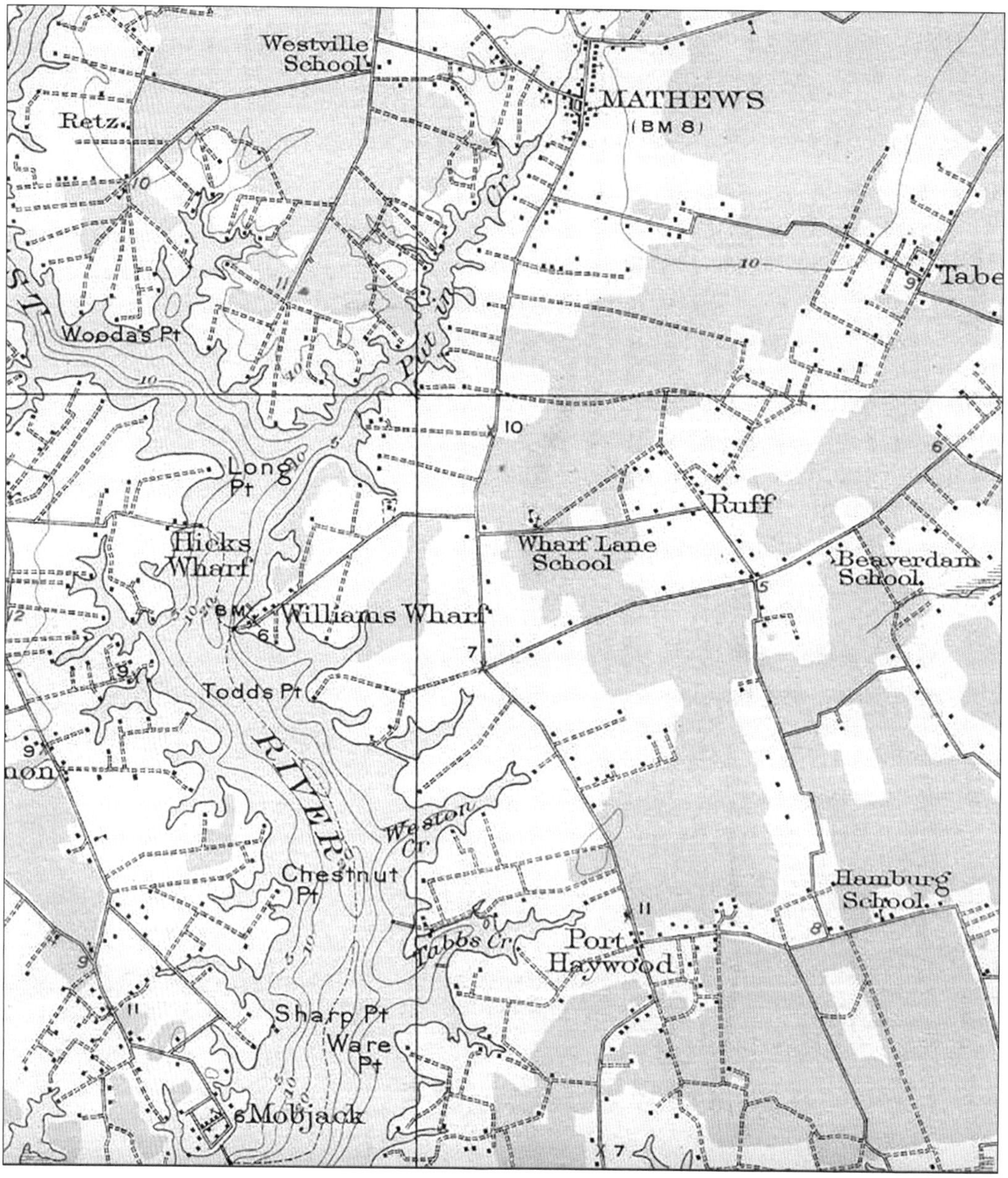


*Figure* 17 This section of the 1916 Mathews County topographical map in fig. 4 depicts the important geographic locations on which most of the early Halls of Mathews lived and worked. It includes land originally patented on the east side of the East River to Matthew Gayle, Philip Hunley, Mark Foster, William Hampton, Thomas Todd, John Degge, and John Collis; the glebe lands, on the west side of Pudding Creek; and all of the known Hall family real estate transactions in Mathews County. US Department of War, Corps of Engineers, US Army, later renamed US Geological Survey.

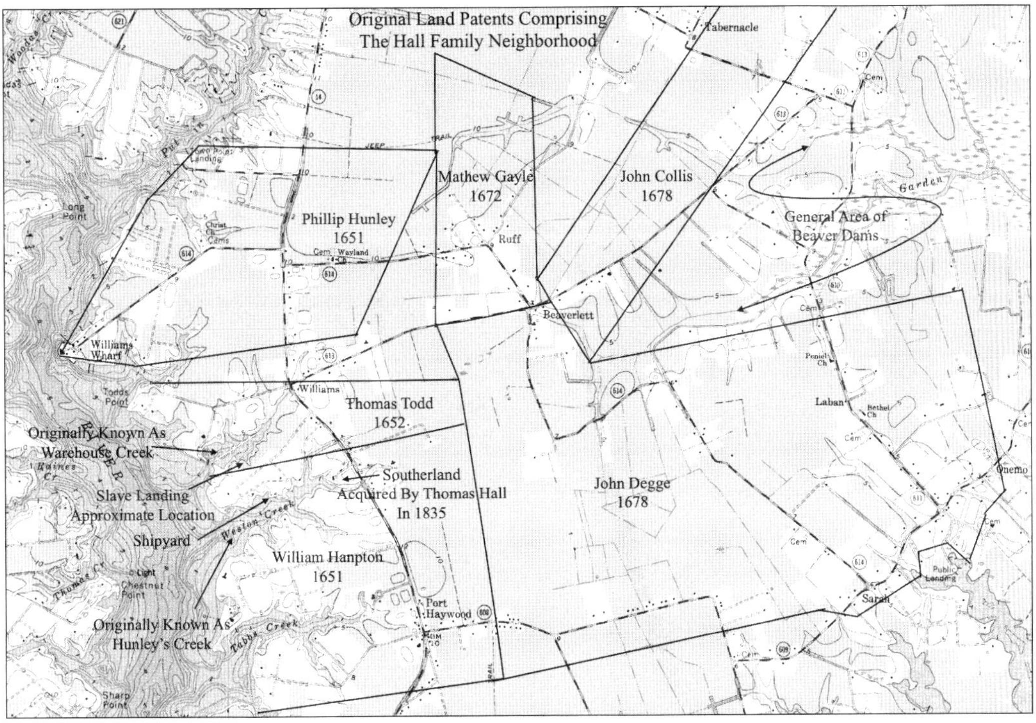


*Figure* 18 Superimposed on the 1965 Mathews County topographical map, plotted to scale from the original patent descriptions using metes and bounds, are the approximate boundaries of the original land patents that encompassed land occupied by the Hall family as well as the Gayles, Hunleys, Degges, Hamptons, and Todds. The location of a shipyard and a slave landing are shown as well as the original names of two creeks. Weston Creek was originally Hunley's Creek, and the creek now containing a tide mill was known as Warehouse Creek in the earliest surveys. A significant void between the Hunley, Gayle, Degge, and Todd patents unfortunately could not be reconciled with the adjacent surveys. It is most probable that it was part of or eventually became part of Philip Hunley's and Thomas Todd's holdings.

Ann Hall's land was located in an important district in the parish and adjoined the main road connecting the northern sections of the county with southern portions to New Point Comfort. In addition to the courthouse, nearby were the principal deepwater port of the parish, Williams Wharf; the Kingston Parish church; notable plantations including Poplar Hall and Woodstock; and shipyards, together with related manufacturing activities. Williams Wharf had warehouses and merchandising establishments to service import and export shipping activity. Shipyards engaged in building coastal and sea-going vessels, small craft for local transportation and fishing, and boat and ship repair services were nearby.* These activities would have required a substantial workforce, and the neighborhood was probably well-populated with skilled craftsmen.

What is not known is the chain of title to the land. It could have been Ann's through inheritance from her family, or it could have come to her when her husband died. It was unusual, however, for land to be recorded in the name of a widow rather than in the name of the estate of her husband until divided. Further, the notation "life interest," if that had been the intent, is not shown, adding to the mystery. Since the land first appeared in the record as belonging to Ann in 1782, it is assumed that Robert was dead by 1781, perhaps years earlier as the last record of him was in 1763. If Ann inherited the land through her family, she may have been from the Gayle, Degge, Collis, or Hunley families, as they had extensive holdings in the neighborhood and all of them together surrounded most of Ann Hall's land.

The original Hall property was for the most part on land originally patented to Thomas Todd, to whom 150 acres was awarded on October 27, 1652. He died without heirs, and the land was re-patented to Thomas Falkener on September 26, 1671, recorded as containing 140 acres. Unfortunately, the chain of title from Thomas Falkener to the Hall family is not known. The land on the patent extending into the East River is today known as Todd's Point.

The patent reads in part:

> To all whosoever Now Know you And I the Said Richard Bonnott esqr do give and grant unto Thomas Todd one hundred and fifty Acres of Land being on a Small Neck of Land lying on the Eastward Side of the Eastermost river in Mockjack bay between the Land of William Hampton and Philip Hunly begining at a Marked pine at the river Side and running along the Marked trees of the said Hamptons East by North three hundred and twenty poles North by west forty five poles west to the Marked tree of Philip Hunly on the river Side three hundred and twenty poles South one hundred and thirteen poles to the first Specified tree of Mr Hampton, The Said Land being due unto the Said Thomas Todd [?] for the transportation of three persons into this Colony and to have and to hold . . .[3]

During the Revolutionary War, farms in Gloucester and neighboring counties provided a

* An 1804 survey by county surveyor George Billups referenced a shipyard (see fig. 34). The metes and bounds together with a sketch of the property place the shipyard on Hunley Creek on land owned by Joseph Degge. The location is approximately 660 yards, 0.38 miles, to the southwest from the Hall property.

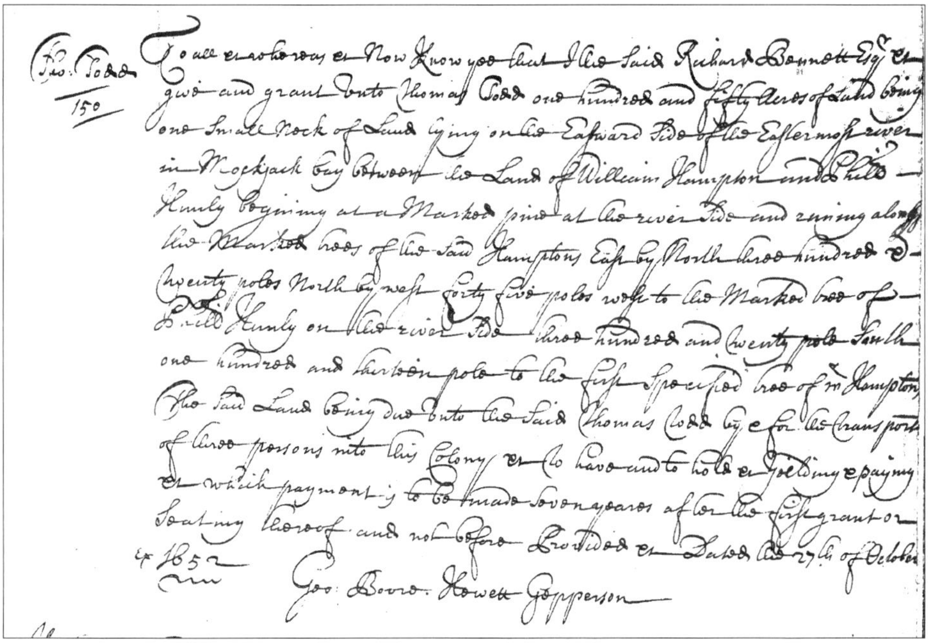

*Figure* 19 Thomas Todd received a land patent on October 27, 1652, for 150 acres in Kingston Parish. The original land owned by the Hall family was partially within the boundaries of Todd's patent. Courtesy of the Library of Virginia, Richmond.

significant part of the food for Continental forces in the area and local militia, often on a promise to receive payment at a later date. On April 5, 1782, a court in Gloucester met to determine a schedule of payments for the variety of provisions sent to the army. Included in the list were these reimbursement fees. The items included give insight into the basic necessities for provisioning an army:

> Grass beef at 4d/# [per lb.], stalled beef 6d/#, Indian corn 12s/bu [per bushel], bacon 1s/#, . . . fresh pork 4d/#, lambs 12s each, country made salt 20s/bu, allum 30s/bu, oats 1s6d/bu, wheat 6s/bu, barley 4s/bu, West India rum 18s/gal., Old rum 24s/gal., French rum 10s/gal., whiskey 8s/gal., . . . a wagon & team 15s/day, an ox cart with driver & 6 oxen 15s/day, cart & driver with 4 oxen 12s/day, . . . a labourers hire 2s6d/day, a horse hire [2s6d]/day.[4]

An example of the magnitude of provisions provided can be seen from the record of claims from some of the farmers in Gloucester: Warner Lewis Jr. received £121.19s.10d for 2,716 pounds of beef, 236 pounds of bacon, and a cart and two horses. George Booth received £122.15s.7d. for a similar mix of provisions. John Hobday received £342.19s.5d., and Sir John Peyton received £239.13s.6d. There were dozens of claims made by small farmers, for example, John Hurst £4.8s.8d. for 200 pounds of beef and 22 pounds of bacon and Lewis Hudgen 8s.6d. for 8½ pounds of bacon.

Ann Hall provided the army with two hundred pounds of beef and was paid £3.6s.8d., indicating that her cattle were grass-fed.[5] The payment was made in October 1781, the month Cornwallis surrendered at Yorktown—a time of total mobilization of the local militia and an all-out effort by the people of Gloucester to support the military in every way possible.

In 1794, the land tax record shows Ann as no longer having land ownership, and in the same entry Thomas Hall is listed as the owner of forty-four and a half acres. Ann probably died in late 1793 or early 1794, at the age of approximately sixty. She was the mother of three veterans, and as a widow by age forty-six, she had the primary responsibility for running the farm and raising a teenage son. She lived through a period of warfare on the nearby Chesapeake Bay and enemy incursions into the surrounding neighborhoods by British seamen and soldiers foraging for provisions. Ann thus made an amazing but not uncommon contribution to the war effort.

The uncertainty of the outcome of the Revolution must have been a constant topic of discussion with the great risk and apprehension of what might happen if the colonists lost to Great Britain. No doubt Ann and her neighbors were remarkable in their ability to adapt to a multiyear period of shortages of manufactured goods and imports of desirable products. She and others like her made an enormous contribution to securing the nation's independence and in creating the society and way of life that followed.

# CHAPTER 7

# Preparations *for* War *and the* Attack *on* Gwynn's Island

A history of a family during the eighteenth century in Kingston Parish, Gloucester County, Virginia, is not complete without including local references to the Revolutionary War. In the lives of the people of Kingston Parish, it was not a distant, abstract series of events but rather was real life and at home in the Chesapeake Bay at New Point Comfort, the Wolf Trap, East River, Pepper Creek, Gwynn's Island, Milford Haven, Gloucester Point, and other locations in the county and throughout Tidewater Virginia. As has been mentioned, in the case of the family of Robert and Ann Hall, all of their children were involved. Their three daughters married men who would serve in the war, and their three sons served. It is unknown whether or not the concentration of war service in the Hall family was typical of the area.

The events leading to a state of war in Virginia and the British colonies of North America were years in the making and became particularly disturbing in 1774. By early 1775, the inevitability of conflict grew more certain, and the Second Virginia Convention, which met March 20–27 in Richmond, resolved to put the colony into a state of defense and to send a delegation to the Second Continental Congress. The Battles of Lexington and Concord took place just a few weeks later on April 19, and on April 20 the royal governor of Virginia, Charles Murray, Lord Dunmore, ordered marines of HM Schooner *Magdalen** to seize gunpowder stored in the magazine in Williamsburg.

---

* The *Magdalen* was a two-masted schooner having a deck length of 48 feet 8 inches and a carrying capacity of 90 3/94 tons. Her crew consisted of thirty men, and she carried six three-pounder guns. The schooner was built in Marblehead, MA, and was purchased by the Royal Navy in 1764. At the time of the gunpowder seizure, she was commanded by Lt. Joseph Nunn. (Rif Winfield, *British Warships in the Age of Sail, 1714–1792: Design, Construction, Careers and Fates* [Barnsley, South Yorkshire, UK: Seaforth Publishing, 2007], 327.)

A supplement to the April 28, 1775, edition of Purdie's *Virginia Gazette* carried news of the gunpowder seizure and several resolutions made by the "committee of Gloucester," including the following:

> The committee having received authentick information, that last Thursday night an officer of one of his Majesty's armed vessels, with a party of armed men, by express command of Lord Dunmore, privately removed the *gunpowder belonging to this colony* out of the magazine, it was unanimously resolved that the removal of the powder from the publick magazine, on board one of his Majesty's armed vessels, by order of the Governour, is exceedingly alarming at this time.
>
> *Resolved*, that his Lordship's verbal answer to the address of the Mayor, Recorders, Aldermen, and Common Council of the city of Williamsburg, on that occasion, is unsatisfactory, disrespectful, and evasive.
>
> *Resolved*, that his Lordship, by this and other parts of his conduct, which have lately transpired, has justly forfeited all title to the confidence of the good people of Virginia.
>
> *Resolved*, that the powder ought immediately to be restored.

The situation grew tense, and Lord Dunmore, fearing for his ability to maintain royal control of the colony, sent a letter to Admiral Graves and General Gage in Boston on May 1, 1775, asking for troops and naval support. In addition, he requested war supplies from Lord Dartmouth in England to arm "Indians, Negroes, & other persons" who would subdue the "refractory People."[1] His concerns proved accurate when on June 8, fearing for his and his family's safety, he fled the Governor's Palace in Williamsburg. He proceeded to the protection of the twenty-four-gun British[*] warship HMS *Fowey*, anchored off Yorktown, and sent his wife and children to England. In that same month, George Washington was appointed commander in chief of the Continental army. It was an eventful spring of 1775, and war with Britain in Virginia was becoming a near certainty.

The news accounts captured the swiftness of changing events and the enormous dislocations to the economy. The following was published on May 4, 1775, in Pinkney's *Virginia Gazette:*

---

* References to British warships and other British activities use "British" and "Britain" instead of "English." After 1707, "Great Britain" became the name of the nation that resulted from the union of England and Scotland.

> At a meeting of the committee of Gloucester, at the courthouse, on Tuesday the 2d day of May, 1775:
>
> *Resolved*, that we will not ship a single hogshead of tobacco to Great Britain until the determination of the continental congress, respecting exportation, be known.

Virginia created the Committee of Safety on July 17, 1775, to make war plans for the defense of Virginia in the interior and coastal regions, especially the Chesapeake Bay. Such defense was essential to keep trade routes open, a vital factor necessary to create credit from exported commodities with which to pay for imported war materials, especially gunpowder and other manufactured goods. This step may have been prompted by activities of the British navy, such as were reported in Pinkney's *Virginia Gazette*, on July 13, 1775:

> GLOUCESTER TOWN, FRIDAY, *July* 13, 1775. It is certain that a boat from the Fowey or Otter landed several armed men on an island in the lower end of this county, who stole 14 sheep and a cow. The owner of them alarmed his neighbors; but before they could arm themselves the robbers had made off. However, the people, who are now well furnished with arms, &c. will be ready to give them a warm reception, should they *favour* them with another visit. *Quere*, Are not the negro slaves, now on board the Fowey, which are under the governor's protection, in actual rebellion, and punishable as such?

Another news account from Purdie's *Virginia Gazette*, August 4, 1775, gives an indication of the degree of organization and cooperation among the counties.

> AT a meeting of the committee of the county of Gloucester, on monday the 24th of July, it was
>
> *Resolved*, that the readiness shown by the volunteers, who marched to the assistance of the lower counties on the late alarms, merits our warmest thanks; and we assure them we should have cheerfully cooperated with them, had it been requisite.
>
> *Resolved*, that the most cordial thanks of the people of Gloucester county are justly due to the worthy inhabitants of those counties who have generously offered their houses as a retreat to our wives and children, in case they should be obliged to abandon their habitations here below.

By the fall of 1775, British warships had effectively blocked vessels from clearing the Virginia capes and, with that, exports to England. The West Indies became almost impossible as well as coastal trade with New England and the Carolinas, other than smuggling operations in small vessels.

In the meantime, in August 1775, Lord Dunmore, now on board the *William*, a merchant ship accompanied by loyalists, moved to the Norfolk harbor. Within a short time, a large fleet of mostly merchant vessels, populated by an increasing number of loyalists and runaway slaves, gathered around the *William*. Dunmore hoped to make the town, shipyards, and port a base for British military activities. At this time Norfolk had a population of approximately 6,000 to 6,500 and was the largest population center in Virginia. A large number of Norfolk's citizens were merchants who depended on open and safe sea routes, and as a result many of them supported the Crown. The town had also become an important center for shipyards, outfitting and provisioning of ships, and thus had a larger manufacturing segment of its economy than anywhere else in Virginia. Norfolk ranked fifth or sixth in population of all towns in the colonies, behind Philadelphia; New York; Boston; Charleston, South Carolina; and perhaps Newport, Rhode Island. Later in the month, on August 23, King George III declared the American colonies in open rebellion, and on December 22 he issued a proclamation prohibiting trade with Virginia and the other colonies.

Preparations for war continued with each county organizing militia units. The committee of Gloucester, consisting of a chairman and thirty-two members, met on September 13, 1775, at the Gloucester courthouse and nominated officers: a lieutenant colonel, a major, several captains and lieutenants, and ensigns for the Virginia State Navy.[2]

By Christmas 1775, the British naval presence in the Norfolk harbor consisted of HMS *Liverpool*, HMS *Otter*, HMS *Kingfisher*, the *Dunmore*, and the *William*.[3]

Relations between the "rebel" elements in Norfolk and the British ships in the harbor deteriorated through the fall of 1775, culminating with a British naval bombardment of the Norfolk waterfront beginning between 3 and 4 p.m. on January 1, 1776. Seizing the opportunity to deny the British from capturing Norfolk to establish a base for military operations, rebels set fire in the early evening hours to buildings on the east side of the town, and, as the wind was from the east, fire quickly spread westward towards the Elizabeth River burning houses, shops, waterfront warehouses, and other structures. Within a few days, the town of Norfolk and its warehouses and wharves were all but totally destroyed. Its inhabitants, being without shelter, were forced to relocate, and in the cold January weather and lacking adequate provisions, the citizens of Norfolk suffered great hardships. In February the few remaining structures were destroyed to end any encouragement for occupation by the British.

Meanwhile the Committee of Safety, now in its sixth month of existence, took steps on

January 11, 1776, to create the Virginia State Navy. The plan included the establishment of squadrons of vessels for the protection of five specific regions of the Chesapeake Bay: the Eastern Shore and the principal rivers in Virginia—the Hampton Roads and James River region, the York River and Mobjack Bay, the Rappahannock River, and the Potomac. These activities took on added significance and urgency with the arrival on February 10, 1776, of HMS *Roebuck*, a forty-four-gun warship. She was under the command of Andrew Snape Hamond who placed his ship in Hampton Roads and vicinity to provide support to Lord Dunmore and to strengthen the British blockade.[4] His resources were increased on February 16, 1776, by the arrival of the twenty-gun HMS *Mercury* accompanied by three transports.

In the eighteenth century, a British warship carrying forty-four guns was a formidable floating battery of cannon capable of firing twenty twelve-pounders,* twenty six-pounders, and four swivel guns. The typical crew for a vessel of this size was 280 sailors, marines, gunners, and officers. A ship of this rating would have had one or more tenders and would have been resupplied by transports. Appendix 6 details most of the British navy vessels that were stationed or made passage in the Chesapeake Bay, at least twenty-six warships including ten ships of the line, carrying from forty-four to sixty-four guns; eleven frigates with twenty to thirty-two guns; five sloops with twelve to fourteen guns; and a variety of smaller vessels. Several of the frigates and sloops were stationed in the Chesapeake for extended periods of time.

Unfortunately, the records of the Virginia State Navy, including construction locations, specifications, crews, and operations, are severely limited and nothing at all like the detailed and methodical records kept by the British navy. The extreme lack of resources, especially foundries for manufacturing cannon; the necessity for importing almost all gunpowder; and a shortage of experienced mariners made creating a fleet of warships capable of matching the British navy unthinkable. Instead, the strategy to meet the British naval threat with galleys seems to have been the best option. They were designed to be built in local shipyards, to have modest numbers of crewmen, to be armed sufficiently to be a strong deterrent to enemy small craft, and to be propelled by sails and oars. Their shallow draft gave them access to safety in upper reaches of rivers and creeks.

The first mention of row galleys, a classification used by the navy board, was in a letter from George Mason to George Washington, dated April 2, 1776: "We are building two row-Gallies, which are in considerable forwardness; & have purchased three Sloops for Cruisers, two of them, being only from forty to fifty Tons Burthen, are to mount 8 Carriage Guns each, 3 & 4 Pounders."

By the summer of 1776, the Committee of Safety took steps to significantly increase

* A twelve-pounder was a cannon that fired a twelve-pound ball, a six-pounder fired a six-pound ball, etc.

galley construction. John Herbert, master shipbuilder, was assigned to identify locations for shipyards on the James River and to employ skilled ship carpenters.[5] Shipbuilding in the Rappahannock district was assigned to his brother Caleb Herbert, and brother Reuben Herbert was to develop shipbuilding capacity on the York River, which included activities in Kingston Parish.

John Earle, a naval architect and student of the history of the Chesapeake Bay, wrote:

> The "Row Galley" of the American Revolution differed from the Greek and Roman galleys of antiquity. The type originated in England during the last quarter of the seventeenth century. It was primarily a sailing vessel with oar ports and oars, or sweeps as they were usually called, for use in calms, to pursue a prize or escape an enemy, and to facilitate navigation of rivers, harbors, etc. This much could be said of any relatively small naval vessel of the period. But the galley type had additional characteristics of fine lines, less depth of hull, and consequently less displacement. Some merchant vessels and privateers* were also built as galleys. They accepted the reduced cargo capacity in exchange for better sailing qualities that facilitated escape from the enemy in war, and in peace the many pirates that infested even the Narrow Seas. Various rigs were used with galleys-ship, brig, schooner, etc. but it would appear that in the minds of some, perhaps many people in the last quarter of the eighteenth century, the lateen rig was associated with galleys, and some were so rigged.[6]

Fourteen galleys were built for the Virginia State Navy during the Revolution (see appendix 7), and the record of cordage, rigging, specifications for spars, and reports by the British navy indicate that at least four and more likely five of the galleys had three masts and were ship-rigged. The remaining galleys would have had two masts and were probably rigged as schooners as this was a rig very familiar to mariners on the Chesapeake Bay at that time. Schooners also did not require large crews of sailors.

Brothers Robert and Spence Hall served on the galley *Henry*, Robert as a master's mate and Spence as a seaman. The *Henry* was constructed in Gloucester County, Virginia, probably on the East River, as that river had the greatest number of shipyards, ship carpenters, and supporting trades in the county.

Construction on the *Henry* probably started in early 1776, with the construction site selection

* A "privateer" was a merchant ship converted to an armed vessel and crewed by civilians. It was authorized by government to attack enemy shipping and capture ships, the value of which was awarded as compensation to the owners and crews.

and preliminary procurement of materials and recruitment of carpenters occurring beforehand, perhaps in late 1775. The first mention of the *Henry* in the minutes of the Virginia Committee of Safety was on June 6, 1776, at which time a warrant was issued to Capt. Robert Tompkins for £150 "upon acc[oun]t to pay the carpenters employed on his Galley [*Henry*] in Gloucester and other expenses." On this same date, it was ordered that Captain Tompkins be permitted to take two eighteen-pounders "now lying at York Town for use of his Galley."[7] The eighteen-pounder was one of the most powerful armaments in the navy at that time. British warships, for example HMS *Emerald*, a thirty-two-gun Niger-class frigate, was armed with twenty-six twelve-pounders and four six-pounders.

Further orders in June and July involved procurement of anchors and rigging; "other necessaries" furnished to Capt. Tompkins; "£20 upon acct for purchase of materials for his Galley"; one hundred pounds of gunpowder and two hundred pounds of lead; and £30 for furnishing necessaries for the *Henry*.[8] On August 30, 1776, the keeper of the public store was ordered to deliver "for the use of the *Henry* Galley five Bolts of Duck and four sides of Leather," and it was ordered that "Stephen Mitchell deliver unto Thomas Gibbs such Iron as he may be in want of for the use of the *Henry* Galley."[9]

Meanwhile, Dunmore, fearing that his position in the Norfolk harbor could not be maintained, especially as the militia was placing cannon at strategic locations along the shore of the Elizabeth River for firing on the British fleet, decided to establish a new military base. He chose Gwynn's Island, located at the northeast corner of Gloucester County, in Kingston Parish, approximately fifty miles by water from Norfolk to the entrance of the Piankatank River.

The Dunmore fleet began the departure from Norfolk on Tuesday, May 21, 1776, under the protection of HMS *Roebuck*, forty-four guns; HMS *Fowey*, twenty-four guns; and HM Sloop *Otter*, fourteen guns. By Friday, May 24, the entire fleet of approximately one hundred vessels of all sizes and rigs was assembled in Hampton Roads. The fleet sailed to Lynnhaven Bay the next day and anchored. On Sunday, May 26, the fleet sailed for Gwynn's Island, arriving during the afternoon and into the evening, anchoring in Hills Bay just within the entrance to the Piankatank River. On Monday morning, British forces landed on Gwynn's Island and over the following weeks converted a rural landscape into an armed encampment with the goal to reestablish royal authority over the colony of Virginia.

Purdie's *Virginia Gazette* on May 31, 1776, reported on Dunmore's activities:

> LAST Sunday lord Dunmore, with his whole fleet, left Hampton road, and came up the bay to Gwynn's island, in Gloucester county, where we understand he has

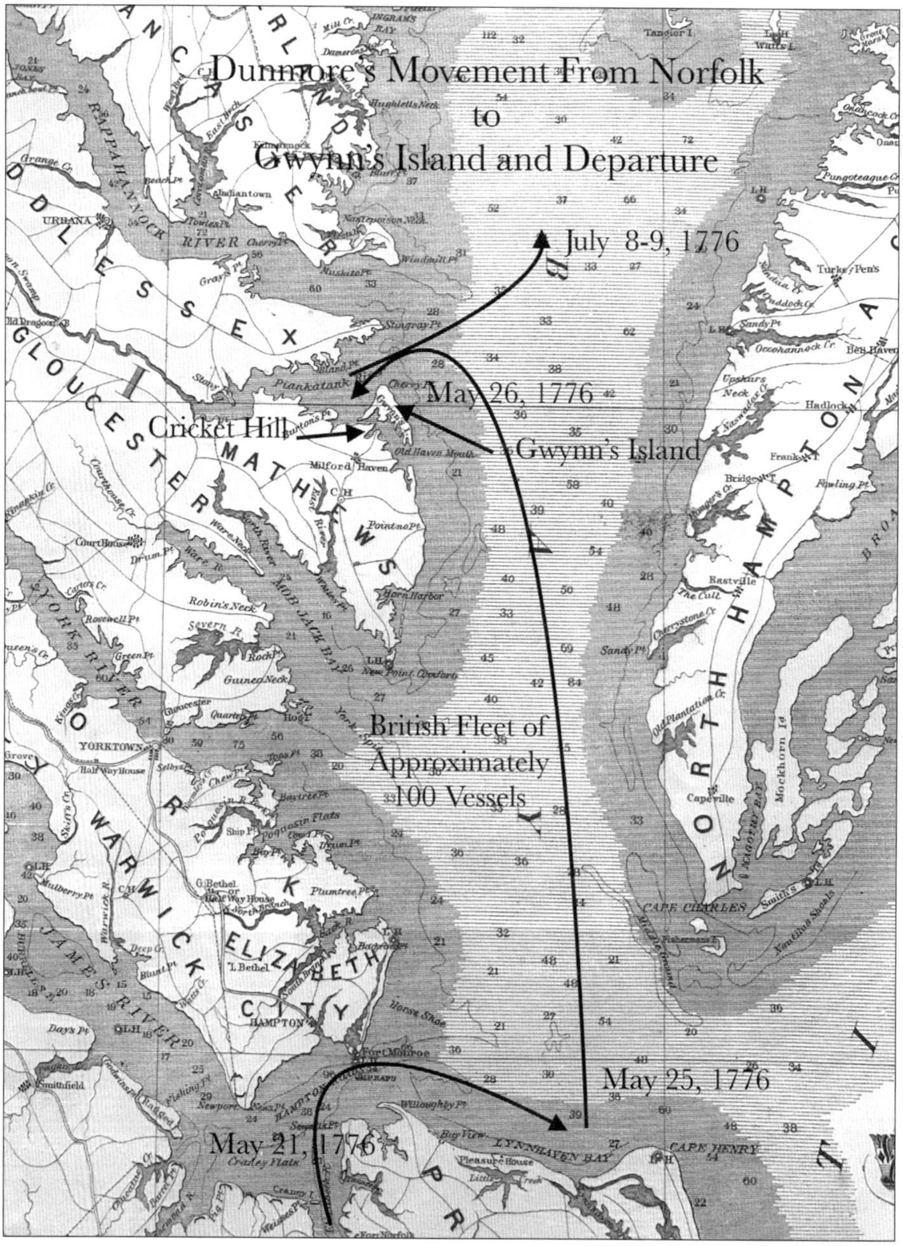


*Figure* 20 The route of evacuation from Norfolk, Virginia, and passage to Gwynn's Island during May 1776 (superimposed on a chart of the lower bay). The fleet of approximately one hundred vessels departed Norfolk on May 21, 1776, assembled in Lynnhaven Roads on May 25, and arrived in Hills Bay at the mouth of the Piankatank River on May 26. The artillery battery at Cricket Hill (indicated by arrow) successfully drove Dunmore from Virginia July 8–9, 1776. From the author's collection.

> landed his black and white troops, to the number of about 500, and is intrenching. This island contains about 2000 acres, occupied by several families, who are possessed of a considerable quantity of stock, and is well watered. A body of regulars and militia, to the amount of 2000 men, quickly assembled, and are watching their motions; and, if opportunity suits, will very likely attempt to beat up their new quarters, very delightful, it should seem, to those pirates and renegadoes in their present sickly, starving, and dirty situation, from their amusing themselves, on the evening of their landing, with a promiscuous ball, which was opened, we hear, by a certain spruce little gentleman, with one of the black ladies.

On June 15, 1776, Dixon and Hunter's *Virginia Gazette* reported:

> We learn from Gloucester, that Lord Dunmore has erected hospitals upon Gwyn's island; that his old friend Andrew Sprowle is dead, and that they are inoculating the blacks for smallpox. . . .
>
> One day this week a small vessel belonging to the enemy, with five hands on board, ran aground on the Gloucester shore, within musket shot, and was taken. The crew jumped overboard, two swam to Gwyn's island, one was shot, and the other two drowned.

In a military maneuver that has never been fully appreciated or broadly known, Brig. Gen. Andrew Lewis, by mid-June, assembled over one thousand members of the Virginia militia and the Continental army in Gloucester County and by early July had increased the number to two thousand. By July 7, Lewis's director of artillery, Dohicky Arundel completed the placement of a battery including two eighteen-pounders, five nine-pounders, and three six-pounders in well-concealed locations on the mainland facing the island. The two eighteen-pounders were placed on Cricket Hill, which was in proximity to the British encampment and several of their warships. An eighteen-pounder cannon in the late eighteenth century weighed 4,200 pounds, was nine feet long, and had a caliber of 5.30 inches. The discharge of one eighteen-pound cannonball required nine pounds of gunpowder.[10] The gun emplacements were within firing range of Lord Dunmore's flagship, the *Dunmore*, and the main encampment of his entourage on the island.

On the morning of July 8, 1776, firing commenced with the eighteen-pound cannon, and before the day was out, Dunmore had begun an evacuation of the island and the withdrawal of his entire fleet. Backed by military units in reserve on the mainland, General Lewis, using the element of surprise, had carefully placed gun batteries to inflict damage to the fleet and shore installations, maintained excellent command and control among his units, and achieved an overwhelming victory against the British in just one day. Dunmore withdrew beginning in the evening of the same day and moved his fleet to the Potomac River and then northward marking the end of British colonial rule of Virginia.

The August 21, 1776, edition of the *Massachusetts Spy*, published in Worcester, Massachusetts, contained a lengthy news account of the events related to Gwynn's Island:

> The following is a particular account of the attack and rout of Lord Dunmore, with his piratical crew, from Gwyn's-Island.
>
> We got to the island on Monday the eighth and next morning, at eight o'clock, began a furious attack upon the enemy's shipping, camp, and fortifications, from two batteries, one of five six and nine pounders, the other mounting two eighteen-pounders. What forces the enemy had were encamped on a Point of the island, nearly opposite, to our five gun battery, covered by a battery of four embrasures, and a breastwork of considerable extent. Besides this, they had two other batteries, and a stockade fort, higher up the haven, where troops were stationed to prevent our landing. In the haven were three tenders, one sloop (the lady Charlotte) mounting six carriage guns, a schooner of two carriage guns, six swivels, and a coho[?]n, and a pilot boat, badly armed; who had orders from Capt. Hammond, of the Roebuck, to prevent our boats passing over to the island, and to annoy the rebels by every means in their power.
>
> Gen. Lewis announced his order for attacking the enemy, by putting a match to the first gun, an eighteen pounder, himself; and the Dunmore being then the nearest to us, at the distance of only four or five hundred yards, the shot passed through her hull, and did considerable damage. Our five gun battery likewise began playing on the fleet, the enemy's camp and works; and the fire soon became so hot that the Dunmore was obliged to cut her cables and haul off, after receving ten shot, some of which raked fore and aft. The Otter lay next her, and it was expected would have taken her birth, but the first we gave her took place, supposed between wind and water, as she immediately slipped her cable likewise, and hauled out on a ca[?]een, without firing a gun. By this time all the fleet, any way near shore, began to slip cables, in the utmost confusion; and had the wind set in with a flood tide, we must have taken great numbers of them. Our eighteen pounders did great execution from the upper battery, which raked the whole fleet; and Capt. Denny, who commanded the other battery soon silenced the enemy at the point, knocking down several tents, which put their camp into great confusion. At half after nine the firing ceased, which was renewed again at twelve, with double vigor, from both batteries; and nothing prevented our pushing to the island during the cannonade, but the want of vessels.

The Gen. being determined to cross next day, gave orders for all the small craft to be collected together from the neighbouring creeks that night, and two brass field-pieces, six pounders, to be carried to a place called Lower Windmill Point, to attack the tender that lay there, and facilitate our crossing. According, in the morning, Capt. Harrison, who had the direction of those field-pieces, began playing upon the tender, which he galled so much, that the schooner ran up a small creek which made into the island, where the crew abandoned her, and the sloop got aground in reach of our cannon; upon which the General ordered Capt. Smith, of the seventh regiment, with his company, to man the canoes and board her, which was done with alacrity. However, before our men came up with her, the crew got into their boat and pushed for the island; but Capt. Smith, very prudently passing the tender, pursued them so close that before they could reach the shore, he exchanged a few shot with them, and took part of them prisoners. The enemy's look outs, perceiving our men close upon the lower part of the island, cried out "the [?] men are coming," scampered off. The pilot boat made no resistance.

Gen. Lewis then ordered two hundred men, under Colonel M'Canaham, to land in the island which was performed as expediciously as our small vessels would admit of. On our arrival, we found the enemy had evacuated the place with the greatest precipitation, and were struck with horror at the number of dead bodies, in a state of putrifaction, strewed, all the way from their battery to Cherry-point, about two miles in length, without a shovel full of earth upon them; others gasping for life; and some had crawled to the water's edge who could make known their distress by beckoning to us. By the small pox, and other malignant disorders, which have raged on board the fleet so many months past, it is clear they have lost, since their arrival at Gwyn's island, over five hundred souls. I myself counted one hundred and thirty graves, or rather holes loosely covered over with earth, close together, many of them large enough to hold a corporal's guard. One in the middle, was nearly done up with turf, and is supposed to contain the remains of the Lord of Gosport, many were burnt alive in brush huts, which, in their confusion, had got on fire. In short, such a scene of misery, distress and cruelty, my eyes never beheld; for which the authors, one may reasonobly conclude, never can make atonement in this world.

The enemy left behind them, in their battery, a double fortified nine pounder, great part of their baggage, with several tents and marquees, besides the three tenders, with their cannon, small arms, &c. also the anchors and cables of the Dunmore, Otter, and many others, to the amount, it is supposed, of twelve or fifteen hundred pounds. On their leaving the island, they burnt some valuable

> vessels, which had got aground. Mr. John Grymes's effects on the island have fallen into our hands, consisting of thirty-five Negroes, horses, cattle and furniture.
>
> Major Byrd, on the approach of our canoes to the island, was huddled into a cart, in a very sick and low condition, it is said, and carried down to Cherry-point, where he embarked. The second shot the Dunmore received cut her boatswain in two, and wounded two or three others; and she had scarcely recovered from the shock when a nine pounder from the lower battery entered her quarter, and beat in a large timber, from the splinters of which Lord Dunmore got wounded in the legs, and had all his valuable china smashed about his ears. It is said his Lordship was exceedingly alarmed, and roared out "Good God that ever I should come to this!" We had our information from one of his people that came ashore after the engagement, who was taken by our scouts; he likewise said, that many were killed in the fleet, which had sustained some thousand pounds worth of damage. The Fowey and Roebuck were the lowermost ships, besides which there were one hundred and odd large sail of vessels, who took their departure on Thursday afternoon, and are supposed to have gone into [the] Potowmack.
>
> In this affair we lost not a man but poor Capt. Arundel, who was killed by the bursting of a mortar of his own invention, although the Gen. and all the officers were against his firing it. His zeal for the service cost him his life.

Thomas Jefferson sketched a map of Gwynn's Island, perhaps many months following the engagement with Lord Dunmore. There is no record of Jefferson having ever visited Kingston Parish during the war years, so the map was probably drawn with the assistance of General Lewis or someone on his staff. During 1776, Jefferson was a delegate from Virginia to the Continental Congress and would not become governor of Virginia until 1777.

Jefferson wrote several notes on the sketch. Beginning in the lower left and then just above: "Gallies may pass into Milford haven quite up to the Enemy's breastworks safe from the fire of the ships, the point of land being pretty high & no large vessel can come into the mouth of the Narrows so as to look down Milford haven." "These two breast works of ours about 500 yrds from the enemy's works." "Narrows about 200 yrds over, 60 yd channel 7 feet at high tide." "This point is ½ mile long, 200 yrds wide and on the end of it is the Enemy's breastworks."

In the lower right corner of the map, the "Creek" is Stutts Creek, with Billups Creek beginning inside and near the mouth of Stutts. The notation reads: "This creek is navigable for boats 3 or 4 miles up and several vessels building on it that may with sail be made into gallies."

Thomas Jefferson was clearly interested in galleys and how they might be deployed. The spring and summer of 1776 was a period of intense planning and construction of galleys, and Jefferson's observations were the first ones recorded involving an ongoing land and naval engagement with the British. No records, however, indicate that any Virginia-built galleys were involved in repelling the British from Gwynn's Island as there were probably none completed and ready for service in early July 1776.

Although no newly constructed galleys were involved in the Gwynn's Island bombardment, a large number of small craft in Milford Haven, from Billups Creek, Stutts Creek, Queens Creek, and others, were used to ferry the militia to the island and to remove abandoned war material left by the British. Local men from Kingston Parish and other areas of Gloucester County were involved, especially in the procurement and handling of small vessels in Milford Haven.

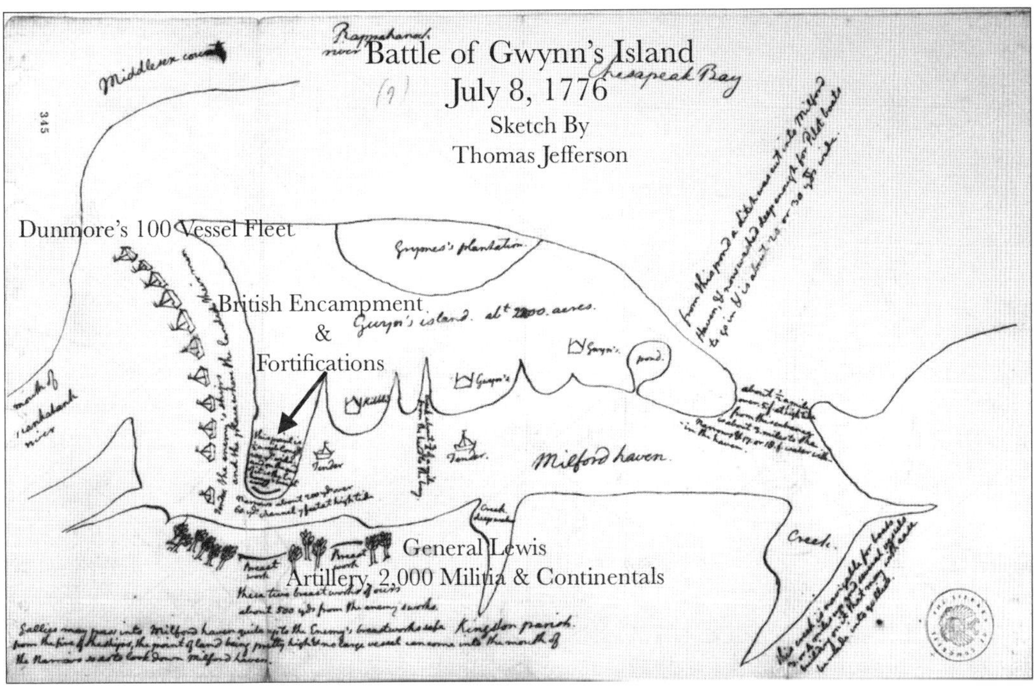


*Figure* 21 Thomas Jefferson sketched the positions of British and colonial forces as they were deployed for the attack on the morning of July 8, 1776, that resulted in victory by the Virginia militia and Continental army units. The superimposed text and arrows show the location of the British fleet, the British encampment, and the location of the colonial forces under the command of General Lewis. Jefferson, who was not present at the time, likely made the map sometime after the battle in a meeting with General Lewis. Courtesy of the Library of Congress, Washington, DC.

Given the massive military presence on Gwynn's Island during the spring and early summer of 1776, it is surprising that anything survived; however, an advertisement in Purdie's *Virginia Gazette*, August 16, 1776, says otherwise:

> *So be LET for one year, on* Wednesday *the 4th of* September, AN exceeding good plantation on *Gwyn's* island, containing 500 acres, whereon is a good dwelling-house, with all other necessary houses, the land rich, and a sufficiency cleared, and under good fence, for 10 or 12 hands. It is remarkable for producing good wheat, clear from the fly, there is a good peach and apple orchard, and the place abounds with fine oysters and fish. At the same time, upon the premises, will be sold the crop of corn as it stands in the field, a few cattle, and some household goods, for ready money. HUMPHREY GWYN.

After Dunmore and his fleet withdrew from Virginia and the Chesapeake Bay, the British navy, for the remaining months of 1776, also largely moved from the bay to other stations, which resulted in a resumption of much needed trade, especially foreign and with the West Indies, for war materials and household goods. An amazing assortment of consumer goods were advertised in Dixon and Hunter's *Virginia Gazette*, on August 24, 1776. They offer an indication of the sophistication of the market. Given wartime conditions, they probably commanded a premium price:

> *For* SALE, OSNABRUGS, Ticklingburgs, Checks, Sheeting, Muslin, Calibanco, Crowningburg, Women's Worsted Hose, do.* black furred Hats, Velvet Hoods, Buckram, Silk and Worsted Ferreting, Binding, Buttons, coloured Thread, Silk Twist, Jacket Patterns, Worsted Crewel, common Necklaces and Bugles, black Gimp, Fans, Hair Sifters, men's coarse and fine Hats, *Scotch* Snuff, best scented Rappee do. chewing Tobacco, Mantelets, Silk Capuchines, Knee Garters, Buckram, Razor Strops, Brushes and Wires for Muskets, Thread Laces, Shoe Tread, Observations on Civil Liberty, *British* Tyranny, or *American* Liberty triumphant, *Watts's* Hymns and Psalms, Psalters, Histories, Pocket-Books, Cutteaus, Fifes, common Sleeve Buttons, Shoe Buckles, Brass Chair Nails, Tobacco and Snuff Boxes, Desk and Cupboard Locks, Cross Garnet and Dove-Tail Hinges, Bridle Bits, Stirrup Irons, Centre and Wimble Bit, Cork Screws, Snuffers, Awl Blades, Shoe Nippers, Steel Pencil Cases, Spectacles, Fishing Tackle, Jews Harps, Slate Pencils, Tailors and Women's Thimbles, *Whitchapel* Needles, Tenon Saws, Hand Saws, Saw Rests, Tongs and Shovels, Augars and Gouges, Bricklayers Trowels, Tea Kettles, Pewter Dishes, Tin Dripping-Pans, Cullenders, Egg Slices, Stone Bottles, Water Pitchers, Queen's China Dishes, Tea Pots and Sugar Dishes, Glass

* Here and following, "do" stands for "ditto."

Bowls and Tumblers, Wine Glasses, Punch Ladles, Rings and Casters, Iron Spice Mortars, Narrow Hoes, Indigo, Pimenta, Coffee, Sole Leather, Harness do. Calf Skins, Men's strong Shoes, a few Medicines, and some other Trifles, too tedious to mention. MATTHEW ANDERSON. GLOUCESTER, *August* 15, 1776.

Construction on the *Henry* was underway in Gloucester during the spring and early summer of 1776; Mathias Gayle testified on February 7, 1839, in conjunction with a pension application, that the *Henry* was launched on June 1, 1776. Rigging and a variety of time-consuming finishing work would have been required before she was ready for service. There must have been cause for great concern for the safety of the *Henry* and East River ship construction when it became clear that Lord Dunmore was moving his headquarters with hundreds of fugitive slaves and royalists to Gwynn's Island.

By mid to late August, the *Henry* had been launched, rigged, armed, and provisioned, and she had been commissioned and had a crew on board because on September 7, 1776, she was ordered to search for British cannon that had sunk near Gwynn's Island. The record does not indicate whether the *Henry* was successful in retrieving the cannon lost by the British. On September 6, 1776, Capt. Robert Tompkins of the *Henry* was issued £783.3s.7d for "Pay of his Company on Board the said Galley." On September 7 the keeper of the public magazine was ordered to deliver to Capt. Tompkins for use of the *Henry* "four hundred Pounds of Gunpowder six Quire of Cartridge Paper One hundred Gun flints and a Worm.*"[11] A few days later, on September 11, several ships, including the *Henry*, were ordered to Yorktown to await orders that would involve moving troops to New York. While there is no record of the *Henry*'s involvement, it is thought that most, if not all, of the Virginia galleys participated in ferrying troops and supplies from the southern Chesapeake Bay to the Elk River in Maryland to join George Washington's army.

Additional stores and equipment were ordered on October 12, 1776, from the keeper of the public store: "twenty five pounds of Dry white Lead one two hour Glass, one large speaking Trumpet, one small Ditto, fifty Shotts, fifty Worsted Caps seventy five pair of Course Stockings, fifty pair of Shoes, thirteen Pieces of Checks, One hundred and seventy five Yards of Oznabrigs, one pound of Lampblack, Ten Barrells of Bread thirty pr of Breeches fifty Jacketts and one Spie Glass for the use of the Henry Galley."[12] The list illustrates the variety of articles needed for the care of the crew and the procurement challenge of colonial storekeepers. Most of the items listed were for clothing and cloth for making garments. "Checks" was a cloth made of linen, and "Oznabrigs" was a coarse cloth used for making sacks, work clothes, and clothing for slaves. Caps made of worsted wool resisted wind and

* A "worm" was a large iron screw affixed at the end of a pole used to extract unexploded charges from the mouth of a cannon.

rain better than common wool. White lead and lampblack were used with linseed oil to make paint. The hourglasses, speaking trumpets (megaphones), and spyglass were essential items for navigation and communicating with a nearby vessel by voice.

On December 13, 1776, the Virginia Navy Board "Ordered that a Warrant Issue to Docr Corbin Griffin. . . . Also for One Pound for Medicine & attendance to the Men belonging to the *Henry* Galley" and "Ordered that a Warrant Issue to Docr. Corbin Griffin for Twenty five pounds seven shilling and three pence for Medicine and Attendance on the Sick Seaman & Marines in the Hospital at York Town." Also on the same date, "Capt Tompkins of the *Henry* Galley Received Orders to Proceed with his Vessel to the head of Elk and take on Board seven hundred Stand of Arms and any other things that the Congress may have lodged at that place in the care of Mr Hollingsworth for the use of this State."[13]

The year 1776 ended with Virginia having successfully constructed a fleet of galleys that were armed, provisioned, and crewed to hinder British foraging parties from nearby enemy ships. It was a remarkable achievement given the scarcity of war materials and the difficulty in finding financial resources to support the navy. It was to be an unusually cold winter, and the suffering of many, including Washington's army at Valley Forge, has been long remembered.

# CHAPTER 8

# Naval Activities *on the* Chesapeake Bay *in* 1777

The last months of 1776 were relatively free from British naval activity, and efforts began in early January 1777 to reestablish normal shipping procedures. Purdie's *Virginia Gazette*, January 17, 1777, provides a glimpse into efforts by the state of Virginia to establish port procedures for entering and departing ships similar to that which had previously existed under British colonial rule. These accounts were preceded by the tragic news of the drowning of William Stevens, a marine on board the *Henry*.

> RICHMOND county, *Jan.* 10, 177[7]. THOSE marines who have not received their pay up to the 8th instant are desired to apply to me for the same. I have in my possession a sum of money due the estate of mr. *William Stevens*, a marine who was drowned last fall from on board the *Henry* galley. Any person who is heir to said deceased may have it by applying to JOHN C. COCKE.
>
> PORT NORFOLK, ELIZABETH RIVER DISTRICT. NOTICE is hereby given to all masters and owners of vessels, and others whom it may concern, that the naval office for this district is now open in the town of *Portsmouth*, where constant attendance will be given by mr. *William Armistead Bailey*, whom I have appointed my deputy, and is qualified to act as deputy in the said office according to law. JOHN KING, naval officer.
>
> PORT HAMPTON, LOWER DISTRICT of *James* RIVER. LET all masters and owners of vessels, and others, whom it may concern, know, that the naval office of this port is open, and the officer expects all the inward bound to enter according to the laws of the commonwealth of *Virginia*, where they may have a permit granted to proceed and dispose of their cargoes in any districts, ports, or places in the said commonwealth; and that the outward bound, when they come to

> clear out, will take care that they have proper certificates for their cargo, with a ballast master's certificate signed and sealed according to law. JACOB WRAY, naval officer.
>
> Pork, beef, flour, tar, turpentine, pitch, ballast, &c. certificates, the master, mate, and boatswain, must be at the office to clear.

The war came very close to home in early 1777, as described in Dixon and Hunter's *Virginia Gazette* for January 24, 1777:

> WE hear the two men of war which came within our capes on Monday last are still hovering about the mouth of York river and New Point Comfort, have taken two salt vessels, and a ship laden with tobacco, from Maryland. Some of the hungry dogs have been on shore at the point, but with what design we cannot tell: No doubt we shall soon hear of bloody battles with the horned tribe, sieges against hog-pens, and violent assaults upon hen-roosts, by those modern heroes of Britain, who, on the dreadful appearance of a rifleman, like amphibious animals, fly to the watery element for security.

The report, although humorous in the second half, is a highly informative account of the menace the people of Kingston Parish endured during the war. The two ships mentioned in the article were HMS *Preston*, fifty guns, the flagship, and HMS *Brune*, twenty guns, both under the command of Commodore William Hotham, who was also responsible for other ships in the region. British ships, such as these two, stationed in the vicinity of the mouth of the York River and Mobjack Bay, made shipping a high-risk endeavor, and galleys of the Virginia State Navy were powerless to confront them directly. Their effectiveness was limited to making it difficult for the British to come ashore in their longboats, tenders, and other small craft to plunder livestock, produce, firewood, and water. British ships were constantly active in the Chesapeake, at times in large numbers, and their crews would make frequent attempts to come ashore to confiscate livestock and crops to supplement their ships' stores. In their pension applications after the war, men who served in the local militia frequently mentioned instances of British attempts to land in the vicinity of New Point Comfort and northward towards Pepper Creek.* The Virginia navy crews were from the surrounding counties, and thus they were in their home waters with strong motivation to protect their families and property from looting by British seamen.

On January 29, 1777, Christopher Tompkins, son of Capt. Robert Tompkins, was recommended to be appointed second lieutenant and commanding officer of the *Henry*. He was

* See appendix 8 for the Revolutionary War Pension Roll, Mathews County, 1840.

issued £180 to be used to recruit seamen for the navy. Capt. John Calvert was ordered to take command of the galleys in the York River and "Proceed immediately to Annoy and Distress the Enemy, which are now lying in the Bay."[1] The *Henry* was probably in the squadron under the command of Captain Calvert.

Another example of war being very close to home is found in a report by the Virginia Council dated February 3, 1777: "Sloop from Martinico bound to Baltimore laden with Powder and Soldiers Cloaths had been chased up East River by some British Ships of War."[2]

The journal of the Virginia Navy Board continued issuing orders during 1777 for materials, crew appointments, and operational assignments. On April 2, for example, it was "Ordered that Mr Thomas Archer deliver Captain [Robert] Tompkins six Barrels of Pork and six Barrels of Flour; Also that Mr William Holt deliver him six Barrels of Pork, six Barrels of Bread, and one hundred Gallons of spirits for the use of the *Henry* Galley."[3]

An entry on April 3, 1777, specifically refers to the *Henry* being stationed in home waters: "Ordered that Captain Robert Tompkins proceed with the *Henry* Galley to Mobjack Bay, there to cruize for the protection of the trade and Inhabitants, and that he use his utmost to comply with this order and prevent any depredations from the Enemy's Ships or Vessels of War."[4]

The following list is the most precise description of the Virginia State Navy in the early spring of 1777. It includes the armament and crew size for each vessel. The *Henry* was the most heavily armed vessel at the time and with a crew of sixty men was equaled only by the brig *Raleigh*.

"A List of the Navy of the Commonwealth of Virginia fit for Duty"
[Williamsburg] April 24, 1777

| | | | |
|---|---|---|---|
| Brig | *Raleigh* 10 four pounders 60 Men (under Cruising Orders) | | |
| Brig | *Northhampton* 10 three & four four pounders | | 50 Men |
| | | | |
| Galley | *Henry*, two eighteen & Six six pounders | | 60 Men |
| Do | *Hero*, two twelve pounders | | 50 Do |
| Do | *Revenge* two eighteen | Do | 50 Do |
| Do | *Manley* two twelve | Do | 40 Do |
| Do | *Protector* one eighteen | Do | 45 Do |
| Do | *Safeguard* one Do | Do | 45 Do |
| Do | *Page* one twelve | Do | 35 Do |
| Do | *Lewis* one Do | Do | 35 Do |
| Sloop | *Scorpion*—eight three | Do | 20 Do[5] |

Robert Hall, as master mate, and brother Spencer were serving on one of the most important ships in the Virginia State Navy and must have witnessed most of the significant missions during 1776 through 1778. However, it appears that not everyone appreciated that distinction. The June 6, 1777, edition of Purdie's *Virginia Gazette* mentions a few deserters:

> DESERTED from the *Henry* galley, *Robert Bernard*, born in *Gloucester* county, who is a tall fellow, very talkative, and speaks much in the blackguard strain. *John Cluverius*, about 5 feet 11 inches high, has an old and homely look, and is as much of a blackguard as the other. They are but indifferent landsmen. Whoever delivers the above deserters to me shall have 10 *DOLLARS* reward for each. ROBERT TOMPKINS, capt. of the *Henry* galley.

The British had an effective blockade of the Chesapeake Bay during 1777 with five warships on the coast, within the capes, and in the lower bay. In late December 1776, Vice Adm. Richard Lord Howe ordered Commodore William Hotham to take command of British activities in the Chesapeake.[6] Hotham sailed on his flagship, HMS *Preston*, with HMS *Brune* to the Chesapeake, arriving in early January 1777, joining HMS *Thames*, HMS *Emerald*,* and HMS *Phoenix*. This five-warship squadron was powerful, far surpassing anything in Virginia or in the entire Continental navy. Storeships, tenders, and ship's boats would have supported the fleet. Armed tenders and the larger classes of ship's boats were used to capture unprotected merchant vessels and for raiding coastal farms for provisions.

The logbook of Capt. Tyringham Howe, of HMS *Thames*, provides one of the few British eyewitness reports of activity of the Virginia State Navy, including everyday life on board, activity on the bay, the weather and tides, and so forth. While the logbook does not identify the specific combatants, it appears that all of Virginia's galleys were involved since it cites eight galleys, two being on the Eastern Shore with six accompanying the frigate *Virginia* sailing out of the York River. The account identifies two galleys having three masts each, and as the *Henry* was the most heavily armed, it is reasonable to assume that she was one of the three-masted vessels. With this rig she would have been considered a "ship," while brigs, schooners, and six of the galleys had two masts.

> Journal of H.M.S. *Thames*, Captain Tyringham Howe

* The *Thames*, a thirty-two-gun frigate of the Richmond class, known for speed and excellent sea-keeping ability, was commissioned in April 1758 at Buckler's Hard, England, and was broken up in September 1803. The *Emerald* was a thirty-two-gun Niger-class frigate launched on June 8, 1762, at Hull, England. She, too, was known to be an excellent sailor. She was broken up at the Deptford, England, shipyard in 1793. Appendix 6 lists all of the ships of the Royal Navy with service in the Chesapeake Bay during the American Revolution.

June 1777, Monday 30th

At Single Anchor in Chesapeake Bay

In General Little Winds and Hazey Weather. 2 PM Heard the Report of guns fired off the Capes. at 4 heard more Guns fired. at 6 Wore away to ½ Cable. 10 PM Saw a Strange Ship standing down New York River. at 12 Saw one more Square Rigged Vessel accompanied by 2 Sloops. Saw the [HMS] *Emerald* at an Anchor Off Cape Henry.

[The moon phase on June 30, 1777, was waning crescent, equivalent to 22 percent of the light of a full moon.]

July
Tuesday 1

Light Breezes and Cloudy Wear. Saw One Ship, a Brig and two Sloops at Anchor in the Mouth of York River. 9 AM Saw One Ship Attended by 2 Square Rigged Vessels and Seven Galleys and other Small Sails Standing down the York Channell Over the Spitt. Set the Single Reef Topsails and Topgallt Sails and Wore away to the Mooring Service in Order to Slip. Employ'd preparing the Ship for Action. at ½ past saw the Frigate [*Virginia*] Anchor on the Egg Island Flatts. All Her fleet did consist of Two Brigs, 6 Galleys, two with three Masts each, with Sloops and Schooners amounting to 17 Sail in all. Do saw One Brigg in the Mouth of Mopsack [Mobjack] Bay, And 2 more Galleys on the Etern Shore by Cherry Stone Point Endeavouring to Join the above Fleet, three other Sail in Sight coming down Chesapeak Bay. 11 Hoisted a Red and White Flagg at the Main Topmast Head and fired at different times 3 Guns as a Signal to the *Emerald*, Lowered the Topgallt Sails and hauled down the Staysails.

Modt Breezes and fair Weather. At Single Anchor in Chesapeake Bay. ½ past Noon saw the *Emerald* hoist a Flag on Her Main Topgallt Mast Head which We Conjectured was to call in all Cruizers. ½ past Noon We hoisted a St George's Ensign at the Fore Topgallt Mast Head which She Answer'd by hauling down Her Signal. the before-mentioned Fleet at Anchor on Egg Island Flatts. at 1 Saw Arm'd Sloops go under the Rebel Frigates Stern and then bore up for Old Point Comfort.[7]

These are the official accounts of the events as recorded by the officers of the watch. On the two dates of these entries, HMS *Thames* was stationed near the entrance to the Chesapeake

Bay. She was anchored between Cape Charles to the north and Cape Henry to the south, north-northeast from the entrance to the Lynnhaven River. She was stationed to observe rebel activity and to blockade the bay in the vicinity of the York River, the lower bay, and the approaches to the Norfolk harbor.

In late summer 1776 and early 1777, the Virginia Navy Board continued to provision the state's naval forces and expand the fleet. The board had authorized the construction of four more galleys. These new vessels were larger than the earlier ones. Previously, galleys were seventy-one feet in length on the keel and had a beam of twenty feet. Average crew size was fifty men.[8] Here are the dimensions of the new ships as transmitted probably during the summer of 1776 to the shipyard on the Mattaponi River under the supervision of George Brett. He was paid six pounds per ton for carpentry work, which included building the hull and decking.

> Eighty one feet Keel Twenty one feet Beam seven and a half feet Hold, Square Stern'd with a Quarter Deck thirty feet long three feet Waist with Quick Work as high as the Sills of the Ports, Ten Gunn Ports. The Plank (except for the Decks) and all the Timbers to be of good sound white Oak of Proper sizes and the Plank for the Decks to be of good two Inches thick Yellow Pine, the whole to be finished in a Workman like manner with as many Ports as can conveniently be Rowed in also Oars, Masts, Yards and all necessary spars fitted to a Cleet and to be delivered by the first day of April next.[9]

The new and larger galleys were named the *Gloucester*, *Tartar*, *Tempest*, and *Dragon*. They were rigged as ships having three masts, were able to carry heavier cannon, had larger crews, and were capable of going on extended cruises at sea. The ratio of keel length to beam was high, 4:1, a ratio associated with vessels having above-average speed, for a given length, all things otherwise the same. The depth of the hold was modest in keeping with vessels with relatively shallow draft, thus enhancing the ability to move into shallow water beyond the capability of British warships.

Work progressed well, for on April 8, 1777, the Virginia Navy Board recorded in its journal:

> Ordered that Captain Thomas Lilly repair to Pepper Creek where the *Gloucester* Galley is now building, and give such directions respecting the finishing the said Galley, with dispatch, as he may judge necessary.[10]

This is the only reference found that gives a specific location for the construction of a galley in Kingston Parish. It appears that her hull and most carpentry work was completed at this time because the order for rigging was issued on April 30, 1777, from the Virginia Navy Board to Capt. Charles Thomas:

| | | |
|---|---|---|
| For Main and fore Shrouds | 200 Fathoms of 5 Inch Rope | |
| Do for fore and Jibb Stays | 30 do | 6 do |
| Bowsprit Shrouds | 20 do | 5 do |
| Mizzen Shrouds | 20 do | 5 do |
| Main & foretopmast Shrouds | 100 do | 3¾ do |
| Mizzen Topmast Shrouds | 35 do | 3¼ do |

3 Cables one of 9½ Inch and 2 of 10 Inches 100 Fathoms long each—also 4½ Inch Houser—with some Coils of 2½ Inch and 3 Inch Rope[11]

This is the only record found that has details concerning the rigging of any of the galleys, which is greatly useful in envisioning the appearance of the *Gloucester* and her sister ships. A sailing vessel with a keel length of eighty-one feet would have had a main deck length of between ninety and ninety-five feet. She had three masts with at least two sails per mast and a bowsprit sufficient for more than one jib. The dimensions of some of the cordage are substantial, with one hundred fathoms being equivalent to six hundred feet and the inches designating circumference. The one hundred–fathom, 10-inch cable would have had a diameter of 3³⁄₁₆ inches and would have weighed approximately 1,920 pounds. The two hundred fathoms of 5-inch cable would have weighed approximately 960 pounds. Galleys must have been equipped with a windlass for handling cables of these sizes.

The journal of HMS *Thames* continues with this entry:

Journal of H.M.S. *Thames*, Captain Tyringham Howe
July 1777
Wednesdy 2

At Single Anchor in Chesapeak Bay
Fresh Breezes and Clear Weather [P.M.] Weighed and came to Sail Standing up Chesapeak Bay all sail set. at 4 Came too between the Horse Shoe and Middle Ground in 6 fms with Small Br. Veered to ⅓ Cable Cape Charles East Distant 6 Leagues, Cape Henry SEbS 5 Leagues. One Galley with 3 Masts and a Schooner in Sight New York River. at 7 Hove in Sight of the Mouth of the River a Frigate [*Virginia*], Two Galleys and a Brigg. People Employed Occasionally. . . .

Saturday 5

Light Breezes and Clear Weather. 3 PM Came out of York River a large Galley with 3 Masts and Anchored near Cherry Stone Point.[12]

A July 2 memo of Captain Howe's reads:

Upon Egg Island Flats was the Frigate [*Virginia*] attended by two Brigs, Six Galleys, two of which had three Masts, the rest amounting to 19 Sail, in all, were Topsail Schooners and Sloops, Two more Galleys were seen upon the Eastern Shore, off Cherry Stone Point, endeavouring to join the above Fleet, besides One Brig in Mocksack [Mobjack] Bay, and coming down the Bay three Vessels more, at a great distance.[13]

The *Thames* report of July 2 was of the considerable activity of the Virginia State Navy and its efforts to escort the recently launched frigate *Virginia* out of the Chesapeake Bay and into the Atlantic where it could be more effectively deployed against British troop transports, storeships, and small enemy warships. These efforts and others similar would never prove successful. The *Virginia*, launched at the yard of George Wells on the Patapsco River in August 1776, was not ready for sea until spring 1777 and did not make her first voyage until June when she sailed to the York River. Encountering superior enemy force, as reported above, she sailed back to the northern Chesapeake and did not sail again that year. In January 1778 the *Virginia* again sailed down the bay but was spotted by HMS *Emerald*, a frigate of thirty-six guns, and was chased back to Baltimore in twenty-one hours. In an April 3 letter, a "Gentleman on board the *Emerald*" wrote that the *Virginia* "sails extremely well." The writer further reported: "On the 30th of March she took the opportunity of a strong northerly wind, and made another attempt to get to sea; but in the night, in order to avoid us as we lay at anchor within and between the Capes, she got entangled with a shoal or bank of land, stuck upon it, and was obliged to anchor, when we took her without opposition."[14]

A July 10, 1777, letter from Capt. Benjamin Caldwell to Lord Howe is one of the few observations disclosing how the British regarded the Virginia State Navy:

[HMS] *Emerald* off the Capes of Virginia 10th July 1777

My Lord. . . .

The *Thames* is Stationed off York Spit at present, & the 1st instant [July 1st] She made the Signal for seeing Ships of Superior force, I got under Sail with the *Raleigh*, but as the Wind was down, and Tide of Ebb; I could only Anchor in a better situation for Her to join me; in the Evening she got under Sail, and came down about half the distance she was from me, and next Morning join'd Company. Captain Howe delivered me a paper with a List of the Armed Vessels, and their situations, which paper I inclose to your Lordship, and Ordered him back to his Station: the *Senegal* was stationed at Cape Charles, (and distroyed Six Vessels, which Captain Molloy will give Your Lordship an Account of,) with the *Raleigh* occasionally, who is now to continue there, as long as Her Water will last; of which She has not much on board. This Ship is at the Tail

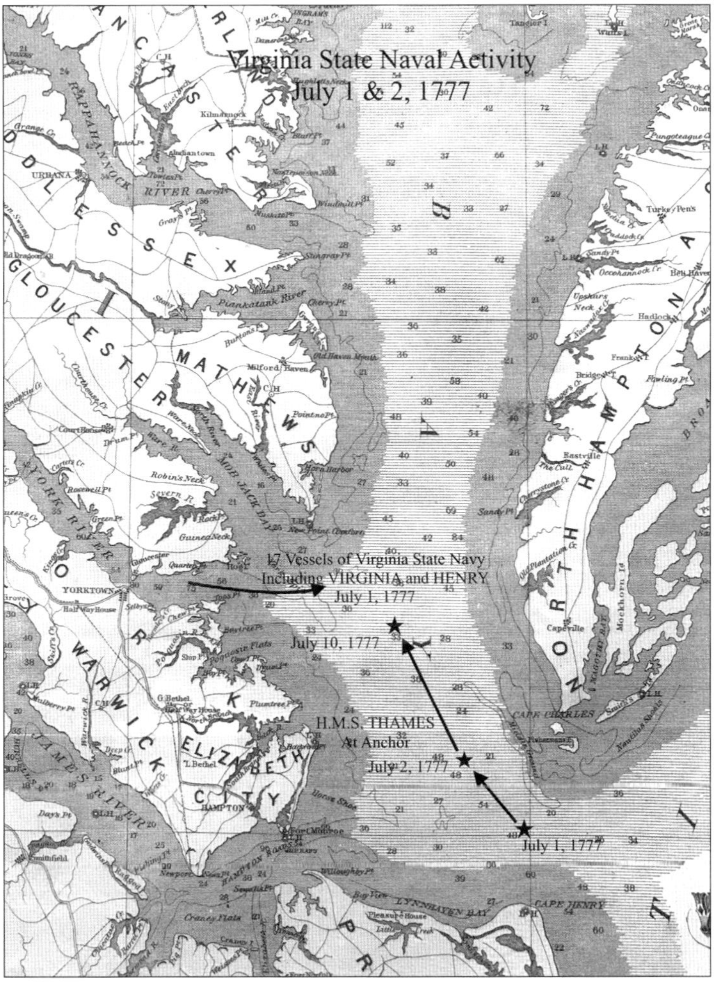


*Figure* 22 The locations of HMS *Thames*, a British frigate, and its movements during July 1–10, 1777 (superimposed on a chart of the lower bay). The logbook of HMS *Thames* provides eyewitness accounts by the officers of the deck of activities of the Virginia State Navy on July 1, 1777. From the author's collection.

> of the Horse Shoe, and the 17th, 19th & 20th in June, three Sloops and One Schooner Boat, came down with Ninety Eight of the people, that were to have gone in the *Albion*, which I gave Passes to, to go to New York.
>
> The 24th we burnt a Sloop with Salt, and the 30th the *Raleigh* with My Boats, drove on Shore, and burnt a French Brig, a little way to the Southward of Cape Henry, Loaded with Sails Cordage, One Hundred Cask of Rum & Bale Goods.[15]

The reference to "seeing Ships of Superior force" acknowledges the remarkable achievement by Virginia in building and purchasing ships, recruiting crews, and procuring gunpowder and other provisions necessary to equip ships for engagement with the enemy. Captain Caldwell's assessment of the situation on July 10 suggests that the Virginia forces might have prevailed against the *Thames* if they had chosen to engage in battle.

The other references in the letter give a perspective on the range of British activities in the Chesapeake, other warships deployed, everyday challenges of providing water and provisions, moving crews from one vessel to another, permission to go ashore in New York, and the great damage inflicted on merchant vessels.

The following order by the Virginia Navy Board on July 11, 1777, indicates that the *Tartar* was well along towards completion, construction having been started in late 1776 or early 1777. It suggests the difficulty in procuring the necessary materials for even the most basic items. Especially interesting is the guidance given to Captain Bright to have his vessel "smok'd" and cleaned to prevent sickness, perhaps suggesting that the *Northhampton* had health-related problems in the past. Sulfur, known as "brimstone," was frequently used to disinfect by burning it in an enclosed area.

> Virginia Navy Board to Captain Francis Bright,
> Virginia Navy Brig *Northhampton*
>
> Sir, The Ballast you are in want of is on Board Capt Taylors Vessel [*Tartar*] and cannot be spared, you must therefore endevour to supply the Place with Shingle Ballast or any thing that will answer the purpose. There is no White lime to be had or you should be furnished with it. We expect and doubt not but you will make all the dispatch in your Power in getting your Vessel cleaned and coming down as soon as Possible.
>
> N.B. You are desired to have your Vessel smok'd & thoroughly cleaned in

> Order to prevent Sickness amongst your Men & be particularly careful in keeping her Clean.[16]

Work continued on the *Tartar*, as seen by information on deliveries of a variety of items. The mention of "Topsails" further documents the type of rig she carried and verifies that there were at least two sails per mast. The effort to secure a crew is evident by references of men from other ships being transferred to the *Tartar*. Payment for planking and timbers was also authorized:

> [July 25, 1777, Williamsburg, Virginia]
> Virginia Navy Board to Captain Richard Taylor, Virginia Navy Ship *Tartar*
>
> Sir, You will receive by Capt [Wright] Westcott [blank] 1lb Twine which is all we can send at present. There is a Quantity of Duck lately arrived at So Quay that we expect in Town every day out of which we intend to supply you with Topsails and shall send it up by the first Opportunity. We have not as yet appointed a Lieutenant to your Ship but shall do it as soon as we have a full Board which we expect will be next week. The Man which came to you from the *Hero* Galley you are desired to keep till further Orders. As we have determined to Sell the Sloop *Scorpion* we have given Orders to Capt Westcott to Turn over all the Sailors he has to your Ship and also the Officers Provided they are willing to go on Board and can be put in the same station and hold the same Rank they had when on Board the *Scorpion*. Capt Westcott is also directed to deliver you the Pig Iron and all the materials he hath on Board belonging to his Vessel except the sails and Rigging.[17]

An August 9, 1777, account for timber for the Virginia navy ship *Tartar*, Captain Richard Taylor, shows a list of items for "Plank and Timber." The list includes quantities of white oak, pine, one-inch pine plank, two-inch pine plank, and so forth. Total value was £37.10s.10d.[18]

In June and July 1777, General Howe began preparations for attacking and capturing Philadelphia and on July 23 sailed from Sandy Hook, New Jersey, with a force of 14,000 troops in transports and warships manned by 5,500 seamen. The fleet of 267 vessels under the command of his brother Vice Adm. Richard Lord Howe consisted of 25 warships and 242 troop and supply vessels. Of the warships, 5 were ships of the line, 64 guns each, and 9 were frigates. The remainder were sloops of war and a fireship. The ships of the line included HMS *Eagle*, HMS *Nonsuch*, HMS *Raisonable*, HMS *Augusta*, and HMS *Somerset*. Among the 9 frigates were HMS *Apollo*, HMS *Emerald*, HMS *Richmond*, and HMS *Solebay*. This was a fleet of enormous power, one that was of great concern to the people of Virginia.[19]

Rather than approaching Philadelphia by way of the Delaware Bay, General Howe decided to approach the city by sailing up the Chesapeake Bay to the Elk River. The fleet reached the Chesapeake on August 14, after an unusually long passage from New York due to prevailing southerly and southwesterly winds, and anchored in the bay on August 15. With excellent navigation, the very large fleet sailed up the bay without interruption.[20] The only loss suffered was the damage inflicted on three transports by lightning.

HMS *Raisonable*, a large man-of-war caring sixty-four guns and a crew of five hundred, remained at York Spit to keep galleys and other Virginia naval vessels blockaded in the York River. The *Henry*, together with the *Hero* and the *Norfolk Revenge*, was ordered to keep watch on its movements.

John Page wrote to Thomas Johnson, governor of Maryland, on August 15 of the appearance of the British fleet in the Chesapeake:

> Sir, We have this Moment received Information that the Fleet which was seen last Tuesday off Accomack County, an Account of which we received last Night by Express, was discovered by Capt Bright of the *Northampton* armed Brig of this State, at 9 o'Clock last Night standing into our Capes. He writes, that he saw above 100 Sail from his Mast-head. We think it may be of great Consequence to your State to have as early Intelligence as possible of this Movement of the Enemy, & therefore have ordered an Express to convey this to your Excellency with all possible Expedition.[21]

HMS *Somerset*, a sixty-four-gun warship with a crew of 520 men, anchored on the night of August 15, 1777, five miles east-northeast of Cape Henry, which is in the Atlantic Ocean just east of the entrance to the Chesapeake Bay and nearly centered between the two capes. At 6 a.m. on August 16, she "came to sail" and at 7 p.m. anchored "all the convoy"[22] in seven fathoms (forty-two feet) of water with New Point Comfort three miles west by north, which would have placed the fleet at anchor between New Point Comfort and Old Plantation Creek on the Eastern Shore. The sight of the British fleet at anchor, until that time the largest fleet ever assembled in the Chesapeake Bay, would have been most impressive and of great concern. News of the arrival of the fleet spread rapidly in the lower Chesapeake, and the menace of war could hardly have been closer. Men of the parish serving on the galleys must have wondered what their missions would be in the days ahead and what might happen to their families on shore.

Journal entries of HMS *Apollo*, a thirty-two-gun frigate, and HM Sloop *Dispatch*, eight guns, offer reports on the movement of the fleet and the concern over the nearby presence of galleys. Evidence of frequent attempts by runaway slaves to seek freedom is seen in the

August 18 report by the *Apollo*, Capt. Philemon Pownoll. The risks of the hardship of life in the military are illustrated by the death of British marine James Clegg, who died at 8:30 a.m. and was committed to the deep at 5 p.m.

> At Sing: Anchor off Rappahannock River
> at 5 AM the Sigl to weigh, weighed as did the fleet, our Sigl to come under the Adml Stern.
> Lt Airs, half past Noon the Adml Bore away and made the Sigl to get into his

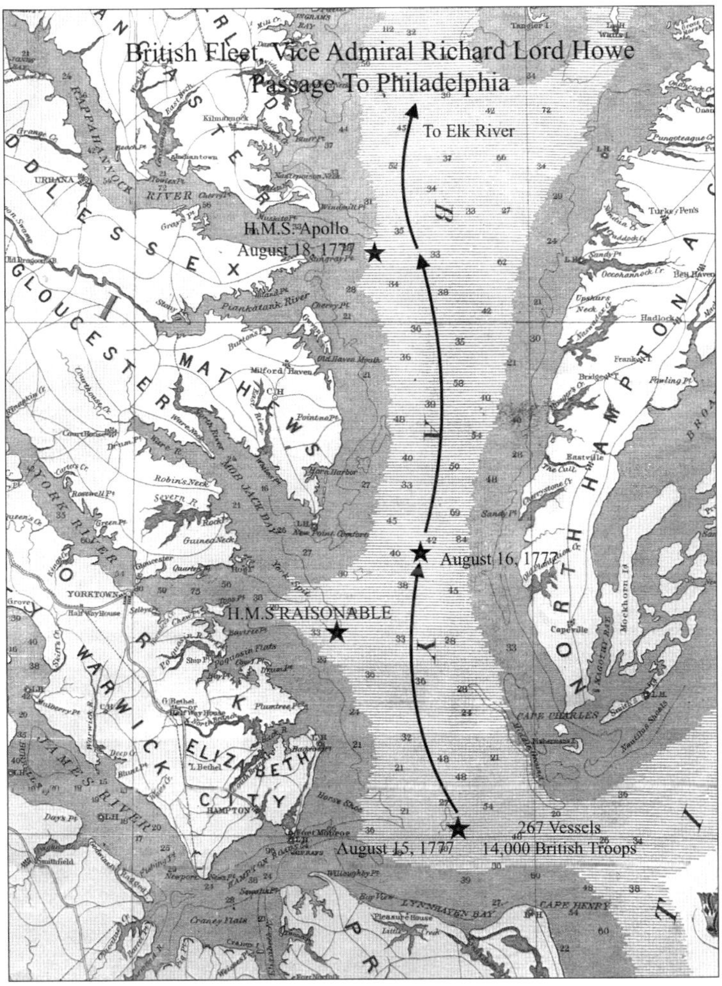


*Figure* 23 The movement of the British fleet, numbering 267 vessels and fourteen thousand British troops, from August 15–18, 1777 (superimposed on a chart of the lower bay). This was the largest British fleet ever to assemble in the Chesapeake Bay during the Revolutionary War: its mission was to capture Philadelphia. From the author's collection.

> Wake, having got into Shoal Water, we anchor'd Pr Sigl, at 2 pm had orders to go [to] Wicomoco River's Mouth to hinder the Boats and Gallies of the Enemy from coming out, anch'd in ¼ less 3 fms, with the *Vigilant*, *Senega*l, and our Gally, row'd Guard off the River Mouth, came on board some Negro Men and Women. . . .
>
> New Point Comfort WbN 5 or 6 Miles
> at 5 A.M. weigh'd pr Signl. ½ past 6 the *Roebuck* md our Signl to come within hail – N.B. Hoisted a White Flagg at our Main Top Mast head as a direction to the Fleet—Saw several Galleys in Shore one of which fired two Shot at us, at 8 Anchor'd with the small Bower in 13 fm. veerd to ⅓ of a Cable. Smith's Point WNW. great Wiccomacoa SW½W. Watts Isld NEbE & Point Lookout NEbN. ½ past 8 departed this Life Jams Clegg Marine. at Noon pass'd by us the Adml & Fleet.
> Fresh breezes & cloudy Wr. at 5 P.M. committed the Body of the above deceas'd to the Deep.[23]

The location of the *Dispatch*, five or six miles and nearly east of New Point Comfort, and the locations of HMS *Apollo*, HMS *Raisonable*, and the many other British ships presented a view to the inhabitants of Kingston Parish of the enormous power of the British navy and surely heightened their concerns over their ultimate fate. The galleys noted "in Shore" most probably included the *Henry* and *Norfolk Revenge*.

Capt. Andrew Snape Hamond, of HMS *Roebuck*, the flagship of the British fleet, wrote a summary of the movements of the fleet from the time after leaving New York in late July until the army units were safely landed in the Elk River. Captain Hamond was responsible for managing the movement of the fleet up the bay. To minimize the navigational difficulties for such a large fleet, he stationed smaller vessels at the significant shallow areas and points of land along the course.

[*Roebuck* off Virginia and in Chesapeake Bay, August 1 to August 31, 1777]

> The Fleet had not sailed 10 leagues before their former ill fortune returned, and the Southerly wind became so fixed that they did not reach the Capes of Virginia untill the 15 Augst and on the next day the whole Anchored off New Point Comfort, Six Leagues up the Bay.
>
> From this time the progress of the Fleet was very rapid; and tho' the Chesapeak Bay is rather an intricate Navigation, and what was never attempted

> before but by very small Merchant Ships, it was effected by the whole Fleet of Men of War as well as Transports in about 5 days, without any accident whatever; all the Shoals & dangers having been marked by small Vessels & boats; for which purpose the *Roebuck* had been sent a head of the Fleet.
>
> [The] 21st was spent in exploring the NEt Branch & the River Elk; and the preference being given to the Latter, Five thousand Men were embarked [the 25th] before day light in the Flat Boats, and proceeded at 4 in the Morning up the River Elk, covered by the *Vigilant*, *Roebuck*, *Apollo*, *Sphynx* & *Swift*, with the remainder of the Army following in Transports. at 10 oclock the first division was landed opposite to Cecil Court House, and before Night the whole disembarkation was finished without the least interuption.[24]

After the fleet moved to the north end of the bay, the Americans were greatly concerned about what the British fleet would do after disembarking army infantry, artillery, and marine units in Maryland. In an August 25 letter to Commodore Walter Brooke, the Virginia Navy Board wrote:

> Sir, You are desired to give Orders to the Captains of the different Vessels in the Naval Service to keep the Strictest Watch on the Enemy as it is more than Probable that they will be attacked by some of their Armed Vessels as soon as they have Landed their Troops. You are desired to Station at Hampton the *Norfolk Revenge*, *Hero* & *Henry* Gallies and grant as few furloughs as possible during this Time of Danger.[25]

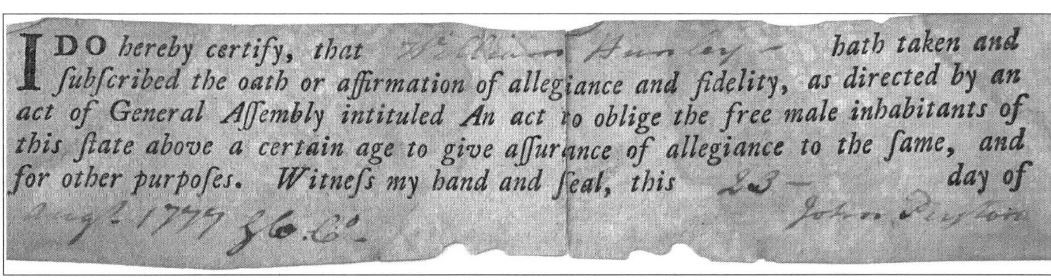

I DO *hereby certify, that* William Hunley *hath taken and ſubſcribed the oath or affirmation of allegiance and fidelity, as directed by an act of General Aſſembly intituled An act to oblige the free male inhabitants of this ſtate above a certain age to give aſſurance of allegiance to the ſame, and for other purpoſes. Witneſs my hand and ſeal, this* 23 *day of* Augt 1777 £6.6 John Preston

*Figure* 24 In 1777 the Virginia General Assembly enacted legislation requiring free males to declare their allegiance to the state and to support the resistance against the increasing hostility by Britain. This became increasingly urgent as the people of Gloucester saw the might of the British navy nearby. William Hunley made the oath on August 23, 1777, in Gloucester County. Most of the men in Gloucester likely made similar pledges as by then many Tories had returned to England or to other British-controlled areas beyond the conflict. Courtesy of the Virginia Historical Society, Billups Papers, Richmond.

The uncertainty of the situation is underscored by new orders to Commodore Brooke just a few days later on September 2. The *Henry* is ordered to Mobjack Bay, its "former Station":

> Sir, You are desired immediately on Receipt hereof to Order one of the Captain Barrons with his Vessel to Gwinns Island in Order to Assist in Transporting of Troops from that place to the Eastern Shore. Capt Barron must be directed to follow such Orders as He may receive from the Commanding officer of the said Troops, respecting their Transportation and keep this matter as secret as possible. You are also to Order Captain [Robert] Tompkins of the *Henry* Galley to his former Station in Mobjack Bay as soon as possible.[26]

In late September the British fleet sailed down the bay without reported intervals of foraging and headed up the east coast for the Delaware Bay. Its mission was to help secure success at Philadelphia, which was occupied by the British army on September 26, 1777.[27]

After the departure of Howe's fleet, the British maintained a blockade of the Chesapeake Bay. On October 3, 1777, the thirty-two-gun frigate *Emerald*; the *Phoenix*, forty-four guns; the *Perseus*, twenty guns; the Sloop *Senegal*, fourteen guns; a topsail schooner; and the tender to the *Roebuck* were all stationed in the lower bay and outside the capes in the Atlantic. This formidable blockade fleet was beyond the capability of the Continental and Virginia State Navy to challenge.

On October 27, 1777, the twenty-eight-gun frigate HMS *Carysfort* reached Hampton Roads and joined the blockade fleet. The thirty-two-gun frigate HMS *Richmond* and the fourteen-gun sloop *Otter* were also in the fleet according to a report dated October 29, 1777.

In the midst of British naval dominance in the lower bay, the *Henry* was on station in Mobjack Bay with Robert Tompkins serving as captain, according to a report dated November 28, 1777. The crew of the *Henry*, including brothers Robert and Spencer Hall, must have become very familiar with the sight of British men-of-war, frigates, and sloops cruising in the vicinity.

The following orders from the Virginia Navy Board, covering the period from October 7 through December 10, offer a detailed look into the vast variety of items needed by ships in the Virginia State Navy and the effort required to manufacture, transport, warehouse, and manage large quantities of wartime materials. In addition to ship

The following account from a September 30 entry in the logbook of the British sloop of war *Haerlem*, twelve guns, sixty-five-man crew, is a wonderful depiction of a storm at sea, thirty-seven leagues (111 nautical miles, 127.7 English miles) southeast of Cape Henry, a position 60 nautical miles east-northeast of Cape Hatteras and in the Gulf Stream. Sea conditions in this region would have been especially severe with strong northeast winds blowing into a northeasterly flow of the Gulf Stream creating unusually high and steep waves.

> Cape Henry No 50°Wt
> Distance 37 Leagues
> In the Night a very heavy Sea from the NE. at ½ Past 6 AM the Sea running very high it broke in upon Deck with Prodigious Violence and laid the Sloop on her beam Ends Stove the Boat to Pieces which with her mast sails and oars and every thing movable upon Decks was washed over board and several of the People much maimed and bruised, the main gratings being Stove by the Boats going away, a quanity of water got down between Decks, to Lighten the Vessel and give the water vent to the pumps, was under the Necessity of h[e] aving over board the Coals and staving several Casks of water in the Hold. at 9 the Vessel righted and got her before the Sea. at Noon being entirely free from water lay'd her too under the Try sail. the Kedge anchor washed from the Bows.
> First Part strong Gales. Middle modt. Latter Clear and Light Breezes. PM Empd Putting the Hold to rights found lost and washd over board by the Sea Shipt in the morning two Harness Cask Containing beef 110 Pieces Pork 170 Pieces Cassks. 6 Butts and 2 Hhds. found a Quantity of Bread damaged and 2 Casks of Pease and 3 firkins of Butter Stove and lost being Crushed to Pieces in the after Hold.[28]

The storm may have been a hurricane but was not recorded as one although it occurred in the hurricane season. The historical record lists a hurricane on August 26, 1777, one that detained George Washington in Elkton, Maryland, and General Howe and his attack on Philadelphia.

supplies, the entries show that the ships' crews were dependent on the navy for clothing and blankets.

> [October 7]
> Ordered that Mr. William Holt deliver to Lieutenant Tompkins five Barrells

> Pork, three Barrells Bread, five Barrells Flour, five Barrells Bread and two Barrells Spirits for the use of the *Henry* Galley.
>
> Ordered that the Keeper of the Public Store two hundred Scupper and five hundred Pump Nails for the use of the *Henry* Galley Capt Tompkins.
>
> [October 16]
> Ordered that Mr. William Holt deliver Lieutenant Joseph Speake twenty Barrels of Bread, six Barrels of Spirits and one Box of Candles for the use of the Galleys at present stationed at Hampton.
>
> [October 20]
> Ordered that Mr. William Holt deliver unto Capt. Taylor the Cordage which hath been lodged with him for use of the *Tartar*, also an Anchor, a Barrell of Brandy and such Pikes, Pole Axes and Iron Crows as he may want for the use of the said Ship.
>
> Ordered that the keeper of the Public Store deliver to Capt. Taylor thirty pounds Sail Twine and eighteen sail Needles for the use of the *Tartar*.
>
> [October 21]
> Ordered that the Keeper of the public Store deliver to Captain Richard Taylor for the use of the people on Board the *Tartar* twenty seven Jackets, thirty yards of Linen one shirt & Cloth to make a pair of Breeches upon his paying for the same.
>
> [October 31]
> Ordered that Mr William Holt deliver to Lieutenant Christopher Tompkins ten Barrels of Pork, six Barrels of Bread, six Barrels of Flour, two barrels of Spirits and one Box of Candles for Use of the *Henry* Galley.

Of special note in the November 1 entry is the reference to Spencer Hall, brother of Robert, master's mate on the *Henry*:

> Ordered that the Keeper of the public Store, deliver to Lieutenant Christopher Tompkins for the Use of the Officers and Sailors on Board the *Henry* Galley the following Articles VIZ for Custis Harman one and three quarter yards Cloth with trimings one pair shoes and seven yards of Stripes. for John Fitzhugh three quarter of a yard of Cloth with trimings, one pair shoes and one pair stockings. [Similar items for Aires Darby, William Brumby, Frederick Byrd,

Richard Saunders, Francis Hern, William Willams, James Minter, Francis Moss, John Bander, Newcomb Dodd, Henry Donohow, Stephen Wilkinson, Nicholas Scarborough, Samuel Cavoner, James Williams, John Wilson, and others] Spencer Hall one yard of Cloth and trimings and a Cap. . . .

[November 11]
Ordered that the Keeper of the Public Store deliver to Captain Charles Thomas as much proper wollens as will make Cloths for thirty negroes belonging to the Public Rope Walk at Warwick.

Ordered that a warrant issue to Captain Charles Thomas for one thousand pounds upon account for the purpose of furnishing necessaries and Building Houses at the Public Rope Walk at Warwick.

[November 27]
Ordered that the Keeper of the Public Store, deliver to Captain Richard Taylor for the use of the Ship *Tartar* sixty five yards of Red and white Bunting, six yards of blue ditto, half pound Thread, six Knots of Logline, one thousand five hundred tenpenny nails and 112 lb of Roping Twine.

Ordered that the Keeper of the Public Store, deliver to Capt. Richard Taylor for the Use of the Men on Board the *Tartar* the following articles to wit thirteen pair of stockings, sixty seven yards of cloth, forty nine yards of Linnen, sixty three shirts, six hats and twelve pair of shoes upon his paying the same.

[November 28]
Ordered that Mr William Holt deliver to Lieutenant Joshua Singleton ten Barrels of Pork, six ditto flour, eight ditto Bread, two ditto Spirits, one Box Candles and one Barrel of tar for the use of the *Henry* Galley.

[November 29]
Ordered that Doct McClurg, deliver to Lieutenant Singleton the following articles Cort Peru: Ibss. Sal: Nitre Ibj, Ol Olivar Ibij, Melt Opt Ibij, Sal Tart ozj: Sperma Ceti Ibi, Sal Diuretic ozere and two Lancets [medical supplies] for use of the *Henry* Galley. . . .

Ordered that the Keeper of the Publis Store, deliver to Lieutenant Singleton forty five yards of Cloth, thirty yards Linen, six shirts, two pair of stockings, and two hats for the use of the people on Board the *Henry* Galley upon his paying for the same.

[December 5]
Ordered that the Keeper of the Public Store, deliver to Captain Richard Taylor for Use of the Officers and Sailors on Board the ship *Tartar* the following Articles VIZ thirty nine pair of stockings, thirty one yards of Cloth, fifteen Jackets, nineteen shirts, fourteen and half Yards Linnen, forty one Blankets, seven hats, seven and half yards Blue Cloth, one and three quarters of a yard Buff ditto, three yds brown ditto, three quarters of a yard Red ditto, one and half yard of white ditto, thirty six yards of white Linen, three Hats and five yards Flannel, on his Paying for the same.

[December 10]
Ordered that the Keeper of the Public Store, deliver to Lieutenant Christopher Tompkins six Gimblets, one drawing knife, two pounds of Brimstone, twenty five Blankets and sixty yards Canvas for Hammacks for Use of the *Henry* Galley.[29]

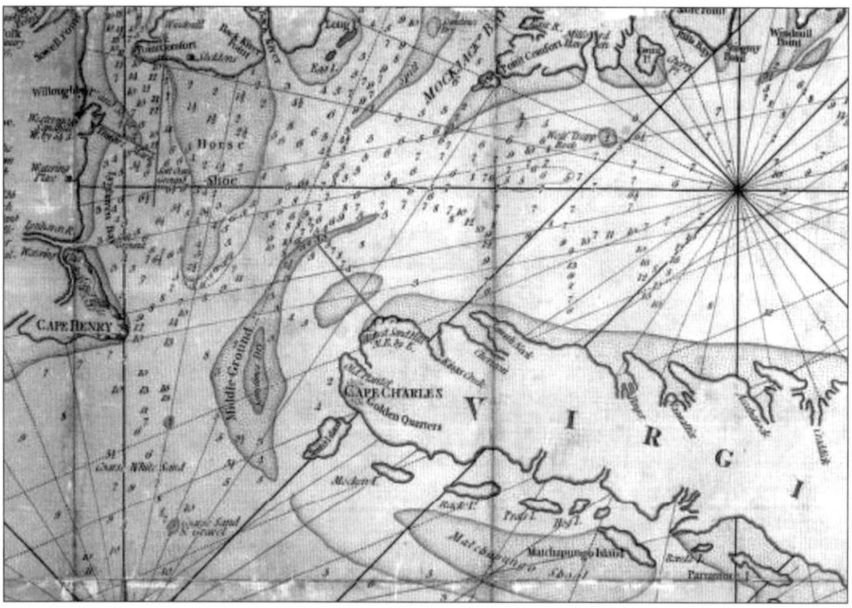


*Figure* 25 By the time of the Revolutionary War, the channels, shallows, tidal currents, and prominent landmarks of the Chesapeake Bay had been extensively surveyed and charted. This section of "A New and Accurate Chart of the Bay of Chesapeake, with All Shoals, Channels, Islands, Entrances, Soundings and Sailing Marks," published by Anthony Smith, July 1, 1776, in London is an excellent example of the detail that was available to mariners at that time. Courtesy of the New York Public Library, Digital Collections, New York, NY.

# CHAPTER 9

# Naval Activities *on the* Chesapeake Bay *in* 1778, Including Robert *and* Spencer Hall

During January 1778 the British fleet was near and menacing to the people of Kingston Parish. Stationed at the entrance of the Chesapeake Bay under the command of Vice Adm. Richard Lord Howe, who commanded the entire British navy on the east coast, were HMS *St. Albans*, sixty-four guns and 500 men; HMS *Phoenix*, forty-four guns and 280 men; HMS *Emerald*, thirty-two guns and 220 men; HMS *Richmond*, thirty-two guns and 220 men; and HM Sloop *Otter*, fourteen guns and 125 men. Altogether, the five warships had a total of 1,345 men and 186 cannon.

January 4, 1778, a Sunday, HMS *Richmond*, Capt. John Lewis Gidoin commanding, reported his position as being northeast by east, four or five leagues from New Point Comfort, the southern tip of Kingston Parish, which would have placed her approximately three miles off the west coast of the Eastern Shore. The *Richmond* weighed anchor at 5 a.m. and gave chase to four vessels to the north. At 7 a.m. she was near the mouth of the Rappahannock River and captured a sloop, and at 10 a.m. she anchored in four and a half fathoms, with the north end of Gwynn's Island to the west. Two of the four vessels being pursued were attempting an escape up the Rappahannock River. In the afternoon, HMS *Emerald* with her tender joined the chase and at 2 p.m. captured another vessel. At 4:30 p.m. the *Emerald*, with her tender, anchored in the Rappahannock, off Carter Creek.

The next day, January 5, HMS *Richmond* chased two vessels in the Rappahannock River and assisted HMS *Emerald* in freeing a merchant ship that had run aground to avoid capture. She was loaded with tobacco and was taken; however, her crew made it safely to shore and avoided capture. The *Richmond* anchored between Carter Creek and Mosquito Point that evening, locations well-known today to residents of Lancaster and Middlesex Counties.

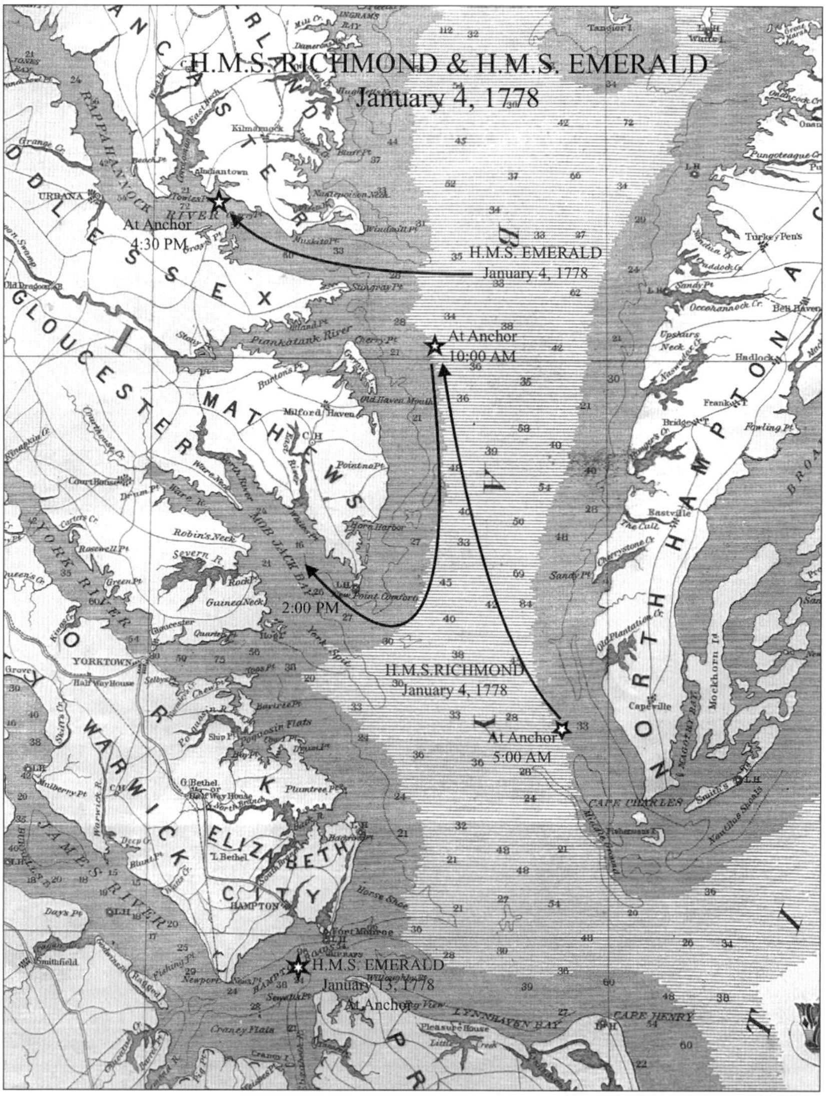


*Figure* 26 During early 1778 the British navy maintained an effective blockade of the lower Chesapeake Bay that severely restricted trade especially for much needed munitions and other war material. Two of the most frequently seen British ships assigned to this mission were HMS *Emerald* and HMS *Richmond*, each armed with thirty-two guns and each with a crew of 220 men. Both ships were known for their excellent sailing qualities, noted for speed and sea-keeping ability. The superimposed text and arrows give an indication of their ability to cover a large area in a relatively short period of time under favorable weather conditions. The appearance of HMS *Richmond* in Mobjack Bay at two o'clock on January 4, 1778, underscores how very close the people of Gloucester County and especially Kingston Parish were to the threat of hostilities. From the author's collection.

January 6, at 5 a.m., the *Richmond* cleared for action and fired four shots to chase "Rebels" from the grounded vessel: they were attempting to salvage whatever could be quickly removed. In conjunction with the *Emerald*, the *Richmond* spent the afternoon removing some of the cargo of tobacco in order to move her into deeper water, which was accomplished by 3 p.m. On January 9, a nine-man prize crew from HMS *Richmond* took the captured ship and most of its cargo to Hampton Roads.

Meanwhile, on January 7, HMS *Phoenix* was fifteen leagues southeast of Cape Henry and at 6 a.m. saw a sail to the north, took out all reefs in the sails, and set the top gallant sails to give chase. By 2 p.m. the chase had reached a location that was two leagues east of Cape Henry, and the *Phoenix* fired several shots at a brig from Guadeloupe bound to Virginia. A boat was sent to remove the prisoners, and a crew from the *Phoenix*, including a petty officer and six men, went on board to navigate her to New York. By 7 p.m. the vessels parted. The weather must have been challenging because at 8 p.m. the *Phoenix* put in second and third reefs in the fore and main topsails and a second reef in the mizzen topsail. At 11 p.m. the topsails were taken in and lowered. The wind velocity and sea conditions were not recorded, but the reduction in sails suggests that the *Phoenix* was in a strong winter gale that was fortunately short-lived.

On January 10, HMS *Phoenix* was sixteen leagues southeast of Cape Henry. A sail was spotted at 8 a.m. to the west, reefs were taken out, and a chase began. The vessel being pursued apparently was faster, and the chase was abandoned. At 1 p.m. another ship was sighted, and a chase began, but visibility made it impossible to continue. At 7:30 p.m. another ship was sighted, and in moderate breezes and hazy conditions the *Phoenix* gave chase. At 9 p.m. she fired a shot at a brig, the *Polly*, Ebenezer Jenkins, master, owned by Seth Jenkins & Co., with a crew of seven seamen, from Nantucket bound to South Carolina. The brig was destroyed*

The ships' journals included other daily events as well, such as deaths of seamen and the occasional neglect of duty:

> January 5, HMS *Richmond*: At 9 that morning the articles of war were read to marine R[ichar?]d Hawkins, who then received twelve lashes for neglect of duty.
>
> January 10, HMS *Phoenix*: At 10 a.m. Seaman John Phillips died, and at 3 p.m. the body of the deceased was committed to the deep. At noon William McFadgan received twelve lashes for neglect of duty.

* Captured ships were frequently destroyed if not useful or valuable and sometimes because there was insufficient crew to man them.

after the crew members were taken as prisoners; she was not carrying a cargo.

The enslaved also played a part in the events. In a bid for freedom, many tried to board the British ships. In a letter dated January 13, 1778, Capt. Benjamin Caldwell of HMS *Emerald*, anchored in Hampton Roads, explained the situation and entreated Patrick Henry, governor of Virginia, to ensure that returned slaves be treated humanely:

> Sir
>
> Having been lately in the Rapahanock, where numbers of Negroes came on board; and as it is not my wish or Intension to distress Individuals, I sent them all on Shore, upon condition, that they should not be ill treated or punished for running away, which I had the strongest Assurances of, from their masters that came for them; yet not withstanding these promises, I have too much reason to fear, they have been extremely ill treated; as many of them came on board two Nights after, they had been returned; complaining much of ill usage, and <u>two</u> with marks of <u>Violent beatings</u>, but as it was not then convenient for me to stay, to inquire into the particulars, I sent them back; as I had given my word, I should receive none; but thought it incumbent upon me to inform you of it; and if a Stop is not put, to such proceedings, both from humanity, and the breach of faith, We shall in future be obliged to keep all that comes to us. I have since my being in this Bay at least, refus'd four hundred, and I am informed the idea on Shore, is, that we land them, to save provisions and water and not from favour; but that is a mistake, for they can always be sent in Prizes, where they are of use, and at this time, thirty would not be inconvenient. The same reason has been given for landing Prisoners, that was given for landing Blacks, but with as little foundation, for when I landed Prisoners last; (the 29th of December,) at which time I wrote to you, <u>there was a convenient and immediate</u> oppertunity of sending them to New York; and mentioned particulars, why they were not sent.
>
> I feel most sensible for this unfortunate war, and the Calamities it occasions, and tho' ambitious to distinguish myself in the execution of my Duty, in Seizing vessels &c hope I do it, with tenderness, to Individuals, and Credit to myself; and I have no doubt Sir, but you will interfere, as far as is in your power, that Justice takes place, with regard to those poor Wretches, I am writing about. I am [&c.]
>
> B. C.[1]

Captain Caldwell wrote another letter on the same day to Vice Adm. Lord Howe giving the official report of the activities since the fifth:

My Lord,

I have great satisfaction, in informing Your Lordship, of our having taken three French men, loaded with Tobacco. On Sunday the 4th instant laying with the *Richmond* in Mocksack [*Mobjack*] Bay, at 2 PM, saw two Sail coming down the Bay; we lay quiet for some time, that they should get down the farther; allowing day Light, to get over the Shoal Water, before we weighd, and then gave Chace; my Tender presently brought us a Brig, and Night coming on, and loosing sight of all other Sails, we Anchored; In the morning, saw the *Richmond* in Chace, of a Sloop and Schooner; and immediately gave Chace; the small Vessels got into Shoal Water, and Captain Gidoin sent his Boats to take them, but as they were Armed, the Boats were called of[f]. We then saw two Sail standing into the Rappahanock-river, and gave them Chace, desiring the *Richmond* to follow with the Prize Brig, then some distance aStern; (as otherwise she might have been Retaken, by the armed Vessels, which we imagine were a kind of Convoy:)

The wind was down the River, and our Pilot was not well enough acquainted to turn the Ship up; but fortunately one of my people, (a regular South Carolina Pilot,) took charge of the Ship, and worked her up in a masterly manner, at 4 PM, the two Sail, a Ship and Snow run a ground; the men left the former, and we took possession of her, and next Evening got her afloat, when the *Richmond* joined me: (with the Brig:) the Snow lay close in Shore, where there was a small Body of Militia, and a Galley in a Creek, near her, therefore I order'd Captain Gidoin, (as his Ship draws less water than mine,) to warp his Ship in, next morning (Tuesday the 6th) by day light, which was done, and upon firing a few Shot, the Frenchmen left the Snow, and the Galley went up the Creek; I then sent as Officer with a Flag on Shore to assure the people, we would not hurt their houses, or do them any kind of damage, if they would not fire upon the Boats, as they must see, both the Village and Snow, were under the Guns; which was agreed to, and in a few Hours she got of[f].

The Ship has Three hundred and Fifty Eight Hogsheads, the Snow One hundred and Ninety Nine, and the Brig Two Hundred, in all seven hundred and Fifty Seven; they were bound to France, but the loss of men, and the Season, had determin'd them to go first to Martinico. I am (&c.)

B.C.[2]

The two letters give insight into the little-known activity of the British navy in the Chesapeake Bay. They provide a vivid picture of the enslaved attempting escape to British ships and an indication of the difficulty of maintaining access to ocean trade routes for imports as well as exports. The reference to a galley shows the enormous challenge the smaller boats faced against a frigate together with their armed boats and tenders. HMS *Richmond*, lurking in Mobjack Bay on January 4, further illustrates how close and menacing the British navy was to the people of Gloucester County. A ship of her size would have been clearly visible around the entire shoreline of Mobjack Bay. The *Richmond* could have bombarded anything on shore without any fear of reprisal.

The journals of HMS *Emerald* and HMS *Richmond* continue on January 20 with the two ships sailing in "Company" in Hampton Roads into the Chesapeake Bay to give chase to two vessels to the north.[3] One of the vessels was the Continental frigate *Virginia*, which outsailed the British ships and retreated to safety up the bay.

One of the few pension applications for service in the Virginia State Navy, dated July 4, 1834, was that of James Gibbs given in the courthouse of Greenup County, Kentucky. It provides the only personal recollection of experiences on board a galley in the Virginia State Navy thus far discovered:

> James (X) Gibbs declares he was born in Lancaster Co., Va., but cannot state the time as he has no record of his birth. When he was large enough he was bound as an apprentice to a sea captain and he thinks he was about the age of 17 when the Revolutionary War first commenced. A short time thereafter his master gave him up and he enlisted as a sailor on board the galley called the *Page* then lying in Carter's Creek, commanded by Capt. James Markham, for three years. The galley lay in Carter's Creek a few days after he went on board repairing her rigging. She then went on a cruise and continued cruising in the Chesapeake Bay and the capes of Virginia. He continued with Capt. Markham on board the *Page* galley about a year. From that vessel Capt. Markham and his crew or a greater part of them were transferred to the ship *Dragon*, then lying off or near the mouth of York River. The *Dragon* sailed on a course in company with ships *Tartar* and *Tempest* and tenders *Patriot* and *Liberty*, the whole being under the command of Richard Taylor. Between the capes of Virginia and Bermuda they gave chase to a British sloop of war. The *Dragon* and *Tartar* being slow sailers, he with a good many other sailors, were transferred from those ships by the commodore's command to the tender called the *Patriot*, then ahead in the chase. The commodore left his ship, the *Tartar*, and took the command of the *Patriot*. About an hour's sun in the evening they came up with the enemy and attempted at once to board the ship. They ran afoul of her, a jib boom passing through some of her quarter galley windows. While lying in this position they attempted to board. The gallant old commodore at the bow of the vessel cheering

> his men in the thickest of the fight was wounded in the thigh and finding himself not supported by the other vessel of the squadron, he gave orders after he had fallen to ______ Brittain who had the command of the tender to fall or sheer off from the enemy. The commodore was very [?] at Capt. Callender's conduct and the next morning refused positively to see Callender who then joined them. After their fight he was returned to the *Dragon* and the whole fleet put back to York River and they put the commodore ashore at Yorktown and he assisted in this duty. They remained at Yorktown refitting about a fortnight.
>
> They sailed on a cruise outside the Virginia capes and lay off on the coast, sometimes at the mouth of Delaware [Bay], off Staten Island, often chasing, oftener chased by the enemy. Finally they put into James River and after serving out faithfully the term of his enlistment he was discharged by Capt. James Markham. He served in consequence of the ship's not getting into port from ten to fourteen days over the term of his enlistment for which he was paid by John Richards, then acting as purser of the *Dragon*.
>
> After he was discharged he entered the merchant service and in a voyage to France the ship was wrecked in the Bay of Biscay, the cargo totally lost, and fifteen or sixteen men drowned. He then lost the discharge Capt. James Markham had given him.
>
> After he left the sea he lived about nine years in Culpeper Co., Va. He then removed to this state about 36 years ago, six of which he resided in Mason County, six or seven on the Ohio River in Lewis County and the remainder in Greenup County. He thinks he is now between 75 and 80 years of age.[4]

The account of James Gibbs's life is a typical example of the careers of young boys who would not inherit a significant acreage or other estate. James was apprenticed at a young age and sent to sea. He faithfully did his duty, enlisted in the cause of the Revolution, saw sea duty and naval warfare, went back to sea after the war, and then moved westward. The dates mentioned in his testimony suggest that he was born in 1759, enlisted in the Virginia State Navy at age seventeen, served until age twenty, and then entered the merchant service and served as a sailor until age thirty. He then lived in Culpeper, Virginia, until age thirty-nine, at which time he moved to Kentucky.

The Virginia Navy Board continued its business of supplying the ships. For example, on January 14, 1778, William Frazier was ordered to deliver to Capt. Richard Taylor two coils of $1\frac{3}{4}$-inch rope, four coils of $2\frac{1}{2}$-inch rope, four coils of 2-inch rope, one coil of $3\frac{1}{2}$-inch rope, and one coil of six-thread ratline for use on the *Tartar*.

The board's journals for at least the first five months of the year lack orders for deployment, other than on April 8 when three ships, one being the *Tartar*, were ordered to Cape Charles to conduct a survey. A May 28 entry shows that Robert and Spencer Hall were transferred from the *Henry* to the larger and more powerful *Tartar*. Robert served on the *Tartar* until some point in 1780 when she was put out of service and then destroyed in April 1781. Other supply entries include the following:

February 3:

> Ordered that a Warrant issue to Captain Robert Tompkins for fifty pounds upon accot for the purpose of furnishing necessaries for the use of the *Henry* Galley.[5]

February 19:

> Ordered that the Keeper of the public store, deliver to Capt. Richard Taylor two claw hammers, eight hundred pump tacks, five hundred ten penny nails, five hundred eight penny ditto, two hundred four penny ditto, ten horn lanthorns. four tin ditto, & eight Gimblets for the use of the ship *Tartar*.
>
> Ordered that the Keeper of the public Magazine, deliver to Captain Richard Taylor sixteen powder horns, forty pound of sheet Lead, and two hundred flints for the use of the ship *Tartar*.[6]

April 8:

> Captains Taylor, Callender and Bright, received Orders to proceed to Cape Charles on the eastern shore for the purpose of taking a survey of every channel and harbour there, which they are to report in writing to the Board.[7]

April 13:

> Ordered that the Keeper of the public store, deliver to Lieutenant Joshua Singleton five hundred pump Tacks for the use of the *Henry* Galley.[8]

May 28:

> Ordered that the Keeper of the public Magazine, deliver to Captain Taylor eight powder horns and eight Cartouch Boxes for the use of the Ship *Tartar*.
>
> Ordered that John Wilson, Jno. Cluvieres, Philip Brumley, William Jarvis, William Piper, and sailors on board the *Henry* Galley be discharged from the same, they having complied with the terms of their Enlistment.

> Ordered that Stephen Wilkinson a sailor on board the *Henry* Galley, be discharged from the same, he being weak and infirm.
>
> Lieutenant Jno. Thomas received Orders to proceed with the Galley under his command to Wicocomico, and there have her properly cleaned and repaired. After which he is to return to his former station in Mobjack Bay there to remain until further orders.[9]

The Treaty of Amity and Commerce and the Treaty of Alliance, between the United States and France, was signed in Paris on February 6, 1778, drastically changing the balance of power. At a March 14 meeting in Lord Weymouth's house, Prime Minister Lord North's cabinet* decided on several military strategy changes that would be sent to King George the next day. Both houses of Parliament would receive a message from the king on the following Tuesday addressing the drastic change in the balance of power and what initial military actions would be made. The cabinet recommended to the king

> That three or four line of battle ships and three other two-decked ships be sent from America for the defence of the Leeward Islands.
>
> That four thousand men be ordered to embark with the line of battle ships for the Leeward Islands.
>
> That ten frigates and six ships [*sloops*] be ordered home from America. . . .
>
> That a Mediterranean squadron be immediately prepared.
>
> That ten thousand of the Militia be ordered to be embodied.[10]

On March 15 Vice Adm. Lord Howe commanded in North America a total of seventy ships, excluding schooners, galleys, storeships, and a hospital ship. Of these the Admiralty Office proposed sending thirteen warships to the Leeward Islands and twenty to England with thirty-seven to remain in North America.[11] Although the British blockade continued, this drastic reduction in the British naval presence on the east coast proved to be a

---

* The prime minister's cabinet consisted of the most powerful men in England. The meeting that day included the prime minister, Frederick North, Lord North; Lord George Germain; John Montagu, Lord Sandwich, 1st Lord of the Admiralty; Henry Howard, Lord Suffolk, head of the Northern Department, the forerunner of the Home Office; and Lord Weymouth, head of the Southern Department, the forerunner of the Foreign Office. The cabinet made all strategic decisions, subject to approval by the king, related to the conduct of the war in North America.

significant factor in the outcome of the war. Table 9.1 illustrates the tactical shift in the British naval presence towards a more maneuverable, flexible fleet primarily organized for blockade duty.

In the spring, French merchant ships and warships began appearing on the Atlantic coast, but while the British navy remained ever present, galleys had not proven to be effective in maintaining commercial shipping. Several of the smaller and first-built galleys were placed in an inactive status in mid-1778; only the four largest, the *Tartar*, *Tempest*, *Dragon*, and *Gloucester* saw service throughout the year.

## TABLE 9.1

***British Naval Forces in North America, under the Command of Lord Howe (March 15, 1778)***[12]

| Guns | Ships | To the Leeward Islands | To England | Remain in North America |
|---|---|---|---|---|
| 64 | 6 | 4 | - | 2 |
| 50 | 5 | 3 | - | 2 |
| 44 | 3 | - | 2 | 1 |
| 36 | 1 | - | - | 1 |
| 32 | 14 | 2 | 6 | 6 |
| 28 | 12 | - | 4 | 8 |
| 24 | 3 | - | 1 | 2 |
| 20 | 8 | 2 | 1 | 5 |
| 16 sloops | 4 | - | - | 4 |
| 14 sloops | 9 | - | 6 | 3 |
| 10 sloops | 2 | - | - | 2 |
| Bombs | 2 | 2 | - | - |
| Fireships | 1 | - | - | 1 |
| Total | 70 | 13 | 20 | 37 |

# CHAPTER 10

# Robert Hall Jr., Son *of* Ann *and* Robert Hall

Robert Hall Jr., the first son of Ann and Robert Hall, was born on September 19, 1758, in Kingston Parish, Gloucester County, Virginia,[1] and died before 1787 at approximately age twenty-eight.

When the Revolutionary War began, Virginia created a navy by purchasing vessels and constructing others specifically designed for naval warfare in the Chesapeake Bay. One of these vessels was the galley *Henry*, which was constructed in Kingston Parish, probably on the East River. Robert, growing up nearby, would have been aware of the shipbuilding project and decided to serve in the newly created navy. He became a member of the crew at age eighteen and was on board the *Henry* in January 1777.[2] He apparently joined the navy between July 1776 and January 1777 because he was not listed on a roster of Virginia State Navy officers and sailors published in the *Virginia Gazette* on July 5, 1776.

Recruiting sailors for the Virginia State Navy was difficult because wages on merchant ships sailing in wartime conditions and the potential for great rewards as a crew member of a privateer offered significant competition for experienced sailors. However, a three-year enlistment promised an award of bounty land. For the young men who did not expect to inherit much if any land, the opportunity of one day owning their own farms attracted a number of men from Kingston Parish and counties in the Tidewater region. Even Robert, who would have inherited his parents' land as the firstborn son, may have been enticed by the sheer vastness of acreage or the financial windfall from selling the warrant.

In his handwritten book, John Pendleton recorded the monthly wages for the Virginia State Navy during the years 1777–1781 as £12.7s.6d. for captains, lieutenants £4.2s.6d., midshipmen £4.2s.6d., masters £7.10s.0d., master's mates £6.0s.0d., surgeons £6.0s.0d., stewards £4.2s6d., and boys £1.10s.0d.[3] These amounts, especially because of wartime inflation, are more useful to show the relative importance of each position as measured by pay rather than the actual income amounts. Some evidence indicates that in some months lesser amounts were paid, and it isn't clear whether victuals were included.

The term "master" in relation to commercial vessels was the same as "captain." First mate would have been second in command. In the navy, however, "sailing master" or "master" was the warrant officer responsible for navigation and sailing and the general management of the ship, including assignment of crew and watches, ordering sail and course changes, stowing provisions and munitions, and ordering repairs and equipment changes. The master was treated as an officer and usually messed with the other officers. The captain of a naval ship was competent to navigate and sail a ship and had the ultimate responsibility for everything that happened with special emphasis on activities associated with military engagement.

Boys commonly began serving on ships as early as fourteen, sometimes younger. Those who were fortunate to have attended school and who had mastered the basics in writing and math and who exhibited leadership potential were able to advance. By the age of seventeen to twenty, many would have become a second or first mate. It was not uncommon for masters of merchant vessels to be in their early twenties. Those who were successful in trading would often retire from the sea by their midthirties. Although no hard evidence has been found that indicates that Robert went to sea at a young age, he had the necessary skill and experience to have become a master's mate quickly after joining the navy, perhaps even when he first enlisted. It is thus highly probable that Robert had experience at sea at a relatively young age and was a seasoned mariner by age eighteen.

On January 28, 1778, Robert was listed as the master's mate in the complete crew roster of the *Henry* (see appendix 4), one of the few crew member lists to have survived. Robert Tompkins was captain at the time, and the crew consisted of seven officers; a surgeon, gunner, carpenter, boatswain, sailmaker, steward, clerk, armorer, quartermaster, master-at-arms, and their assistants; and thirty-two seamen and marines. Of the fifty-two-man crew, only two names had the notation "3 years," which was an agreed term of service: Robert Hall and Peter Foster, carpenter's mate. Peter Foster was Robert's brother-in-law, having married his sister Nanny on October 27, 1776. Another member of the *Henry* crew was Spencer Hall, Robert's younger brother, who would have been seventeen years of age in January 1778.

The *Henry* was frequently mentioned in the records. However, members of the crew, other than captains, were rarely mentioned by name. Two mentions of Robert and Spencer suggest that they were valuable crew members. On March 30, 1778, the Virginia Navy Board

> Ordered that the Keeper of the publick store, deliver to Robert Hall ten quires

> of Cannon cartridge and five of musket paper, and two hundred and fifty pump Tacks for the use of the *Henry* Galley.
>
> Ordered that the Keeper of the public magazine, deliver to Robert Hall two hundred gun flints seven pound of Lead, and one iron pot for the use of the *Henry* Galley.[4]

Shortly after, on April 7, six six-pounder cannon with their apparatus were transferred from the *Henry* to the *Tartar.* Three four-pounders in possession of the navy were sent to the *Henry* as replacements. On April 8, Lt. Joshua Singleton received orders to take command of the *Henry.* The two entries taken together suggest that Robert may have been the senior officer on board pending the arrival of Singleton.

In the last entry pertaining to Halls serving on the *Henry*, on May 28, 1778, the Virginia Navy Board "Ordered that the commanding Officer of the *Henry* Galley turn over Robert Hall and Spence Hall, to Captain Richard Taylor of the Ship *Tartar.*"[5] Statements by Lieutenant Singleton suggest that Robert was promoted to sailing master in January 1779, at age twenty.[6]

The *Tartar*, a larger vessel than the *Henry*, was launched in 1778 and was principally stationed in the Chesapeake Bay to prevent pillaging of crops and livestock by the British and to help deny them access into the principal rivers. Galleys also engaged in coastal patrol off the capes of Virginia to help minimize privateering activities of British loyalists.

On November 30, 1779, the Virginia House of Delegates "*Resolved*, That the ships Tartar and Dragon, and the gallies Henry, Manly, Hero, Page, Lewis and Safeguard, be no longer retained as a part of the Virginia navy."[7] On October 28, 1847, the commissioner of pensions declared:

> Robert Hall was a master in the Virginia State Navy, left service upon the reduction of the navy and was discharged 24 Jan. 1780. The heirs were allowed at $152.08 per annum from the date of his discharge to 1 Jan. 1786, in which year or the next he died. This amount is payable to Thomas Green of Richmond, Va., attorney of Peter G. Foster, administrator of Robert Hall.[8]

Robert left the service one day before he would have qualified for a share of tea, coffee, loaf sugar, brown sugar, and rum, "A list of necessaries wanting out of the public store for the officers on board the ship Tartar for two months from 25 Nov. 1779 to 25 Jan. 1780."[9] The order included the names of all of the officers of the *Tartar* during the time interval mentioned. The commanding officer was Capt. William Saunders. Robert was not included.

In January 1780, Robert was twenty-one years old and a veteran of the Revolutionary War, having served for three years, half that time on the *Henry* and half on the *Tartar*. The record shows that he was a master's mate by January 1778, although he may have enlisted at that rank, and a master by January 1779.

Robert's rank in the navy required certain qualifications and skills that were prerequisites to his military service, and thus he must have served for a number of years prior to the Revolution as a mariner. As a sailing master, Robert would have been proficient in math and would have had a working familiarity with trigonometry; he would have been highly knowledgeable about weather patterns and about navigation by dead reckoning, including determining latitude by the sun and the North Star, determining the speed of a ship, course made good, and traverse boards; he would have had familiarity with the nautical almanac and plotting using coastal and sea charts, along with numerous other skills required to be an accomplished sailing master. Reading and writing were essential requirements to manage the many activities required to operate a ship, and a sailing master had to be an accomplished leader of men.

The only way to learn these skills in the eighteenth century was on board a ship, so Robert must have had several years of experience prior to joining the navy. As he was just eighteen years old when he joined the crew of the *Henry*, he must have gone to sea at a young age, perhaps as early as fourteen years old or earlier, to have qualified for his rank as early as he did. He may not have crewed on a transatlantic crossing, but he would have surely made coastal passages, perhaps to New England, the Carolinas, and the West Indies as well.

While the record is silent concerning Robert after his discharge from the navy, he likely continued as a mariner in some capacity. Service on privately owned vessels, especially on privateers, was highly profitable at that time, and Robert would have been extremely well-qualified for service on an armed private vessel.

In addition, there is no record of Robert having been married and no record of children. If there were any, they were all dead by 1847 when his siblings and their offspring petitioned the court in Mathews County for a share of Robert's pension and other benefits, if any. The last mentions of Robert in the record occurred in the land tax books of Mathews County in 1797, 1798, and 1799: in each of those years Thomas Hall is shown as owning forty-four and a half acres along with twenty and a half acres from Robert Hall. Robert, whose estate must not have been settled yet, may have inherited the tract from his father in 1781 or early 1782. Unfortunately, Robert's twenty and a half acres are not shown in earlier tax records.

As a veteran with three years' service, and with his rank of sailing master, Robert was entitled to 2,666⅔ acres of bounty land located in present-day Kentucky, which was part of Virginia until June 1, 1792.

To designate the bounty land for Revolutionary War veterans, the Virginia General Assembly established a military district by a resolution passed on December 19, 1778, and defined the area:

> That it is the opinion of this committee, that a certain tract of country to be bounded by the Green river and a south east course from the head thereof to the Cumberland mountains, with the said mountains to the Carolina line, with the Carolina line to the Cherokee or Tennessee river, with the said river to the Ohio river, and with the Ohio river to the said Green river, ought to be reserved for supplying the officers and soldiers in the Virginia line with the respective proportions of land which have been or may be assigned to them by the general assembly.[10]

The tracts were in a vast area of present-day Kentucky and southern Ohio that was set aside to reward veterans who had served no less than three years of continuous duty; service in the state militia was not considered. On June 22, 1779, the General Assembly of Virginia established the Virginia Land Office, which was responsible for proving claims and processing documents for approval by the governor's office. The first warrant was issued in 1782.

With his father dead, and his brother Spencer having moved to Salem, Massachusetts, Robert's youngest brother, Thomas, took up the family business of securing the pension and war benefits to which the family was entitled.

Thomas engaged an attorney in Richmond and appeared before what was most likely an administrative panel or officer of the court to review and pass judgment on bounty land and pension claims. On September 5, 1787, Thomas qualified as being the brother and representative of Robert Hall. On the same day, testimony was presented from statements that had been previously made by Lt. Joshua Singleton concerning Robert's length of service and rank. He certified that "Robert Hall engaged on board the *Henry* galley in Jan. 1777 and served as master's mate until Jan. 1779."[11]

Other procedures may have been involved, but the outcome was favorable: on September 14, 1787, a "certificate was issued by Virginia for £173.5.2 for the balance of full pay of Robert Hall." On September 28, "William Reynolds, assignee of the representative of Robert Hall [Thomas Hall], is entitled to the proportion of land allowed a master of the State Navy for three years' service." The final legal action concerning this case occurred on October 6, 1787, with the issuance of "Warrant 4311 for 2,666⅔ acres was issued by Virginia to William Reynolds, assignee of Thomas Hall, representative of Robert Hall."[12]

The warrant was sold, land sight unseen, as was often the case. While thousands of veterans moved to Kentucky after the war, large numbers were not in a position that would have permitted them to leave their homes and farms and start anew in what was then the wilderness. The capital to acquire the necessary farming equipment, the labor necessary be it family and/or slaves, and the risk of settling in a mostly unpopulated territory, initially without churches, merchandising stores, and other conveniences, all made having cash instead of land an often-preferred option. This was especially the case with widows and children of deceased veterans who were entitled to bounty land.

It is not known how much the Hall family received from the sale of the warrant or when the sale took place. However, beginning in May 1779, the state of Virginia authorized the sale of treasury warrants to patent tracts of land west of the Allegheny Mountains, primarily in the present state of Kentucky, for the purpose of helping to reduce Revolutionary War–related debt. The state initially offered land at the rate of £40 per one hundred acres. A random analysis of the more than twenty thousand Virginia treasury warrants

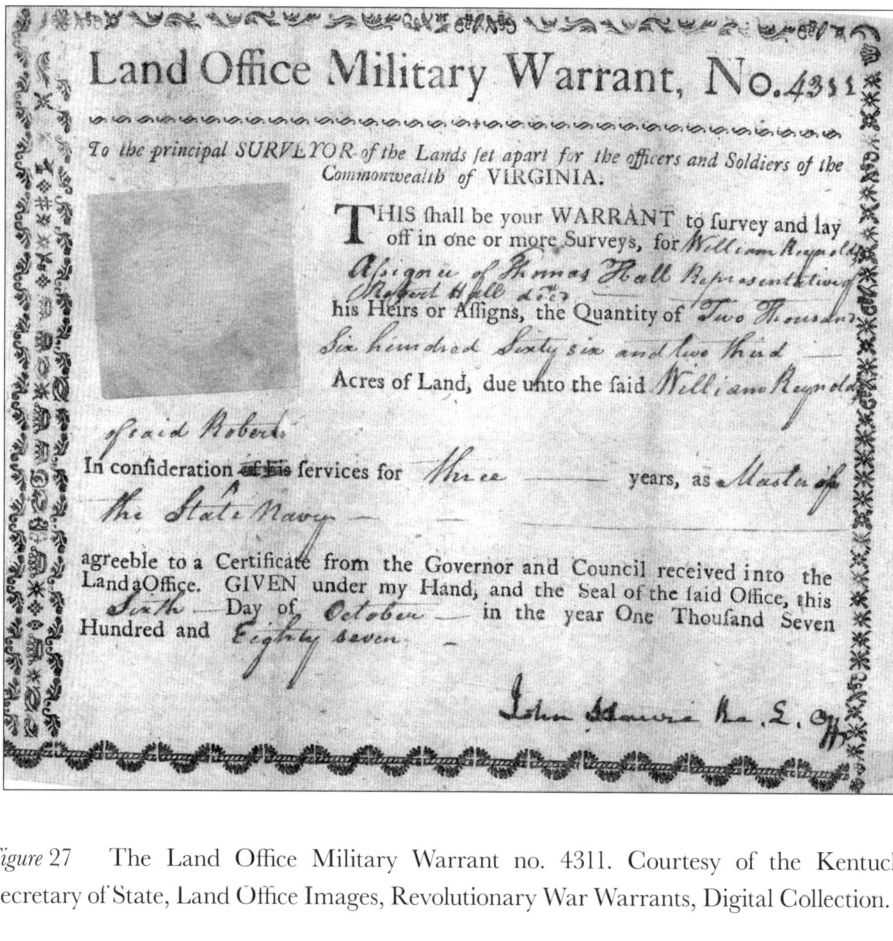
Land Office Military Warrant, No. 4311

*To the principal SURVEYOR of the Lands set apart for the officers and Soldiers of the Commonwealth of* VIRGINIA.

THIS shall be your WARRANT to survey and lay off in one or more Surveys, for William Reynolds Assignee of Thomas Hall Representative of Robert Hall dec'd his Heirs or Assigns, the Quantity of Two Thousand Six hundred Sixty six and two third Acres of Land, due unto the said William Reynolds of said Robert. In consideration of his services for three years, as Master of the State Navy agreeable to a Certificate from the Governor and Council received into the Land Office. GIVEN under my Hand, and the Seal of the said Office, this Sixth Day of October in the year One Thousand Seven Hundred and Eighty seven.

John Harvie R. L. Off.

*Figure* 27 The Land Office Military Warrant no. 4311. Courtesy of the Kentucky Secretary of State, Land Office Images, Revolutionary War Warrants, Digital Collection.

shows thousands of sales at the initial offered price. However, between the summer of 1780 and the summer of 1781, the price was increased to £160 per one hundred acres for at least the next few years.*

Regrettably, these valuations are of only limited use in estimating what the Hall family might have received from the sale of the warrant because the Hall acreage was large, requiring a significant investment, and a buyer would not have known how long he would hold the warrant before a patent would be awarded or exactly where the land would be located. These factors suggest that the value of warrants for land in Kentucky was deeply discounted compared to the market price of the land. Assuming a value in the range of £20–25 per one hundred acres, the Hall family might have received as much as £533–666, or an average price of 4s.6d. per acre. Even if the amount was half as much, the sale must have represented a windfall to the family.

Warrant no. 4311 gave the holder a very large tract of land, 4.167 square miles, equivalent to 4.85 percent of the 85.93 square miles of land in Kingston Parish. And its location was in a desirable region of Kentucky, although the acreage's potential for agricultural development was probably not known at that time. A deed for 2,000 acres begins as follows; a second deed was for the remaining 666⅔ acres.

> Henry Lee, Esquire Governor of the Commonwealth of Virginia. To all to whom these presents shall come Greeting: Know ye that by virtue of part of a Military Warrant No. 4311. Issued the 6th day of October 1778. This is Granted by the said Commonwealth unto William Reynolds. a certain Tract or parcel of Land containing Two thousand Acres by Survey bearing date the eighth day of September 1791. lying and being in the District set apart for the Officers and Soldiers of the Virginia State Line, on the East side of the South fork of Little Barren River, and bounded as follows To wit: Beginning at two Sycamores a Sugar tree and a mulberry at the lower side of the mouth of Sulphur Lick Creek. thence up the South fork of little Barren River with its meanders.[13]

The land can be found in northern Metcalfe County with Campbellsville to the northeast, Columbia to the east, Glasgow to the southwest, and Edmonton to the south. The

* The new price appears to have remained constant and was the value recorded for over fifteen thousand transactions until late 1783 when treasury sales ended. Speculators were very active in this market buying large holdings that would subsequently be divided into smaller parcels. Resold acres were likely sold at a premium to provide a profit for the speculator. Thus, a small farmer acquiring a few hundred acres might have paid £175 per one hundred acres or perhaps much more as the era of hyperinflation began, one that would last through the decade.

northernmost part of the property is at the fork of the Little Barren River where it divides into the South Fork Little Barren River and the East Fork Little Barren River. The coordinates at that spot are latitude 37.125° north and longitude 85.632° west. Mammoth Cave National Park is to the west.

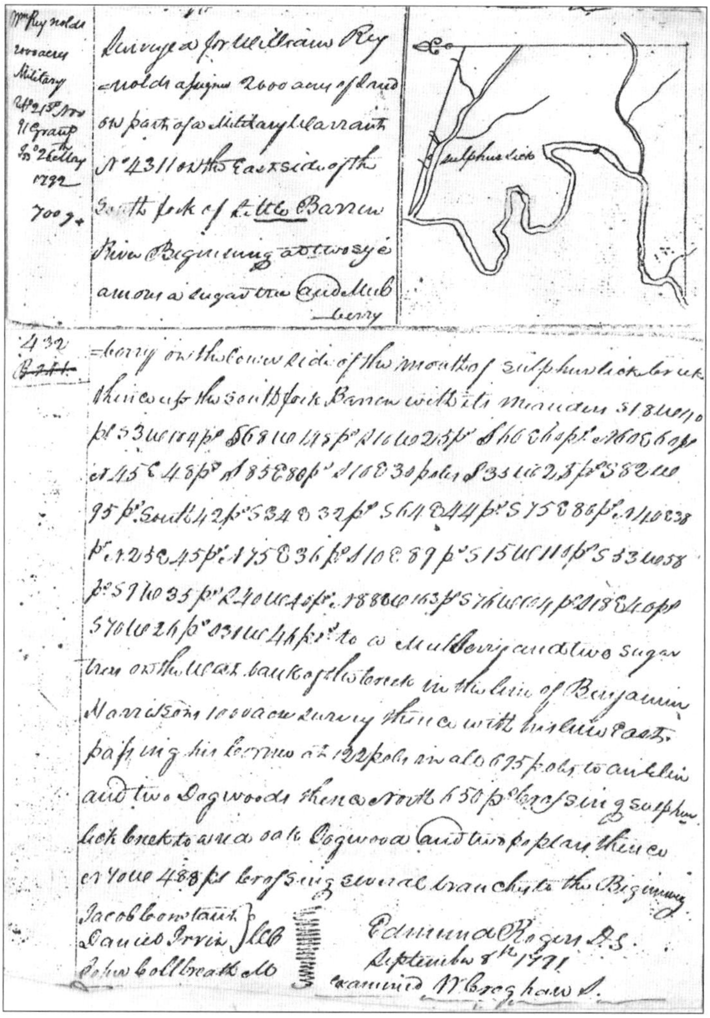

*Figure* 28 This survey of 2,600 acres was made for William Reynolds and was part of Military Warrant no. 4311. The detailed metes and bounds are shown together with a drawing of the area. The survey was signed by Edmond Regan on September 8, 1791, suggesting that the property was not purchased until almost four years after the assignment to William Reynolds, representing Thomas Hall. It is not known when the Hall family received payment. Courtesy of the Kentucky Secretary of State, Land Office Images, Revolutionary War Warrants, Digital Collection.

# CHAPTER 11

# Spencer Hall, Son *of* Ann *and* Robert Hall

Spencer Hall, the second son of Ann and Robert Hall, was born on November 28, 1760, in Kingston Parish, Gloucester County, Virginia. The origin of his first name, perhaps from a family connection with the Spencers in nearby Petsworth Parish, is not known; however, if his parents followed English naming customs, he would have been named for his mother's grandfather. At the time of his birth, his mother would have been approximately twenty-six years old and his father about thirty. The Hall household in 1760 included daughters Ann, age four, and Elizabeth, about five or six, and son Robert, age two. The orphan Hugh Brooks was probably also living with the family.

Nothing more is known about Spencer until sometime in mid to late 1776 when at the age of sixteen, or soon to be, he joined the Virginia State Navy as a seaman. The next record of Spencer was just before his seventeenth birthday as a member of the crew of the *Henry* on November 1, 1777, when he was issued "one yard of Cloth and trimings and a Cap." He appeared three months later, on January 28, 1778, on the crew roster of the *Henry*, at which time he was paid £3.4s.13d. for thirty-one days' service. The last mention of Spencer in the *Naval Documents of the American Revolution* was on May 28, 1778, when he and his older brother, Robert, were both transferred to the *Tartar*. Although a record has not been found concerning his leaving the service, his name appears later as qualifying for a land grant for his service in the Revolutionary War, indicating that he served at least three years. However, no record of a bounty land claim for Spencer has been found.

The record shows Spencer, at age twenty-one, in Salem, Massachusetts, on December 20, 1781, the day of his wedding or the date of stating his intention to marry Mary Cottee (Cottle) Ober, age seventeen. Spencer's bride was part of the Ober family of Beverly that had a strong tradition in maritime affairs. Since the *Tartar* went into inactive status in November 1779, Spencer and other members of the crew were probably discharged from the service in late 1779 or very early in 1780. His brother Robert was discharged on January 24, 1780, and Spencer probably left the service at the same time. In fewer than two years, Spencer had found a wife and established himself in Salem.

The demand for skilled sailors in New England was very high at that time, and the opportunity to earn a share of the proceeds from the sale of captured ships and their cargoes was a strong incentive that drew sailors from great distances. To be competitive in attracting skilled seamen, merchant vessels were forced to offer higher wages than prewar levels. Perhaps, on leaving the navy Spencer signed on board a merchant vessel or privateer that traded between the Chesapeake and New England. Since he ended up in Salem, there is a strong likelihood that his vessel's home port was in Salem or nearby Beverly. Both of these ports were significantly engaged in privateering activities during the Revolutionary War. Opportunities at home in the Chesapeake Bay were limited as British naval control was very effective in 1780 and in 1781 until the French fleet became engaged.

The vast majority of American naval warfare during the Revolution was sponsored by private investors, many of whom became very wealthy and were responsible for the rapid economic growth in Salem, Beverly, and other New England ports in the years leading up to the War of 1812. The 158 privateers based in Salem and Beverly captured 440 enemy ships that were classified as prizes—over half of all prizes captured by privateers from all of the colonies.[1] By comparison, the Continental navy had 31 commissioned vessels in 1776 and during the war captured 196 enemy ships, but losses to the British reduced the fleet to 7 by 1782. A total of 449 privateers from all the colonies captured upwards of 800 British ships and imprisoned twelve thousand British seamen over the course of the war.

With 6,665 citizens in 1783, Salem in the 1790 census ranked sixth in population after Charleston, South Carolina; Baltimore; Philadelphia; Boston; and New York. With more than fifty thousand feet of wharves, the largest fleet of trading vessels was mostly small schooners exporting cod and barrel staves to the West Indies and returning with sugar and molasses, which was converted into rum. In 1791 there were seven distilleries capable of producing between five and six hundred thousand gallons of rum annually. Slavery was also a highly lucrative trade, and New England ports, especially Salem and Boston, profited greatly.

The volume of commerce and the variety of cargoes handled through the port of Salem after the Revolution were remarkable:

> Hemp from Luzon, pepper from Sumatra, coffee from Arabia, palm oil from the west coast of Africa, cotton from Bombay, duck and iron from the Baltic, tallow from Madagascar, salt from Cadiz, wine from Portugal and the Maderas,

> figs, raisins, and almonds from the Mediterranean, teas and silks from China, sugar, rum, and molasses from the West Indies, ivory and gum-copal from Zanzibar, rubber, hides, and wool from South America, whale oil from the Arctic and Antarctic, and sperm from the South Seas.[2]

During 1783–1789, an average of three ships per month sailed from Salem southward, with Baltimore being the most frequented port. Large quantities of flour were imported, and naval stores (primarily tar and turpentine) were needed in Salem's numerous shipyards. Exports included rum, wine, and mahogany furniture. Cargoes to the West Indies were made up of dried fish, barrels of pickled mackerel, salt beef, salt pork, boards and shingles, barrel staves and hoops, cheese, butter, and candles.[3]

During the 1790s, shipyards were an important part of Salem's economy and supported a number of skilled trades including ship carpenters, spar makers, caulkers, painters, and the makers of cabinets, rope, blocks, pumps, and sails. Riggers were also an important trade as were the blacksmiths who specialized in anchors and chains. Rowboats, carried on ships, were typically made in shops specializing in small boat manufacture. Ship chandlers (firms that provided provisions for ships), harbor pilots, navigation instrument and chart shops, clothing and shoe shops, and other trades were also important components to the local economy.

Spencer most likely met Mary Cottee Ober in mid to late 1780, or very early in 1781. Baptized on October 7, 1764, in St. Peter's Episcopal Church in Salem, Mary was the daughter of Israel and Abigail* Ober, who were married on September 9, 1753, in Salem. Israel Ober, born in 1734, was a mariner and died at the relatively young age of thirty-nine on August 8, 1773.† Abigail lived for seventy-five years and died in May 1811. Israel and Abigail had seven children, three girls and four boys. Mary was their last-born daughter. At the time of her birth, she had five siblings: Johanna, age ten: Israel, age eight; Abigail, age seven; James Levette, age four; and Jonathan, age two. Her younger brother, William, was born in 1766.

The extended Ober family was prominent in Beverly, Massachusetts, especially in maritime pursuits, and they were significantly engaged in Beverly home-ported merchant vessels and privateers. Few if any families had a similar number of relatives engaged in the maritime activities of the Revolutionary War. Observed by Octavius T. Howe, an early nineteenth-century New England maritime writer, "Most of the vessels sailing from Beverly in the first three years of the war were manned by Beverly crews and always

---

* Abigail's parents were Jonathan Archer Jr. and Abigail Archer, née Allen.

† He was buried in the Hospital Burying Ground in Salem.

included a strong contingent of Lovetts, Herricks, Gages, Thorndikes, Batchelders, Ellingwoods, Fosters, Obers, and Woodberrys, and the two latter families could have officered and manned a large privateer with men of their own name."[4]

The maritime roster of the Ober family is impressive: Israel Ober, Mary's oldest brother, was the captain of the sloop *Fish Hawk*, commissioned on September 1, 1780, and captain of the sloop *Little Vincent*, December 4, 1781; his brother James Ober was captain of the brigantine *Freedom*, September 17, 1781; John Ober was the first lieutenant on the brig *Washington*, May 8, 1777; Nathaniel Ober was first mate on the sloop *Fish Hawk*, November 20, 1777; Nicholas Ober was the prize master on the *Saratoga*, September 4, 1780; and Mary's brother William Ober was first mate of the *Rambler* at some time during 1780 and 1781. Finally, Richard Ober was captain of the privateer *Fanny*, a snow, commissioned January 15, 1778, as well as, at various times, first mate on the brigantine *Starks*, first mate on the ship *Resourse*, captain of the *Resourse*, and captain of the brigantine *Fortune*, November 7, 1781.[5]

According to a mention in the diary of William Bentley, a well-know Anglican preacher of Salem, the Ober family also converted land into a shipyard by June 1794. The land was

At least three of Mary Ober Hall's brothers died relatively young. Israel Ober, baptized June 6, 1756, died at sea in October 1793, at age thirty-seven. Jonathan, baptized November 14, 1762, died in January 1789, at age twenty-six, from "lung fever [pneumonia]." William, baptized August 17, 1766, and married to Betsy Robinson in 1794, committed suicide in July 1816, at age fifty. Nothing has been found concerning Mary's other siblings other than the marriage of Abigail, baptized on August 7, 1757, to Joseph Lambert in 1782.[6]

An Ober died as a result of the sinking of the schooner *Brutus* on Monday, March 8, 1802. She apparently was driven ashore in a gale and at half past seven o'clock in the evening struck a rock, which penetrated the hull. The crew discharged her cargo of coffee in an attempt to lighten the vessel, but she began to break up at half past nine. With the help of the main mast, all but one of the crew reached the shore. They walked during the night "across the Cape" in snow with temperatures near zero. Captain Brown died before the crew reached a lighthouse. Others died of exposure, including one Ober, who was recovered "almost choaked with sand" and died the next day.[7]

This could have been James Levette Ober, Mary's only brother not accounted for, but it could just as well have been another member of the family.

near "Becket's."[8] Spencer Hall knew a James Becket who was joint owner, one-third, with Spencer of the ship *Mary Ann*. Spencer could easily have met Mary through any of these connections.

One of Mary's relatives appears to have been involved in the slave trade as first mate on the schooner *Felicity*. Her captain was William Fairfield, and she sailed in September 1788 for the Cape Verde islands to secure a cargo of thirty-five slaves. The ship departed the coast of Africa on March 13, 1789, and after thirteen days at sea, the captives "Rised upon us. At half-past seven," seized some of the firearms, and killed the captain. The crew, after killing two of the Africans, subsequently regained control, and "we put them In Irons and Chained them." The slaves were sold at Cayenne, French Guiana, in South America, and the *Felicity* returned from Martinico in the Dominican Republic to Salem on June 30, 1789, now under the command of one Captain Ober.[9]

Mary Cottee Ober Hall gave birth to their first child, Spence Jr., on August 26, 1782, just eight months after their marriage. The child died as a result of "diarrhea" three weeks later on September 15, suggesting perhaps a premature birth.[10]

A year later a daughter, Mary, was born on August 17, 1783. Nothing further is known about her, but she too may have died at a very young age because a second daughter was born on December 17, 1785, and given the name Polly, which was a nickname for "Mary." Polly lived only ten years and died on December 30, 1795.

Mary and Spencer had three more children. A second son, Spencer Jr., was born on December 2, 1787. Israel Ober was born on July 19, 1790, and James Levette was born on January 27, 1793. Spencer had returned from a voyage to Africa on November 7, 1792, and he may have been at home for the birth of James, but by midyear he would have begun a second voyage to Africa from which he did not return.

Spencer Hall was often at sea and enjoyed good success in his commercial ventures, accumulating enough capital and sources of credit to become a partial, perhaps majority, owner of a schooner, the *Polly*. Unfortunately, a strong Atlantic gale in December 1786 drove the *Polly* onto a Barnstable, Massachusetts, beach and inflicted sufficient damage to cause the vessel and cargo to be put up at auction. Barnstable is near the center of the shoreline of Cape Cod at the southern end of Cape Cod Bay. Winds from northerly directions make the bay a dangerous place for a sailing vessel especially in heavy weather conditions. Fortunately, there was not a report of loss of life, and the cargo and ship were not destroyed.

The following advertisement was published on March 26, 1787, in the *Essex Register*, the newspaper of Salem, Massachusetts:

For the Benefit of the Insurers,
Will be Sold by PUBLIC VENDUE,
At BARNSTABLE,
On FRIDAY next, 30th instant,
At TWELVE o'Clock precisely,
The well-built Schooner POLLY,
Burthen 100 Tons, Only two Years old,
With all her APPURTENANCES,
as she now lays at BARNSTABLE.

Said Schooner was Stranded on Barnstable Beech the 10th of December last, where she suffered considerable Damage; but has since been got off, and now lays in Barnstable Harbour, where the Inventory may be seen, by applying to

Capt. Spence Hall, or David Scudder.
ALSO,
30 or 40 Molasses Hogsheads, 89 Shaken ditto, with Heads.

In December 1786, Spencer was just twenty-six years old and only seven years had elapsed since serving in the Virginia State Navy. He was captain of a schooner of somewhat larger than average size, and while the ownership of the vessel is unconfirmed, the advertisement suggests that Hall and Scudder were at least partial owners. And the name, *Polly*, was the nickname of his wife, Mary, further suggesting his ownership.

Spencer had much to be proud of, having accomplished more than many do in a lifetime. As captain of a seagoing sailing ship, he would have been proficient in navigation and all aspects of managing a ship's crew, the maintenance and working of the ship, the administrative tasks associated with paying port duties, procuring and negotiating for cargoes and their discharge, and countless other skills required to own and operate a ship.

Clearly, he was educated and skilled in the mathematics necessary for navigation and the ability to read and write. How, when, and where he learned is unknown, but this progress would have been unattainable without having mastered academic and practical sailing skills at an early age.

On January 2, 1790, three years after the grounding of the *Polly*, Spencer registered the seventy-one-ton schooner *Mary Ann*, constructed in 1789. Now twenty-nine years old, he was listed as owner and master, in partnership with James Becket.[11]

The three years since the loss of the *Polly* must have been financially rewarding to be able to purchase the majority share of a newly constructed ship. Assuming that during that time he continued going to sea as mate or captain, he perhaps had enough capital to acquire minority shares in the vessels on which he served. Unfortunately, tragedy at sea was to reoccur with the loss of his newest ship, the *Mary Ann*.

The *Berkshire Chronicle*, Pittsfield, Massachusetts, on March 25, 1790, published the following news item: "SALEM, March 2. . . . Capt. Spencer Hall, of this port, was lately cast ashore on Cape Hatteras."

This shipwreck occurred less than two months after acquiring the *Mary Ann*, on what was probably her first voyage under Spencer's ownership. Cape Hatteras, North Carolina, one of the most treacherous parts of the East Coast, known as the graveyard of the Atlantic, was especially dangerous during winter and early spring months, being highly susceptible to strong northeast gales. Sea conditions offshore are often violent, with winds out of the northeast blowing against the northeast-flowing Gulf Stream. Very steep wave formations in this part of the Atlantic are especially dangerous. An estimated several thousand ships have been lost over the centuries on Cape Hatteras.

Further information about the loss of the *Mary Ann* comes from William Bentley's diary:

> [February] 21. Sunday. Snow fell in the morning—dined with Col. Pickman. News that Capt. Spence Hall of this end of the Town has lost both his Vessel & Cargo upon Cape Hateras as you enter upon the Carolina Coast. The Vessel belonged ⅔ to the Capt., who has insured £150. The other third to James Becket, who has not insured. The Vessel was taken by execution from N. Silsbee.[12]

Based on the appraisal in Spencer's estate made years later of the eighty-two-ton schooner *Union*, which Spencer purchased in the fall of 1790, valued at £300, the £150 in insurance would have covered a significant portion of his loss of the *Mary Ann*. Fortunately there was not a report of loss of life; presumably the crew along with Spencer all made it safely to the Cape Hatteras beach.

Spencer, somehow able to recover quickly from hardships, was back in the news just seven months after Cape Hatteras. The "Ship News" in the *Essex Register* has him returning as the captain of the *Mary* from "St. Andeara" (Sant Adrià de Besòs, near Barcelona) in Spain on August 30 after a forty-five-day sail, overall a three- or four-month voyage.

On October 4, 1790, just five weeks after completing the voyage from Spain in the *Mary*,

Spencer was listed as the owner and master of the eighty-two-ton schooner *Union*, constructed in 1783 in Kingston, Massachusetts, located thirty-six miles south-southeast of Salem on the west side of Kingston Bay, part of the greater Plymouth Bay.[13]

The record is silent on the *Union*'s activities in the first two years of his ownership, but in 1792 Spencer became involved in the slave trade. Why Spencer made this dramatic change in occupation is unknown. Perhaps he succumbed to it out of desperation. He did have significant debts, especially from the loss of the *Mary Ann*, and a successful voyage involving the slave trade was typically highly profitable. It would have been an option since his home port, Salem, was deeply involved in the slave trade, as were numerous other New England seaports. A slave-trading voyage would begin by carrying a cargo of rum and manufactured goods to the African coast to be traded for slaves, who would typically be sold in South America or the West Indies, with the return passage to Salem or other east coast ports with a cargo of sugar, molasses, and other commodities from southern ports. The molasses would be converted into rum, and the trading cycle would begin again.

In the same, March 25, 1790, edition that the *Berkshire Chronicle* published the notice of the Cape Hatteras shipwreck, two other news items give a sense of life in the times:

SALEM, March 2.

Early on Monday evening last Week, a Barn in Beverly, on a Farm tenanted by Mr. John Potter, took Fire, and was consumed, together with a large Quantity of Hay, several Hundred Weight of Flax, &c. Twenty-eight Head of Horned Cattle, three Horses, two sucking Calves, a Sheep and two Lambs, perished in the Flames.

Capt. Radx, arrived here from the West-Indies, on his homeward passage, in lat. 36° 39', long 70° 50', fell in with the ship Flora, Capt. Dennis Sennitt, from Norfolk, in Virginia, bound to England, with a cargo of wheat—the Captain was drowned—the vessel had sprung a leak—and the pumps were so choaked that the people could not free her—they therefore left the ship, and took passage with Capt. Radax to this port.

Capt. Radax, on his passage from this port to the West-Indies. In lat. 32° 13', lon. 60°, met with a brig sunk, all but her quarter-deck and forecastle, and her masts gone. She had a single deck, and appeared to be about 90 tuns.

Spencer's last voyages were on board the *Union*, and during a stop in Charleston, South Carolina, he executed his will, in his own vessel, on September 20, 1792. Slave trading, while profitable, was dangerous because of a variety of diseases on the coast of Africa for which American and European visitors had little immunity. Spencer clearly wanted his estate to be properly managed, and he was certainly acquainted with the risks he would likely encounter. His will reads as follows:

> State of South Carolina.
>
> In the Name of God Amen. I Spence Hall of the State of [ blank ] Mariner considering the uncertainty of this mortal life and being of sound mind memory and understanding blessed be almighty God for the same do make and publish this my last will and testament in manner and form following. First I will and desire that all my just debts and funeral expenses be duly paid and satisfied. Secondly I give and bequest unto my loving Wife Polly Hall all and singular the rest and residue of my Estate both real and personal or of what nature or kind the same may be or wheresoever the same shall be found, to use possess and enjoy as long as she shall remain and continue single and unmarried. But if my said Wife should marry or die then I give and bequeath all and singular my said Estate unto my Children which I now have & may hereafter have, their heirs Executors Administrators and Assigns for ever to be equally divided between them share and Share alike. Lastly I do hereby nominate and appoint my said Wife Polly Hall sole Executrix of this my last Will and Testament hereby revoking all former and other Wills by me heretofore made, and declaring this and no other to be my last Will and Testament. In Witness whereof I have hereunto set my hand and Seal this Twentieth day of September in the Year of Our Lord One thousand Seven hundred and ninety two.
>
> Spence Hall
>
> Signed sealed published and declared by the said Spence Hall as and for his last Will & Testament in the presence of us who at his request in his presence and in the presence of each other have subscribed our names as witnesses hereunto.
>
> Thos. M. Woodbridge
> John Batton
> John Ward[14]

The voyage to Africa probably originated in Charleston, South Carolina, and the *Union* made excellent time during the passage because she had completed the voyage and returned to New York by November: voyage completed in New York, November 7, 1792; slaves purchased in unspecified location on West Coast of Africa, 94 slaves embarked, 77 slaves disembarked in the West Indies; schooner, registered in New York; Spence Hall, captain.[15]

The total distance sailed, assuming straight-line courses, was approximately nine thousand nautical miles. If Spence sailed to Africa on the day after signing his will, he would have completed his voyage in forty-eight days. The *Union* was clearly a fast schooner, and Spencer was obviously an accomplished captain.*

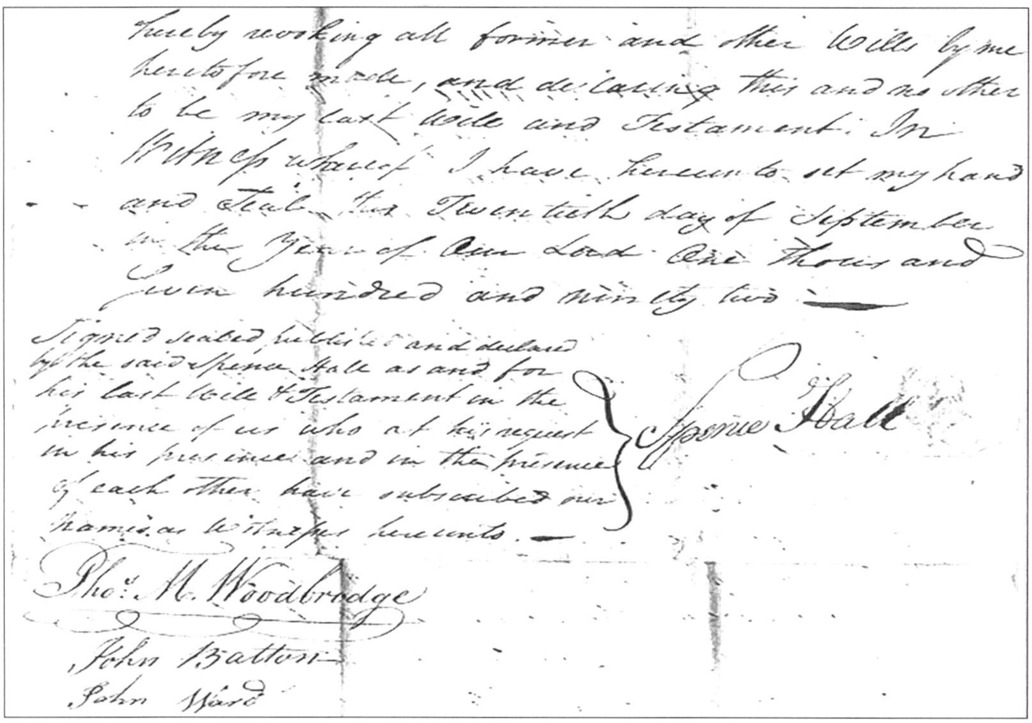

hereby revoking all former and other Wills by me heretofore made, and declaring this and no other to be my last Will and Testament. In Witness whereof I have hereunto set my hand and Seal the Twentieth day of September in the Year of Our Lord One Thousand seven hundred and ninety two —

Signed sealed published and declared by the said Spence Hall as and for his last Will & Testament in the presence of us who at his request in his presence and in the presence of each other have subscribed our names as Witnesses hereunto. —

Spence Hall

Thos. M. Woodbridge
John Batton
John Ward

*Figure* 29 Capt. Spencer Hall signed his will in Charleston, South Carolina, on September 20, 1792, on board his schooner, the *Union*. Courtesy of the Massachusetts Archives, Boston.

* Assuming three days in Africa to load a cargo of slaves, and three days to off load in the West Indies, the *Union* would have averaged a daily distance of 214 nautical miles at a remarkable average speed of 8.9 knots (nautical miles per hour). Her hull speed, assuming a waterline length of 72 feet, would have been approximately 9.5 knots. If the *Union* had similar dimensions for its rated tonnage as other high-performing schooners of the late eighteenth century, her keel length would have been 65 feet 6 inches, her beam 19 feet 10 inches, and her depth of hole 7 feet 4 inches. Her length on deck would have been approximately 78 feet 6 inches, and her cargo capacity, or burden, would have been approximately 112 tons.

Less than a year later, in 1793, having arrived at Bunce Island, Africa, on the *Union*, Spencer Hall was dead. The African coast was feared for its deadly diseases, including yellow fever, malaria, and smallpox. Spencer likely died of one of them. His second-in-command, Capt. R. Fisher, continued in Spencer's absence and completed the voyage on October 30, 1793: slave trading at Sierra Leone, 94 slaves embarked; first region of slave purchase, Senegambia and offshore Atlantic; principal place of slave purchase, Rio Nunez; 77 slaves disembarked; subsequent fate unknown; principal place of slave landing, Suriname in South America.[16]

Bunce Island, also Bance Island in the eighteenth century, is twenty miles inland on the Sierra Leone River, the point at which seagoing vessels could navigate no further due to the depth of the channel. Beginning in the seventeenth century, the area became active in the forced exportation of Africans. In 1750, the firm of Grant, Sargent, and Oswald of London became owners of the island, a very small, narrow land area approximately one-third mile in length, and increased its capacity to receive and export Africans by building additional structures and a shipyard and significantly enhancing the island's fort.

The firm remained active in the slave trade until 1800. In the last two decades of its existence, it specialized in slaves for the rice plantations in South Carolina, with Charleston being the principal port of entry. Bunce Island is located in what was known as the Rice Coast of West Africa, a region where rice had been cultivated for centuries. Africans from the Rice Coast were recognized as being especially skilled in its cultivation.

Contemporary reports noted the large number of graves of slave traders on Bunce Island, especially captains whose families could afford gravestones. Spencer Hall is likely buried on the island:

> The schooner *Union* of Salem in New England. When she arrived on the Coast she was commanded by one Hall who dying at Bance Island, was succeeded in the Command by his Mate. She took on board a Cargo of Slaves from Rio Nunez with which she left the Coast bound to the West Indies, or Surinam about the latter end of October last [1793]. The name of the Master who carried her off was Fisher.[17]

William Bentley expressed a low opinion of those involved in the slave trade when he noted Spencer's death in his diary:

The letter that documents the death of Spencer Hall, along with a related letters, also gives insight into the nature of the slave trade and the treatment of slaves at sea:

> The Ship *Willing Quaker* Adamson Master belonging to Boston or Salem in New England. She arrived at the mouth of the River Sierra Leone on the ___ of April 1793, thence she went to the Bananas and the Isles de Los, and whilst she staid on the Coast lay mostly at one or other of these places. She took in Slaves at both places. In the month of July she left the Isles de Los with upwards of One hundred Slaves on board, bound it is supposed to Surinam. A. W. Hutchinson came out as Supercargo, but some difference arising between him and Adamson he was left on the Coast whence he took a passage to the West Indies in the schooner *Union* of Salem,. R. Fisher Master, also freighted with Slaves.

Captain Adamson carried a letter from one of the ship's owners to King Naimbanna of Sierra Leone directing that seven slaves owed to him as the result of earlier trading be paid to Adamson in men and boys. The instructions from the owner to the captain charged him to see that the captives was young and healthy; without defects in limbs, teeth, and eyes; and with as few females as possible. They were to be kept "well fed, well used, and . . . clean and dry." The men were to be kept in irons, and the gratings (ventilated hatches) were to be locked at sunset, suggesting that the captives were brought on deck during daylight. The price desired was fifty dollars per head.[18]

> Reports that Capt. Spence Hall died in the Guinea Trade. He has left a wife & six[?] children, belonging to the english Church in this Town. He has been an unfortunate man, & thus sought "base means for his redress."[19]

Bentley's comment also suggests that Spencer's two ship mishaps and perhaps other trading losses gave him no choice but to venture into the high-risk but highly profitable slave trade to help meet his financial obligations. Bentley was somewhat disingenuous in his comment given that a large part of the Salem and Beverly economies thrived on the slave trade by being vendors of a large array of provisions, shipbuilding, and repair with the associated requirement for manufactured items and the payrolls of all involved.

The *Salem Gazette* imparted the requisite information on May 6, 1794: "NOTICE is hereby given to all such persons as have any demands against the estate of SPENCER HALL, late of Salem, mariner, deceased, to bring in their accounts forthwith to MARY HALL, Executrix."

The appraisal of the estate began on December 13, 1794, and it was not completed until April 1800. Six years was a long time to settle an estate, and thus there must have been unusual complications. A list of claims dated October 16, 1796, includes £129 owed to William Ober and £160 owed to Abigail Ober out of a total of £312.77 owed. Spencer thus had financed his last ship, and perhaps earlier ones, through loans from his wife's family.[20]

The inventory of his estate, dated December 13, 1794, is extensive and contains items that would only have been in the home of someone who had achieved a level of moderate wealth. The inventory is headed by the schooner *Union* with an estimated value of three hundred pounds. The following is a partial list: a mahogany desk, a stand table, a square table, a four-foot mahogany table, a card table, eight birch chairs, two round green chairs, six leather bottom mahogany chairs, a mahogany bureau, two feather beds, an oak bed and "bed under," a bedstead with mahogany posts, a mahogany easy chair, two looking glasses, sheets, pillowcases, napkins, blankets, towels, tablecloths, pictures, books, a Bible, two trunks, silver spoons, fifteen wine glasses, a Hadley's quadrant, a compass, a spinning wheel, two copper teakettles, three copper kettles, a frying pan, a toaster, a fender, two shovels and tongs, a pair of flat irons and smoothing box, two pairs of bellows, a gin case and bottles, knives and forks, and two brass candlesticks.[21]

*Figure* 30 Located on the Sierra Leone River, in what is known as the Rice Coast of West Africa, the fort was a principal marketing center for receiving slaves from the interior and marketing them to merchants. Sketched in 1805; courtesy of the British Library, London.

Spencer's schooner, the *Union*, was quickly sold and reregistered to Clifford Crowninshield on January 6, 1795. James Devereux was listed as master.[22]

At the time of his death, Spencer and Mary had four living children: Polly, age eight, who would die two years later; Spencer Jr., age six; Israel, age three; and James, who was just eight months old. The record does not provide information about Mary concerning the years that followed and how she supported the family. However, Spencer's two known slave-trading voyages—there may have been more—were probably lucrative, and she would have had the profits from them and the proceeds from the sale of the *Union* and perhaps other items in the estate. And being an Ober, she may have shared in the estates of other members of her family.

Spencer Jr. followed in his father's footsteps and went to sea after just reaching his sixteenth birthday. He signed on as a seaman on the *Belisarius*, departing Salem on December 31, 1803, bound for the Isle de France. Spencer completed numerous voyages between 1803 and 1816, an average of one voyage per year. He visited the East Indies in southeast Asia, the West Indies including Saint Lucia in the Caribbean on six occasions, "Malaca,"* the Indonesian island of Sumatra on two occasions, and Messina in Italy. He was a seaman on the first four voyages, became a second mate for the next two, and then mate on the following five voyages.[23]

Following his voyage to the West Indies in June 1809, holding the rank of mate, Spencer Jr. married Rachel Gwinn in Salem on November 12, 1809.[24] He was twenty-one years old. On December 14, 1809, he set sail for the West Indies on board the schooner *George & Susan* as mate, a rank he would hold on the same schooner for five voyages, all of which were to the West Indies, including Saint Lucia.

He was issued three seamen's protection certificates, used to prove citizenship. The last one, certificate no. 3067, was issued on September 17, 1810, and was probably of special importance due to the growing tensions at sea with Great Britain that resulted in the War of 1812.

On a voyage bound for Messina that departed on April 1, 1812, on the schooner *Sally*, Spencer, twenty-five years old, was listed as master.

At some point before November 1814, at the age of twenty-six, Spencer joined the ranks of a privateer crew. Salem provided a large number of merchant ships that were reregistered and repurposed to become privateers, merchant ships armed for naval

---

* Likely either Malacca in Malaysia or Málaga in Spain.

combat at sea without cargo of any kind other than provisions for the crew and ammunition to protect themselves as well as capture enemy merchant ships. A vessel sailing under a letter of marque, another type of privateer, was a merchant ship armed for its protection against the enemy but carrying a cargo of military significance or a cargo needed to establish credit for trading in munitions and other materials necessary for warfare. In the War of 1812, thirty-one privateers sailed from Salem including four ships, two brigs, four sloops, and twenty-one schooners. Shipowners and other investors financed these vessels because of the opportunity for large profits.

A captured enemy merchant ship would be auctioned, including its cargo, in Salem or some other convenient port, and the proceeds shared among owners and the crew according to an agreed formula. A well-established schedule of the portion belonging to the crew rather than set wages created a strong incentive to pursue the enemy, incurring great risks and hardships, to realize the greatest profit.

Privateers played a vital role in the War of 1812, as they had during the Revolution, with 1,300 enemy vessels captured by 517 privateers. US Navy ships, numbering 23 vessels, captured 254 British ships.[25]

In the roster of officers of "the private armed ship America on her fifth cruise," "Commenc'd the 24th of November, 1814 and ended April 8th, 1815,"[26] Spencer Jr. was listed as one of six prize masters. A prize master was responsible for taking command of a captured ship, sailing her to a convenient port, obtaining the necessary legal approvals, and organizing the auction sale of the cargo and ship. The fact that the *America* had six prize masters demonstrates the high probability of capturing numerous British merchant ships, as each captured ship would require a prize master and crew. Once ashore, the prize master and his crew would most often be delayed for some time before rejoining their ship.

Remarkably, there is an account of the engagement that resulted in Spencer Jr. becom ing a prize master. The location was in the Irish Channel (now known as the North Channel), which provides access to the Irish Sea:

> Jan. 26th [1814]. At 2 P.M. saw a sail bearing N.N.W.; called all hands to make sail in chase. At 3 sent up Royal masts and yards; and set all necessary sail. At 8 came up with the chase; it proved to be the British brig *Sovereign* from Cork bound for Liverpool, John Brown commander. Took on board the prisoners and put on board Mr. Hall, prize master with six men and ordered her to America. Her cargo consisted of coals, crates, butter, etc. [27]

The *America* landed in Portsmouth, New Hampshire, to gather her crew and, after refitting, sailed on her fourth cruise beginning on October 31, 1814. She captured twelve ships on this cruise.

At 350 tons, the *America* was the largest ship engaged in privateering that was homeported in Salem. She carried twenty cannon and a crew of 150 men.[28] While she was a privately owned vessel, her organization was similar to a naval ship. Her captain was listed as commander, and there were three lieutenants, a sailing master, a surgeon, a purser, a captain of marines, a gunner, a gunner's mate, and a carpenter. A typical schedule of shares would have awarded one share to each able-bodied seaman with the scale increasing by rank to between ten and twenty shares for the commander. Assuming a captured 150-ton vessel with cargo sold at auction for £2,500, the proceeds would have been reduced by the cost of repairs to the ship with the net amount divided equally between the owners and the crew. If repairs in this example cost £100, the crew, assuming 150 men, would have divided their share of £1,200, with the commander, using a typical schedule of shares, receiving £90, a very large sum in 1814. Seamen would have received £6 each, and Spencer, in this example, as a prize captain, would have received £24, enough to acquire a significant ownership interest in a small ship. Success over several voyages enabled privateer men to acquire significant wealth, especially the officers.

Spencer Hall Jr. next appears as one of two commanders of the *Castigator* with the rank of first lieutenant. Her second commanding officer was First Lt. Stephen G. Clark. She was a very small vessel of ten tons, two masts, and two lateen sails. She carried one "car'nade," firing six-pound cannonballs. Her crew numbered twenty men, and they were most certainly armed with muskets. The record of prizes shows three captures by the *Castigator*. She was built in Salem in 1813 and was wrecked in the Salem harbor on September 23, 1815.[29]

Not yet thirty years old, Spencer Jr. died in Salem following his last voyage, which was aboard the *Mary Eliz*, bound for Sumatra. She had departed Salem on April 7, 1816. The December 28, 1816, edition of the *Essex Register* reported the following:

> DIED, . . . In this town, Capt. Spencer Hall, aged 29. Funeral to-morrow afternoon, immediately after divine service from his late dwelling house in Carlton Street. Friends and relations are requested to attend without further notice.

Spencer Jr.'s two younger brothers also went to sea. Israel was issued a seamen's protection certificate, no. 1553, on October 10, 1805, at age fifteen. He married Abigail Taylor on September 22, 1811, when he was twenty-one, and he and Abigail had five children:

Abby Taylor, born March 13, 1812; James Leavitt, born November 17, 1814; Rachel, born March 15, 1816; Thomas Dodge, born June 27, 1819; and William Spencer, born April 8, 1823.

Brother James received his seaman's protection certificate, no. 2962, on May 21, 1810, at age seventeen. Not long after, on January 2, 1811, the *Essex Register* reported the sad news: "Lost overboard from brig Active, 7 days after leaving Salem, James Leavitt Hall, aged 18, a young man highly and justly esteemed." Israel named his first son after his lost-at-sea brother.

At the time of Spencer Jr.'s death in 1816, Mary was fifty-two years old and had lost five children, with Israel being the only one to survive.

There is no record that Mary ever remarried, and just as the surviving veterans and widows of the Revolutionary War in Mathews County applied for pensions as a result of new legislation by Congress in 1832, Mary engaged an attorney in Salem to seek what she might be entitled. The following testimony was entered into the court in Salem, Massachusetts, on July 9, 1833, when she was sixty-nine years old:

> Know all men by these presents that I Mary Hall of the Town of Salem in the County of Essex and the State of Massachusetts, widow and devisee of Spence Hall formerly of the Parish of Kingston and County of Gloucester, being that past now Mathews county in the state last aforesaid, do constitute and appoint Philip Sale of the said County of Mathews and State of Virginia my agent and attorney for me and in my name, to demand and receive from the Register of the Land Office of Virginia in Richmond any and all Warrants that I may be intitled for Bounty Lands due for the services of the said Spence Hall, and his brother Robert Hall in the Navy of Virginia during the Revolutionary War;
>
> also to receive from the Auditor of Public Accounts of the said state of Virginia all arrears of pay, depreciation or other equivalent therefor that I am intitled or that may hereafter be provided or become due for their said services and to grant receipts or other discharges for the same as fully and effectually as though [I] were personally present,
>
> and for the purpose of enabling our said attorney more effectually to carry the afforesaid powers into execution he is here impowed to create one or more substitutes for that purpose; hereby ratifying all my said Agent and attorney or his substitutes or either of them may do by virtue hereof.

In testimony whereof I have hereunto set my hand Seal this 9th day of July 1833.

Signed Sealed & delivered } Mary Hall
in presence of }
J. P. Saunders }
Joshua Chase }[30]

She would live another four years, during which she seems to have received nothing for her claim. Her death was reported in the *Essex Register* on April 28, 1837: "In this city, Mrs Mary Hall, aged 73. Funeral this afternoon, from her late residence, No 21, Essex street—friends and relatives are invited."

# CHAPTER 12

# Thomas Hall Sr., Son *of* Ann *and* Robert Hall

Thomas Hall Sr., the last known child of Ann and Robert Hall, was born about 1764. He was a veteran of the Revolutionary War and became a shipbuilder, of schooners, and lived a long, productive, and profitable life.

Thomas first appeared in the record on the tax list of Kingston Parish in 1791 at approximately twenty-seven years old. He was listed with his mother, Ann, living on forty-four and a half acres with one slave and two horses. Four years earlier, the tax list of 1787 showed Ann as having one slave over the age of sixteen and two under that age and no horses, mares, colts, or mules but seven cattle. Thomas was not listed, but his omission appears to have been caused by a damaged original record, or he was not residing with his mother at that time.

In 1794, the tax list showed Thomas as the owner while his mother Ann was no longer listed. It is assumed that she died between 1791 and 1794 when in her late fifties. Thomas, now age thirty, had probably lived with his mother most of his life except for military service during the Revolutionary War and perhaps employment away from home in his early twenties. He did, however, marry in 1790.

Other than tax lists, the first record of Thomas's youth appears years later, on July 14, 1834, when he gave testimony at the Mathews County Courthouse as part of his application for a Revolutionary War veteran's pension. Congress on June 7, 1832, adopted legislation that granted eligibility to veterans who had served at least two years for a pension of full pay for life. Under the act, a pensioner's widow or child could collect money due from the last payment until the date of death.

In preparation to prove relevant facts for the testimony concerning Revolutionary War pension applications, someone requested a search of county records for deeds and heirs sometime before March 1834. Unfortunately, it is not known what was found. The clerk recorded the following searches in the fee book: the deed from Robert Hall to Thomas Hall and copy of the same; the heirs of Francis Brown; that Francis Brown died intestate; same in the case of Robert Hall's heirs; same in the case of Deggs Weston's heirs; and proof that Robert Hall's land warrant was lost.

Thomas in 1834 was a seventy-year-old lifelong resident of Mathews County, having lived on the same land, perhaps in the same house, for most of those years. He testified as follows:

> I entered the service in 1779 by order of Sir John Payton Coln. to Richard Billups Capt. to enrole me. When Arnold went up James River they wanted some men to go to Williamsburg to guard the capital. I being a young man just old enough to go on this list they took me with them. We started and marched to Gloucester Court House. Hearing that Arnold had retreated and was coming up York River we stopped at Gloucester Court House and there we were stationed for some time and then we marched back again and was discharged of that tour of duty. I served three months on that tour of duty. In 1780 I was called out under the same Capt. & Coln. to go to Point Comfort to do duty where there was a steady guard kept on the account of the British having possession of Point Comfort Beach to prevent them from comming up in the neighborhood to plunder it. On that tour of duty I served three months. In the latter part of the same year I was called out in like order under the same officers on the account of some barges coming up east river to try to land on the shore. There we had a little firing upon them. We were stationed at the mouth of the river for some time and then marched to point comfort where the guard was usely [usually?] kept. On that tour of duty I served six weeks. Whilst stationed at point comfort we had to fire on the enemy many times on the account of they attempting to come up in the neighborhood to plunder. We never had any engagements with them that was worth speaking about. In 1781 I was called out when all the Gloucester militia was called out to go down to Gloucester Town where Corn Wallis had blockaded york river up with his fleet and marched to Gloucester Court House where we were stationed there for a little while and then marched to hubards old field. There we stopt a little while and then marched down to ware Church. There I was taken sick and had to come home. I did not get down to Gloster town where they had the engagement on that tour of duty. I served two months and a half.
>
> I served all the time as a private and for such service I claim a pention. I hereby relinquish every claim whatever to a pention or annuity except the present and declare that my name is not on the pension Roll of the agency of any state. I was

born in 1764 in Gloucester County, Kingston parish. I have no record of my age. I was living in Gloucester County, Kingston parish when called into service. I have lived there ever since I was called into service as a militia man. I never received notification discharge. I was acquainted with Coln. Boswell Coln. Cascy Coln. Payton. I can prove my service by Richard Hurst who served in the same company as I did and Mathias Gayle who served with me in a nother company. They can testify to my character as sworn to and subscribed.

In open court the day and year aforesaid.

Thomas Hall

Now Richard Hurst and Mathias Gayle residents in the County of Mathews do hereby certify that we are well acquainted with Thomas Hall who has subscribed and sworn to the above declaration that we believe him to be 70 years of age that he is reputed and believed in the neighborhood where he resides to have been a soldier of Revolutionary war and that we concur in that Opinion. Sworn to and subscribed in open Court the day and year aforesaid.

Richard Hurst
Mathias Gayle[1]

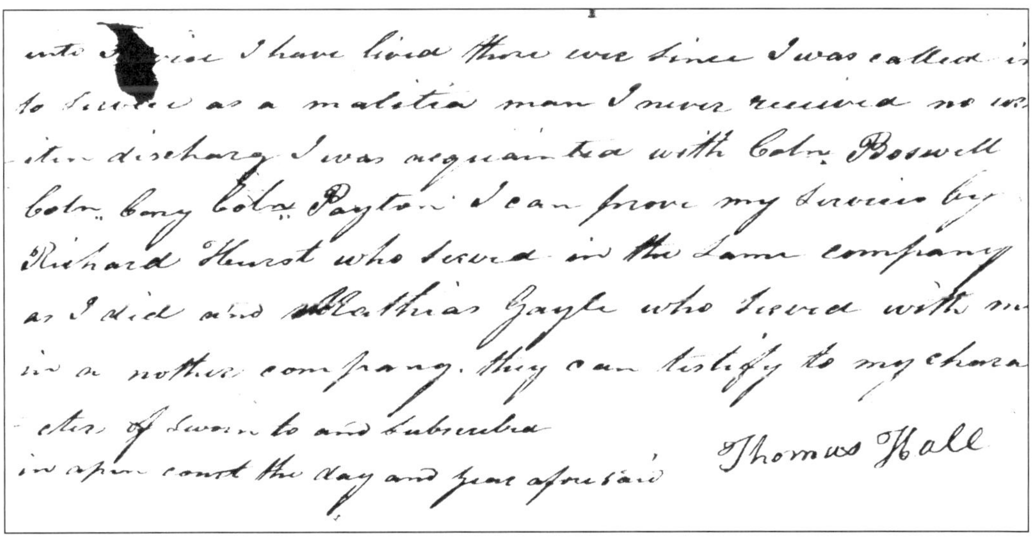
into [illegible]vice I have lived there ever since I was called in
to Service as a malitia man I never received no wr
iten discharg I was acquainted with Coln Boswell
Coln Cany Coln Payton I can prove my Service by
Richard Hurst who served in the same company
as I did and Mathias Gayle who served with me
in a nother company. they can testify to my chara
cter as sworn to and subscribed
in open court the day and year aforesaid Thomas Hall

*Figure* 31 The signature portion of Thomas Hall's sworn statement made on July 14, 1834, to prove his service in the Revolutionary War as application for a pension. Courtesy of the National Archives, Washington, DC.

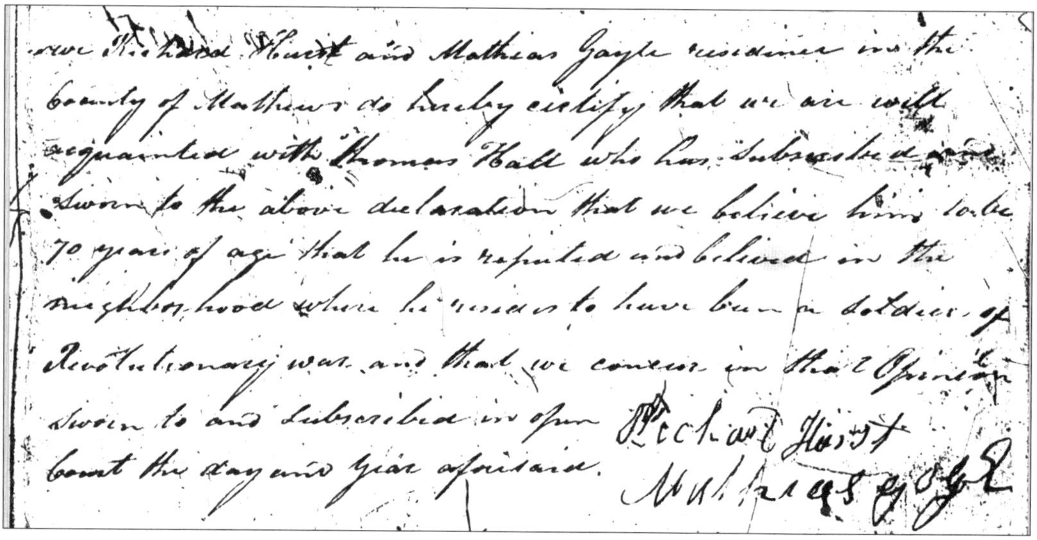

we Richard Hurst and Mathias Gayle residing in the
County of Mathews do hereby certify that we are well
acquainted with Thomas Hall who has subscribed and
Sworn to the above declaration that we believe him to be
70 years of age that he is reputed and believed in the
neighborhood where he resides to have been a soldier of
Revolutionary war and that we concur in that Opinion
Sworn to and subscribed in open Richard Hurst
Court the day and year aforesaid. Mathias Gayle

*Figure* 32 Richard Hurst and Mathias Gayle were in attendance with Thomas Hall on July 14, 1834, and certified his residency, age, and Revolutionary War service. Courtesy of the National Archives, Washington, DC.

Thomas was credited with nine months and seventeen days of service in the regiment of Colonel Payton in the Virginia army with the rank of private. The certificate, no. 27897, was dated August 23, 1834, and placed him on the Virginia pension roll in the amount of thirty-three dollars per annum. In court with him that day were longtime friends, neighbors, and fellow veterans Richard Hurst and Mathias Gayle.

Thomas testified that he entered the service as a young man, just old enough to serve. If he had been born in the first half of 1764 and entered the service in mid to late 1779, he would have just turned sixteen years old. During the time Thomas was marching "to Williamsburg to guard the capital,"* Thomas's two brothers, Robert and Spencer, were nearing the end of their service on the *Tartar* and their three-year careers in the Virginia State Navy.

Benedict Arnold had entered the Chesapeake Bay on December 30, 1780, with a fleet of British warships including forty-four-gun HMS *Charon*, four frigates, HMS *Fowey*, three

* It is not clear exactly when Thomas was on this mission and which capital he is referring to since the capital moved from Williamsburg to Richmond in April 1780. Thomas referenced Williamsburg, but, according to the testimony of William Hurst and William Diggs on October 6, 1836, Mathias Gayle, who was in the same unit as Thomas, was called out to go to Richmond. Another possibility is that the unit may somehow have positioned troops in Williamsburg to defend Richmond.

sloops, two brigs, and sixteen other vessels. Several of the ships sailed directly up the James River and landed eight hundred men at Westover plantation who then marched to Richmond. They destroyed several buildings, including warehouses as well as the important foundry at Westham. Hoping to encourage rebels to desert the Virginia militia and join the British army, and to increase citizen support for the Crown, Arnold purposefully targeted public property and avoided destroying private property. The fleet moved back down the James River on January 10, 1781, and established winter quarters in Portsmouth, Virginia, beginning on January 19.[2] On March 20, 1781, twelve British warships arrived in the Chesapeake to provide reinforcements for Arnold, followed by an additional twenty ships that arrived on March 26 with two thousand British troops. Arnold's last military actions in Virginia, in conjunction with Gen. William Phillips, occurred from mid-April through the middle of June 1781 when British forces occupied Williamsburg and on April 21 destroyed the Virginia State Navy yard, a twenty-gun ship and warehouse on the Chickahominy River.[3] On April 27, the British destroyed most of what remained of the Virginia State Navy at Osborne's, a plantation and landing on the south side of the James River approximately ten miles below Richmond.

What followed was a series of British and American maneuvers that ultimately concluded with the siege of Yorktown and the British surrender to George Washington in October 1781. Prior to that, the British had landed at Gloucester Point in August 1781 to erect fortifications to protect the army encampment across the York River at Yorktown and the British ships anchored in the river. In addition, they wanted to prevent the Virginia militia from constructing cannon placements at points from which they could fire on British activity in the river. From early August and most of September, British troops frequently engaged in foraging across Gloucester County for provisions for the army in Yorktown and the British garrison at Gloucester Point. The British also considered Kingston Parish a strategic location for protecting their activities in Gloucester, as was reported on August 15, 1781, in the *Pennsylvania Gazette*, Philadelphia:

> It is *reported*, that a detachment of Earl Cornwallis's army, under command of Brigadier-General O'Hara, have landed in Gloucester county, Virginia, near the mouth of the York river, in the vicinity of which, on New-Point-Comfort, it is asserted, they are to erect a strong fortification.

The first conflict of the Yorktown campaign actually started at Gloucester Point on September 29 and 30 when 1,500 men in the Virginia militia attacked the strong British position and earthworks that by then included nineteen cannon and seven hundred men. The Virginia militia, under the command of John Mercer, defeated the British on October 2 and, in doing so, significantly diminished the strategic position of the British in Yorktown and eliminated a critical supply line from Gloucester Point.[4]

Thomas Hall's account of British barges attempting to enter the East River is one of the few references of enemy activity so close to his neighborhood and the parish village, which at that time was called Westville and is now known as Mathews Courthouse. The distance from the mouth of the East River to where the Hall family lived was two and a half miles. Thomas seems to have been stationed at New Point Comfort, a point of land easily assaulted by British tenders, longboats, and barges attempting to come ashore to seize provisions, including livestock, firewood, and crops, and to refill water casks. The distance by road from his house to New Point Comfort was six miles, with another mile to the lighthouse. The west side of the point extending to the lighthouse had a water depth of ten feet within less than one hundred feet of the shore. Depths of twenty feet were found less than a mile from the southern tip of the point, adequate depth for most of the ships used by the British navy. For example, twenty-eight-gun frigate HMS *Carysfort* had a draft of fourteen feet in the stern while the sixty-four-gun, two-decked HMS *Eagle* required seventeen feet.

Thomas missed being involved in the final days of the war leading to the surrender in October 1781 of the British army by Lord Cornwallis at Yorktown. He had marched with his unit as far as Ware Church but returned home due to illness. His unit continued to just north of Gloucester Point to help contain the British, who were attempting to maintain that strategic location. He never received an official notification of discharge and evidently was not called into service again after October 1781.

In 1782, at age nineteen, Thomas was a veteran of the Revolutionary War and the man of the house. His father had died probably about two years earlier; his older brother Spencer was living in Salem, Massachusetts; and his older brother Robert seems not to have been living at home at this time. His sisters, Betsey, Nanny, and Joicey, were all married by this time and living elsewhere. Thomas would live about another twelve years with his mother, until she died.

In about 1790, Thomas married Mary Gayle, a family long associated with the Halls, including military service and living in the same neighborhood.* At this time Thomas would have

* Based on the fee book for the clerk of the court in chancery suit for 1793, Mary had nine siblings: Sarah Gayle, who married Randolph Miller; a second Sarah, who married John Pead of the same neighborhood; Mathias Gayle; Joseph Gayle; John Edwards Gayle, born August 11, 1769; Catharine Gayle, who married Holder Hudgins; and Caty Gayle, who was born on August 15, 1766. The court action involved the appointment of the infants, under the age of twenty-one, Christopher Gayle and Thomas Gayle. (Billups Papers, 65 B49, Earl Gregg Swem Library, College of William & Mary, Williamsburg, VA, and Emma R. Matheny and Helen K. Yates, comps., *Kingston Parish Register, Gloucester and Mathews Counties, 1749–1827* [Richmond, VA, 1963], 54.)

been approximately twenty-six years old and Mary about twenty. Mary's parents are thought to have been Thomas Gayle and Joyce Gayle, perhaps cousins, who were married on December 15, 1763, in Kingston Parish.[5] Thomas Gayle owned land nearby, 189 acres in 1790.[6]

Thomas Hall may have gone to sea in the years after the Revolutionary War. Francis Armistead of the District of East River referenced a Captain Hall transporting pipes of wine in a letter written on June 5, 1807, to "any Officer of the Revenue of the United States." The letter "certif[ies] that four Pipes of London Particular Maderia Wine imported in the Schooner Eliza Capt Hall on the 6th day of August 1806 and entered at the Port of New York." The letter continues with a list of the pipes of wine, including the number and gallons, and states that it "was regularly imported into this district from the afore said Port of New York." The wine was owned by John Patterson, a well-known resident of Mathews and near neighbor of Thomas Hall, and the letter explains that Patterson lost the certificates required for each pipe. Francis Armistead was instructing the Revenue Service not to seize the cargo for want of the certificates.[7]

The origin of the letter being the District of East River and the well-known Mathews names, Patterson and Armistead, give strong circumstantial evidence that "Capt Hall" is Thomas Hall. The future shipbuilder would have had significant experience and mastery of ship handling and with what was required for constructing a well-found vessel. If this was in fact Thomas Hall, he would have been a mariner for at least several years prior to 1806, beginning as an ordinary seaman and over time learning the art of navigation and the other skills required to be a captain. In 1806 Thomas was forty-two, suggesting that he may have previously spent many years at sea; twenty-five years had elapsed since he had served in the Revolution.

After the wedding, Thomas and Mary probably continued to live in the household of his mother. Although the census of 1810 for Mathews County, with pages missing, does not include the Hall household, Thomas and Mary had at least four children by then. Their first child, Sarah Ann, was born in 1794. Robert was born about 1800, Thomas Jr. about 1802, and John W. between 1803 and 1806. A second daughter, Mary Ann, was born in 1813 or 1814.*

The earliest record to survive for the Hall household is the US Census for 1820. Although the enumeration began in August 1820 and ended thirteen months later at the end of August 1821, census instructions required that the count be made as of August 1, 1820; however, it is believed that the count was often recorded on the day of the census taker's visit. On the day

* The children's birth years are calculated from the 1850 census. Unfortunately, church records of births, marriages, and deaths were no longer maintained after the demise of the Church of England following the Revolutionary War, and state of Virginia laws did not require demographic record keeping at that time.

of the census, Thomas Hall's household included eleven white people, seven males and four females, and nineteen slaves, eight males and eleven females. Other than Thomas and Mary, age fifty-six and fifty, eight whites were eighteen or younger, six boys and two girls. There was one white female who was between sixteen and twenty-six who may have been their married daughter, Sarah Ann. She married William Hurst on November 17, 1808, but may have been staying with her parents at the time of the census as William was frequently at sea. Two of the six white males and one of the younger white females can be identified as children of Thomas and Mary, but the remaining four males and one younger female are unknown. They were under the age of ten and were probably not children of Mary given her age. The census recorded the occupation of two white males as being in "Manufactures" with none in agriculture or commerce. Manufactures in Mathews at this time was most often shipbuilding.

The nineteen slaves may have been members of one family as there were a male and female each over the age of forty-five, four males and six females between the ages of fourteen and forty-five who may have been their children, and three males and four females under the age of fourteen who may have been grandchildren. Some of the male slaves likely worked in Thomas Hall's shipyard.

Other than land transactions, little is known of the activities of Thomas during the twenty-nine years from the time of his marriage in 1790 until the first documentation concerning shipbuilding in 1819, at age fifty-five. But, it is likely that he spent most or all of his adult years at sea and in boat and ship construction.

Where land ownership is concerned, Thomas continued to own forty-four and a half acres and in 1797 acquired an additional twenty and a half acres from the estate of his brother Robert, who died about 1787. In 1800 his holdings were reduced by thirteen and a half acres. The tax book for that year shows two entries, one for forty-four and a half acres and one for seven acres, suggesting that the parcels were not adjacent. However, beginning in 1806 Thomas was taxed for fifty-one and a half acres recorded as one entry; thus, perhaps the two parcels in fact did adjoin. The entry remained the same until 1814 when Thomas acquired an additional acre, bringing the total to fifty-two and a half acres, a holding that would remain unchanged until the disposition of his estate in 1840.

In addition, Thomas acquired fifty acres in 1818 and sold thirty-seven and a half acres of the tract to John R. Lewis in 1819. It is not known what happened to the remaining twelve and a half acres because in 1819 Thomas was taxed for just the first fifty-two and a half acres.

Thomas Hall obtained a retail merchandising license in 1802 and may have renewed it in subsequent years although the surviving record is mostly incomplete. It was not uncommon for shipbuilders to also engage in trade, but other than the issuance of the license there is nothing in the record that describes the location or nature of retailing or how long Thomas might have remained in the retail business.

In 1814 Thomas acquired twenty-five acres of glebe land and resold the entire parcel a year later to Molly Terril and others. He acquired additional land in the Glebe Neck from Mann Billups as surveyed on January 21, 1830. The parcel contained approximately forty-five and one-quarter acres, and Thomas continued to own it until his death when it was sold to Elijah Barnum.[8]

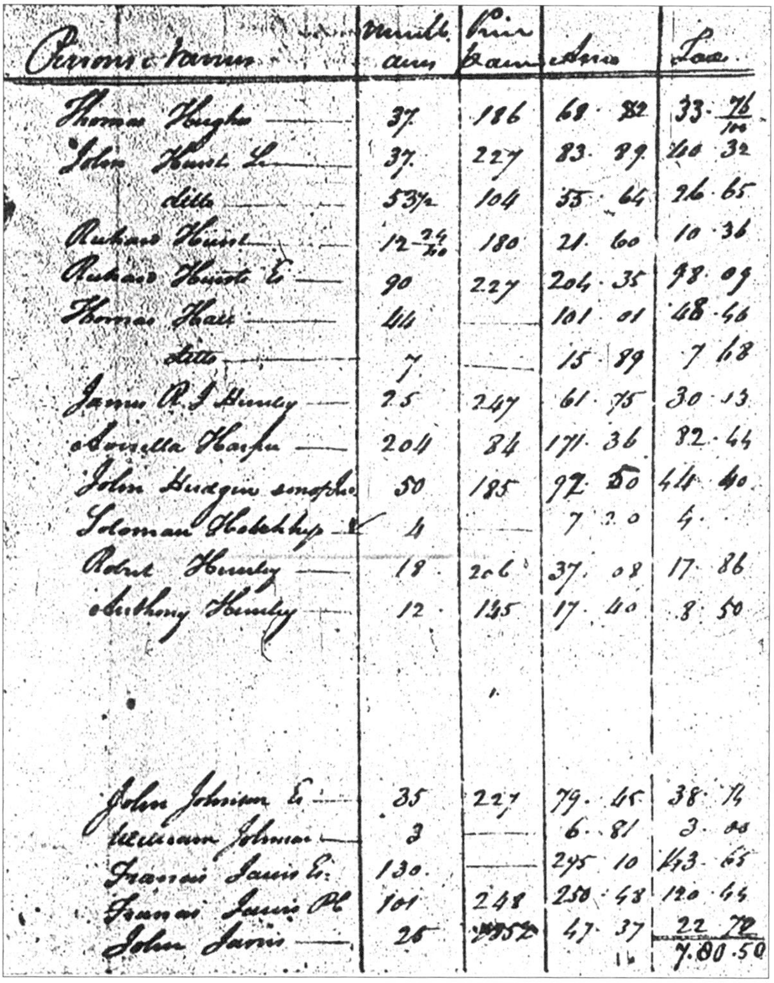

| Persons Names | [illegible] | [illegible] | [illegible] | Tax |
|---|---|---|---|---|
| Thomas Hughes | 37 | 186 | 68·82 | 33·76/100 |
| John Hurst Sr | 37 | 227 | 83·89 | 40·32 |
| ditto | 53½ | 104 | 55·64 | 26·65 |
| Richard Hurst | 12 24/40 | 180 | 21·60 | 10·36 |
| Richard Hurst Jr | 90 | 227 | 204·35 | 98·09 |
| Thomas Hall | 44 | | 101·01 | 48·46 |
| ditto | 7 | | 15·89 | 7·68 |
| [illegible] | 25 | 247 | 61·75 | 30·13 |
| [illegible] | 204 | 84 | 171·36 | 82·44 |
| John Hudgins [illegible] | 50 | 185 | 92·50 | 44·40 |
| [illegible] | 4 | | 7·20 | 4· |
| Robert [illegible] | 18 | 206 | 37·08 | 17·86 |
| Anthony [illegible] | 12 | 145 | 17·40 | 8·50 |
| John Johnson Jr | 35 | 227 | 79·45 | 38·14 |
| William Johnson | 3 | | 6·81 | 3·00 |
| Francis [illegible] Sr | 130 | | 295·10 | 143·65 |
| Francis [illegible] | 101 | 248 | 250·48 | 120·44 |
| John [illegible] | 25 | [illegible] | 47·37 | 22·72 |
| | | | | 7·80·50 |

*Figure* 33 The ledger page of the 1800 tax list showing Thomas Hall with two parcels of land, one for forty-four acres and the second for seven acres. He is preceded by several entries related to the Hurst family. Courtesy of the Library of Virginia, Richmond.

In 1820 Thomas purchased four acres from the estate of Caleb Hunley, land that Hunley had owned from at least 1782, the year of the first tax list. This property was located four miles southeast from the courthouse in the East River district. It had a building valued at forty dollars; however, this was the first year that buildings were listed, and thus it may have been on the property for some time. This parcel would remain his until his death. This parcel may have been on Hunley Creek, now Weston Creek, and it may have been the location of Hall's shipyard. Four acres would have been adequate space for a yard building schooners. Other than this parcel, there is no record of Thomas owning waterfront property suitable for a shipyard, and thus he may have worked on leased land or on land of one of his partners or a family member.

A survey made by George Billups, county surveyor, sometime between 1804 and 1810, references a shipyard that suggests another possibility for the location of Thomas's business:

> Explanation of this plate or Figure—Begining at: A. a corner in (Joseph?) & (Hundley?) Gayle Runing thence S 29* W 103 poles to B. a corner in [?] Gayle thence S 7½ W 29 po. to C. a corner in said line near Gayles dweling house thence S 59 E by the shipyard to ye creek at D. thence meandering with the creek to E in [?] & [?] Hundley thence N 56 E 47 poles to F a corner White Gum on ye main Road thence Runing with ye main Road to the Begining Containing 53 Acres & 36 poles.
>
> The dividing line between Wm. Tomkins & Jos. Deggs Begining Runing to J. a small ceder on ye S. side of ye creek that makes to ye house thence to H near G. containing 14 Acres Ann Diers part. Begining at H. Runing N 68 E 60 poles to I thence Runing by marked trees persimon & grape thence to a small marked sassafras at K. 42 poles from A Containing 16 Acres the Remainder for Wm. Tomkins. Surveyd & divided by me
>
> G Billups CS [county surveyor]

The property was bounded on the south by Hunley Creek, on the east by the main road, and on the north and west by a Gayle family property. It was located just to the north and on the opposite side of the main road from Thomas's fifty-one and a half acres. The proximity suggests the strong possibility that his shipbuilding activities took place there, on land owned by either Gayle or Degge, but more likely Gayle as the survey did not indicate that the surveyed parcel actually contained the shipyard.

* A symbol for "degrees" appears inconsistently after relevant numbers in this survey.

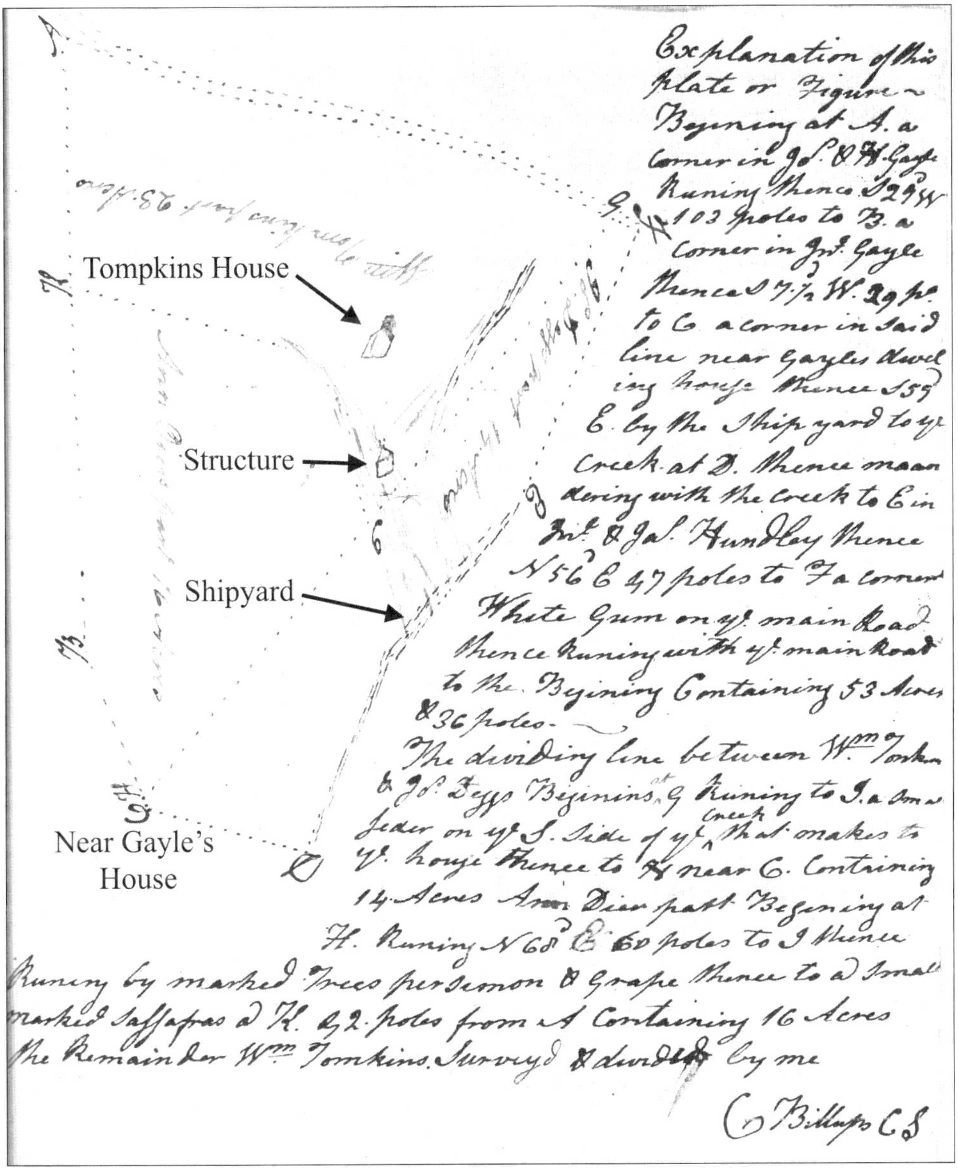


*Figure* 34 This survey, by G. Billups, the county surveyor between 1804 and 1810, identifies the location of a shipyard less than 0.4 miles by road from Thomas Hall's residence and possibly the yard he used to construct schooners in the late 1810s through the 1820s. While the sketch appears crude, the survey was remarkably accurate, and the land shown can be located today. The superimposed text and arrows show the approximate locations of the Tompkins and Gayle houses and the shipyard located on Hunley's Creek, now known as Weston Creek. From the Christopher Tompkins Papers, courtesy of the Virginia Historical Society, Richmond.

Adjoining this property to the west was a fifty-four-acre tract sold to John Patterson by John Gayle and Francis, his wife, and Josiah Gayle. The description in the indenture, dated June 11, 1805, based on a survey made by George Billups in March 1804, follows:

> Begining at A a corner on the creek in Joseph Degges's line at the ship yard thence N. 66° W. 26½ Poles to B a corner Sycamore stump on Joseph Degges & Nancy Dyers lines but now not to be seen. thence N. 3. E. 28 Poles to C. a corner in the said Nancy Dyers line. thence 27½°. E. 102 Poles to D. a corner on the lines of Joshua & Matt Gayle & William Tompkins calld in an old Survey the Read Oak Stump but not to be seen at this day. thence runing on the said Joshua & Matt Gayles line down the branch to a pine stump near the slave landing upon the head of the creek commonly calld the warehouse creek so noted in old Surveys of these lands. thence down the warehouse creek & up the creek commonly calld Hunleys creek agreably to their several meanders & with the shore of East River between the mouths of said creeks to the begining place containing by the aforsaid Survey fifty four acres.[9]

This property description mentioning "old Surveys of these lands" is one of the few that references landmarks of a much earlier period. The date of "old Surveys" is not known, but given the absence of landmarks from the early surveys, for example, "Read Oak Stump but not to be seen at this day," a gap of at least fifty years would not be unreasonable. Based on the survey, Warehouse Creek is the creek just north of Weston Creek, the one that was damned to create a tidal raceway for a mill. The "slave landing" suggests a feature of the late seventeenth and early eighteenth centuries. Its location was on the south shore of the creek at a spot with deep water close to shore. Small boats and flats would have been used to transport cargoes to and from anchored vessels in the East River. A slave pen was probably nearby. The slave landing and warehouse references suggest a commercially active neighborhood, especially with its proximity to Williams Wharf.

Beginning in 1802 and continuing until 1844, Williams Wharf on the East River, just two miles by road from the home of Thomas Hall, became an official port with a customhouse and a government agent authorized to register new ships into service, record changes in ownership, and document changes in the nature of trade of a vessel. The neighborhood was an active center for shipping and the trades necessary to provision and maintain ships. The East River hosted numerous shipyards, from small craft used for local river transport and fishing to large oceangoing schooners and brigs.

Shipyards for building average-size schooners, up to about 120 tons, did not require a large land area. The primary requirement was a relatively protected bank of a creek having a gentle slope and sufficient depth for launching a vessel. The yard would have had designated areas for sawing and shaping wood timbers, for constructing the ship, and for storing materials. Some yards also had forges for iron fabrication. There was often a shed or barnlike structure for storing tools and for fabricating small boats and specialized components of the schooner. This space would also have been used for "lofting," transferring the lines from a model, drawing, or pattern from a previously built ship to the unshaped timbers that would be used to build the ship.

The primary work of a small shipyard was typically repair, as merchant ships of the period were worked hard and needed periodic maintenance. There was probably a small boat under construction at all times to fill in between large vessel repair work or during inclement weather if a shed was available.

The construction of a new ship was undertaken as a speculative venture of the shipwright and others or on the order of a merchant or another shipowner. If the construction was on speculation, the project would have been done during reduced demand for repair services, which was typically a more profitable use of the yard.

Another possibility for Thomas's shipyard involves the Gayles, his wife's family. On May 1, 1805, William B. Tompkins purchased a $4^{120}/_{160}$–acre tract of land from John Patterson for the sum of seventy-five dollars. The property and two additional parcels had previously been in the estate of Matthew Gayle. Matthew Gayle was a shipbuilder, and his shipyard was in the neighborhood, as indicated in an advertisement from the *Virginia Gazette*, April 2, 1779:

> The subscriber has for sale, the hull, masts, and yards of a new vessel, intended for a brig, completely finished and ready to launch, of the following dimensions: $56^1/_2$ feet keel straight rabbit, 20 feet 2 inches beam, and 8 feet hold. She was built by *Matthew Gayle*, at *East* river warehouse. For terms apply to the printer, or *Francis Willis*, Esq; in *Gloucester* county. JOSEPH SMITH.

The description of the Patterson tract, a good example of how descriptions were made in deeds at the time, places the location adjacent to Hunley Gayle's land, which adjoined Thomas Hall's property along the northern boundary:

> Bounded on the north by the Main County road as it now runs on the East by the Land of said William B. Tompkins on the south by Nancy Dyers Land on the West by Gayles Land. Begining at D. calld a corner read oak Stump markd in the Platt in Joshua & Matt Gayles Line thence S 27° E 14 Poles to E on the main road & corner at the road. thence S 47° E $18^1/_2$ Poles to F a corner on the side of the main road in Gayle & Tompkins line near Thomas Hall's thence runing in a direction with the dividing Line between Thomas Hall & Hunley Gayle S 65° W 42 Poles

> to G a mark & corner on Tompkin's ditch noted in the Platt. thence with the Ditch N 31° W 4 Poles to intersect the Line between John Gayle's & Tompkins's Land.[10]

Hunley Gayle was also a shipbuilder, having launched the 103-ton schooner *Virginia* in 1826. He and Hall may have built ships in the same yard given the proximity of their lands and to Hunley Creek. Hunley was apparently a prosperous farmer, and the description of his estate sale gives a general added understanding of material conditions of families in the neighborhood. The following advertisement is from the October 29, 1833, *Richmond Enquirer*:

> VALUABLE NEGROES, STOCK, &c. FOR SALE.—On Wednesday, Oct. 30th, (if fair, if not, the next fair day,) *we will sell*, at the late residence of Hunley Gale, in Matthews county, the whole of his personal *estate*, consisting of about 16 very valuable *slaves*, stock of horses, cattle, sheep and hogs, farming utensils, household and kitchen furniture, and the crop of corn, oats and fodder. The slaves will be sold for cash, and the other property on a credit of 9 months. Bonds, with approved security, will be required of the purchaser, before the property is removed. The sale will be continued from day to day until the whole is sold. CHRISTOPHER TOMPKINS, JOHN D. JARVIS, Exec'rs of Hunley Gale.

The War of 1812 included a period of approximately two years, 1813–1814, of frequent British naval activity in the lower Chesapeake Bay, and especially in the vicinity of New Point Comfort and Mobjack Bay, that was similar to naval activity during the Revolutionary War some thirty-five years earlier. The people of Mathews County were in a dangerous situation without effective naval resources to discourage British activity. Residents could clearly see enemy ships in the bay and even in their neighborhoods along the North and East Rivers.

William Hurst, Thomas Hall's son-in-law, enlisted at the beginning of the war, served for more than two years, 1813–1815, and was honorably discharged in Mathews County in February 1815. William's service was unusual in that he first was a soldier in a rifle company that was attached to the Sixty-First Regiment of the Virginia Militia, but after three months he was made master of a small vessel engaged in carrying messages between Mathews and Fortress Monroe in Hampton and provisions from Norfolk and other points of supply to military units in Mathews County. He was given the assignment because he had been a sea captain before the war and was well-acquainted with navigation in the Chesapeake Bay. On one occasion William's vessel was chased by a Brittish ship, and to save his crew, he ran his vessel aground and escaped ashore. The British burned and totally destroyed William's vessel.

On March 28, 1855, William appeared in the Mathews County Courthouse to apply for bounty land. He stated that he had earlier been granted eighty acres as authorized by congress in September 1850. Sixteen years later, on September 29, 1871, William's widow, Sarah

Ann, appeared at court to apply for a pension based on William's service. She stated that her husband died in Mathews County on October 14, 1857, and that their wedding occurred on November 17, 1808, officiated by the Reverend William Williams. At the time of their wedding, William was twenty-one years old and Sarah Ann was just fifteen. Sarah Ann's brother Thomas stated that he had been at the marriage of William and Sarah Ann, which took place in his father's house. He further said that he had been with William when he died and assisted in his burial.[11]

Little is known about ships from Mathews being involved in the War of 1812. However, William Tompkins of Mathews County asked the British consul in Norfolk for a letter requesting respectful treatment should he be boarded by a British ship. The consulate provided the following:

> British Consul's Office, Norfolk,
> Virginia, 6 April 1811
>
> Sir,
>
> The Bearer Mr. Tompkins, who is a Gentleman of much respectability, being about to proceed to Lisbon in the American Brig Mohawk, Samuel Smith Commander, with a Cargo of Flour and Corn, I beg leave to introduce him to whatever Civilities and good offices he may stand in need of and it may be agreeable to you to shew him.
>
> With great respect, I have the honour to be, Sir,
> Your most obedient humble Servant,
> Jno. Hamilton
>
> [To] The Captain, or Commander,
> of any of His Majesty's Ships
> or Vessels of War.[12]

Newspapers recorded several events involving Mathews County and the war. The following chronological series of reports offers a perspective of how the War of 1812 affected the people of Mathews.

> The following is extracted from a letter received by a gentleman in Norfolk, from his friend, dated East River, March 11.
>
> "We are this day all under arms; the enemy, occupies Mobjac Bay, and one of

their launches and two tenders chased a pilot boat into the mouth of East River this morning. The little fleet of sharp vessels that lay in Severn have all moved into East River, and some of them as high up as they can get. Two large Baltimore schooners about 300 tons each, armed, having together about 100 men, are moored across the river before my door; it is expected an attempt will be made to cut them out this night.—We have on duty one company of artillery with two field pieces, and three companies of infantry, placed in a situation to act with the armed vessels in case of an attack.

"Capt. Sinclair with his flotilla, commands the mouth of the Pianketank river; he ran into that place two nights ago, and found anchored there a large suspicious looking schooner; he ordered one of his boats to fire a shot ahead of her, she immediately returned a broadside; a sharp action commenced: the schooner cut her cables and got off, but in a dreadful shattered situation, her booby hatch, quarter boards, rails and many other pieces, with an officer's military hat were found afloat in the morning, and we have a report to-day that a schooner has been seen sunk off Gwinn's Island, with her yards standing.

"The British have captured within these 3 or 4 days, within New Point Comfort and Gwyn's Island, 8 or 10 vessels, some of them with 5 or 600 barrels of flour, and report says a vessel with 500 barrels of Pork, from George Town bound to Norfolk, said belong to Mr. Masosn, and for the navy, has also been captured." (*Poulson's American Daily Advertiser*, Philadelphia, PA, March 25, 1813)

TROUBLE WITH THE BLACKS.

*Baltimore Whig office, April* 3, 1813.

IMPORTANT INFORMATION.

By capt. Weems, direct from Hampton, we learn that the British squadron still retained their former position in Hampton Roads; that a conspiracy among the negroes had taken place, but was detected. . . .

At Gloucester court-house, an attempt was made by the blacks to murder three slaves, who refused to join in the conspiracy. Several troops of horse have been ordered out to seize suspected blacks. (*Columbian*, New York, NY, April 5, 1813)

Eight negroes have been condemned to be hanged in Mathew's county, for personating Englishmen in the night, and robbing a Mr. John Ripley. (*Providence Gazette*, Providence, RI, April 10, 1813)

The schr. Bona. Dameron, from Havanna for this port, was captured 3d ult. off New Point Comfort, and carried to Bermuda. (*Alexandria Daily Gazette, Commercial & Political,* Alexandria, VA, April 16, 1813)

The sch Little Jane, Mitchell, bound to Norfolk, returned this morning, having gone down as far [as] Rappahannock, where he fell in with the Comet, and was informed that a 74, a frigate, 3 schooners and a lugger were off New Point Comfort. The schooners were under way, standing off and on, in sight of the ships. Left there on Sunday afternoon. Capt. Gordon had gone down near enough to ascertain their force, and was watching their motions. (*Baltimore Patriot*, Baltimore, MD, June 2, 1813)

The boat FRIENDS' ADVENTURE, captain Drake, which sailed from Norfolk on Friday, the 26th ult. bound to Baltimore, with a cargo of tar, was chased on shore at New-Point Comfort, about 2 o'clock on Saturday morning, by 5 of the enemy's barges, belonging to two brigs at anchor off that Point; the vessel and cargo totally lost to the owners—a part of the tar, we understand, has been saved by the people on shore. (*Columbian*, New York, NY, December 6, 1813)

The enemy landed at New Point Comfort on the 29th ult. and destroyed the oil used for the light house; they nearly demolished the dwelling house of the keeper, and fixed the British flag on the top of the light house! (*Norfolk Herald*, Norfolk, VA, January 25, 1814)[13]

*Copy of a letter to the Editors, dated Matthews county, (Vir.) March 18.*

"SIRS—I yesterday visited the camp, near New-Point Comfort; and had the pleasure of seeing one of the handsomest skirmishes, I ever witnessed. About 10 o'clock, captain Weedon, who commands at this post, received information from a trooper, that the enemy showed a disposition to cross over on the main, with about fifty or sixty men. In a few minutes, about the same number was ordered to advance and meet them, which was promptly obeyed, with the captain at their head. The fire commenced equally severe on both sides for about fifteen minutes, when the enemy was compelled to take shelter under the cover of some sand hills. At this moment a barge came in to their assistance, and commenced a fire from a 12 pound cannon, which was returned from a concealed six; which was continued with great warmth for a few minutes, when she had to make the best of her way to the beach, being in a sinking condition, having several shot through her.—Here sirs, it will give me great pleasure to speak of captain Weeden, as he deserves.—More determined bravery never was displayed by any man, although being in the most imminent danger throughout the whole of this affair; having his horse shot down at the most trying moment, yet no signs of fear or confusion was discovered. I am happy to inform you we lost not a man; and while we have such officers as him, we have every thing to hope and nothing to fear." (*Baltimore Patriot*, Baltimore, MD, March 25, 1814)

About seventy negroes from Gloucester and Matthews County, Virginia, have lately joined the British. (*Rhode-Island American, and General Advertiser*, Providence, RI, April 5, 1814)

We learn by letters from Lancaster county, Va. under date of the fst inst. that the force of the enemy at New Point Comfort, on the 30th ult. consisted of one frigate and one schooner, only; that during the preceding week considerable desertion among the blacks took place in the neighborhood of Gloucester court-house, to the number of twenty-eight in one night, and that measures have been adopted to prevent their future elopement. (*Columbian*, New York, NY, April 11, 1814)

*Extract of a letter from Leaven Gayle, Lieut. Colonel of the 61st Regt. to the Adjutant General of Va. dated Mathews County, May 26.*

"The principal station of the enemy in our Bay is Tangier Islands, but they continue a line of cruizers of light and large vessels from thence to Lynhaven Bay; a part of them continually hovering close in, along the shores from New Point Comfort to the mouth of the Rappahannock River, and within 15 or 20 days past they have ascended our principal water courses, say East, North and Piankitank Rivers, in large force, with barges of the largest class, not less than six in number with from 30 to 40 men in each barge, up to the head of the navigation, and have taken the soundings of these rivers. They generally approach in the night, when none of their vessels are in immediate view, and arrive at the head of the water-courses about day-light. The first visit of the enemy in this way, was on the night of the 1st instant to East River, when they captured the fine schooner Grecian, of Baltimore; the loss to the owner by this capture in vessel and cargo is computed at $35,000 and not a cent insured." (*Commercial Advertiser*, New York, NY, June 10, 1814)

*MOVEMENTS OF THE ENEMY.*

> By a gentleman from below we learn verbally, that on Wednesday last, the British made an attempt with their barges to land in Matthews county and burn a fine new ship on the stocks belonging to Mr. Tabb, but were opposed by the militia and repulsed with loss.—A second attempt it is thought has been since made, as a frigate and brig were observed to go down to Lynnhaven and return on Tuesday —and a firing was heard on Saturday in the direction of Matthews, the result of which, when our infermant left York, was not known. (*Baltimore Patriot*, Baltimore, MD, June 13, 1814)

> A report from Williamsburgh, Virginia, states, that a number of British barges were attacked near New-Point, in Matthew's county, by our troops, and after a sharp contest the barges sheered off, leaving 5 of our militia-men killed and 6 wounded—the loss of the British not known. (*Rhode-Island Republican*, Newport, RI, June 29, 1814)

The War of 1812 brought disruption to Mathews County in many ways, including the economy. When the war ended, however, there was a strong rebound in trade and in the demand for ships, schooners, and other types of vessels. It is unknown when Thomas Hall joined the ranks of shipbuilders, but the first record of his shipbuilding activities was the enrollment, the registration of a new vessel, that occurred on December 17, 1819, for the schooner *Sarah Ann*. Built in Mathews County in 1819, she was described as having one deck, two masts, a square stern, no quarter galleries, and no figurehead. Her dimensions were length of keel, 55 $^{8}/_{12}$ feet; width, 18 feet $1^{1}/_{2}$ inches; and depth of the hold, $6^{1}/_{2}$ feet. She was rated at 55 $^{60}/_{95}$ tons. Mathews shipwrights were noted for building high-performance schooners, and Thomas's schooners seem to have typified the reputation.[14]

The *Sarah Ann*'s owners were Thomas Hall; William Hurst, Thomas's son-in-law; Christopher Tompkins, a wealthy neighbor; and James H. Roy, also a wealthy landowner, all of Mathews. Thomas is identified as the master ship carpenter and Hurst as her first master, or captain. The *Sarah Ann* was probably named for Thomas's daughter, who was also William Hurst's wife. She was initially registered for coastal trade, but she was reregistered on March 21, 1820, for foreign trade and again on April 21, 1821, when owners William Hurst, who continued as master, James H. Roy, and Thomas Hall sold their interests. The next owner was Raymond G. Savignace of New York City. The schooner's ownership changed again in 1824 and 1825, with the 1825 entry recorded as being in New Orleans, afterwhich the record is lost.

The accounts at John Patterson's store in Mathews provide an understanding of the times from a retail perspective. According to his account, between July 1 and December

16, 1819, William Hurst purchased sugar, coffee, rum, tobacco, linen, whiskey, cloth, silk, buttons, thread, pepper, scissors, and two blankets. Matthew Gayle, from August 1819 to January 1820, purchased tobacco, cigars, ribbon, gloves, buckshot, flints, a vest pattern, silk, a toothbrush, a wool hat, a pair of suspenders, yards of cloth, and a pair of stockings.[15]

Between June 19 and December 23, 1819, James Saunders, perhaps related to John H. Saunders who married Thomas's granddaughter Sarah, sister of Thomas Spencer Hall, purchased ribbons, muslin, silk "per wife,"* salt, nails, a cashmere shawl, cotton, a cotton ball, pins, a yard of flannel "per wife," and a stone pot. Thomas Hall paid the entire amount on December 23, an indication that Saunders may have been employed by Thomas. Saunders may have been an apprentice because he was registered as the builder of the forty-nine-ton schooner *Spread Eagle*, which was launched in Mathews in 1824.

Saunders owned land on the west side of Pudding Creek that was once part of the glebe land and had been formerly owned by John R. Lewis. The tract containing twelve and a quarter acres was surveyed on September 5, 1818, by Issac Foster, county surveyor, and adjoined a second tract owned by Saunders on the south side of the surveyed parcel. It too was on the creek.[16] As mentioned earlier, Thomas Hall also owned land nearby on glebe land, and he purchased additional glebe land for his daughter and son-in-law, William Hurst.

Mary Hall, Thomas's wife, purchased a quarter yard of "Bombayett" on March 14 and a bottle of snuff on August 7, 1820. The purchases were charged to Thomas Hall on October 13, 1820.†

The account books for John Patterson's store list a large number of items and materials used in ship construction, including numerous entries made during October through December 1819 for Thomas Hall. Although the account is titled "Schooner Thomas Hall," the entries are for the account of Thomas Hall, the owner of the schooner *Sarah Ann*, which was then being constructed, not the schooner *Thomas Hall*, which was built in 1822.

Included in the account were gallons of oil, over a quarter ton of iron, canvas, a barrel of tar, gallons of paint oil, white lead (used in paint), nails, putty, brushes, lampblack (used in paint), varnish, red lead (used in paint), turpentine, yellow paint, screws, a pair of hinges, padlocks, cupboard locks, panes of glass, steel, a set of knives and forks, three spoons, a

* "Per wife" meant that it was ordered by his wife.

† Accounts often were not settled until customers had the cash.

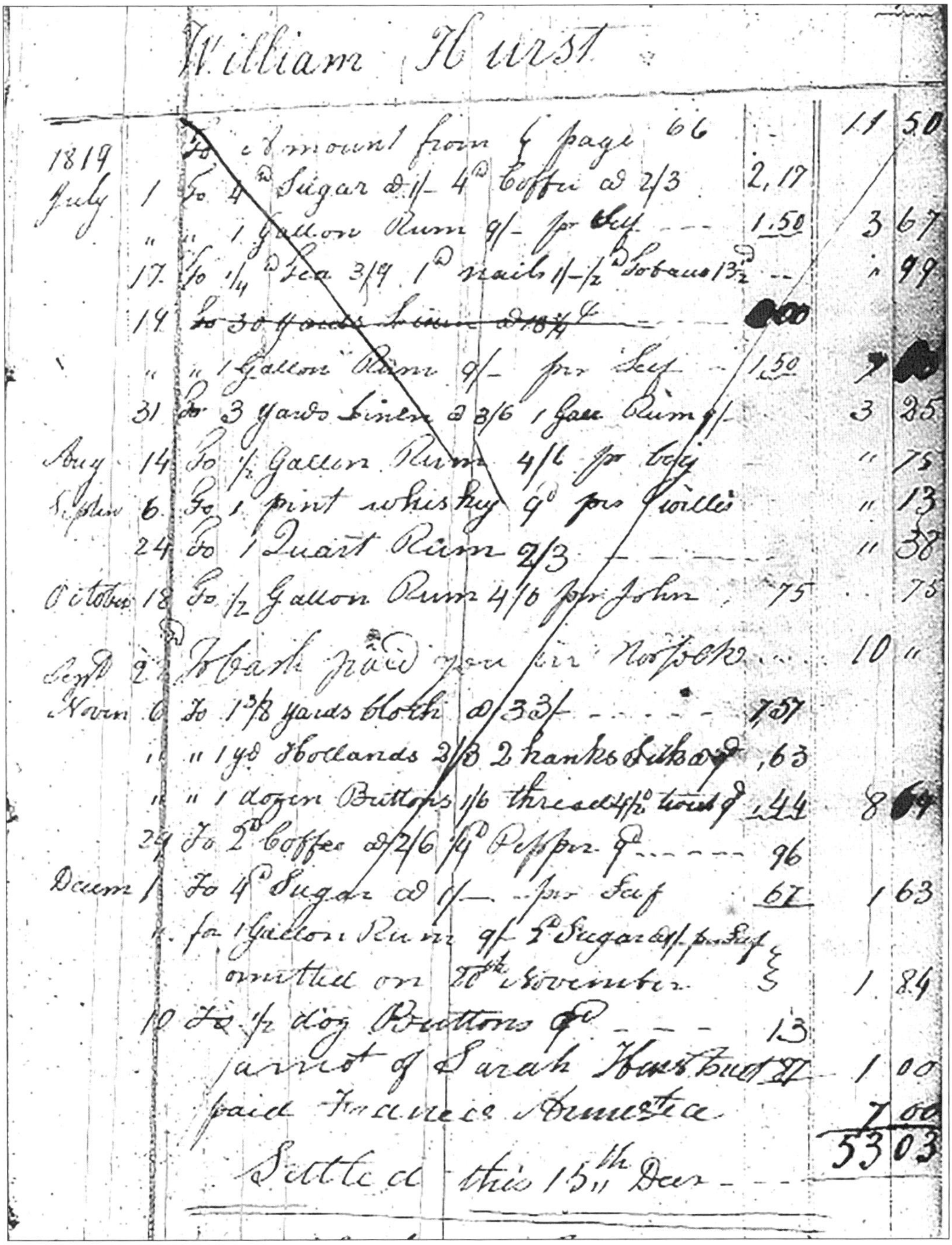

William Hurst

| | | | | |
|---|---|---|---|---|
| | | To Amount from page 66 | | 11.50 |
| 1819 July | 1 | To 4 lb Sugar @ 1/- 4 lb Coffee @ 2/3 | 2.17 | |
| | " | " 1 Gallon Rum 9/- pr [illegible] | 1.50 | 3.67 |
| | 17 | To 1/4 lb Tea 3/9 1 lb nails 1/- 1/2 lb Tobacco 13 1/2 | | .99 |
| | 19 | ~~To 30 yards Linen @ 1/4~~ | [illegible] | |
| | " | " 1 Gallon Rum 9/- pr [illegible] | 1.50 | [illegible] |
| | 31 | To 3 yards Linen @ 3/6 1 gall Rum 9/- | | 3.25 |
| Aug | 14 | To 1/2 Gallon Rum 4/6 pr [illegible] | | .75 |
| Septem | 6 | To 1 pint whiskey 9d pr [illegible] | | .13 |
| | 24 | To 1 Quart Rum 2/3 | | .38 |
| October | 18 | To 1/2 Gallon Rum 4/6 pr John | .75 | .75 |
| Sept | 2 | To Cash paid you in Norfolk | | 10 " |
| Novm | 6 | To 1 3/8 yards Cloth @ 3/3 | 7.57 | |
| | " | " 1 yd Hollands 2/3 2 hanks Silk @ [illegible] | .63 | |
| | " | " 1 dozen Buttons 1/6 thread 4 1/2 [illegible] | .44 | 8.64 |
| | 24 | To 2 lb Coffee @ 2/6 1/4 lb Pepper 9d | .96 | |
| Decem | 1 | To 4 lb Sugar @ 1/- pr [illegible] | .67 | 1.63 |
| | " | for 1 Gallon Rum 9/- 4 lb Sugar @ 1/- [illegible] omitted on 20th November | | 1.84 |
| | 10 | To 1/2 doz Buttons @ [illegible] | .13 | |
| | | amount of Sarah Hurst [illegible] | | 1.00 |
| | | paid Frances Armistead | | 7.00 |
| | | | | 53.03 |
| | | Settled this 15th Decr | | |

*Figure* 35 A page from an account book of John Patterson's store showing purchases and payments for William Hurst from July 1 through December 16, 1819. Courtesy of the John D. Rockefeller Jr. Library, Colonial Williamsburg Foundation, Williamsburg, VA.

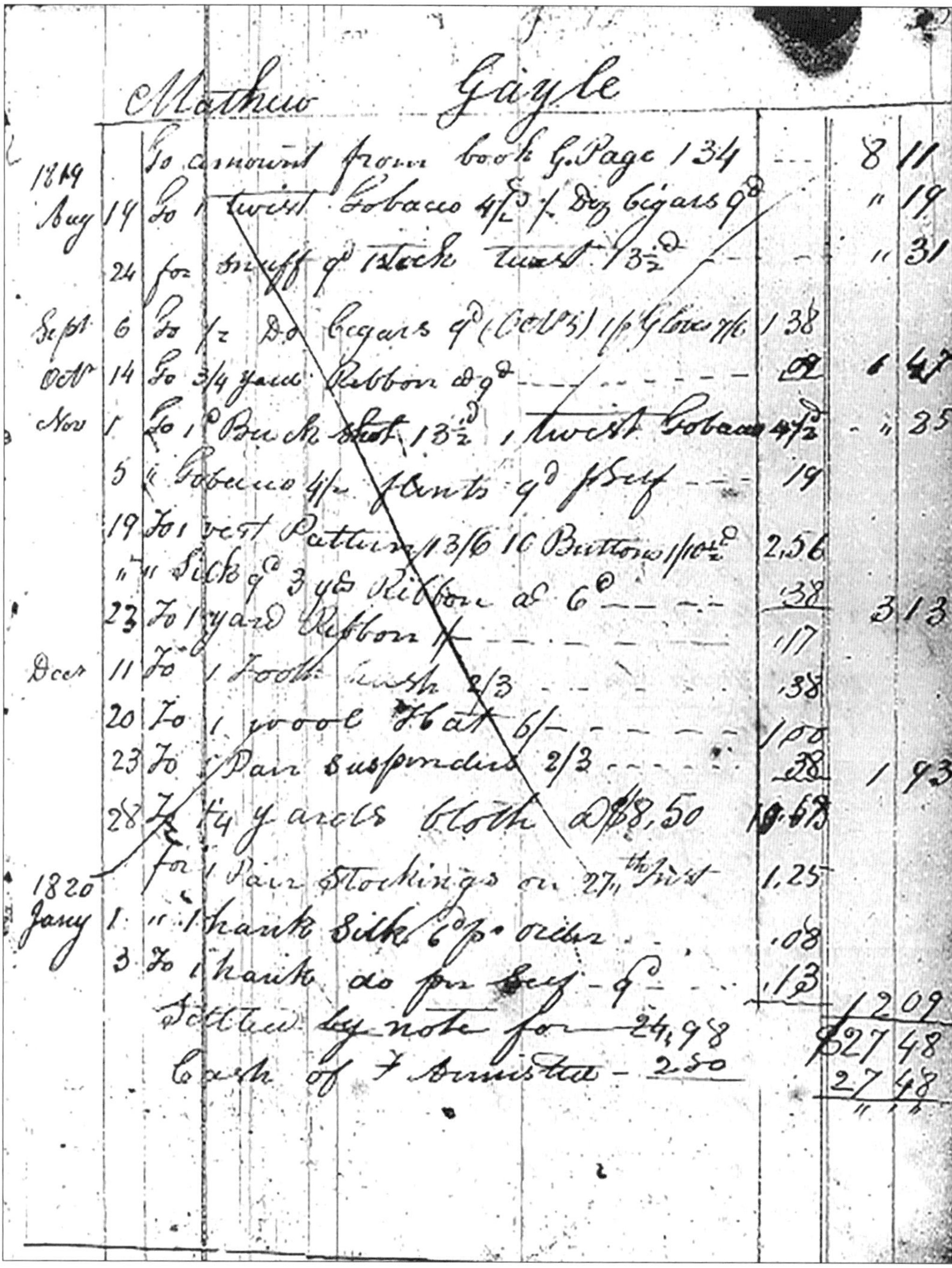
Mathew Gayle
To amount from book G. Page 134 ... 8 11
1819 Aug 19 To 1 twist Tobacco 4½d ½ Doz Cigars 9d ... " 19
24 for snuff 9d Black twist 1 3½d ... " 31
Sept 6 To ½ Do Cigars 9d (Oct 5) 1/6 Gloves 7/6 1 38
Octr 14 To 3/4 yard Ribbon @ 9d ... [illegible] 1 47
Nov 1 To 1 lb Buck shot 13½d, 1 twist Tobacco 4½ ... " 25
5 " Tobacco 4½ Pants 9d Self ... 19
19 To 1 vest Pattern 13/6 16 Buttons 1/10½d 2,56
" " Silk 9d 3 yds Ribbon @ 6d ... 38 3 13
23 To 1 yard Ribbon ... 17
Decr 11 To 1 Tooth brush 2/3 ... 38
20 To 1 wool Hat 6/ ... 1 00
23 To 1 Pair suspenders 2/3 ... 38 1 93
28 To 1¼ yards Cloth @ $8,50 [illegible]
For 1 Pair Stockings on 27th Inst 1,25
1820 Jany 1 " 1 hank Silk 6d p. order .08
3 To 1 hank do for Self 9 .13 12 09
Settled by note for 24,98 27 48
Cash of F Armistead 2 50 27 48

*Figure* 36 A page from an account book of John Patterson's store showing purchases and payments for Matthew Gayle from August 19, 1819, through January 3, 1820. Courtesy of the John D. Rockefeller Jr. Library, Colonial Williamsburg Foundation, Williamsburg, VA.

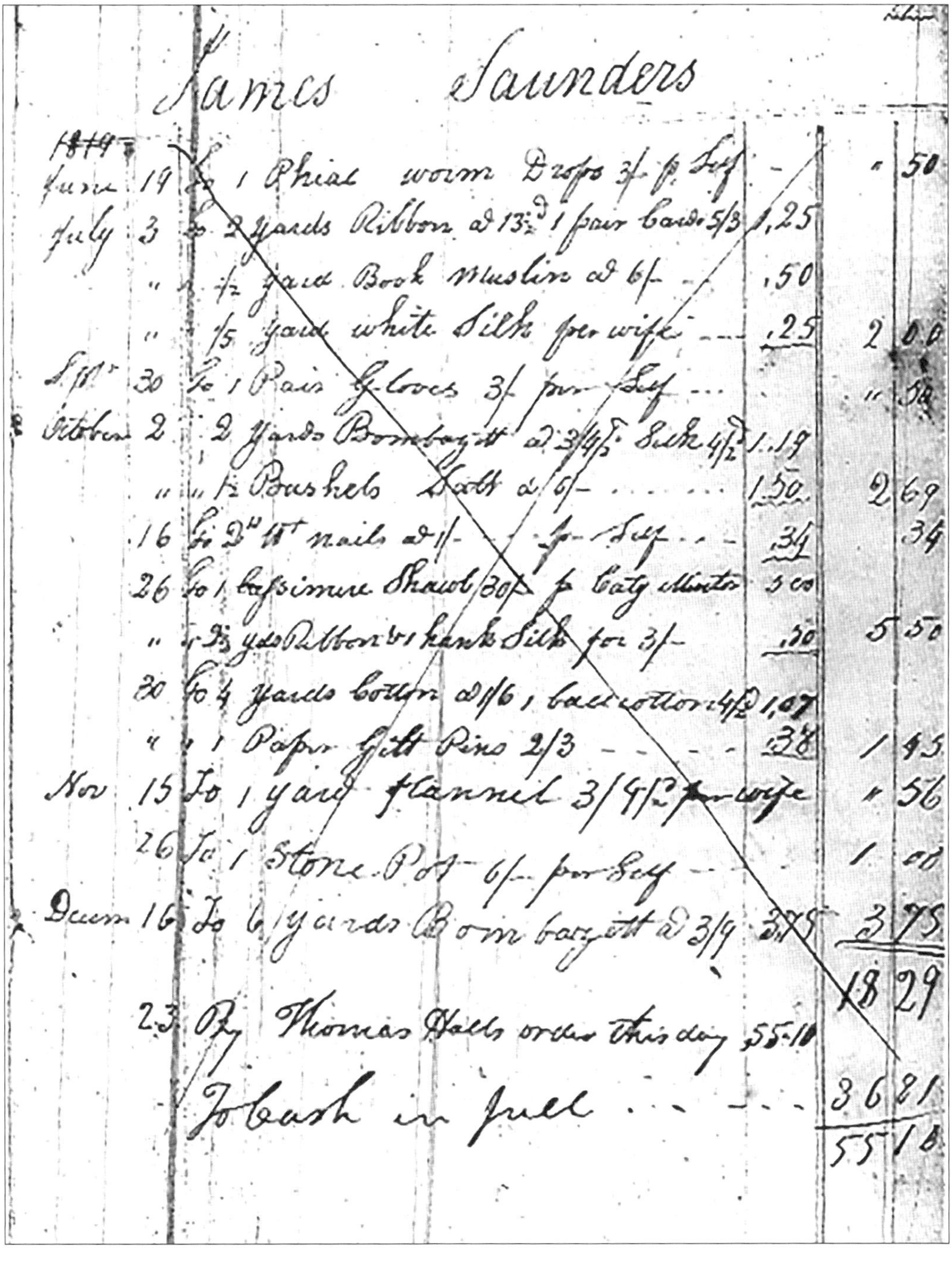

James Saunders

| | | | | |
|---|---|---|---|---|
| 1819 | | | | |
| June | 19 | To 1 Phial worm Drops 3/ p Self | | 50 |
| July | 3 | To 2 yards Ribbon at 13½d 1 pair Cards 5/3 | 1,25 | |
| | " | 1/2 yard Book Muslin at 6/ | ,50 | |
| | " | 1/5 yard white Silk per wife | ,25 | 2 00 |
| Septr | 30 | To 1 Pair Gloves 3/ per Self | | 50 |
| October | 2 | 2 yards Bombazett at 3/4½ Silk 4½ | 1.19 | |
| | " | 1½ Bushels Salt at 6/ | 1.50 | 2 69 |
| | 16 | To 2lb 4d nails at 1/ p Self | .34 | 34 |
| | 26 | To 1 Cassimere Shawl 30/ p Caty Minter | 5 00 | |
| | " | 1½ yds Ribbon & 1 hank Silk for 3/ | ,50 | 5 50 |
| | 30 | To 4 yards Cotton at 1/6, ball cotton 4½ | 1,07 | |
| | " | 1 Paper Gilt Pins 2/3 | .38 | 1 45 |
| Nov | 15 | To 1 yard flannel 3/4½ per wife | | 56 |
| | 26 | To 1 Stone Pot 6/ per Self | | 1 00 |
| Decem | 16 | To 6 yards Bombazett at 3/9 | 3.75 | 3 75 |
| | | | | 18 29 |
| | 23 | By Thomas Halls order this day | 55.10 | |
| | | To Cash in full | | 36 81 |
| | | | | 55 10 |

*Figure* 37 A page from an account book of John Patterson's store showing purchases and payments for James Saunders from June 19 through December 23, 1819. Courtesy of the John D. Rockefeller Jr. Library, Colonial Williamsburg Foundation, Williamsburg, VA.

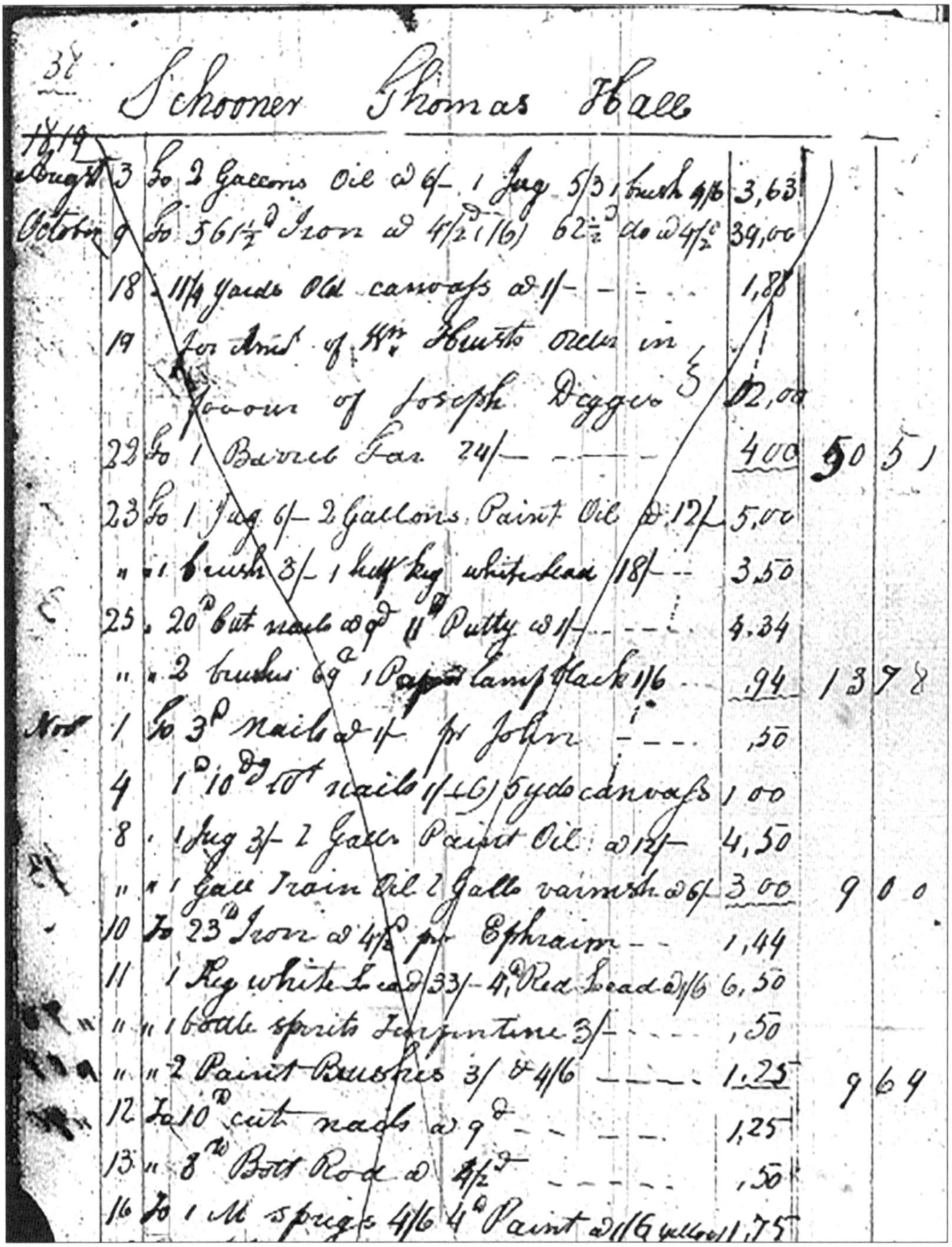

38

Schooner Thomas Hall

| 1819 | | | | |
|---|---|---|---|---|
| August | 3 | To 2 Gallons Oil @ 6/- 1 Jug 5/3 1 brush 4/6 | 3,63 | |
| October | 9 | To 561½ Iron @ 4½ (16) 62½ do @ 4½ | 39,00 | |
| | 18 | 1¼ yards Old canvass @ 1/- | 1,88 | |
| | 19 | For Amt of Wm Hewitts order in favour of Joseph Diggers | 12,00 | |
| | 22 | To 1 Barrel Tar 24/- | 4,00 | 50 51 |
| | 23 | To 1 Jug 6/- 2 Gallons Paint Oil @ 12/- | 5,00 | |
| | " | 1 brush 3/- 1 half keg white lead 18/- | 3,50 | |
| | 25 | 20 cut nails @ 9d 11 Putty @ 1/- | 4,34 | |
| | " | 2 brushes 69 1 Paper lamp black 1/6 | ,94 | 13 78 |
| Nov | 1 | To 3 nails @ 1/ pr John | ,50 | |
| | 4 | 1 10d 10d nails (1/6) 5 yds canvass | 1 00 | |
| | 8 | 1 Jug 3/- 2 Galls Paint Oil @ 12/- | 4,50 | |
| | " | 1 Gall Train Oil 2 Galls varnish @ 6/ | 3 00 | 9 00 |
| | 10 | To 23 Iron @ 4½ pr Ephraim | 1,44 | |
| | 11 | 1 Keg white Lead 33/- 4 Red Lead @ 1/6 | 6,50 | |
| | " | 1 bottle spirits Turpentine 3/- | ,50 | |
| | " | 2 Paint Brushes 3/ & 4/6 | 1,25 | 9 64 |
| | 12 | To 10 cut nails @ 9d | 1,25 | |
| | 13 | 8 Bolt Rod @ 4½ | ,50 | |
| | 16 | To 1 M sprigs 4/6 4 Paint @ 1/6 yellow | 1,75 | |

*Figure* 38 A page from an account book of John Patterson's store showing purchases and payments for "Schooner Thomas Hall" from August 3 through November 16, 1819. Courtesy of the John D. Rockefeller Jr. Library, Colonial Williamsburg Foundation, Williamsburg, VA.

coffee mill, a coffeepot, three tumblers, a hammer, two tin pans, and a number of other items. The total bill was $136.55 of which $39 was for iron, the single largest purchase. These items suggest the final phase of completing the vessel, painting and equipping the cabin.

Nothing in the record has been found to offer any suggestion concerning when or how Thomas learned the highly skilled profession of shipbuilder. But, considerable knowledge and years of experience were necessary to become a master ship carpenter, the individual having ultimate responsibility for all aspects of constructing the ship: procurement of materials; design of the ship, in most cases; accounting; recruiting workers; equipping the ship with hardware, anchors, masts, sails, and rigging; and successfully launching the vessel. Thomas at some point most certainly was an apprentice in a local shipyard, probably on the East River, and then, when having mastered the skills necessary, attracted investors and built his first ship. His ownership share could have been payment for part of his work. Before building the *Sarah Ann*, he most likely built smaller craft for local use and, by demonstrating his shipbuilding skills, gained the confidence from others of his ability to execute a larger project.

Thomas may have had the benefit of working as an apprentice in one of the better-known shipyards on the East River, such as Thomas Smith's. Smith was an accomplished and well-known builder, and as early as 1785, perhaps well before then, he built ships similar in size to what Thomas would build thirty-five years later. In 1785, when Thomas would have been twenty or twenty-one, old enough to make his own decisions concerning employment, the following advertisement was published in the *Maryland Journal* on April 8. It gives an example of the capabilities of Kingston shipwrights and the type of vessels that were routinely built on the East River:

> TO BE SOLD,
>
> A SHIP on the Stocks, in great forwardness, which may be completed and launched soon, of the following Dimensions, viz. 73 Feet Keel, straight Rabbit, 27 Feet Beam, 12 Feet in the lower Hold, and 5½ Feet betwixt Decks, built of the best Oak Plank and Timber, of suitable Size and Thickness, strong and substantially put together, and as a Mediocrity has been observed in her Construction, will indubitably sail very fast, and stow Tobacco to Advantage.——She stands on fine navigable Water upon East River, in the County of Gloucester, Virginia, near to the Place where the Subscriber lives, who will be always ready to communicate the Terms to any Person inclinable to purchase. THOMAS SMITH.

The vessel was a "ship," meaning it had three masts and was square-rigged, unlike the fore and aft rigs of two-masted schooners. Ships were the least frequently constructed vessels in

Kingston Parish at that time, with schooners being the most prevalent followed by sloops and brigs. Smith's ship, according to its advertised specifications, would have had a registered tonnage of 194 and an approximate burden of 270 tons. Her length-to-beam ratio, 73/27, was that of a merchant ship designed to maximize cargo capacity at the expense of speed. The claim that the ship "will indubitably sail very fast" must be taken as speed compared to merchant ships having similar dimensions. That this larger-than-average vessel for East River construction was built on speculation suggests a strong demand for ships during the second half of the 1780s, possibly a result of rebuilding the merchant fleet after the extensive destruction during the Revolutionary War.

Thomas continued building schooners, completing the *Thomas Hall* in 1822. Her enrollment was dated October 15, and owners included William Hurst, master; James H. Roy; and Thomas Hall. Her enrollment changed on April 30, 1823, to foreign trade and would remain primarily in that status for the duration of the surving record. Much larger than the *Sarah Ann*, the *Thomas Hall* was rated at $96^{13}/_{95}$ tons with a length of 66 feet, a width of 21 feet 6 inches, and a depth of hold of 8 feet. But, as before, there were no galleries or figurehead, and she had a square stern. The rig was the same, a two-masted schooner. This vessel may have been built on speculation because the port of registry changed to Baltimore, Maryland, on July 18, 1825, and on April 25, 1826, the owner of record was Thomas C. Reardon of Baltimore. The last record of the *Thomas Hall* was dated December 15, 1836, registered in the port of Bristol, Rhode Island.

The last record of a schooner built by Thomas was for the *Alexander*, the largest of the three known vessels, with a rated tonnage of $114^{60}/_{95}$. She had a length of 72 feet 6 inches, a width of 22 feet 2 inches, and a depth of the hold of 8 feet $4^{1}/_{2}$ inches. She was of the same rig and construction as the first two vessels and was first registered on November 21, 1826, for foreign trade under the ownership of William Hurst, also master, and Thomas Hall, now age sixty-two. Thomas and his son-in-law now had sufficient capital to no longer need other partners. On February 20, 1830, Joseph R. Gayle became master with no change in ownership. Gayle, married to Mary Ann, was also Thomas's son-in-law. Gayle continued as her master until March 2, 1831, when the registration was surrendered at Wilmington, Delaware, with the notation "Vessel totally lost."[17] What happened to the *Alexander* and who bore the financial loss is unknown although her master, Joseph Gayle, was not killed by whatever happened. The origin of the ship's name is also unknown, and curious given that the first two schooners built by Thomas were probably named for family members.

The three schooners built by Thomas Hall were well-designed and were fast sailors based on an analysis of their dimensions. The sailing performance and cargo capacity of ships, brigs, sloops, and schooners were the result of the designers' selection of the ratios of length

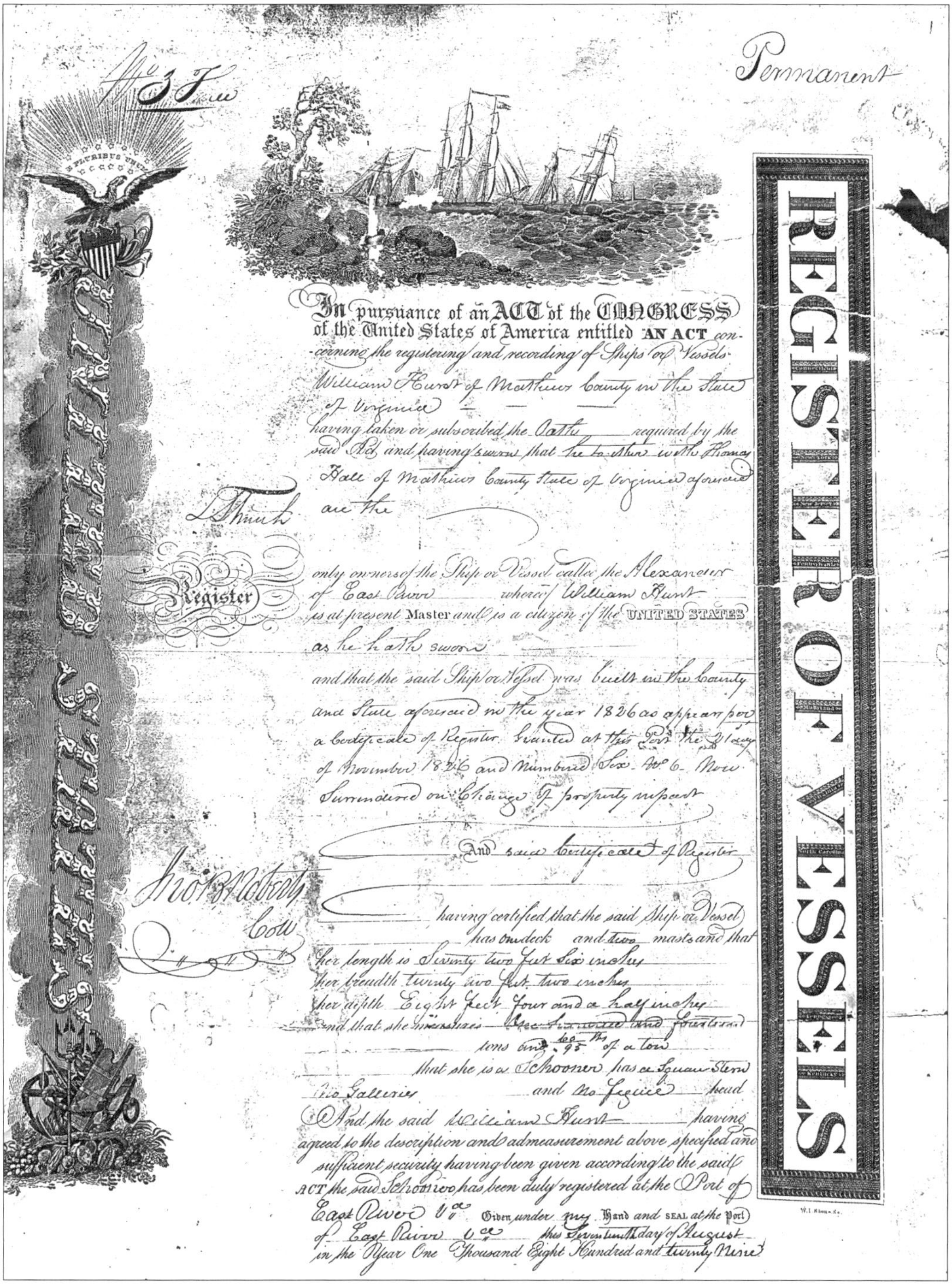
Permanent

REGISTER OF VESSELS

E PLURIBUS UNUM

UNITED STATES

Register

In pursuance of an ACT of the CONGRESS of the United States of America entitled AN ACT concerning the registering and recording of Ships or Vessels William Hurst of Mathews County in the State of Virginia having taken or subscribed the Oath required by the said Act, and having sworn that he together with Thomas Hall of Mathews County State of Virginia aforesaid are the only owners of the Ship or Vessel called the Alexander of East River whereof William Hurst is at present Master and is a citizen of the UNITED STATES as he hath sworn and that the said Ship or Vessel was built in the County and State aforesaid in the year 1826 as appears by a certificate of Register granted at this Port the 21 day of November 1826 and Numbered Six No. 6. Now surrendered on Change of property

And said Certificate of Register having certified that the said Ship or Vessel has one deck and two masts and that her length is Sixty two feet six inches her breadth twenty two feet two inches her depth Eight feet four and a half inches and that she measures One hundred and fourteen tons and 60/95ths of a ton that she is a Schooner has a Square Stern no Galleries and no figure head

And the said William Hurst having agreed to the description and admeasurement above specified and sufficient security having been given according to the said ACT the said Schooner has been duly registered at the Port of East River Va. Given under my Hand and SEAL at the Port of East River Va this Seventeenth day of August in the Year One Thousand Eight Hundred and twenty Nine

*Figure* 39 The US Register of Vessels for the *Alexander*, owned by William Hurst and Thomas Hall of Mathews County. Courtesy of the National Archives, Washington, DC.

to beam and beam to depth of the hold, the distance from the underside of the main deck to the bottom of the hull. There was always a compromise in designing a vessel for speed versus cargo capacity. The decision would be based on the anticipated cargoes and ports served. A vessel designed for speed did not have the same cargo capacity as a ship of equal length designed to maximize cargo. In general, the narrower the beam of a vessel for a given length, the faster she would sail. Thomas Hall's designs, based on an analysis of the significant dimension relationships, were closely matched to a sample of fourteen schooners and four brigs noted for above-average speed and good sea-keeping abilities. The analysis showed that the *Alexander*, Thomas's last ship, was probably above average in sailing performance.*

The era of greatest schooner construction in Mathews County was the four decades 1790 through 1830. Records shows that during 1791 to 1800 142 schooners were constructed, 118 from 1801 through 1810, 90 from 1811 to 1820, and 103 from 1821 until 1830. The actual number was probably many more as the surviving records are not thought to be complete. After 1830, construction declined to 77 schooners through 1840 and 65 through 1850. During those years other types of vessels were constructed, including a relatively small number of brigs, sloops, and ship-rigged vessels.[18] But schooners defined Mathews County shipbuilding, and its small shipyards were widely known for producing exceptional vessels both in quality of construction and sailing performance.

During the period that Thomas Hall was building schooners, total construction of all types of vessels averaged 12.4 per year from 1811 through 1830.[19] By any measure, this represented a major industry for Mathews County, and the resulting economic impact was very important in providing employment in the shipyards and the many supporting manufacturing and supply businesses.

The ten years during which Thomas Hall constructed ships, assuming he began planning the construction of the *Sarah Ann* in late 1817, were characterized by the construction of mostly small schooners. Of the eighty-seven launched during the ten-year period 1817 through 1826, thirty-nine, or 45 percent, were smaller than forty tons and just fifteen were larger than one hundred tons, leaving thirty-three schooners in the forty- to one hundred–ton range. However, during those ten years, the size of schooners became larger: three schooners greater than one hundred tons were launched during 1817 through 1821 and

* Dimensions of schooners built during the relevant time period were taken from *The History of American Sailing Ships* by Howard I. Chapelle (New York: W. W. Norton, 1935). The formula used to determine tonnage for registration by the captain of the Port of East River, Mathews County, was ((Length – (Beam * 0.6)) * Beam * Depth)/95. Length was equal to the length of the keel, and beam was measured at the widest point. Tonnage of cargo, a vessel's burden, was typically 30–40 percent greater than registered tonnage.

*Figure* 40 The *Young Brutus*, a Baltimore clipper schooner, illustrates the typical schooner constructed in Mathews County during the 1820s, including the three built by Thomas Hall. From Howard I. Chapelle, *The Search for Speed Under Sail, 1700–1855* (New York: W. W. Norton, 1967).

twelve from 1822 through 1826. Thomas Hall tended to build larger vessels, as his schooner launched in 1819 was the largest that year, as was his schooner constructed in 1822. His last known schooner, the *Alexander*, was launched in 1826 and tied for fourth largest out of fourteen launched that year. The trend towards larger schooners was in reaction to market demand for greater capacity for shipping larger cargoes carried on relatively fast vessels for mostly foreign trade.

Advertisements of the period provide an understanding of the types of vessels typically constructed in Mathews County and the resulting economic dependence on the industry. The advertisements reveal interesting details regarding construction with the pervasive use of copper fasteners and seasoned timber. There is a mention of the use of a model, the lines of which were used for the construction of a brig, suggesting perhaps a "standard" design for that shipwright. There was also flexibility in how a new vessel would be rigged, either as a schooner or a brig, each class of vessels having two masts. Careful attention about how a vessel would be utilized was of utmost importance in selecting rig, dimensions, and economical crew size.

A Vessel now on the *Stocks*, and can be launched in 3 or 4 weeks, of the following dimensions, viz: 62 Feet Straight Rabit, 25½ do. Beam, 13 do. Hold, 17 do. Rake Forward, 4 do. do. Aft, Iron fastened, will measure about 220 Tons, and supposed to stow 300 Hogsheads Tobacco, or 2,500 Barrels Flour. . . . Apply to Mr. JOHN BILLUPS, in Milfred Haven, Mathews County. (*American Beacon and Commercial Diary*, Norfolk, VA, May 3, 1817)

A NEW SCHOONER, *Built in Matthews County, of the best Seasoned Materials*; A high decked vessel—Burthen, 135 tons, carpenter's measurement. She lays at Dickson's Wharf, and will be sold a great bargain. (*American Beacon and Commercial Diary*, Norfolk, VA, May 8, 1818)

A BRIG, now on the Stocks in Matthews County, of the following dimensions—60 feet straight rabbit, 24 feet beam and 12 feet hold—can be launched in two weeks. She is copper-fastened, and in every respect a first rate vessel. (*American Beacon and Norfolk & Portsmouth Daily Advertiser*, Norfolk, VA, October 3, 1818)

The schooner CARRIER, an excellent vessel, 39 tons burthen, sails well, was built in Matthews county, Va. in August last, of the best materials.—She is remarkably well found, and well calculated for a small West-Indiaman, or bay craft. (*Alexandria Gazette & Daily Advertiser*, Alexandria, VA, January 15, 1819)

A NEW, handsome, copper fastened and fast-sailing SCHOONER, $24^{4}/_{94}$ tons, built in Matthews county, Virginia—she has a new suit of best Russia Duck Sails, and running Rigging complete. (*Baltimore Patriot & Mercantile Advertiser*, Baltimore, MD, November 4, 1820)

A NEW BRIG, Built in Matthews County, Virginia, of the best white oak, 217 tons carpenter's measurement, copper fastened, with lower masts, boom and bowsprit, well secured with beams and knees, and expected from her model and general appearance to sail uncommonly fast. (*Baltimore Patriot & Mercantile Advertiser*, Baltimore, MD, March 2, 1821)

FOR SALE, FREIGHT OR CHARTER, The very fine fast sailing brig ROSANNA, copper fastened and coppered with heavy copper, carries about 1200 barrels, about 18 months old, built in Matthews county, Virginia, of the best seasoned timber, by capt. MILES KING, for his own use, fitted and found in the best manner, and considered by good judges to be a first rate

> vessel. ALSO, FOR SALE, The Hull, Masts and Spars complete of a first rate *clipping* Brig or Schooner, now building in Matthews county by Capt. MILES KING, and can be launched in about three weeks; she is about 190 tons burthen, copper fastened to the bends, decks copper nailed, built of the best materials, and expected to sail as fast as any vessel of her class. (*Baltimore Patriot & Mercantile Advertiser*, Baltimore, MD, August 9, 1822)
>
> FOR SALE, *The fast sailing copper fastened and coppered Brig VIRGINIA, 235 tons burthen,* built in Mathews County, Virginia, about four years old, was coppered with heavy copper last year.
>
> She has nearly two suits of sails, and a large inventory, and may be sent to sea at a trifling expense. (*Baltimore Patriot & Mercantile Advertiser*, Baltimore, MD, August 21, 1822)
>
> FOR SALE, A remarkably fine new BRIG, built in Matthews' County, Virginia, of the best materials, under the immediate direction of Captain MILES KING—burthen 188 tons, Carpenters' measurement, about 230 tons Custom House measurement; expected to carry 1600 barrels, and to sail as fast as any vessel. She is copper fastened, and can be ready for sea in a week, and will be sold low. (*Baltimore Patriot & Mercantile Advertiser*, Baltimore, MD, June 7, 1823)
>
> FOR SALE, The well known copper fastened and coppered Brig MARY, burthen 272 tons, and will carry 2300 bbls. The Mary was buit in Matthews county, Virginia, of the best materials, under the particular inspection of Capt. Miles King. She is well found, and would require very little expense to fit her for a voyage to India, from whence she has just returned. (*Baltimore Patriot & Mercantile Advertiser*, Baltimore, MD, July 30, 1823)

Between July 30, 1823, and July 1831, another sixteen Mathews-built vessels, mostly schooners, were advertised in the *Baltimore Patriot*. Many of these vessels were built on speculation, with Baltimore being the primary market for Mathews-built vessels. The next advertisement in Baltimore newspapers for a Mathews County–built sailing vessel did not appear until twenty-eight years later on May 6, 1859.

The 1820s marked the beginning of the end of large-scale ship construction on the East River. After about 1830, steam propulsion became competitive with sail, and of necessity ship construction moved to larger ports with the infrastructure for machine shops and iron fabrication.

As the era of large-scale shipbuilding in Mathews began to decline, much greater attention was devoted to improving agricultural methods. As a result of better land management, farms in Mathews and nearby counties enjoyed increasing yields. James H. Roy of Green Plains, Mathews County, one of the owners of Thomas Hall's first schooner, observed in 1819:

> The agriculture of the counties of Gloucester, Middlesex and Mathews, and I might say, of the whole Senatorial district, is improving. Great attention is now paid to the raising and carrying out all kinds of manure; deep ploughing and turning in a good coat of vegetable matter is allowed to be right, and is pursued. . . . Our crops consist of barley, wheat, corn, and Indian peas, for market—the tobacco crop being almost entirely abandoned, even in the county of Middlesex, where a few years ago it was much attended to. Oats in the chaff, or chopped, and mixed with a small quantity of Indian meal, together with blade fodder or hay, is the common food for horses; the corn stalk, with every thing that grows upon it, save the ear and blade, together with barley or wheat straw, is the ordinary winter's provision for cattle. . . . I have before said that great attention is now paid to manuring. The mode of raising this is different. I prefer the mode of confining the cattle all the winter and a part of the spring to a warm dry cow house, to which all the corn stalks raised on the farm are carried and deposited for consumption and manure. My cattle are in much better condition in the spring than they formerly were, and I make five times as much manure. . . .
>
> . . . The modern mode of raising hogs, to wit, by suffering them to graze on the clover in the day, and to have them penned at night, (thereby saving much manure,) is certainly preferable to any other. . . .
>
> A fair experiment of the relative value of horses and oxen for agricultural purposes, has not been made. The most judicious manager with us is partial to oxen. My own opinion is this: if persons of good judgment were employed in breaking them, and giving them an early habit of quick motion, at the same time training them to be governed by leading lines, a pair of good oxen would be equal to a pair of ordinary mules or horses, and they would not cost half as much. . . .
>
> We have no fences with us more permanent than wood. To the estate on which I reside, consisting of about 650 acres of arable land, there are 100 acres of wood land attached: this I find scarcely equal to the purposes of fire wood & rail timber; but I am not an economist in fuel, having very many

> negro quarters where there should be fire. Mr. Rootes, who resides at White Marsh, and who (from the excellent quality of his land) is not disposed to keep more in wood than necessary, thinks that one tenth of an estate in timbered land will be sufficient for the support of the balance; probably his opinion on this subject is more correct that mine.[20]

Entries from the account book of Christopher Tompkins, Thomas's 1819–1821 partner in the schooner *Sarah Ann*, offers insights into the local trade and transportation activities on the East River in the late 1820s:[21]

> [1828]
>
> [December 31]
> Lucia Harrison went up E. River to load with C Capt.[?] Hudgins corn
>
> [1829]
>
> [January 8]
> Schooner Lucia G. Harrison returned from up East River having Recd. from
> Capt.[?] Hudgins—229 [bushels] corn
> John Tabb—200
> Geo. W Bray—16½ bushels
> 2 bales cotton from B Tompkins
>
> [January 12]
> Lucia G Harrison sailed for N York
> shipped William Hurst @ $13 per Month
>
> [February 11]
> Lucia G Harrison arrived from New York, discharged Wm. Hurst
>
> [March 11]
> Lucia G. Harrison loaded & has on board
> 22½ Bls. corn from Brookes Miller
>
> 142 Do. from Mrs Degges
> 300 Do. from Capt.[?] Hudgins
> 464½ = 2322½ bushels @ 45c $1045.12

[April 7]
Signed Thomas Hall's John on board the Lucia G Harrison @ $9 Per Month
George Weston returned on board
Lucia G Harrison has on board
540 bushels corn
60 bales cotton
212½ bushels [corn]
28 bushels Peas & beans
4 Bls Potatoes for Mr. Roy

[June 15]
Agreed with John Brommly to build a vessel 38 foot Keel—17½ foot beam & 6½ foot hold. —to have Patent Rudder, copper fastened, & butt [?] all [?] & everything complete for $960.

[June 22]
William M. Thomas sailed for Baltimore to take charge of Brig Matilda

[July 6]
Agreed with James Davis to build a vessel 34 foot Keel 16 foot beam @ 4½ foot hold with a quarter Deck & copper fastened @ $20 per Ton

[July 19]
Signed Thomas Halls John at $ 9 per Month on board the Lucia G Harrison & she went up Ware River

[July 22]
Agreed to give John Brommly $600 to build a boat 33 foot Keel 15 [foot] 9 [inch] beam 5 foot hold. quarter deck & [?] to be copper fastened & finished complete. deck plank 2 inches thick

[September 24]
L. G. Harrison returned from Loyds with 2375 bushels wheat 1 [?] & 2 boxes bound to N. York @ 80c[?] per bushel

The account book recorded transactions from May 1827 through February 1831 and, while pages are missing, gives a detailed understanding of the scope of Tompkins's business activities. He was in the freight transportation business, delivering mostly farm commodities from surrounding farms to major markets, including Norfolk, Baltimore, Richmond, and New York. Wheat, corn, cotton, peas, beans, and large quantities of lumber were exported in his vessels from Mathews County. He also raised crops and in some cases bought the crops of other farmers for his own account.

He owned a number of schooners and at least one brig. The account book is full of names of captains and others he hired from time to time, including slaves, whose owners typically received the earnings. The book includes the details of his purchase of Poplar Hall and its 1,260 acres. On April 2, 1830, he recorded a purchase price of $14,466.60. He paid one-third in cash, one-third due in twelve months, and one-third due in twenty-four months. The surveyor's fee was $20.

The last two pages give a detailed listing of the cost of materials and labor to build a seventy-ton schooner, the *Richard Hunley*. The carpenter's bill for the hull was $1,400, a rate of $20 per ton. Other items included $100 for joiner work for the interior, $20 for a boat, $81.93 for the blacksmith, $304.90 for the sailmaker, $30 for blocks, $255.62 for the rope maker, $67 for two sixty-seven-pound anchors, and $14.70 for the plumber. The total cost for the *Richard Hunley* was $2,450.15.

The April 7, 1829, entry shows that Thomas Hall's son John W. signed on board the *Lucia G. Harrison*, and again on July 19, 1829. John would have been about twenty-seven years old. He was hired at an agreed-upon rate of pay for a specific voyage and, once completed, was without employment until another crew position could be found. He may have worked on Thomas's farm during intervals between voyages.

The entries for the voyage and return of William Hurst, Thomas Hall's son-in-law, on January 12, 1829, and February 11, 1829, are illustrative of the employment practices for mariners and the types of voyages undertaken at all times of the year. At a master's pay, William's $13 compensation per month gives a useful indicator of the value of a dollar. On an annual basis, assuming full-time employment, which was not often the case, a master would earn $156 per year.

At $2,450.15, the cost of the new schooner *Richard Hunley* equated to almost sixteen years of annual compensation for William Hurst. At $14,466.66, the cost of Poplar Grove equated to almost six new schooners and ninety-three years of wages for a master of a ship. Shipowner, merchant, and farmer Christopher Tompkins was clearly an enterprising businessman of skill, attention to detail, and hard work and was a wealthy member of the neighborhood.

The US Census of 1830 recorded the number of members of the household by age ranges, with the head of household being the only name listed. It also included the number of slaves by age ranges. Thomas Hall reported a male between sixty and seventy, himself; a male between twenty and thirty, probably his son Robert; two females between thirty and forty, one of which was likely Robert's wife, Elizabeth, and the other is unknown; an unknown female between ten and fifteen; and one male and one female between the ages of five and ten, who were likely Robert and Elizabeth's children, Thomas Spencer and Sarah. Since she does not appear in the census, Thomas's wife, Mary, must have been dead by 1830, when she would have been sixty-five or sixty-six years old.

As measured by the number of slaves on the property, the Hall household was prosperous for the times. The 1830 census lists nineteen, the same as in 1820, including three males under ten, two males ten to twenty-three, one male twenty-four to thirty-five, two males thirty-six to fifty-four, and one male over fifty-five. There were six females under the age of ten, one female ten to twenty-three, and three females twenty-four to thirty-five. The numbers suggest that there were at least two families and more likely three, with nine small children under the age of ten.

Thomas made a significant land acquisition in late 1834 or early 1835* with the purchase of two parcels from Christopher Tompkins. The first, surveyed on January 6, 1825, by John Hayes, extended his original forty-four and a half acres southward by seventy-eight and a quarter acres along the east side of the main road.[22] It was bounded on the east by the land of Anthony H. Hudgins and on the south by the land of Miles King.

The second parcel was eight and a quarter acres directly to the west, across the main road from the first parcel. This land was at the head of Weston Creek, earlier known as Hunley Creek. Today the property is known as Sutherland and includes a dwelling house that may or may not have been on the property at the time Thomas Hall purchased it. The land tax records do not show any buildings on either of the two parcels in 1835 through 1837. However in 1838, when Thomas deeded the property to his son-in-law Joseph R. Gayle, the tax record shows a value of $200 for buildings. The value of buildings increased in 1840 to $900, suggesting that the structure was built during 1838 and 1839 and was completed in 1840. An accurate estimate of the age of the house, which still exists, has not been determined, but the architecture, building materials, and construction methods suggest the decades of 1800–1840. It is possible that the house was moved to its current location from a nearby property, which would mean the house is older, perhaps constructed in the 1820s. It is believed that the subsequent enlargement to the house was constructed in 1850. By 1843, around which time Joseph R. Gayle moved with his family to Baltimore, Maryland, he had sold the

---

* The Mathews County Fee Book for January 1835 has the entry, "Thomas Hall Recording deed from C. Thompkins to you. $1.50." (Mathews County Clerk's Office, Mathews, VA.)

property. Thomas Weston became the new owner, and at some point the creek was renamed for him. There is no evidence that Thomas Hall ever lived on the property, although it seems likely that he did given the timing with the end of his life.

The house has been maintained to a high standard and has had several additions and renovations over the years. The original structure was a story and a half with two rooms and side passage arrangement on the first floor and a similar second-floor plan. Each of the four rooms had a fireplace, the foundation was brick, the roof was covered with shingles, and board siding was used on the outside walls. The length of the front, facing the main road to the east, was twenty-six and a quarter feet and the depth was twenty-eight and a half feet. The side passage, on the south side of the house, was nine and a quarter feet wide. The front first-floor room measured fifteen and a quarter feet by fourteen and a quarter feet; the back first-floor room was fifteen and a quarter feet by twelve and a quarter feet. The house was typical for middle- to upper middle–income families in the early 1800s.

*Figure* 41 Sutherland, acquired in late 1834 or early 1835 by Thomas Hall. The original house has been carefully restored and is an excellent example of early nineteenth-century domestic architecture in Tidewater Virginia. The screen porch and the structure to the right of the dormer windows are twentieth-century additions.

An architectural survey conducted by the NIAHD[*] field school in 2013 supports the estimated date of construction as during the first thirty or forty years of the nineteenth century. The survey identified the two chimneys on the north side as having a 1:3 brick bonding pattern and degraded mortar joints, indicative of the early nineteenth century, rafters in the attic of the original wing pegged at the apex with mortise and tenon joinery, and pit-sawn timbers in excellent condition.

Thomas Hall, age seventy-five, Revolutionary War pensioner, is the only one listed in his household in the US Census of 1840. He died that year, on August 23, at the age of seventy-six. By 1840, his son John W. was dead, his daughters were married and living elsewhere, and his grandchildren Thomas Spencer and his sister Sarah, now aged seventeen and eighteen respectively, were living elsewhere, as was their cousin John, the grandson of Thomas and son of John W., also a teenager. Thomas Hall Jr. had married in 1835, and by 1840, he and his wife, the former Lucina Summers, had two small children under the age of five.

The census also shows that Thomas Hall's property in 1840 included twenty-one slaves, twenty owned by Thomas and one owned by his son Thomas Jr. Eight were under the age of ten, four males and four females. Three males and three females were between ten and twenty-three, one female was between twenty-four and thirty-four, two males and three females were between thirty-six and fifty-four, and one male was over fifty-five. The age ranges and number of individuals continue to suggest three families, with the census showing ten engaged in agriculture and none in manufacture, or shipbuilding.

What is not known is exactly where the Halls were living. They were somewhere on the original forty-four and a half acres or the adjoining property acquired by Thomas Sr. or at Sutherland. The order in which names were listed in the census suggests that they were living in proximity.

In summary, Thomas and Mary Hall's five children all married and settled in Mathews County. Their first child, Sarah Ann, and William Hurst were married on November 17, 1808, in Mathews County, she being about sixteen years old and William about twenty-three. In 1810, William and Sarah Ann purchased $8^{52}/_{160}$ acres of land that had previously belonged to the glebe of Kingston Parish.[†] Four years later, on July 28, 1814, Sarah Ann and William sold the property to John Patterson for $128. The deed used the name "Sally," as she must have been called, it being a nickname for Sarah.[23]

---

* The National Institute of American History and Democracy (NIAHD) is a partnership between the College of William and Mary and the Colonial Williamsburg Foundation.

† An act of the General Assembly of Virginia, on January 22, 1810, appointed commissioners for the sale at public auction of the glebe that included Perrin Smith, Holder Hudgins, Richard Billups, Gabriel Miller, Anthony Hudgins, and Sands Smith.

There is a record of just one child, John, born in 1832, when Sarah Ann would have been about thirty-nine or forty and William about forty-seven. John W. Hurst appears in the 1850 census as being eighteen years old living with his mother and father. Also in the same household was Elizabeth Hall, age forty, who probably was the widow of John W. Hall, Sarah Ann's brother.

As previously mentioned, William Hurst was a business partner with Thomas Hall, his father-in-law, and the inscription on his tombstone, an unusual epitaph, reads: "CAPT. WILLIAM HURST. Son in Law of *Thomas Hall decd* who departed this life Oct'r 14th 1857. In the 72nd year of his age." The association must have been especially close.

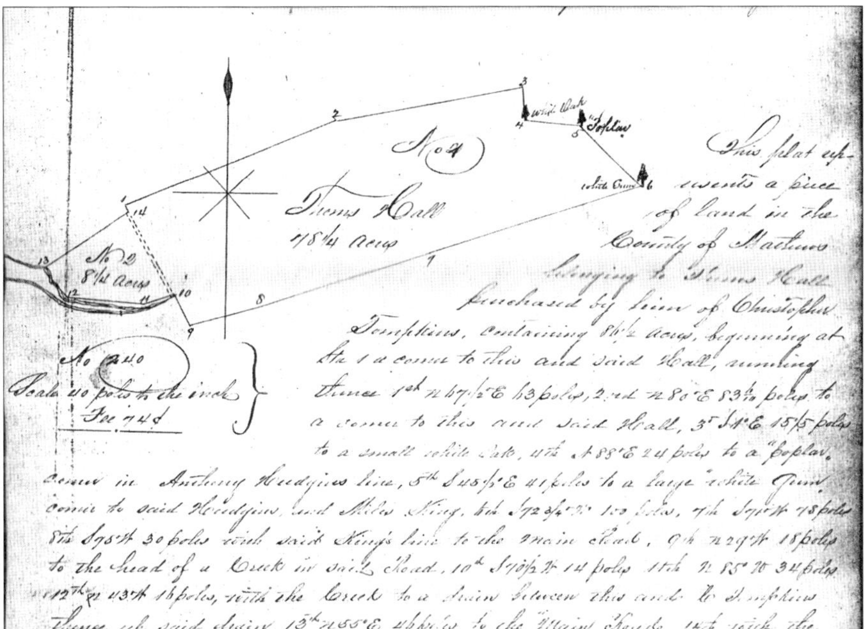

*Figure* 42 The survey shows the land owned by Thomas Hall in 1834, including a survey made on January 6, 1825, by John Hayes for seventy-eight and a half acres and a second survey by W. M. Brownley for eight and a half acres made on September 22, 1834. The original forty-four and a half acres of the Hall family begins on the northern boundary of the seventy-eight-and-a-half-acre tract. The tract to the west is now called Sutherland. From Land Books nos. 1 and 2, courtesy of the Mathews County Clerk's Office, Mathews, VA.

Thomas Hall had purchased the land on which William and Sarah Ann lived at a public sale of land owned by the estate of Warner Lewis. Christopher D. Tompkins was the trustee, and the sale was recorded on January 18, 1826.[24] This was the same year in which the schooner *Alexander* was launched, which was owned by Thomas Hall and William Hurst. The property consisted of seventy-one acres and was bounded on the east by Pudding Creek, on the north by the land of George Brownley, on the west by William L. Smith's land, and on the south by the land of John Lewis. This property never appeared on the land tax records of Thomas Hall, so it would appear that he gave the land to his daughter Sarah Ann and her husband, William. After William died, Sarah Ann made a will, signed on December 3, 1877, that provided for all of her property, including her farm, which had been expanded to eighty-four acres, and all personal property, to be left to her nephew George W. Gayle.[25]

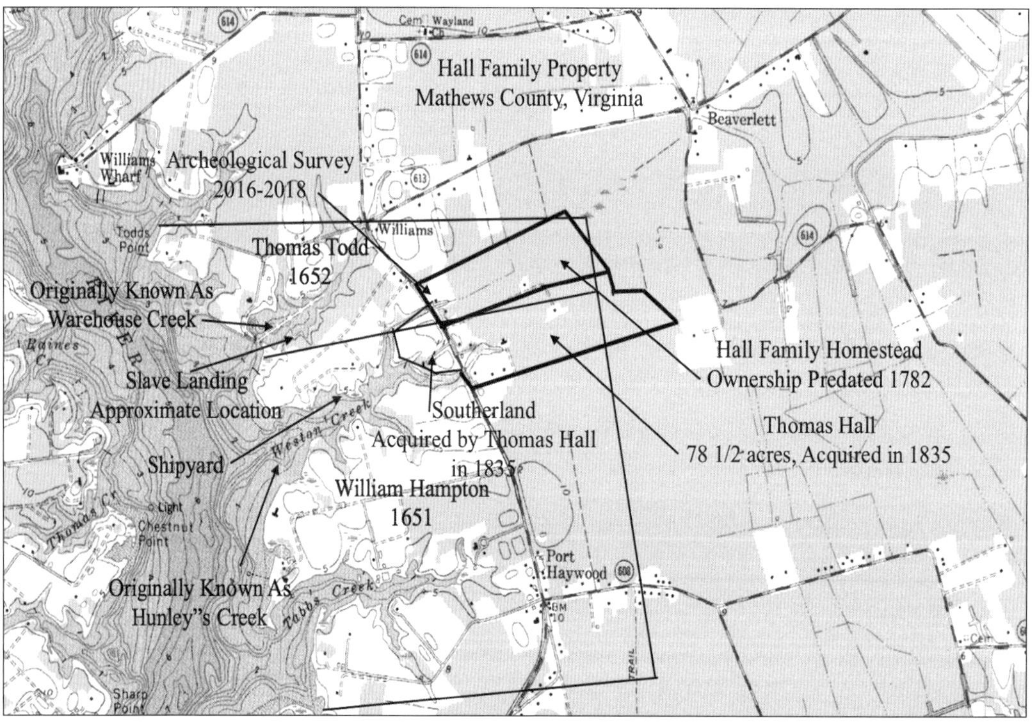


*Figure* 43 A section of the 1965 topographical map of Mathews County showing the boundaries of the 1652 Thomas Todd land patent and the 1651 William Hampton land patent (superimposed)—the two combined contained most of the land that would eventually be owned by the Hall family. The original Hall homestead, predating 1782, and subsequent additions are shown as related to the original land patents by Todd and Hampton. Also marked are the shipyard on Hunley's Creek, now Weston Creek, and the slave landing on Warehouse Creek.

Thomas and Mary's youngest child, Mary Ann, who married mariner Joseph R. Gayle, had four children: Sarah Ann, born 1834; Ann, born 1836; Joseph, born 1842; and George William, born 1848 in Baltimore, Maryland. Father Joseph died during a sea voyage on July 22, 1863. The notice of his death appeared in the *Baltimore Sun* newspaper on October 7, 1863:

> *Death of a Baltimore Ship Master.*—A letter from Rio de Janeiro, to O. Morton Stewart, brings intelligence of the death of Capt. Joseph R, Gayle, master of bark Paladin. He died at sea on the outward passage, on the 22d of July last, in lat. 9 north.

At the time, Joseph was about fifty-three years old, and Mary Ann was about fifty. The widow Mary Ann Gayle was listed in the US Census of 1870 as living in the Westville District of Mathews County with her older sister, Sarah Ann Hurst, also a widow, along with Mary Ann's son George, age twenty-two.

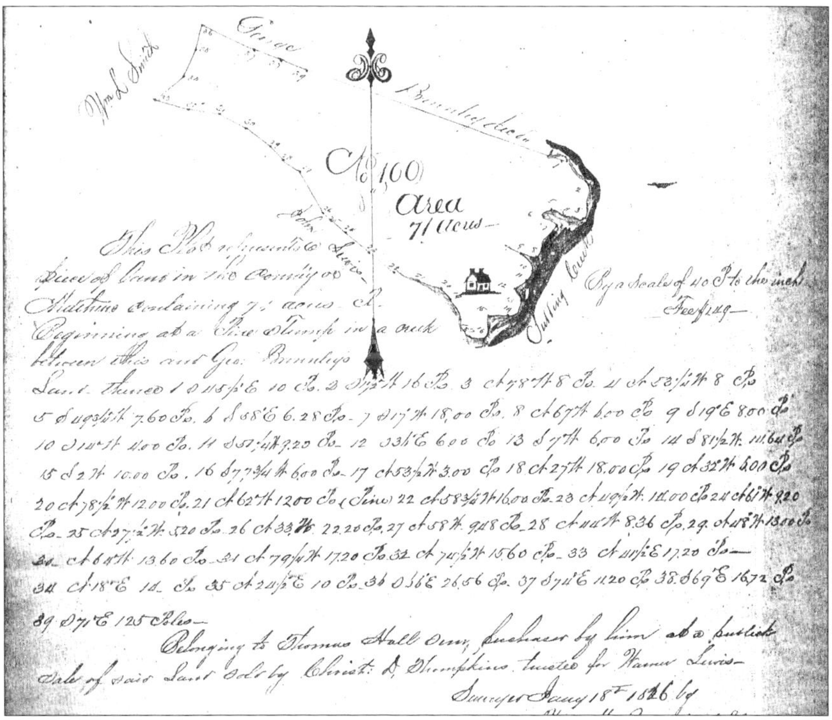


*Figure* 44 The seventy-one-acre tract owned by William and Sarah Hurst was surveyed on January 18, 1826, by W. M. Brownley and was located on the west side of Pudding Creek. The dwelling house is sketched with some precision, a story and a half with a chimney at each end and situated near a point of land extending into the creek. From Land Book no. 1, courtesy of the Mathews County Clerk's Office, Mathews, VA.

Thomas and Mary's youngest son, John W., appears in the 1841 land tax records owning twenty-six acres left to him by his father when he died in 1840. In 1843, the acreage was owned by John's orphan,* who owned the land until 1844. After that it was shown as being owned by the estate of his father, who died at the age of approximately forty. Nothing further is known about either father or son.

Chapter 14 goes into further detail about Thomas and Mary's first son, Robert, and his son, Thomas Spencer Hall.

Chapter 15 goes into further detail about Thomas Hall Jr., Thomas and Mary's second eldest son, and his family.

*A New and Comprehensive Gazetteer of Virginia, and the District of Columbia*† presents a comprehensive description of Mathews County as it was in the early 1830s, with most of the chapter devoted to a description of the rivers and creeks and other topographical features.

---

* A child under age twenty-one without a father was considered an *orphan*, a legal term providing certain legal protections.

† In 1835, Joseph Martin of Charlottesville, Virginia, published *A New and Comprehensive Gazetteer of Virginia, and the District of Columbia*, a collection of the history, statistics, and condition of many Virginia counties. It opens with a general description of Virginia including boundaries, geography, geology, bodies of water, climate, and other "Natural Curiosities." Descriptions of politics and society follow, including population, government, laws, religion, education, the military, hospitals, prisons, manufactures, agriculture, commerce, and fiscal matters. A chapter specifically on Mathews County is shown in appendix *5*.

Martin assembled his *Gazetteer* from many contributors as well as his own writings. Dr. William Shultice, the author of the chapter on Mathews County, was a young physician from Fredericksburg, Virginia, who became one of four licensed physicians in Mathews and a large landowner. He acquired Springdale in late 1832 or early 1833 from Richard Billups Jr., who had purchased the property from Joice Respess in 1823 (Richard Billups, Virginia Bible Records, 1784–1920, Virginia Historical Society, Richmond). Springdale was 1.8 miles north from Sutherland on the Main Road. Shultice was a keen observer and his report on the county, prepared approximately during 1830–1833, is wide-ranging and detailed.

William Shultice was an accomplished physician and became active in county affairs. Christopher Tompkins became a business partner and friend. On September 13, 1831, Dr. Shultice wrote Prof. William Gibson in Philadelphia to introduce Tompkins, who was visiting the city "for the purpose of obtaining the advice and assistance of the Faculty. He is afflicted with the Gravel." The letter goes on to describe Tompkins's condition of kidney stones, later in the letter also being called "calculus," which is the Latin word for small pebble. The end of the letter reads, "Any assistance which your Faculty may enable you to render the Colonel will be a source of additional gratification to me, both as an admirer of your individual ability and a lover of Science." He signed it, "With respect, your friend and pupil." The letter is in the Virginia Historical Society, Richmond.

> [The] land in this county . . . is of a medium quality as regards fertility. It produces corn and oats, but is not so well adapted to wheat, from its extreme humidity. . . . The soil is generally a sandy loam, with a substratum of clay. . . .
>
> The natural growth of timber on this land is oak, which ship carpenters say, will vie with the live oak, pine, chesnut and gum. The land after cultivation, if permitted to lie out, invariably puts up a growth of pine. . . .
>
> . . . The people of this county are engaged in ship building, maritime and agricultural pursuits. Until recently the two former occupied their principal attention; so entirely were they engaged in ship building some years back, that the cultivation of the soil, was almost entirely neglected. . . . lately vessel building has decreased, and agriculture receives more attention. About 20 years ago [1810–1815], there were annually built one hundred vessels of various sizes and denominations, from large ships down to the smallest craft; at the present period there are built, every year, from 20 to 30 vessels of different burdens. There are belonging to this county about 200 ship carpenters.[26]

The *Gazetteer* continues with these observations: the county has ten windmills, two tide mills and one gristmill (water powered). There are no freshwater streams running through the county due to its levelness. Wells are generally dug eight to ten feet deep, with thirty-foot wells being nearly inexhaustible. There are springs of excellent water, but they are rare. The predominant religion is Methodist. Westville, the county courthouse, "contains about 30 houses, 4 mercantile stores, 1 tanyard, 3 boot and shoe factories, 1 tailor, 2 blacksmiths, 1 saddler, 1 carriage maker, and 1 tavern. The public buildings are a very neat, new C. H., 2 jails, 1 for criminals and the other for debtors, and a clerk's office. These houses are all well built of brick. Westville is a port of entry; there are 2 regular packets which ply between this place and Norfolk weekly, and 1 that runs from it to Baltimore. Population 150, including 3 regular physicians."[27] The countywide population in 1830 was 7,666.

The inventory of Thomas Hall's estate no longer exists, nor does his will, but his landholdings totaling 147 acres, shipbuilding, and ownership of numerous slaves suggest that his estate was sizable for the period. As recorded in the Mathews County tax records, his land was divided among his heirs as follows: Thomas Hall Jr. 36 acres; Robert Hall's orphans, Sarah Hall and Thomas Spencer Hall, 24 acres; John W. Hall 26 acres; Joseph R. Gayle, husband of Mary Ann Hall, 34 acres; and William Hurst, husband of Sarah Ann Hall, 27 acres.

# CHAPTER 13

# The Daughters *of* Ann *and* Robert Hall

Ann and Robert Hall's three daughters were all born in Kingston Parish: Elizabeth "Betsey" Jordan, born about 1754; Ann "Nanny," born on September 19, 1756; and Joyce "Joicey," born on February 17, 1763.

The name of their first daughter, Elizabeth "Betsey" Jordan, suggests that Ann's mother or Ann's father's mother was named Elizabeth, if the family followed traditional English naming patterns. The name "Jordan" was never used again, and its source is not known. Ann "Nanny" may have been named for her mother or her father's mother, as was frequently the case for the name of a second daughter.

At about age nineteen, Betsey married William Foster, the son of Richard and Susannah Foster (née Bland), on October 30, 1773, in Kingston Parish. They had one son, William Foster Jr., who was born on December 29, 1775. William Sr. died sometime during 1775 or 1776, perhaps before the birth of his son. Betsey, with the infant William Jr., married Francis "Frank" Brown on February 9, 1777. They would have six children: Robert, Spencer H., Susan, Nancy Ann, Elizabeth, and Francis. Only the birth year for Nancy Ann, 1782, is known. She married her cousin, Joshua Gayle, born in January 1782, the son of Mathias and Joyce Gayle (née Hall).

Francis Brown served as steward on the *Henry* with his two brothers-in-law Robert Hall and Spencer Hall as well as with Peter Foster, the husband of his sister-in-law Nanny.* The position of steward included the responsibility for all victual provisioning and on-board cooking. It is not known how long he served or when he died.

---

* The list of crew members can be found in appendix 4.

Nanny married Peter Foster Sr. on October 27, 1776,[1] at the age of twenty-one. Peter was also twenty-one, having been born on March 22, 1756, in Kingston Parish. They had eight children: Susannah Ransom, born September 3, 1777; Ann, born May 5, 1780; Elizabeth, born October 4, 1782; Richard, born January 26, 1785; Peter Jr., born May 11, 1787; Mary "Polly," born October 24, 1789; William Edward, born September 26, 1795; and Harriet, born October 20, 1798.

Peter Foster served for three years in the Virginia State Navy on board the *Henry* as the carpenter's mate. Starkey Moss was the carpenter. The carpentry function on a wooden sailing ship was an important part of ensuring the seaworthiness of the vessel and critical to repairing damage from storms and enemy cannon fire and included maintenance of the vessel's masts, yardarms, booms, steering mechanism, and bilge pumps. In many respects it was the position most equivalent to today's chief engineer.

Ann and Robert's third daughter, Joyce, married Mathias Gayle in 1780, and they had four children: two daughters, Betsey and Nancy, dates of birth and other information unknown, and two sons, Joshua, who was born in January 1782, and Bartlett born in 1785. Joshua married his cousin Nancy Ann Brown, and they had four children. Bartlett evidently had the benefit of an education because he became a doctor. Dr. Bartlett Gayle married Martha Buckner, and they had five children. The fifth, Charles S. M. Gayle, was also a doctor.

Joyce's husband, Mathias, served with his brother-in-law Thomas Hall in the Revolutionary War. On October 6, 1836, in the Mathews County Courthouse, William Hurst and William Diggs, both aged seventy-five,

> declare they were acquainted with Matthias Gayle and Joice Hall before and since their marriage and think they were married in 1780 and he died about 1794. They think he entered service under Capt. Robert Gayle in 1777 and served a tour of duty at New Point Comfort consisting of two months and was then discharged, after which he was called out again the same year under the same officer at the same place and served two and a half months. In 1778 he was called out under the same officer and served one month and the place aforesaid and in like manner served a tour of two months. In 1779 he was called out to go to Richmond on account of the British going up James River and marched to Gloucester Court House and then through King and Queen and King William and there heard that the British had returned down the river, and then was ordered to Williamsburg where he was stationed some time. Then he was ordered to York where he stopped some time. In all he served about three months under Capt. Philip Tabb. He returned home and

> was again called out under Capt. Ro. Gayle at New Point and served one month. In 1780 he was called out and served at New Point two months under Ro. Gayle. In 1781 he was called out (when all the militia of Gloucester was) under Capt. Gayle and marched to Gloucester Court House, then to Hubbard's old field, then to Ware Church, then to Sewel's old field, where he was stationed some time. Then he was marched to Gloucester Town where a battle was fought. In all he served three months. He was engaged in many little skirmishes while stationed at New Point. He was born in Gloucester County, Kingston Parish, where he resided during his life.[2]

On October 6, 1836, in the Mathews County Courthouse, Joyce Gayle, aged seventy-four,

> Declares she is the widow of Matthias Gayle who was a soldier under Capt. R. Gayle who had command of a militia company and continued to the end of the war. She heard him speak of being at Gloucester Town when the great battle was fought. She was married to Matthias Gayle in 1780 by Parson Fountain and her husband died in 1794.

On September 20, 1837, Thomas Hall "Declares he was well acquainted with Matthias Gayle. He was married to his sister Joice Hall in 1779 or 1780." On July 2, 1838, Dr. Bartlett Gayle "Declares he has always understood the oldest child of his mother was born in Jan. 1782 and were he now living would be 56 years old." The result of these court appearances over a period of a year and a half was the award of a pension to Joyce Hall Gayle.[3]

# CHAPTER 14

# Thomas Spencer Hall, Son *of* Elizabeth *and* Robert Hall III, Grandson *of* Thomas *and* Mary Hall, *and* Great-Grandson *of* Ann and Robert Hall

Thomas Spencer Hall, the son of Elizabeth and Robert Hall III, the grandson of Thomas Sr. and Mary Hall (née Gayle), and the great-grandson of Ann and Robert Hall, was born in September 1823. His sister, Sarah Ann, was born the previous year, in 1822. There were no other known siblings.

Little is known about the life of Thomas Spencer's father, Robert, who was Thomas and Mary's second of five children and first son. He was born in Mathews County about 1800 when his mother would have been thirty years old and his father thirty-six. He married Elizabeth, whose last name is unknown. The marriage likely occurred in 1820 or 1821, when Robert would have been twenty or twenty-one years old.

Robert appeared in the record for the first time on August 28, 1819, at about age nineteen, as a customer in John Patterson's account book. Patterson, a successful merchant, landowner, and politician, owned a store near Williams Wharf that was patronized by members of the Hall family for purchases that included materials and supplies for Hall-built schooners. The first entry under Robert's name was "By Thos Hall's order for [$]50.00." Thirteen items were purchased on that day including two yards of cloth at $9 per yard, three yards of lining, two and a half yards of cashmere for $8.75, padding and small buttons, three and a half yards of linen, a fine hat, a pint of whiskey, and several other items. The total charged that day was $33.36. The pint of whiskey cost $.13.

Robert or someone else charging purchases to his account visited Patterson's store on

September 7, 8, 9, 13, 16, 18, 21, 27, and 30. Items included a vest pattern, one and a half yards of cambric, three yards of ribbon, eight hanks of silk, four yards of ribbon, three-quarter yards of lace, one ball of cotton, whiskey, buttons, thirteen and three-quarter pounds of bacon, rope, buttons for vest pattern, nutmeg, sugar, one ounce of indigo per John Minter, and a jug of rum. The purchases of ribbons, lace, material for a vest, and a variety of cloth suggest that Robert may have been married at this time.

The entries for the account of Robert Hall continue with five visits to the store in October 1819 and four visits in November. Purchases included whiskey, rum, tobacco and whisky for John Minter (who was mentioned four times), rum for Randolph, salt, flannel cloth, a shaving box and brush, and a chamber pot. The total carried forward to the daybook, which no longer exists, was $20.94.

There is evidence that Robert assisted his father in his shipbuilding business. The $50 cash balance in the Patterson account book was probably part of Robert's compensation. In December 1819 his father completed and launched the *Sarah Ann*, and on December 15, 1819, Robert purchased coffee, sugar, candles, writing paper, salt, and a gallon of whiskey for the ship. On January 31 and February 14, 1820, he purchased oil, whiskey, coffee, and sugar. On March 2, 1820, the entry was made, "By cash in full $37.19." These items were no doubt part of the initial provisioning of the vessel.

On March 20, 1820, Robert purchased oil, a bushel of peas, six yards of canvas, thirty-five and a half fathoms of tarred rope, six pounds of rice, rum, whiskey, writing paper, and a slate. On March 22, he purchased nails and paper tacks for the schooner, and $50.71 was paid to "Wilson" for provisions and $1.75 for freight from Norfolk. The account at this time had a balance of $52.46, which was paid by James H. Roy, $25 and $1.22; William Hurst, $17.16 and $13.12; and Tompkins, $13.12. At this time Roy, Hurst, Tompkins, and Thomas Hall were the owners of the *Sarah Ann*. The account continues with a half barrel of tar purchased on June 8, a bottle of turpentine on the 12th, and a couple of gallons of whiskey, sugar, coffee, pepper, candles, nails, a slate, and a half barrel of flour on the 21st. The balance of $11.13 was paid in full on July 19.

In another customer account book of an unknown merchant in Mathews Courthouse in 1821, probably that of John Patterson, entries for sixteen items under "merchandise" for Robert Hall were recorded for the year. In 1822, there were nineteen entries for Robert. In July 1822, an account for the schooner *Thomas Hall* was opened, and entries were recorded, without a description of the merchandise, in July, August, September, and October. September 22, 1822, shows an entry for notes receivable from Robert Hall in the amount of $189.85, a significant sum considering that land was valued at this time at approximately $10–12 per acre and the monthly wage of a merchant seaman was approximately $9.

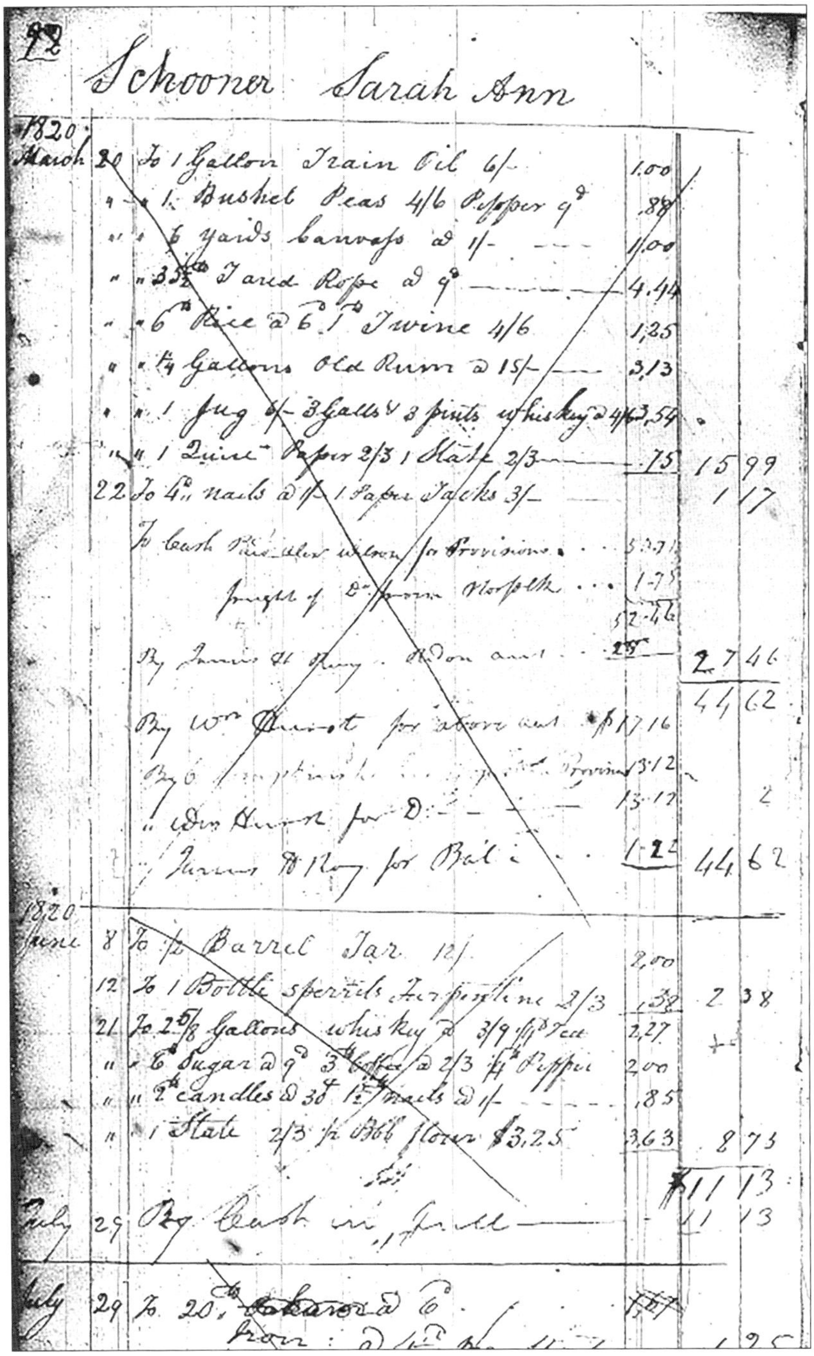


*Figure* 45 A page from an account book of John Patterson's store showing purchases and payments for "Schooner Sarah Ann" from March 20 through July 29, 1820. Courtesy of the John D. Rockefeller Jr. Library, Colonial Williamsburg Foundation, Williamsburg, VA.

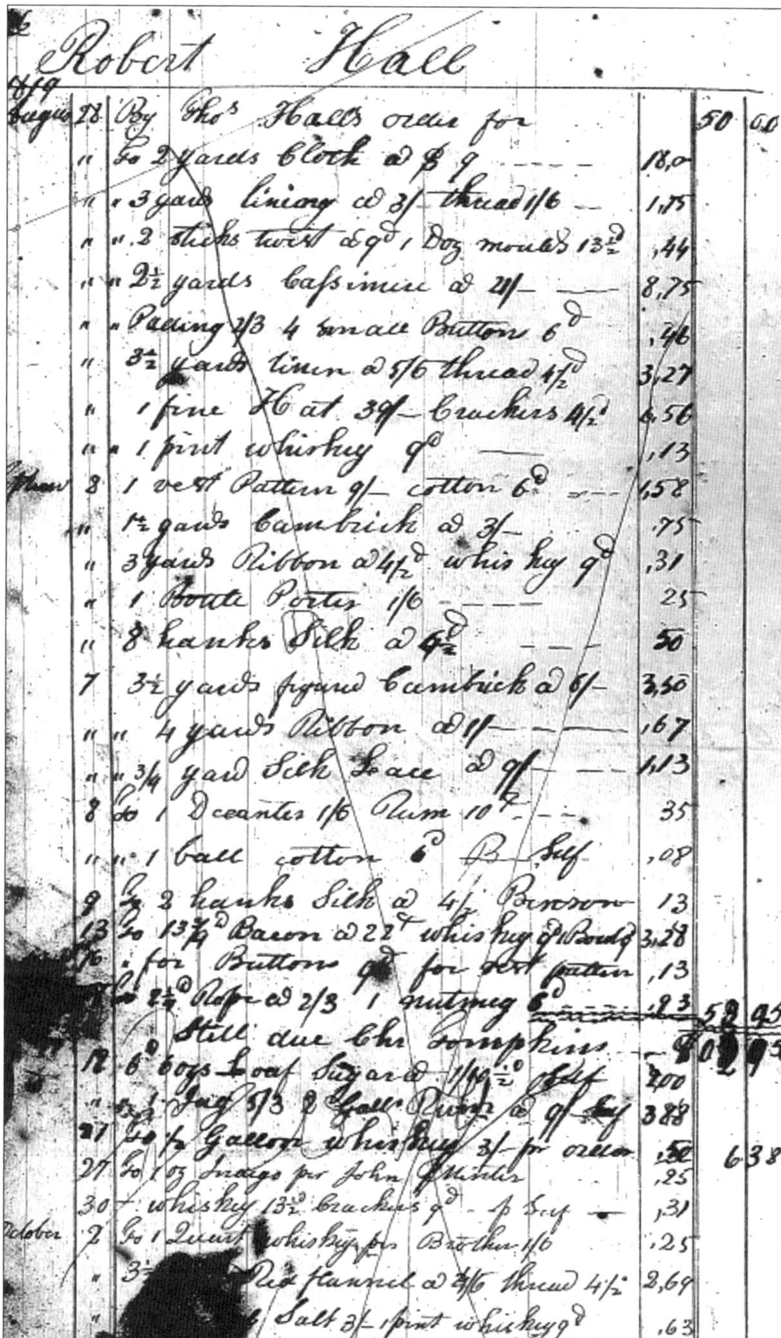

Robert Hall

1819 August 28 By Thos Hall's order for — 50.00
" To 2 yards Cloth @ $9 — 18,00
" " 3 yards lining @ 3/- thread 1/6 — 1,75
" " 2 sticks twist @ 9d, 1 Doz moulds 13½d — ,44
" " 2½ yards Cassimere @ 21/- — 8,75
" " Padding 2/3 4 small Buttons 6d — ,46
" 3½ yards linen @ 5/6 thread 4½d — 3,27
" 1 fine Hat 39/- Crackers 4½d — 6,56
" " 1 pint whiskey 9d — ,13
Sept 3 1 vest Pattern 9/- cotton 6d — 1,58
" 1½ yards Cambrick @ 3/- — ,75
" 3 yards Ribbon @ 4½d whiskey 9d — ,31
" 1 Bottle Porter 1/6 — 25
" 8 hanks Silk @ 4½d — 50
7 3½ yards figured Cambrick @ 6/- — 3,50
" " 4 yards Ribbon @ 1/- — ,67
" " 3/4 yard Silk Lace @ 9/- — 1,13
8 To 1 Decanter 1/6 Rum 10d — 35
" " 1 ball cotton 6d B. Self — ,08
9 To 2 hanks Silk @ 4½ Benson — 13
13 To 13 7/9 Bacon @ 22d whiskey 9d [illegible] — 3,28
16 for Buttons 9d for vest pattern — ,13
To 2¼ Rope @ 2/3 1 nutmeg 6d — ,93 — 58.45
Still due Chr Tompkins — [illegible]
12 6 boxs Loaf Sugar @ 1/10½ Self — 2,00
" To 1 Jug 5/3 2 Gall Rum @ 9/- Self — 3,88
27 To ½ Gallon whiskey 3/- pr order — ,50 — 6.38
27 To 1 oz Indigo per John Miller — ,25
30 whiskey 13½ Crackers 9d p Self — ,31
October 2 To 1 Quart whiskey for Brother 1/6 — ,25
" 3½ Red flannel @ 4/6 thread 4½ — 2,69
" Salt 3/- 1 pint whiskey 9d — ,63

*Figure* 46 A page from an account book of John Patterson's store showing purchases and payments for Robert Hall from August 28 through October 5, 1819. From the John D. Rockefeller Jr. Library, Colonial Williamsburg Foundation, Williamsburg, VA.

Additional entries for Robert Hall were made in October, November, and December 1822. The last entry under the name of Robert Hall was in January 1823, the year his son, Thomas Spencer, was born.*

The dates of the entries coincide with the October 15, 1822, initial registration date of the *Thomas Hall* suggesting that Robert was involved with the schooner's construction and fitting out. However, Robert is not listed as having an ownership interest in any of the three ships his father constructed, and he was never listed as master. He may have gone to sea from time to time as others in the family did, but there is no record of his having been engaged in that occupation. It is reasonable to assume that he was familiar with ship construction, as he would have been nineteen years old when the *Sarah Ann* was registered on December 17, 1819, and twenty-six at the time of the initial registration of the schooner *Alexander* on November 21, 1826, the last known vessel built in Thomas Hall's shipyard.

Unfortunately, Robert was dead by the end of 1833, at about thirty-three years of age. In the five years prior to his death, shipbuilding in Mathews County began a significant decline, and thus it is possible Robert went to sea as the demand for shipwrights contracted.

The Mathews County fee book has the following entry made in December 1833: "Elizabeth Hall widow of Robert Hall deceased. Order allowing your a/c vs Ro Hall's admor [allowing the administrator an advance for Elizabeth Hall against Robert Hall's estate]: for b[o]ard & clothing of Sarah Ann & Thomas Hall 18 copy 18 filing."[1] The fee was for petitioning the court for an advance from Robert's estate for the care of his children. At this time his son, Thomas Spencer, was ten, and his daughter, Sarah, was eleven. There is no record concerning where Elizabeth and her two children lived, but it is assumed that they were in the household of Thomas Hall Sr. or nearby on family land. Thomas Spencer, having lost his father at age ten, must have had a close relationship with his grandfather and probably learned much from him. Although little is known about his life other than from the census and land records, he apparently became a skilled blacksmith who owned his own shop in New Market, now Deltaville, and continued his trade in Hartfield.

Thomas Spencer Hall's life spanned a period of great change in ship construction. When he was born in 1823, ocean-going shipbuilding, mostly two-masted schooners, was an important segment of the Mathews County and Virginia economies, a segment in which he would have probably entered, especially given his grandfather's and father's involvement in ship construction. However, by the time he moved to Middlesex County, twenty-four years later in 1847, steamships were making significant inroads into commercial shipping.

---

* During this period entries were also made for Thomas Hall Sr., two in 1821, twenty-five in 1822, and three in 1823, the last one recorded in May.

As discussed in the previous chapter, beginning around 1830, Mathews experienced a significant reduction in the construction of ocean-going schooners, brigs, and ships, and the number of shipyards and the need for shipwrights in local yards declined because the manufacturing process for steam engines, propellers and shafts, and other related equipment required iron and steel. Thus shipbuilding migrated to large ports such as Norfolk and Baltimore that were equipped with the necessary infrastructure including rolling and milling machines for metal fabrication, metal presses, metal furnaces, and metal lathes.

During this same period, advances in agricultural technology transformed farming methods from little-changed traditions dating from the colonial era to horse- and mule-drawn mechanized equipment for many of the tasks required in field cultivation and harvesting. Regular steamship schedules from wharves in Mathews to Baltimore and Norfolk became commonplace and increased the volume of passenger and freight traffic, including fresh produce, fish, and shellfish, up and down the bay. The local economy thus entered a period of transition from a dependence on shipbuilding and repair to greater dependence on agriculture and commercial fishing.

Seven years after the death of Robert, in October 1840, the Mathews County Fee Book recorded the appointment of Joseph R. Gayle, Thomas Spencer's uncle, to be the administrator for the estate of his father-in-law, Thomas Hall Sr., who died in August of that year. Thomas Spencer and his sister, Sarah, and their cousin John W. Hall were to inherit land from their grandfather's estate. The three being "infants," the court appointed William Hurst and his wife, Sarah Ann, and Thomas Hall Jr., the children's guardians, to represent their interests in the settlement of the estate and the management of the inherited property until the children were of age at twenty-one.[2]

The term "infant" in the 1840s indicated a child under the age of twenty-one. Thomas Spencer was seventeen years old at the time and his sister, Sarah, was probably eighteen. John W.'s age is not known. A child, beginning at age fourteen, could select his or her own guardian, usually a trusted family member or close friend of the parents. In most cases there was no purpose in petitioning the court for appointing a guardian unless there was an inheritance involved. The guardian had the responsibility of managing the estate until the infant reached his or her majority. Sarah and Thomas Spencer inherited twenty-four acres. They continued to be listed as orphans until 1843 and as joint owners of real estate until 1844. In 1845 John H. Saunders, who had become Sarah's husband, had purchased the land.* The assessed value of the twenty-four acres in 1845 was $288, half of which presumably went to Thomas Spencer.

---

* In his will, John H. Saunders refers to his wife as "Nannie."

Thomas Spencer next appeared in the record on April 21, 1846, at age twenty-three, approximately a year following the sale of his share of the land from his grandfather's estate. On that date he acquired 105 acres of land in Middlesex County for $500 from John J. Burk.[3] The property was bounded on the south by the Piankatank River, on the north by John J. Bass, on the west by Henry Barrick, and on the east by A. M. Hicks. Some of the purchase price probably came from the inheritance of his grandfather's estate.

A year later on July 31, 1847, he sold the property to Anthony D. Hudgins of Mathews County for $700.[*4] The description of the acreage is different, suggesting changes in adjacent ownerships. In the 1847 deed, the property was bounded on the north by Henry Barrick's land and others, on the south by the Piankatank River, on the east by the Chesapeake Bay, and on the west by Wood and others.[†]

In the deed of April 21, 1846, Thomas Spencer was the sole owner, but the deed of July 31, 1847, listed "Thomas S. Hall and Elizabeth his wife."[5] This was the first mention of Thomas Spencer having a wife. Elizabeth S. Saunders was the daughter of Jacob Saunders[6] of Mathews County and the sister of John H. Saunders, who had married Thomas Spencer's sister, Sarah. Thus, brother and sister married sister and brother. Elizabeth was born about 1828. Their marriage probably occurred between mid-1846 and early 1847, when she would have been about nineteen years old. A son, John R., was born early in 1848.

Tragically, Elizabeth died during childbirth or shortly thereafter. The 1848 tax records for Middlesex County show Thomas Spencer owning 105 acres (Stingray Point Farm had not yet conveyed) and 30 acres on Broad Creek with a life interest. This second parcel, in proximity to Stingray Point, belonged to his deceased wife's father, and they are thought to have made it their home after the marriage. Thomas Spencer probably purchased Stingray Point Farm after his engagement to Elizabeth since it was very close to her father's land.

Thomas Spencer's sister, Sarah, and her husband, John H. Saunders of Mathews County,

---

* Hudgins apparently experienced financial difficulties because in a deed recorded on June 14, 1848, the property was placed in the hands of a trustee, Thomas R. Bull, with terms for eventual payment of the purchase price to Thomas Spencer Hall. The trustee subsequently sold 9⅓ acres of Stingray Point Farm to John Norton for $112 on November 13, 1849. The description for land adjoining the parcel included the property of Hudgins on the east, Thomas Western on the west, Elizabeth Greenwood on the south, and on the north the property of John Boss and Jacob Saunders, the father of Thomas's deceased wife, Elizabeth. (Middlesex County Court House, Deed Book 20, page 413.)

† As was noted in chapter 1, this parcel was part of Stingray Point, where John Smith nearly died in July 1608.

had two children, Thomas A. Saunders and Nannie E. Saunders.[7] In addition, they cared for the infant son of Thomas Spencer and Elizabeth, John R.[8]

Within two years following the death of his first wife, Thomas Spencer, age twenty-six, married Pelina Jane Carter in December 1849. Her father, Hiram Carter, served as witness, and the Reverend R. A. Christian performed the ceremony. Pelina was just sixteen years old, and with infant John R. soon to return to his father's house, she began her marriage with a two-year-old stepson. Pelina and Thomas Spencer's first child was a son, William Thomas, who was born on February 9, 1851. Thomas Spencer and Pelina had nine more children over the following sixteen years.

Pelina was one of six children, four sons and two daughters, of Hiram Carter and his wife, Emily Pendleton Steptoe Pollard Tankersley Carter. Hiram and Emily were married on

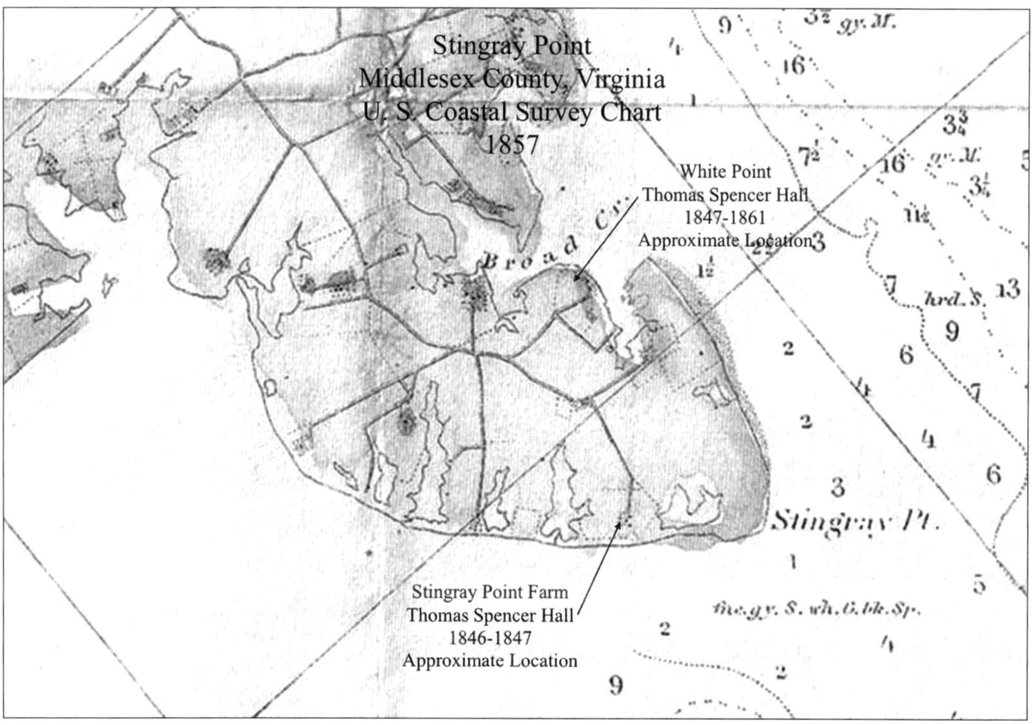


*Figure* 47 This illustration of Stingray Point in 1857 is especially significant given its date and the dates of occupation by Thomas Spencer Hall on Stingray Point Farm and White Point within Broad Creek (superimposed). The actual field survey measurements were made several years earlier, mostly in the mid-1840s. From the first published chart of the Rappahannock River, made by the US Coast Survey, known as the Coast and Geodetic Survey beginning in 1878.

On November 24, 1834, when he was about forty-two, Hiram Carter purchased 133½ acres of land from Washington B. Callis for $1,400. The tract was located "on the public road from Sandy Bottom and Miles' store adjoining the lands of William T. Miles, Griffen Cundiff, and land formerly owned by E. Deagle."[11] The property may have included structures: on the property today stands a restored house thought to have been built between 1815 and 1825. However, the house may have been built by Hiram Carter in 1835 or 1836, especially given that the purchase price, which was $10.48 per acre, suggests a land-only transaction.

The house in its original configuration consisted of a center hall, a stairwell with reverse landing to the second floor, and two flanking rooms, each with a fireplace. The second floor had the same configuration as the first floor, including two additional fireplaces. An open first-floor porch and an enclosed porch room overhead on the second floor covered the entrance. The foundation and the two chimneys were brick, and the siding was clapboard. The property also included a one-room house with a loft above that was believed to have been used as slave quarters and a separate kitchen building, which had a fireplace large enough in which to stand.[12] There is no surviving record listing other structures such as a barn and outbuildings that may have been on the property.

The Carter family owned the property for twenty-four years and sold it on March 9, 1858, to William H. Kelly of Baltimore, Maryland, for $1,800. It included the original tract of 133½ acres. Hiram was still alive at this time as the deed recorded his appearance at the closing.[13] The property, at present known as the Kelly House, is one of the few remaining early nineteenth-century structures in Middlesex County. See figure 48 on the next page.

February 18, 1818, in Lancaster County, where they are thought to have been born.[9] They probably moved to Middlesex County before 1820, the year in which Hiram first appeared in the US Census. Based on his ages listed in the censuses of 1820, 1830, and 1840, he was born between 1790 and 1794.[10]

In a deed recorded on January 6, 1851, in Middlesex County, John H. Saunders purchased ninety-six acres of Stingray Point Farm from Anthony H. Hudgins for $800.[14] At this time Thomas Spencer was living on the thirty acres on Broad Creek. The 1853 tax record for Middlesex County shows in the entry for Hall, Thomas S., that his residence in Middlesex, on an estate held for life, was thirty acres on Broad Creek, twenty-one miles from the courthouse. It had a land value of $18 per acre including buildings and the total value of the land and buildings as $540 ($150 added to the land on account of buildings).[15]

*Figure* 48 The home of Hiram Carter on land acquired in 1834 and sold in 1858. Now known as the Kelly House, it has been completely restored and is an excellent example of an early nineteenth-century Tidewater central passageway design with flanking rooms on either side on the first and second floors.

Thomas Spencer and Pelina lived on the property, known as White Point, for twelve years, during which time they had seven children who joined John R. In 1861, Thomas Spencer sold his interest in the thirty acres on Broad Creek and moved his family eight miles inland to Hartfield, where he had purchased five and a half acres from William H. and Mildred Hudgins for $500.[16] The deed was recorded on August 22, 1861. The property was bounded on the north by the main county road and the land of Ammon Didlake, on the south and east by the Bath estate, and on the west by the land of the heirs of Robert T. Mountain.

A few days earlier, a deed recorded on August 4, 1861, showed that Thomas Spencer had sold his interest in the thirty acres[17] to his brother-in-law John H. Saunders for $400. John's father, Jacob Saunders, who would have been between sixty-one and seventy-one years old based on the census records, or his estate owned the property, and Elizabeth would have probably inherited it if she had lived. The property was eventually left in the estate of Jacob Saunders to the children of John H. Saunders and Elizabeth's son, John R. Hall.

Thomas Spencer, thirty-eight years old in 1861, and Pelina, twenty-eight, would have three more children after their move to Hartfield. Their move from property at the easternmost end of Middlesex County, bound by the Chesapeake Bay, may have been a decision based on fears of the unfolding war or a business move to have his blacksmith shop located in a more central part of the county.

A skilled blacksmith, Thomas Spencer owned his own shop in New Market, now Deltaville, and then Hartfield. Blacksmiths at this time repaired broken and malfunctioning farm equipment, fabricated specialized items such as the iron tongs used to harvest oysters, were the repair shop for wagon wheels and axles, and practiced the traditional service of shoeing horses and mules. The work was hard, working conditions were less than desirable, and income was modest at best. Nine years after the family's move to Hartfield, Thomas Spencer Hall died in late 1870 or early 1871 at age forty-seven. He was buried on his property between his house and the main road in what is now an unmarked grave.

The years following the Civil War were difficult throughout the South. In Middlesex County, many inhabitants lived at little more than a subsistence level, largely dependent on what could be produced on their own land. Thomas Spencer Hall's estate was inventoried and appraised on April 18, 1871, and auctioned on May 17. The listings provide a useful perspective on the material condition of an average household at the time. Some of the items listed include blacksmith tools, a grinding stone, a no. 1 C&B plough, a buggy, a horse cart, a sorrel horse, a sorrel stallion, 14 shoats, a sow, a red cow, a white cow, a cooking stove, 3 beds and furniture, blankets and quilts, a mantle clock, a looking glass, a washstand and basin, 6 Windsor chairs, 4 chairs and small table, lamps, an oil can, 10 knives and forks, 2 tubs, a cupboard with plates, 4 stone jars, an old carpet, 150 bales of fodder, 28 pounds of bacon, 76½ pounds of lard, and 10½ bushels of corn.[18]

There were liens on the estate, and most of the items were sold to reduce debt. However, the court allowed Pelina to keep some of the items necessary for everyday living including the red cow, the horse, the stove, two beds, a table and six chairs, the plough, fodder, and bacon. Most of the remaining items in the estate were purchased by family members including John R. Hall, who purchased the grinding stone, looking glass, and a lamp; John H. Saunders, who bought the blacksmith tools and the white cow; and William T. Hall, who purchased three knives and forks, two stone jars, and the old carpet. Pelina purchased most of the remaining items, perhaps with money given to her by her children and by members of the Carter family. Her household thus retained most of the everyday things she was accustomed to have.

Missing from the inventory of Thomas Spencer Hall's estate was his five and a half acres of land and his house and farm buildings. These assets were held as collateral on the debts owed. It appears that the obligations were not satisfied until 1880, when on June 28 a special commissioner of the Circuit Court of Middlesex County conveyed with a special warranty of title the five and a half acres, "being the same tract on which Thomas S. Hall resided at the time of his death," to his son Addison Hall.[19]

The records of the appraisal and sale of the estate show that the appraised values were much higher than what was eventually realized from the estate sale, which was held on May 17, 1871. For example, the blacksmith tools appraised at thirty dollars sold for ten, the buggy sold for five dollars but was appraised at ten.

At the time of his death, Thomas Spencer and Pelina had nine children[*] in addition to John R.: William Thomas,[†] born February 9, 1851; George Warren, born January 22, 1852; James B., born November 3, 1854; Addison, born January 10, 1856; Alice B., born January 25, 1858; Emma Jane, born January 25, 1860; Beauregard, born April 10, 1861; Lorena Belle, born December 15, 1864; and Mary S., born in 1866 and may have died as an infant. At his death, six of his children were not yet sixteen years old. Brothers William Thomas and George Warren, ages twenty and nineteen respectively, must have assumed responsibility for providing for the care and feeding of the large household.

William, in particular, was vital because he had learned the blacksmith trade and worked with his father. William continued being a blacksmith in Topping, Middlesex County, where he lived in a house given to him and his bride, Nannie A., by her parents, John D. and Nancy Miller, as a wedding gift. They were married on November 23, 1875, when William was twenty-four and Nannie twenty.[20] The wedding gift was made in a deed recorded on September 17, 1877, and contained "five acres and thirty poles."[‡] The plat description references an adjoining "woodshop of J. D. Miller."[21]

In 1870, Sarah and John H. Saunders sold the thirty-acre White Point tract to their nephew John R. for five dollars and in consideration of the "love & affection, which the said John H. Saunders & Sarah A., his wife, bear towards the said John R. Hall." The property boundaries were described as having Broad Creek to the north, the lands of Robert J. Bass on the east, on the south the main road leading from New Market to Stingray Point, and on the west the lands of Nathan Christopher, deceased. The deed was recorded on February 6, 1870.[22] John R. was twenty-two years old, and there is no record of his having married by this date.

---

* It appears that one child had died.

† William Thomas was the author's great-grandfather.

‡ There are 160 square poles in one acre, so 30 poles would be 0.1875 of an acre.

Three years later John H. Saunders repurchased the property, for five dollars, in a deed recorded on May 17, 1873.[23] Saunders then traded the thirty-acre White Point tract on the same day in exchange for nineteen acres in the lower part of Middlesex County adjoining the lands of Josiah D. Ailworth, Robert D. Watson, and others. Saunders may have been putting his affairs in order. He was approximately fifty-six years old and was apparently in poor health because on August 20, 1873, he created and signed his will. He was dead by November 26 when his will was proved and recorded.[24] He left all of his property to his wife, Sarah A. Saunders, sister of Thomas Spencer Hall, and at her death the property was to be divided between their two children: Thomas A. Saunders was to receive the land on which his parents had resided, and Nannie E. Taylor, wife of David A. Taylor, was to inherit White Point. As recorded in the will, the two tracts adjoined.

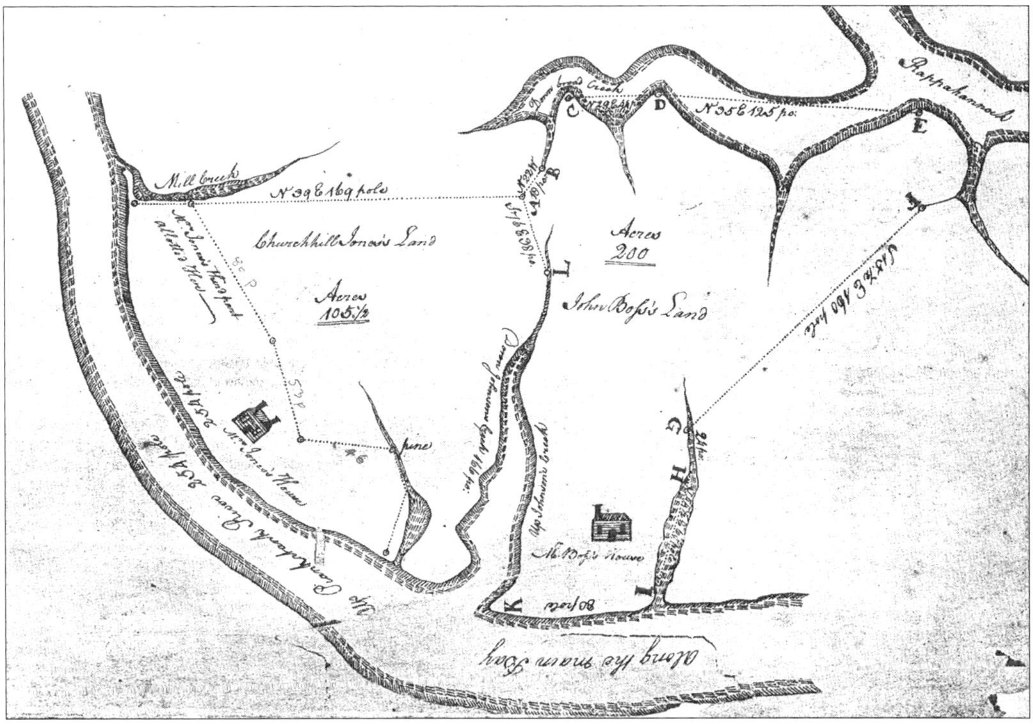


*Figure* 49 The earliest known survey of Stingray Point, dated September 4, 1773, contains a two-hundred-acre tract of land that included White Point and most of the southern shore of Broad Creek. The northerly direction is generally to the right. Two houses are shown, one owned by "Mr. Boss," a story-and-a-half structure with one chimney, and one owned by Mr. Jones, a story and a half with a chimney at each end. On a current topographical map, the survey stations marked "I" and "K" would be in the Chesapeake Bay, indicating approximately four hundred feet of erosion over more than two hundred years. From Map Books nos. 1 and 2, Middlesex County Courthouse, Saluda, VA.

When John R. Hall died in early 1876, at age twenty-eight, he left in his estate forty-nine and a half acres, which sold for $871 to David A. Taylor, the husband of his cousin Nannie, in a deed recorded on August 25, 1876.[25] The southern boundary of the combined parcels was the main county road and the land of Addison Carter, one of the brothers of his stepmother, Pelina. The other boundaries were Broad Creek on the north, R. Boss on the east, and Nathan Christopher on the west.

Pelina died in 1914 and was buried in the Lower Church. Beside her grave is a monument for her husband, Thomas Spencer, but he was buried on his land at Hartfield, and the grave is now unmarked. The Lower Church is believed to be on the same site as the first church, the "Old Peankatank Church," which was erected around 1657.[26]

A surviving document in the National Archives contains an invaluable genealogy of the Hall family based on Robert Hall Jr. It was originally submitted in the court of Mathews County to obtain any outstanding benefits derived from Robert's service in the Revolutionary War. It has been the Rosetta stone to researching the Hall family and provided the critical link between Mathews and Middlesex Counties:

> Virginia. In Mathews County Court, Monday the 10th day of May 1847. It has been made to appear to the satisfaction of the court that Robert Hall, a Master in the Navy in the revolutionary war, died intestate in the latter part of 1786 or in the early part of the year 1787 leaving Thomas Hall, Betsy Hall, who married Francis Brown, Nancy Hall, who married Peter Foster, Joicey Hall, who married Mathias Gayle, and the children of Spencer Hall, his sole heirs at law. Thomas Hall died intestate in 1840, leaving Sarah Hurst the wife of William Hurst, Mary Gayle the wife of Joseph R. Gayle, Thomas Hall, Sarah Hall who married John Saunders and Thomas Hall the children of Robert Hall and John Hall a minor who was a son of John Hall, his sole heirs at law. Nancy Foster who died leaving Richard Foster, Peter Foster Jr., William Foster, Susan R. Foster who married William Foster who is since dead leaving two children Harriett & William Foster. Ann Foster who married Robert Debnam, Elizabeth Foster who married Joshua G. Brown who is since dead leaving five children: viz. Peyton I., Ann who married Beverly Waddle, Caroline who married Henry Baker, Selina F. who married Nathan Walker & Wilson R. Brown and Polly Foster who married James Brownly, his sole heirs at law.
>
> Joicy Gale who was Joicy Hall died leaving Bartlet Gayle, Joshua Gayle, Nancy Gayle and Betsy Gayle her sole heirs at law. Betsy Brown who was Betsy Hall died leaving six children. viz: Robert Brown, Spencer H. Brown, Susan who

married ____ Oliver, Ann who married Joshua Gayle, Elizabeth Brown and Francis Brown who married _____ Walden, her sole heirs at law.

In Mathews County Quarterly Court, May 10, 1847. On the motion of Peter G. Foster who made oath & together with Richard Foster his security, entered into & acknowledged a bond in the penalty of one thousand dollars conditioned[?] according to Law, certificate is granted the said Peter G. Foster for obtaining letters of administration of the Estate of Robert Hall deceased in [?] form of Law.

Know all men by these presents, that I, Peter G. Foster, administrator of Robert Hall deceased, who was a Sailing Master in the Virginia Navy of Revolutionary War: do hereby constitute, nominate and appoint Thomas Green of Richmond, his lawful attorney, to prosecute any claims to Land or money that may be due from the State of Virginia & United States, or either, on account of the Revolutionary service of said Robert Hall: & to demand [?] from the proper offices in Richmond and Washington, any Land warrant or warrants [?], to hold and assign the same, or to surrender them at the General Land office in order to obtain Certificates of Scrip in lieu thereof, which he is authorized to receive, sell & assign. Or if said warrants be already surrendered, then to demand & secure the certificates & to sell & assign the same.

If no scrip can be obtained, he is authorized to secure warrants which may have been surrendered, and to locate or sell the same, as he may think best. Said attorney is also authorized to prosecute by suit or petition, & to demand & secure from the State of Virginia & the United States, any halfpay or commutation, & interest that may be due, particularly under the Act of 5th July 1832; and to substitute and appoint one or more attorneys under him, with a general or special authority to do all he is permitted to do, & revoke the same at pleasure. I hereby ratify & confirm whatever said attorney or his substitutes may lawfully do in the promises. As witness my hand and seal this tenth day of May 1847.

Peter G. Foster
Administrator of Robert Hall, decd.[27]

Additional information comes from another pension application:

10 May 1847. Mathews Co., Va. William Hurst declares he married the daughter of Thomas Hall who was the brother of Robert Hall. Thomas Hall

> got him to transact business for him as he lived to be a very old man. He often heard Thomas speak of the warrant he got for the Revolutionary services of his brother Robert Hall and that he disposed of it to a man named Reynolds. Thomas Hall died 23 Aug. 1840 leaving three children, Sarah Hurst, Mary Gayle and Thomas Hall, and three grandchildren, John Hall, Sarah Saunders and Thomas [Spencer] Hall.[28]

The court appearance of Peter Foster and others on May 10, 1847, occurred between the purchase of Stingray Point Farm by Thomas Spencer Hall on April 21, 1846, and its sale to Anthony H. Hudgins on July 31, 1847, and his marriage to Elizabeth Saunders in late 1846 to early 1847. This was a time of significant changes in the family, the local economy, the growing tensions in the national political spectrum, and the migration from Mathews County to Middlesex County. The economic well-being of the next generation of Halls would be challenging during the years leading up to the Civil War and the thirty years following, a time of social and economic distress.

## CHAPTER 15

# Thomas Hall Jr., Son *of* Thomas *and* Mary Hall *and* Grandson *of* Ann *and* Robert Hall

Thomas Hall Jr., the second son of Thomas and Mary Hall (née Gayle), was born in Mathews County about 1802. His brother Robert, born about 1800, was named for his grandfather while Thomas was named for his father. While census records do not give evidence, it is thought that the two brothers and their families lived in proximity, and probably on the original family land.

In 1835, Thomas Jr., at age thirty-three, married Lucina "Lucy" F. Summers, who was sixteen. She too was born in Mathews County and was the child of Mary and William Summers.

The land tax records for the years 1791 through 1800 do not list William Summers, nor does the personal property tax record of 1791. However, the tax record of 1792, and continuing through 1800, shows William Summers as having one white male over the age of sixteen in his household, suggesting that he was new to the county in 1792, or that he was without property or was not a head of household prior to 1792.

By 1820, his family had grown. The US Census recorded the Summers household as consisting of six males: two under the age of ten, two aged ten to sixteen, one aged sixteen to twenty-six, and one over the age of forty-five. The census shows three members of the household engaged in agriculture. Also listed were two females: one under the age of eleven and one aged twenty-six to forty-five. The female less than eleven years old must have been Thomas's future wife, Lucina.

The census of 1830 recorded the Summers family as having one male fifteen to twenty years old, one male twenty to thirty, and one female forty to fifty. William was probably dead at this time, and the sons were living with their mother. Inexplicably missing from this census was a female who would have been the age of Lucina. The census of 1840 had just one reference to the family, one Dudley Summers, age twenty to thirty, engaged in manufacturing. The age suggests that Dudley was the youngest son of Mary and William. By this time Thomas Hall Jr. was Dudley's brother-in-law.

Thomas Jr. and Lucy had eight children: John Spencer, born in 1836; Mary Ann, born on November 26, 1839; William Thomas, born on July 11, 1842; Lucy Frances, born in 1845; Sarah "Sallie" Elizabeth, born on March 14, 1848; Virginia Maude, born in 1851; Martha "Mat" Ellen, born in 1853; and James "Robert," born on December 8, 1854.

Listed in Thomas Jr.'s household in the census of 1840 were his son John Spencer, age approximately four; his daughter Mary Ann, about one; and his wife, Lucina, who would have been about twenty-one. The census also includes one female between the ages of sixty and seventy. She was most likely Lucina's mother, Mary, who would have been approximately sixty or more given that her husband, William, deceased, was born at least before 1776, according to the personal property tax records. At about thirty-eight, Thomas Jr. had one slave, a male between the ages of ten and twenty-four. He and the slave were recorded as being engaged in agriculture. Since seventy-five-year-old Thomas Sr. likely lived nearby and owned twenty slaves, all listed in the census, it is highly likely that Thomas Jr. also utilized some of his father's slaves.

By the time of the US Census of 1850, Thomas Jr., age forty-eight, and Lucina, age thirty-one, had five children, ages four to thirteen. Having inherited slaves from his father, who died in 1840, Thomas Jr. now owned one male slave, age twenty-six; a female slave, age twenty-five; and two elderly slaves, a male age ninety and a female age eighty-eight, perhaps husband and wife. The other fourteen or fifteen slaves owned by Thomas Hall Sr. probably were sold by his estate.

The US Census of 1850 included a population schedule that listed the names of individuals by household, a schedule of slaves showing the owner and age of each, and an agricultural schedule. By 1850 the local economy in Mathews had become highly dependent on agriculture. The census recorded 141 farmers, 97 mariners, 77 ship carpenters, 45 laborers, 44 house carpenters, 17 merchants, 16 shoemakers, 8 physicians, 7 teachers, 6 blacksmiths, 6 tailors, 4 clergy, 4 bricklayers, 5 constables including the sheriff, 4 shipwrights, 3 wheelwrights, 3 coach makers, 2 clerks, 2 painters, 2 lighthouse keepers, 2 attorneys at law, 2 cabinetmakers, 1 pilot, 1 boat builder, 1 machinist, 1 jeweler, 1 innkeeper, and 1 harness maker.

The total number of persons reporting a profession totaled 503 out of 675 dwelling houses.

Of these, farmers represented the largest primary occupation accounting for 28 percent of all employment, mariners represented 19 percent, ship carpenters 15 percent, laborers 9 percent, and house carpenters 9 percent. Shipbuilding in Mathews County declined rapidly after 1830, and it is thought that the great majority of the county's ship carpenters worked in shipyards in the Hampton Roads region. Maritime-related occupations, including mariners, ship carpenters, shipwrights, pilots, boat builders, and lighthouse keepers, totaled 182, 36 percent of all occupations in Mathews County.

According to the 1850 agricultural census, which reflected inventories from 1849, Thomas Jr. owned thirty-six acres. Twenty acres were in cultivation, and sixteen acres were in an unimproved condition, which often meant a woodlot and/or untended fields. Thomas Jr.'s land, structures, animals, and crops were valued at $800, which breaks down as follows: The farm value was estimated to be $500, and the faming implements $15. His farm animals—two cows, two oxen, two cattle, and ten swine—were valued at $82. In the barn or waiting to be harvested were 160 bushels of corn, 10 bushels of peas, 15 bushels of sweet potatoes, $15 worth of produce and other market garden items, ten pounds of butter, one ton of hay, and $40 worth of animals slaughtered. These values total $652, which indicates a value of $148 for structures, fencing, and other improvements. The value of slaves was not included in estimating farm values.

The value of Thomas Jr.'s farm animals and crops was small in comparison to most of the farms in the county in 1849. Table 15.1 shows the number of farms as measured by the value of their crops and animals as recorded on the 1850 census. It appears that values were established in a very general way, orders of magnitude by estimate being the primary method of classification.

Table 15.1 shows that 146 farms, half of the total 294 farms listed in Mathews County, had farm values of $1,100 or less. The total value of these farms was $90,000 or 14.5 percent of $622,200, the total of all farms. On the other hand, only 39 farms, just 13 percent of total farms, those with values greater than $4,000, accounted for half, $311,100, of the total farm values of the county. The largest 11 farms, 4 percent of all farms, accounted for 25 percent of total countywide value. Thus by the mid-nineteenth century, a consolidation had occurred with large farms having the capital to become even larger. The result was a significant concentration of a large share of total farming value being accounted for by a small percentage of Mathew's farm families.

Mathews County farms were remarkably similar as measured by the animals they raised and utilized in cultivation. In a random sample of farms varying in size from values of $500–16,000, all of them had at least one cow, with farms of $500 in value averaging 1.4 cows per farm to larger farms having a value of $1,000–2,000 averaging 2.9 cows per farm. These

**TABLE 15.1**

***Number of Farms and Farm Values, 1850, Mathews County, Virginia[1]***

| Farm Value | No. of Farms | Cumulative Farms | Farm Values | Cumulative Values |
|---|---|---|---|---|
| < $100 | 3 | 3 | $300 | $300 |
| 200 | 10 | 13 | 2,000 | 2,300 |
| 300 | 19 | 32 | 5,700 | 8,000 |
| 400 | 8 | 40 | 3,200 | 11,200 |
| 500 | 36 | 76 | 18,000 | 29,200 |
| 600 | 15 | 91 | 9,000 | 38,200 |
| 700 | 6 | 97 | 4,200 | 42,400 |
| 800 | 7 | 104 | 5,600 | 48,000 |
| 900 | 3 | 107 | 2,700 | 50,700 |
| 1,000 | 36 | 143 | 36,000 | 86,700 |
| 1,100 | 3 | 146 | 3,300 | 90,000 |
| 1,200 | 11 | 157 | 13,200 | 103,200 |
| 1,300 | 6 | 163 | 7,800 | 111,000 |
| 1,500 | 24 | 187 | 36,000 | 147,000 |
| 1,600 | 3 | 190 | 4,800 | 151,800 |
| 1,800 | 3 | 193 | 5,400 | 157,200 |
| 2,000 | 28 | 221 | 56,000 | 213,200 |
| 2,500 | 13 | 234 | 32,500 | 245,700 |
| 3,000 | 17 | 251 | 51,000 | 296,700 |
| 3,500 | 4 | 255 | 14,000 | 310,700 |
| 4,000 | 11 | 266 | 44,000 | 354,700 |
| 4,500 | 5 | 271 | 22,500 | 377,200 |
| 5,000 | 2 | 273 | 10,000 | 387,200 |
| 6,000 | 6 | 279 | 36,000 | 423,200 |
| 7,000 | 1 | 280 | 7,000 | 430,200 |
| 8,000 | 1 | 281 | 8,000 | 438,200 |
| 10,000 | 5 | 286 | 50,000 | 488,200 |
| 12–16,000 | 6 | 292 | 77,000 | 565,200 |
| 27,000 | 1 | 293 | 27,000 | 592,200 |
| 30,000 | 1 | 294 | 30,000 | 622,200 |
| Total | 294 | | $622,200 | |

numbers suggest that cows were kept primarily for the farm family and their workers' consumption. All farms had swine, 13.7 on average for small farms and 21.9 on average for the larger farms. The next highest were cattle, with 94 percent of all farms having at least one. The average was 2.7 for small farms compared to 5.5 on larger farms.

Horses were used on 78 percent of the farms, with the average for all farms being 1.4. They were primarily devoted to transportation: pulling the ubiquitous two-wheeled farm cart and farm wagons and for personal conveyance. Teams of oxen, most often two animals per team, were the principal means of cultivation, they being capable of pulling plows and heavy loads, such as logs from the forests, without requiring excess care and feeding. Oxen were on 71 percent of all farms in groups of two, four, and six, with the average being 2.6 per farm. Sheep were recorded on 41 percent of the farms without a particular number per size farm except for the very largest farms with values above $15,000 where the number of sheep averaged 32.

The 1850 census listed 141 individuals who stated that farming was their principal occupation. However, the 1850 agricultural schedule lists 294 farms. The difference of 153 households shows that farming was an important second occupation for a large percentage of county households. There were 675 dwellings in the 1850 census, 294 of which, or 44 percent, were engaged in farming activities. There were far more households that, while not engaged in commercial farming, had small kitchen gardens for self-sufficiency.

The total white population in 1850 was 3,641, 1,662 males and 1,979 females. The number of men and women over the age of twenty who could not read or write was 417. There were 456 children in school. There were forty-eight white marriages within the past year. Four people were classified as "Idiotic" and three were "Deaf & Dumb." In addition to white families, enslaved individuals totaled 2,928, 1,430 males and 1,498 females. There were 147 free blacks and biracial individuals, 67 males and 80 females.

Table 15.2 summarizes the demographics of Mathews County in 1850. It shows that the white population represented 3,641 persons out of a total of 6,716, or 54.2 percent. Slaves, free blacks, and biracial individuals numbered 3,075 persons, or 45.8 percent of the total.

On May 21, 1866, Thomas Jr., sixty-four years old, sold his real estate to his sons John Spencer and William Thomas for fifteen dollars per acre. The description of the property as recorded in the deed is as follows:

> Containing forty three and two thirds acres, being the same more or less, being the land upon which the said Thomas Hall now resides, and adjoins the lands of Thomas G. Weston and George E. Tabb, thirty six acres of the said land the said Thomas Hall derived title to by the death of his father the late Thomas

**TABLE 15.2**

***1850 Population of Mathews County, Virginia***[2]

| | Whites | Free Blacks and Biracial Individuals | Slaves | Total |
|---|---|---|---|---|
| Males | 1,662 | 67 | 1,430 | 3,159 |
| % of total | 52.6 | 2.1 | 45.3 | 100.0 |
| Females | 1,979 | 80 | 1,498 | 3,557 |
| % of total | 55.6 | 2.3 | 42.1 | 100.0 |
| Total | 3,641 | 147 | 2,928 | 6,716 |

> Hall, and the residue thereof, to wit: seven and two thirds acres the said party of the first part purchased of Josiah Diggs and adjoins the land of the said Thomas G. Weston and Christopher S. Browne, being wood land.[3]

Unfortunately, the surveys necessary to determine the exact location of Hall's 43⅔ acres do not exist, and thus it cannot be determined if this parcel was part of the original land once owned by Ann Hall. However, the circumstantial evidence makes a strong case for this parcel to be the same one that the Halls had occupied since sometime in the early eighteenth century.

On that May 21, 1866, a little more than a year had elapsed since the end of the Civil War. It was a time for families to reassemble their lives, rebuild their farms and occupations, and begin a new life under extreme economic and political hardships. The enslaved had been freed, but in most instances these men and women continued in the employment of their former owners working for wages or as sharecroppers or tenants.

The readjustment to peacetime conditions was especially applicable for William Thomas and John Spencer, who were the only members of the Hall family of Mathews and Middlesex Counties to serve in the Civil War. John Spencer enlisted "in the field" on October 9, 1862, and served throughout the war including the surrender at Appomattox. He died in January 1891 in Mathews County.

William Thomas was eighteen years old when the war started in April 1861 and on July 20, 1861, having just turned nineteen, he enlisted. He joined the Mathews Light Artillery, Company H, 61st Virginia Militia, which became Armistead's Company, Virginia Light Artillery, on May 14, 1862. It was under the command of Capt. Andrew D. Armistead and consisted of approximately seventy men. The unit served throughout the war and was with the Army of Northern Virginia at the surrender at Appomattox on April 9, 1865.

William Thomas was awarded the Legion Medal for his service in the Confederate army in 1912 at the age of seventy. He died on April 30, 1922, at age seventy-nine and was buried with his wife, Amanda, on Far Back Farm, Mathews County. She had died twenty years earlier on July 3, 1902. Far Back Farm, which adjoined the original Hall family property on its southwest boundary, had earlier been owned by Anthony H. Hudgins. His tombstone, beside his wife's, remains to this day and has a Confederate flag engraved at the top of the monument and at the bottom are the words "At Rest."

William and John's father, Thomas Hall Jr., died on May 1, 1867, in Mathews County, Virginia, at approximately sixty-five years old. His death marked the end of the continuous family ownership of the original Hall homestead of the eighteenth century. While in following years the Hall family spread in many directions across the United States, to this day there still remain members of the family in Mathews County and a great many live elsewhere in Virginia.

# EPILOGUE

During the years following the Civil War and for the first two decades of the twentieth century, a span of fifty-five years, life in Mathews County and its economy remained essentially unchanged. Slight declines in farm employment were offset by increases in commercial fishing, employment in shipyards in the Hampton Roads region, and men serving in the merchant marine.

The 1850 US Agricultural Census counted 43,094 acres of farmland, which was a significant 78.3 percent of the total land area of the county. Sixty years later, in 1910, farm acreage was essentially unchanged at 43,205 acres. However, beginning in the 1920s, a marked decline in agriculture began and became a neverending downward trend for the next eighty years. This was typical of many rural counties in Virginia and elsewhere and was primarily the result of rapid industrialization, the advent of motorized transportation, and improved roads. These factors changed commodity markets and created higher wage employment opportunities in nearby cities and a greater awareness of careers in other occupations. From 40,091 acres in 1920, an acceleration of reduced farming began and by 1925 had fallen 11 percent to 35,681 acres.

During the 1930s, Mathews experienced the extreme hardships associated with the Great Depression. However, Mathews families had the ability, as was the case in most rural regions, to be largely self-sufficient by farming and fishing, which served them well during those difficult years. After the depression and with the need for additional skilled trades in Virginia's shipyards as World War II unfolded, acres devoted to farming declined to just 23,942 acres in 1945, 21,576 acres in 1950, 12,763 acres in 1959, and 8,421 acres in 1997. In 2002, there were only 6,635 acres of farmland. The number of farms decreased from 1,387 in 1910 to 961 in 1945 and to 713 in 1950. In 2002 just 47 farms remained in Mathews County.

The dramatic decline in farming and its impact on the character of the county have been significant and have changed most aspects of life over the years. The familiar farming landscapes prevalent in the first half of the twentieth century, neighborhood general stores and post offices, tractors and dirt roads literally disappeared in relatively few years, well within the memory of many of the now elderly inhabitants of Mathews County. Likewise, the scores of white Chesapeake Bay dead rise workboats, moored in every creek that in years past worked pole nets, crab pots, and oyster beds, are gone. The once open topography with cultivated fields, pastures, farmhouses and barns, fencing and ditching, grazing cattle, and men and women at work in fields and barnyards is gone and has been replaced by forests that now cover two-thirds of the county. The large number of near-home employment opportunities once provided by farming and commercial fishing have been replaced mostly by employment outside of the county. Occupations within Mathews are primarily in education, local government, retail, construction, and services.

However, even with these significant changes, there remains today an enduring culture that would be recognized by past generations, one that greatly values patriotism, self-sufficiency, hard work, support of one's neighbors, and strong families that care for their children. The people of Mathews County are deeply committed to their community, and they do a disproportionate share of service beyond the county and to the nation. Especially noteworthy were their great sacrifices during World War II, particularly in the merchant marine.

Mathews County remains a unique, appealing, and special place in which to live because it has thus far kept its traditional values and culture during a time of displacement and rapid change elsewhere in all aspects of life in the twenty-first century. The county is located in an ideal climate zone, has unmatched waterfront, and is convenient to metropolitan areas in Virginia. It has a long, rich heritage historically rooted in the early formation of colonial Virginia, the Revolutionary War, the War of 1812, and subsequent military engagements. These traits may prove to be important assets in the years to come as people from other parts of the United States seek a better place in which to live. Mathews County will remain among the most appealing for a long time to come.

# APPENDIXES

## APPENDIX 1

### Kingston Parish
### Gloucester County, Virginia
### Land Grants[1]

| Family Number | Last Name | First Name | Title Code | Year | Date | Acres | Persons | Neighborhood |
|---|---|---|---|---|---|---|---|---|
| 1 | Gwynn | Hugh | B | 1635 | Dec. 19 | 1,000 | | PR-MH |
| 2 | Lilly | John | A | 1642 | June 20 | 350 | 7 | MH |
| 3 | Connydon | John | A | 1642 | July 1 | 200 | 4 | PR-MH |
| 4 | English | Abraham | A | 1642 | July 10 | 350 | 7 | MH |
| 5 | Price | Arthur | C | 1642 | July 10 | 1,000 | | PR-MH |
| 6 | Hockaday | William | A | 1642 | Aug. 11 | 1,100 | 11 | PR-MH |
| 7 | Curtis | Thomas | C | 1642 | Aug. 15 | 700 | | BC |
| 8 | Rigby | Peter | A | 1642 | Aug. 16 | 450 | 9 | MH |
| 9 | Sayes | Thomas | A | 1642 | Aug. 20 | 350 | 5 | BWC |
| 10 | English | William | A | 1642 | Sept. 19 | 100 | 2 | PR-MH |
| 11 | Tyman | William | A | 1642 | Oct. 8 | 100 | 2 | MH |
| 12 | Symmons | Thomas | A | 1642 | Oct. 10 | 350 | 7 | NR |
| 13 | Bennett | Richard | A | 1642 | Oct. 13 | 100 | 2 | MH |
| 14 | Turner | Abraham | A | 1642 | Oct. 20 | 200 | 3 | WR |
| 15 | Dawber | Edmond | B | 1642 | Nov. 28 | 1,100 | | NR |
| 16 | Boyce | Christopher | A | 1642 | Dec. | 2,000 | 41 | PR |
| 1 | Gwynn | Hugh | A | 1643 | Jan. 17 | 1,700 | 37 | MH |
| 17 | Glasscocke | Thomas | A | 1643 | Aug. 30 | 200 | 4 | PR |
| 18 | Worleidge | Lt. William | A | 1643 | Oct. 16 | 550 | 12 | ER |
| 19 | Hoddin | John | A | 1643 | Oct. 17 | 150 | 3 | NR |
| 19 | Hoddin | John | A | 1643 | Oct. 17 | 950 | 19 | NR |
| 20 | Levitt | George | A | 1643 | Oct. 19 | 1,000 | 20 | NR |
| 21 | Read | George, Gent | A | 1648 | Nov. 2 | 2,000 | 30 | PR |

| Family Number | Last Name | First Name | Title Code | Year | Date | Acres | Persons | Neighborhood |
|---|---|---|---|---|---|---|---|---|
| 6 | Hockaday | William | A | 1649 | June 6 | 900 | 18 | MH |
| 22 | Moon | Abraham | C | 1650 | June 6 | 500 | | MH |
| 23 | Gundry | John | A | 1650 | Aug. 13 | 200 | 4 | DC |
| 24 | Hull | Richard | A | 1650 | Aug. 13 | 300 | 6 | PC |
| 25 | Holder | William | A | 1650 | Aug. 13 | 200 | 2 | HH |
| 25 | Holder | William | A | 1650 | Aug. 13 | 200 | 4 | HH |
| 26 | Morrison | Winefried | A | 1650 | Aug. 13 | 300 | 6 | PC |
| 27 | Smith | John | A | 1650 | Aug. 13 | 300 | 6 | HH |
| 28 | Watts | John, Gent | A | 1650 | Aug. 13 | 200 | 4 | HH |
| 29 | Worleich | William | A | 1650 | Aug. 13 | 100 | 2 | HH |
| 29 | Worleich | William | A | 1650 | Aug. 13 | 300 | 6 | MB |
| 29 | Worleich | William | A | 1650 | Aug. 13 | 650 | 11 | MB |
| 30 | Cheesman | Edmond | A | 1650 | Sept 16 | 50 | 1 | GC |
| 31 | Plummer | William | B | 1650 | Oct. 7 | 400 | | MB |
| 32 | Morgan | William | A | 1650 | Oct. 26 | 300 | 6 | PC |
| 33 | Singelton | Henry | A | 1651 | | 320 | 6 | ER |
| 34 | Elliott | Anthony | A | 1651 | March 20 | 1,150 | 18 | NR |
| 35 | Hampton | William | A | 1651 | March 20 | 700 | 14 | ER |
| 36 | Hunley | Philip | A | 1651 | June 29 | 613 | 12 | ER |
| 37 | Armistead | William | A | 1651 | July 1 | 1,231 | 20 | ER |
| 37 | Armistead | William | A | 1651 | July 1 | 600 | 12 | ER |
| 38 | Grigson | Richard | A | 1651 | Sept. 13 | 300 | 6 | PC |
| 38 | Grigson | Richard | A | 1651 | Sept. 13 | 150 | 3 | PC |
| 39 | Welch | Edmond | A | 1651 | Oct. 12 | 400 | 8 | NR |
| 40 | Foote | Thomas | A | 1652 | Jan. 26 | 150 | 3 | HH |
| 24 | Hull | Richard | D | 1652 | Jan. 26 | 250 | | PC |
| 41 | Winefield | Widow Morrison | G | 1652 | Jan. 26 | 100 | 2 | HH |
| 42 | Bayly | Richard | A | 1652 | Jan. 29 | 400 | 4 | NR |
| 43 | Ripley | Richard | A | 1652 | Jan. 29 | 400 | 8 | WH |
| 44 | Preston | Thomas, Jr. | A | 1652 | Aug. 2 | 500 | 10 | ER |
| 45 | Ransom | Peter | C | 1652 | Sept. 2 | 1,100 | | NR |
| 46 | Pead | John | A | 1652 | Sept. 21 | 150 | 3 | WH |
| 44 | Preston | Thomas, Jr. | A | 1652 | Sept. 28 | 200 | 4 | ER |
| 47 | Dudley | Richard | A | 1652 | Sept. 24 | 200 | 4 | NR |

| Family Number | Last Name | First Name | Title Code | Year | Date | Acres | Persons | Neighborhood |
|---|---|---|---|---|---|---|---|---|
| 48 | Thomas | Curtis | A | 1652 | Sept. 20 | 450 | 5 | BC |
| 49 | Ludlow | George | A | 1652 | Oct. 25 | 2,000 | 24 | PR |
| 50 | Todd | Thomas | A | 1652 | Oct. 27 | 450 | 8 | WH |
| 50 | Todd | Thomas | A | 1652 | Oct. 27 | 150 | 2 | ER |
| 51 | Halliard | Thomas | A | 1652 | Nov. 1 | 450 | 9 | ER |
| 52 | Thomas | William | A | 1652 | Nov. 16 | 700 | 7 | NR |
| 53 | Lendall | Robert | A | 1652 | Oct. 18 | 150 | 2 | ER |
| 54 | Normansell | Richard | A | 1652 | Nov. 28 | 450 | | ER |
| 55 | Mackenny | William | G | 1652 | Dec. 3 | 450 | | ER |
| 56 | Thomas | John | A | 1652 | Dec. 6 | 400 | 8 | ER |
| 57 | Morris | Thomas | A | 1652 | Dec. 6 | 200 | 4 | MH |
| 58 | Long | Richard | A | 1652 | Dec. 6 | 350 | 8 | MH |
| 59 | Smithy | John | A | 1652 | Dec. 6 | 100 | 2 | MH |
| 1 | Gwynn | Hugh | A | 1652 | Dec. 6 | 300 | 11 | MH |
| 27 | Smith | John | A | 1652 | Dec. 8 | 150 | 3 | HH |
| 60 | Bannister | John | C | 1653 | | 350 | | HH |
| 61 | Needles | John | A | 1652 | March 10 | 300 | 7 | HH |
| 62 | Ludlow | Col. George | B | 1652 | March 12 | 2,000 | | PR |
| 45 | Ransom | Peter | H | 1653 | June 6 | | | NR |
| 63 | Bedlam | William | C | 1653 | July 1 | 150 | | HH |
| 64 | Carey | Richard | A | 1653 | Oct. 13 | 1,000 | 17 | QC |
| 64 | Carey | Richard | A | 1653 | Oct. 13 | 350 | 7 | ER |
| 50 | Todd | Thomas | A | 1653 | Oct. 15 | 600 | 8 | ER |
| 65 | Billups | George | C | 1653 | Nov. 25 | 100 | | MH |
| 65 | Billups | George | C | 1653 | Nov. 25 | 500 | | MH |
| 66 | Callis | Joane | C | 1653 | Nov. 25 | 450 | | NR |
| 67 | Cable | George | A | 1653 | Nov. 25 | 200 | 4 | MH |
| 68 | Collins | George | A | 1653 | Nov. 25 | 350 | 7 | ER |
| 69 | Hale | Francis | A | 1653 | Nov. 25 | 400 | 8 | HH |
| 57 | Morris | Thomas | C | 1653 | Nov. 25 | 400 | | MH |
| 70 | Morgan | Thomas | A | 1653 | Nov. 25 | 200 | 4 | NR |
| 71 | White | John | A | 1653 | Nov. 25 | 100 | | ER |
| 72 | Burton | Richard | A | 1653 | Dec. 20 | 360 | 10 | QC |
| 73 | Welch | Edmond | A | 1654 | | 900 | 19 | QC |

| Family Number | Last Name | First Name | Title Code | Year | Date | Acres | Persons | Neighborhood |
|---|---|---|---|---|---|---|---|---|
| 32 | Morgan | William | A | 1654 | Feb. 25 | 550 | 8 | PC |
| 74 | Thompson | George | D | 1654 | Feb. 25 | 200 | 4 | PR |
| 74 | Thompson | George | A | 1654 | Feb. 25 | 400 | 8 | PR |
| 75 | Foster | Mark | A | 1654 | June 6 | 100 | 2 | ER |
| 76 | Pritchard | Walter | A | 1654 | June 6 | 250 | 5 | WH |
| 44 | Preston | Thomas | A | 1654 | June 7 | 150 | 2 | ER |
| 77 | Higgenson | Col. Humphrey | B | 1654 | Sept. 20 | 800 | | PR |
| 58 | Long | Richard | C | 1653 | Nov. 25 | 430 | | MH |
| 78 | Hampton | John | A | 1655 | July 14 | 150 | 3 | BD |
| 79 | Lucas | Edward | A | 1655 | July 14 | 150 | 3 | GC |
| 59 | Smithy | John | A | 1655 | July 14 | 300 | 6 | GC |
| 24 | Hull | Richard | G | 1655 | Oct. 9 | 400 | | HH |
| 80 | Iverson | Abraham, Jr. | G | 1656 | March 26 | 100 | | NR |
| 81 | Kibble | George | A | 1656 | June 4 | 740 | 8 | PR |
| 82 | Smith | Capt. John | G | 1656 | Oct. 8 | 400 | | MH |
| 83 | Brumfield | Edward | D | 1657 | June 6 | 1,100 | 22 | PR |
| 84 | Layne | Henry | A | 1657 | Oct. 10 | 50 | 1 | ER |
| 1 | Gwynn | Hugh | A | 1657 | March 11 | 165 | 4 | MH |
| 85 | Chapman | John | D | 1657 | March 15 | 250 | | PR |
| 86 | Poyndexter | George | A | 1657 | March 15 | 350 | 7 | MH |
| 87 | Teage | John | A | 1657 | March 16 | 150 | 3 | HH |
| 36 | Hunley | Philip | A | 1658 | June 11 | 300 | 6 | ER |
| 88 | Walker | Lt. Col. John | G | 1658 | June 11 | 100 | 2 | MH |
| 89 | Chapman | John | C | 1658 | Sept. 15 | 400 | | PR |
| 90 | Forest | Henry | A | 1658 | Sept. 25 | 550 | 8 | MH |
| 91 | Dudley | Richard | A | 1659 | | 299 | 6 | NR |
| 75 | Foster | Mark | A | 1659 | March 6 | 500 | 10 | ER |
| 92 | Hill | Charles | D | 1659 | March 15 | 150 | 3 | GC |
| 92 | Hill | Charles | D | 1659 | March 15 | 150 | 3 | GC |
| 93 | Borum | John | G | 1661 | Nov. 20 | 400 | | HH |
| 94 | Carles | Joane | G | 1661 | Nov. 20 | 200 | | NR |
| 95 | Mann | John | G | 1661 | Nov. 20 | 600 | | ER |
| 33 | Singelton | Henry | G | 1661 | Nov. 20 | 400 | | ER |
| 96 | Smart | William | G | 1661 | Nov. 20 | 450 | | WH |

| Family Number | Last Name | First Name | Title Code | Year | Date | Acres | Persons | Neighborhood |
|---|---|---|---|---|---|---|---|---|
| 97 | Thomas | Marke | E | 1661 | Nov. 24 | 350 | | HH |
| 98 | Grigg | Robert | A | 1662 | April 19 | 370 | 8 | GC |
| 98 | Grigg | Robert | G | 1662 | June 1 | 250 | | WH |
| 99 | Wyatt | Edward | B | 1662 | July 20 | 1,230 | 3 | PR |
| 100 | Williams | Rowland | G | 1662 | March 18 | 300 | | GC |
| 101 | Medcalf | Gilbert | G | 1664 | | 810 | | PR |
| 65 | Billups | George | A | 1664 | March 18 | 250 | 5 | GC |
| 102 | Ranson | James | F | 1664 | Feb. 10 | 110 | | NR |
| 103 | Medcalf | Gilbert | A | 1664 | Sept. 25 | 560 | 9 | PR |
| 104 | Dudley | Richard | A | 1665 | Sept. 4 | 105 | 3 | ER |
| 80 | Iverson | Abraham | A | 1665 | Oct. 10 | 230 | 5 | NR |
| 105 | Aylmer | Justinian | F | 1666 | April 4 | 300 | 2 | PC |
| 106 | Knight | Guy | A | 1666 | Aug. 27 | 400 | 8 | MH |
| 107 | Smith | Thomas | G | 1666 | Aug. 27 | 100 | | MH |
| 108 | Wray | John | A | 1667 | March 15 | 240 | 5 | QC |
| 109 | Bohannan | John | A | 1667 | Dec. 20 | 220 | 4 | ER |
| 110 | Boram | Anne | A | 1667 | Dec. 17 | 148 | 3 | HH |
| 111 | Colles | Thomas | A | 1667 | Dec. 17 | 200 | 4 | NR |
| 111 | Colles | Thomas | A | 1667 | Dec. 20 | 220 | 4 | ? |
| 112 | Curtis | George | A | 1667 | Dec. 20 | 400 | 8 | BC |
| 104 | Dudley | Richard | A | 1667 | Dec. 20 | 300 | 6 | QC |
| 104 | Dudley | Richard | A | 1667 | Dec. 20 | 300 | 6 | QC |
| 113 | Leonard | Roger | A | 1667 | Dec. 20 | 300 | 6 | ER |
| 32 | Morgan | William | F | 1667 | Dec. 20 | 50 | 1 | MB |
| 114 | Prouse | Henry | A | 1667 | Dec. 20 | 200 | 4 | ER |
| 102 | Ranson | James | A | 1667 | Dec. 20 | 300 | 6 | NR |
| 33 | Singelton | Henry | E | 1667 | Dec. 20 | 300 | | ER |
| 115 | Seatonne | George | G | 1668 | Aug. 16 | 300 | | PR |
| 116 | Shapley | John | G | 1668 | Oct. 1 | 350 | 3 | MH |
| 117 | Curtis | John | A | 1668 | Oct. 27 | 160 | 2 | NR |
| 118 | Collins | Thomas | A | 1669 | July 19 | 250 | 5 | WC |
| 119 | Shipley | Mary and Sara Long | F | 1669 | July 4 | 350 | | MH |
| 46 | Pead | George | F | 1671 | Sept. 25 | 150 | | WH |

| Family Number | Last Name | First Name | Title Code | Year | Date | Acres | Persons | Neighborhood |
|---|---|---|---|---|---|---|---|---|
| 120 | Falkener | Thomas | D | 1671 | Sept. 26 | 140 | | ER |
| 31 | Plummer | William | D | 1671 | Sept. 29 | 150 | | PC |
| 121 | Nevett | Hugh | A | 1671 | Oct. 6 | 230 | 5 | BC |
| 36 | Hunley | Philip | A | 1672 | Aug. 19 | 160 | 4 | ER |
| 122 | Elliott | William | A | 1672 | Oct. 8 | 200 | 4 | QC |
| 123 | Gayle | Matthew | A | 1672 | Oct. 8 | 284 | 6 | ER |
| 124 | Beverley | Robert | A | 1672 | Oct. 10 | 500 | 10 | QC |
| 99 | Wyatt | Conquest | A | 1672 | Oct. 10 | 50 | 1 | QC |
| 81 | Kibble | Mary | E | 1672 | Oct. 11 | 500 | | PR |
| 125 | Guyton | John | A | 1673 | March 19 | 188 | 4 | MH |
| 126 | Pore | Edmund | A | 1673 | March 18 | 77 | 2 | ER |
| 127 | Ryland | Thomas | A | 1673 | May 23 | 120 | 3 | HH |
| 124 | Beverley | Robert | C | 1673 | Oct. 6 | 1,000 | | PR |
| 128 | Arrundell | Peter | A | 1673 | Oct. 23 | 150 | 4 | PR |
| 129 | Bristoe | Major Robert | A | 1673 | Oct. 23 | 230 | 5 | MB |
| 122 | Elliott | William | A | 1673 | Oct. 23 | 340 | 7 | NR |
| 130 | Goodson | John | A | 1673 | Oct. 20 | 100 | 2 | NR |
| 106 | Knight | Guy | A | 1673 | Oct. 23 | 23 | 1 | MH |
| 131 | Putnam | Thomas | H | 1673 | Oct. 23 | 333 | | MH |
| 116 | Shapley | Richard | F | 1673 | Oct. 23 | 130 | | MH |
| 116 | Shapley | Richard | G | 1673 | Oct. 23 | | | MH |
| 116 | Shapley | John | A | 1673 | Oct. 23 | 80 | 2 | MH |
| 124 | Beverley | Robert | D | 1673 | Nov. 6 | 150 | | GC |
| 124 | Beverley | Robert | D | 1673 | Nov. 6 | 150 | 3 | GC |
| 132 | Snelling | Alexander | F | 1674 | April 8 | 43 | | ? |
| 133 | Wright | Henry | A | 1674 | April 8 | 140 | 3 | ? |
| 65 | Billups | George | A | 1674 | April 9 | 500 | 6 | GC |
| 37 | Armistead | Capt. John | A | 1674 | Sept. 21 | 400 | 9 | ER |
| 134 | Edmond | ? | A | 1674 | Sept. 21 | 150 | 3 | ER |
| 135 | Bennett | Robert | F | 1675 | Jan. 26 | 330 | 6 | ER |
| 136 | Curtis | George | E | 1675 | Jan. 26 | 800 | | PR |
| 137 | Kemp | Col. Matthew | E | 1675 | Jan. 26 | 173 | | PR |
| 109 | Bohannan | Dunken | E | 1675 | March 6 | 340 | | ER |
| 138 | Fentry | Stephen | E | 1675 | March 6 | 300 | | QC |

| Family Number | Last Name | First Name | Title Code | Year | Date | Acres | Persons | Neighborhood |
|---|---|---|---|---|---|---|---|---|
| 125 | Guyton | John | C | 1675 | March 6 | 125 | | MH |
| 139 | Johnson | Jacob | E | 1675 | March 6 | 300 | | QC |
| 140 | Kemp | Col. Matthew | A | 1675 | March 6 | 229 | 5 | PR |
| 141 | Lindsay | James | C | 1675 | March 6 | 390 | | QC |
| 142 | Nevells | John, Infant | F | 1675 | March 6 | 100 | | ER |
| 143 | Tomkins | Hannah | D | 1675 | Oct. 4 | 200 | | WR |
| 37 | Armistead | Capt. John | D | 1678 | Sept. 21 | 220 | 5 | ER |
| 144 | Dickson | Christopher | D | 1678 | Sept. 21 | 160 | 3 | ER |
| 145 | Armistead | Ralph | C | 1678 | Sept. 26 | 48 | 1 | DC |
| 146 | Beard | William | C | 1678 | Sept. 26 | 380 | 8 | MH |
| 147 | Bromley | Archabell | C | 1678 | Sept. 26 | 350 | 7 | WH |
| 148 | Collis | John | A | 1678 | Sept. 26 | 620 | 12 | BD |
| 149 | Degge | John | C | 1678 | Sept. 26 | 200 | 4 | ? |
| 149 | Degge | John | D | 1678 | Sept. 26 | 1,800 | 35 | BD |
| 36 | Hunley | Philip, Jr. | C | 1678 | Sept. 26 | 200 | 4 | ER |

## Neighborhood Codes

| | | | |
|---|---|---|---|
| Beaver Dams | BD | North River | NR |
| Blackwater Creek | BC | Pepper Creek | PC |
| Dyers Creek | DC | Piankatank River | PR |
| East River | ER | Queens Creek | QC |
| Garden Creek | GC | Wading Creek | WC |
| Horn Harbor | HH | Ware River | WR |
| Milford Haven | MH | Winter Harbor | WH |
| Mobjack Bay | MB | | |

## Title System Codes

| | |
|---|---|
| Original Land Grant Based on Headrights | A |
| Land Granted by Court Order | B |
| Other Original Grants | C |
| Re-patent, Escheat Land, Death without Heirs, and Felonies | D |
| Re-patent, Sale of Land | E |
| Re-patent, Inherited Land | F |
| Re-patent, Assignment of Rights | G |
| Re-patent, Resurveyed Land | H |

## APPENDIX 2

### 1704–1705 Rent Roll of Virginia[2]

| County | No. Acres < 101 | No. Acres 101–1,000 | No. Acres > 1,000 | Total No. Acres | Owners <101 | Owners 101–1,000 | Owners > 1,000 | Total No. Owners |
|---|---|---|---|---|---|---|---|---|
| James City | 7,580 | 47,738 | 53,462 | 108,780 | 93 | 171 | 26 | 290 |
| Charles City | 2,476 | 24,954 | 24,629 | 52,059 | 26 | 56 | 11 | 93 |
| Warwick River | 3,108 | 25,291 | 9,286 | 37,685 | 42 | 76 | 4 | 122 |
| Elizabeth City | 3,543 | 20,353 | 5,664 | 29,560 | 51 | 61 | 4 | 116 |
| York | 5,823 | 37,359 | 17,950 | 61,132 | 77 | 117 | 11 | 205 |
| Northhampton | 4,697 | 59,666 | 36,808 | 101,171 | 55 | 184 | 19 | 258 |
| Accomack | 2,868 | 103,070 | 90,962 | 196,900 | 34 | 285 | 44 | 363 |
| Surry | 5,812 | 60,908 | 49,369 | 116,089 | 70 | 171 | 25 | 266 |
| Isle of Wight | 4,990 | 71,897 | 61,646 | 138,533 | 54 | 185 | 23 | 262 |
| Nansemond | 7,077 | 104,597 | 5,550 | 117,224 | 91 | 280 | 4 | 375 |
| Norfolk | 6,316 | 67,890 | 39,478 | 113,684 | 77 | 196 | 26 | 299 |
| Princess Anne | 3,418 | 57,155 | 38,155 | 98,728 | 41 | 151 | 23 | 215 |
| Henrico | 3,935 | 75,255 | 86,624 | 165,814 | 48 | 181 | 32 | 261 |
| New Kent | 12,684 | 97,013 | 64,173 | 173,870 | 150 | 318 | 29 | 497 |
| Gloucester | 7,306 | 86,818 | 53,574 | 147,698 | 98 | 250 | 33 | 381 |
| Petsworth Parish | 1,800 | 27,040 | 12,292 | 41,132 | 21 | 74 | 9 | 104 |
| Kingston Parish | 1,759 | 29,196 | 15,582 | 46,537 | 27 | 77 | 11 | 115 |
| Abingdon Parish | 2,035 | 11,091 | 15,300 | 28,426 | 29 | 40 | 7 | 76 |
| Ware Parish | 1,712 | 19,491 | 10,400 | 31,603 | 21 | 59 | 6 | 86 |
| King William | 4,770 | 34,980 | 61,200 | 100,950 | 51 | 138 | 28 | 217 |
| King and Queen | 7,457 | 84,964 | 66,101 | 158,522 | 84 | 292 | 26 | 402 |
| Prince George | 6,239 | 83,647 | 37,332 | 127,218 | 74 | 221 | 22 | 317 |
| Middlesex | 3,649 | 18,549 | 26,810 | 49,008 | 44 | 65 | 13 | 122 |
| Essex | 9,288 | 77,976 | 53,316 | 140,580 | 106 | 229 | 35 | 370 |
| Totals | 113,036 | 1,240,080 | 882,089 | 2,235,205 | 1,366 | 3,627 | 438 | 5,431 |
| | 5.06% | 55.48% | 39.46% | 100.00% | 25.15% | 66.78% | 8.06% | 100.00% |

## APPENDIX 3

### 1704–1705 Rent Roll of Virginia[3] Landowners by Average Acres

| County | < 101 acres | 101–1,000 acres | > 1,000 acres |
|---|---|---|---|
| James City | 82 | 279 | 2,056 |
| Charles City | 95 | 446 | 2,239 |
| Warwick River | 74 | 333 | 2,322 |
| Elizabeth City | 69 | 334 | 1,416 |
| York | 76 | 319 | 1,632 |
| Northhampton | 85 | 324 | 1,937 |
| Accomack | 84 | 362 | 2,067 |
| Surry | 83 | 356 | 1,975 |
| Isle of Wight | 92 | 389 | 2,680 |
| Nansemond | 78 | 374 | 1,388 |
| Norfolk | 82 | 346 | 1,518 |
| Princess Anne | 83 | 379 | 1,659 |
| Henrico | 82 | 416 | 2,707 |
| New Kent | 85 | 305 | 2,213 |
| Gloucester | | | |
| Petsworth Parish | 86 | 365 | 1,366 |
| Kingston Parish | 65 | 379 | 1,417 |
| Abingdon Parish | 70 | 277 | 2,186 |
| Ware Parish | 82 | 330 | 1,733 |
| Average Acres for Gloucester Parishes | 75 | 347 | 1,623 |
| King William | 94 | 253 | 2,186 |
| King and Queen | 89 | 291 | 2,542 |
| Prince George | 84 | 378 | 1,697 |
| Middlesex | 83 | 285 | 2,062 |
| Essex | 88 | 341 | 1,523 |
| Average Acres for All Counties | 83 | 342 | 2,014 |

## APPENDIX 4

### Crew Roster of the Galley *Henry*

Shown are the number of days of wages for the month, thirty-one days in most instances, followed by wages in pounds, shillings, and pence. Officers have allowances for rations indicated below their wages.

"A Pay Role of Mens Wages Belonging to the *Henry*. Galley—"[4]

[*Williamsburg, 28 January 1778*]

(No. 1.)

From 28. Decemr. to Januy. 28.

| | | | |
|---|---|---|---|
| Robert Tompkins. Captn. | 31 Dys. | | 8/. 12 8 .. |
| Rations . . . for Ditto | 31 | | 3/. 4 13 .. |
| Joshua Singleton. 1st Lieut. | 31 | | 6/. 9 6 .. |
| Rations . . . . . . Ditto | 31 | | 2/. 3 2 .. |
| Christopher Tompkins 2d Lieut. | 13 | | 4/6. 2 18 6 |
| Rations . . . . . . . Ditto | 13 | | 2/. 1 6 .. |
| Francis Read 1st Midshipman | 31 | | 3/. 4 13 .. |
| Rations . . . . . Ditto | 31 | | 1/. 1 11 .. |
| Robert Dodson Midshipman | 31 | | 3/. 4 13 .. |
| Rations . . . . Ditto | 31 | | 1/. 1 11 .. |
| William Dunford. Master | 31 | | 5/. 7 15 .. |
| Rations . . . . Ditto | 31 | | 1/. 1 11 .. |
| Robert Hall Masters Mate | 31 | 3 years} | 3/. 4 13 .. |
| Rations . . . Ditto | 31 | | 1/. 1 11 .. |
| John Swope Surgn. | 31 | | 8/. 12 8 .. |
| Rations . . Ditto | 31 | | 1/. 1 11 .. |
| Ambrose Arnando Gunr | 31 | | 3/. 4 13 .. |
| Starkey Moss Carpenter | 31 | | 4/. 6 4 .. |
| John Warton Boatswain | 31 | | 4/. 6 4 .. |
| Peter Foster Carpents. Mate | 31 | 3 years} | 3/. 4 13 .. |
| Edward Wollage Boatsns Mate | 31 | | 2/6. 3 17 6 |
| Francis Horn Sailmaker | 31 | | 3/. 4 13 .. |
| Francis Brown Stuard | 31 | | 3/. 4 13 .. |
| William Lucas Clark | 31 | | 2/. 3 2 .. |

| (No. 1.) | | |
|---|---|---|
| From 28. Decemr. to Januy. 28. | | |
| Francis Moss Armorer | 31 | 4/. 6 4 .. |
| James Willis Quarter Master | 31 | 3/. 4 13 .. |
| Nucomb Dodd . . Ditto | 31 | 2/6. 3 7 6 |
| William Lucas Master Arms | 31 | 2/6. 3 17 6 |
| John Revell | 31 | 2/. 3 2 .. |
| James Minter | 31 | 2/. 3 2 .. |
| John Bander | 31 | 2/. 3 2 .. |
| Willam Jarvis | 31 | 2/. 3 2 .. |
| Dunford Moore | 31 | 2/. 3 2 .. |
| Richard Saunders | 31 | 2/. 3 2 .. |
| Philip Brumley | 31 | 2/. 3 2 .. |
| William Pippen | 31 | 2/. 3 2 .. |
| John Cleuverius | 31 | 2/. 3 2 .. |
| John Wilson | 31 | 2/. 3 2 .. |
| Edward Moore | 31 | 2/. 3 2 .. |
| Turn Over — | | £ 166.4 .. |
| Amount Brought Forward | | £ 166.4 .. |
| James Peters | 31 Dys | 3/. 4 13 .. |
| Michael Donoven | 31 | 3/. 4 13 .. |
| Spence Hall | 31 | 3/. 4 13 .. |
| Henry Donohow | 31 | 3/. 4 13 .. |
| Hugh Bingham | 31 | 3/. 4 13 .. |
| Jerry Malone | 31 | 3/. 4 13 .. |
| Michael Cuningham | 31 | 3/. 4 13 .. |
| Patrick Welch | 31 | 3/ 4 13 .. |
| Samuel Cavener | 31 | 3/. 4 13 .. |
| James Williams | 31 | 3/. 4 13 .. |
| John Clark | 31 | 3/. 4 13 .. |
| Enoch Edwards | 31 | 3/. 4 13 .. |
| John Prosser | 31 | 3/. 4 13 .. |
| John Fitzhugh | 31 | 3/. 4 13 .. |
| George Hall | 31 | 3/. 4 13 .. |

| (No. 1.) | | | |
|---|---|---|---|
| From 28. Decemr. to Januy. 28. | | | |
| Ayers Darbey | | 31 | 3/. 4 13 .. |
| Custis Harman | | 31 | 3/. 4 13 .. |
| John White | | 31 | 3/. 4 13 .. |
| Charles Lucas | | 31 | 3/. 4 13 .. |
| Stephen Wilkeson | | 31 | 3/. 4 13 .. |
| James Lucas | | 31 | 3/. 4 13 .. |
| George Edwards | | 31 | 3/. 4 13 .. |
| Fredrick Byrd | | 31 | 3/. 4 13 .. |
| Williams Williams | | 31 | 3/. 4 13 .. |
| Banister Pippen | | 31 | 3/. 4 13 .. |
| Voss Foster | | 31 | 3/. 4 13 .. |
| Nicholas Scarborough | | 31 | 3/. 4 13 .. |
| William Brumley | | 31 | 3/. 4 13 .. |
| | | | £ 296. 8 .. |
| Voss Foster Deserted | Disalld | | 4 13 .. |
| | | | £291.15 .. |

## APPENDIX 5

***A New and Comprehensive Gazetteer of Virginia, and the District of Columbia***
Joseph Martin
Charlottesville, Virginia, 1835, pp. 226–229

### MATHEWS

Mathews was created by act of Assembly, in 1790, and formed from a part of Gloucester county. This county is a peninsula, extending into the Chesapeake bay, united to the main by a narrow neck of land scarcely a mile wide, and its boundaries are almost entirely of water. It is bounded on the north by Piankatank river, which separates it from Middlesex, and by the Chesapeake; on the south by the Chesapeake and Mob-Jack bays; on the east by the Chesapeake; and on the west by North river and Mob-Jack bay and a narrow neck of land uniting it to Gloucester—extending in lat. from 37° 22' to 37° 30' N. and long. from 0° 38' to 0° 48' E. of W.C. This county is indented by numerous inlets from the bay, which cut and divide the land into a number of small necks, that are bounded on each side by a creek or river. The principal rivers are the Piankatank, East, and North rivers. The former is a bold stream, about a mile wide at its mouth, and extending itself 30 or 40 miles into the interior, terminates in the Dragon swamp. East river is about the same width of the Piankatank at its mouth, which opens into Mob-Jack bay; it runs about 8 or 9 miles up, in the centre of the county, four miles from its mouth it sends off a branch, named Pudding creek, at the head of which is situated the court house. North river likewise enters into Mob-Jack bay; it does not differ much in size from the two rivers just described, and runs up into Gloucester, for the distance of 15 miles. These rivers are all salt, of course, as they derive their waters from the bay, a little fresh water mingles with them at their heads, but does not materially affect their saltiness, except after very heavy and long continued rains. Besides these rivers, there are creeks almost too numerous to be named. Muddy creek is at the upper part of the county, and forms part of the line of separation from Gloucester: it is a very inconsiderable creek, and enters the Piankatank. Cob's creek is rather larger, it is about a mile long, and enters the same river 3 or 4 miles above its mouth. Queen's creek is much more considerable in size, being a fourth of a mile wide, and three miles in length; it enters the Piankatank at its mouth. About three miles below Queen's creek, is the mouth of Slut's creek, which opens into Milford Haven, it is of the same size with Queen's creek. Two miles below are Lilley's and Billup's creeks, they are small and near each other; they enter Milford Haven. A part of the bay which flows in between the main land and Gwyn's island, and extends from the mouth of Piankatank to Billup's creek, is called Milford Haven, and is a secure harbor for vessels. At the lower extremity of the Haven is situated a small, uninhabited island, named Rigby's, between which and the main, is a passage called the Thoroughfare. A short distance below this is Garden creek, which is a small stream that enters into the Chesapeake. Off the mouth of this creek is a shoal, extending five miles out in the bay, named the Wolf Trap, and on which is stationed a light boat. Winter Harbor is a creek or inlet from the bay, which is narrow at its entrance, after running a few hundred yards widens, and diverging extends itself into small branches, which run a mile or two in the land. Horn Harbor is another inlet just below the former, being much larger but not extending itself any farther in the land. Dier's creek is an inconsiderable stream, just below Horn Harbor. The point of land lying below Dier's creek, is the lowest extremity of the county, named New Point Comfort; it is a sandy point which juts out into the bay, and on which is erected a Light House. After leaving New Point Comfort and ascending on the south side of the county, about one mile above is Harper's creek, which is small. Pepper creek two miles above is more considerable. Two or three miles higher up, is the mouth of East river, between which and the mouth of North river is a point called White's. Entering the North river a short distance from its mouth, is Godsey's creek, and 4 or 5 miles higher is Black Water creek, opening in the North river and running a mile or two into the interior.

This county is only 20 miles long, and in its widest section not more than 8, and area 127 sq. miles, varying from that width, down to a point, so that it will be seen from the sketch of the water courses, that the land is divided into many sections or necks:—thus Chapel neck is a small body of land lying between North river and Black Water:—White's neck lies between North and East rivers, and consists of a considerable body of land which terminates at White's point. The land lying between Cob's and Queen's cr. is called Cow neck, and terminates in two points denominated Iron and Burton's points. Between Queen's and Slut's creeks, is situated Crab neck, at the north corner of which neck is a place called Cricket hill. Lying between Lilley's and Billup's creeks, is Lilley's neck. Between Winter and Horn Harbors, is a small point of land named Potatoe neck. The body of land which is situated between Horn Harbor and East river, extending from thence to the lowest extremity of the county is known at Point Comfort.

The most remarkable feature in the topography of this county is its extreme levelness. The banks of the Piankatank river are somewhat elevated and from thence the land descends in an almost uninterrupted plain, until it terminates in the waters of the bay. It was evidently at some period covered by the sea, or bay, as the whole face of the country incontestibly proves. There are about 60,000 acres of land in this county, which is of a medium quality as regards fertility. It produces corn and oats, but is not so well adapted to wheat, from its extreme humidity; the country lays so remarkably level, that it is a very laborious and difficult operation to drain and lay dry the land. The soil is generally a sandy loam, with a substratum of clay; there is little or none of silicious earth, nor does it contain any calcareous matter. Marl has been found in some parts of this county, and if sought, could no doubt be obtained in most places by digging to a sufficient depth. In digging wells, coccle shells, oyster shells and the shells of many testaceous animals, not known at the present day, are found 20 feet below the surface; together with wood, roots, weeds and a variety of undecomposed vegetable substances. Recently, the leg bone of an animal, supposed to be an ox, although much larger than that animal now exists, was found twenty feet below the surface, which is lower than the bed of the contiguous river. These facts present matter for interesting speculations to the minds of the geologist and naturalist.

The natural growth of timber on this land is oak, which ship carpenters say, will vie with the live oak, pine, chesnut and gum. The land after cultivation, if permitted to lie out, invariably puts up a growth of pine.

Mathews contains a population of 7666 souls, of which number 3481 are slaves, and 190 free negroes. The people of this county are engaged in ship building, maritime and agricultural pursuits. Until recently the two former occupied their principal attention; so entirely were they engaged in ship building some years back, that the cultivation of the soil, was almost entirely neglected, and it was necessary to import corn for home consumption—hence it is that this county has been behind others in agricultural skill; lately vessel building has decreased, and agriculture receives more attention. About 20 years ago, there were annually built one hundred vessels of various sizes and denominations, from large ships down to the smallest craft; at the present period there are built, every year, from 20 to 30 vessels of different burdens. There are belonging to this county about 200 ship carpenters, a great number of them find employment in the Navy Yards and other places during the summer months, and return to their homes on the approach of winter. The low price at which vessels are built render it rather unprofitable, and the workmen cannot all find employment at home.

East river is a port of entry, and has a Collector, and Inspector of the revenue attached to it; there are 1700 tons of shipping belonging to this port, among which is one ship, one brig, and a number of schooners and small skippers. Some of them make voyages to almost every part of the commercial world, hence it is, that many of the young men are trained to the perils of the sea.

This county is supplied with meal by means of wind and tide mills, there being 10 wind and 2 tide mills, with one common grist mill; consequently the people do not feel much inconvenience from long, dry seasons, except in procuring water for the cattle. The land, lying almost on a dead level, there cannot be any fresh water streams running through it, and consequently in dry seasons every cattle hole, at which the stock was watered dries up, and they suffer much from thirst. Sometimes, in excessive drought, the inhabitants have difficulty in procuring water to drink themselves. Wells are generally dug 8 or 10 feet deep, so that the water they contain is that which filtrates through the earth, and when the ground becomes dry, the water ceases to flow; but recently wells have been dug 30 feet, when large veins of water have been found, which are inexhaustible. There are a few springs of excellent water, but they are rare. The manufacture of castor oil has been carried on by only one press, a few years since the palma christi bean was extensively cultivated, but it is now reduced.

On the east side of the county is an island comprehended within its limits and known by the name of Gwyn's island; it contains 2000 acres of land, and 200 inhabitants. It is surrounded by the waters of the Chesapeake; it has two points, that to the north is called Cherry Point, and that to the south Sandy Point. There is a tradition, that Pocahontas, in attempting to swim across the Piankatank river, was near drowning, but was rescued from a watery grave by an individual, to whom, as a reward for his services, she gave this island. After Lord Dunmore was driven from Williamsburg, he took up his quarters on this island, where he remained some time.

The predominant religion of the people is the Methodist; there are in this county seven meeting houses belonging to that denomination, two of which belongs to the reformed Methodist; there are two Baptist meeting houses, the congregations attached to which are rather thin; there are a few Episcopalians and Universalists, who, however have no places for public worship; the latter never had any church, and the churches held by the former, under the old established English church, have fallen into dilapidation and decay. There is a Sunday school kept at almost every house of public worship in the county, and several common schools, but no academy. Population in 1810, 4227—in 1820, 6920—in 1830, 7666. It belongs to the fourth judicial circuit and second district. Taxes paid in 1833, $955.98—in 1834, on land, $380.13—1694 slaves, $423.50—559 horses, $33.54—18 coaches, $46.10—14 carryalls, $16.20—86 gigs, $50.60—Total, $950.07.

TOWNS, VILLAGES, POST OFFICES, &C.

Bell Isle, P. O. in the northern part of the county, 13 ms. S. E. of R. and 182 S. S. E. of W.

MATHEWS C.H. or *Westville*, P. V. and *seat of justice*, is situated near the centre of the county. It lies in 37° 35' N. lat. and 0° 40' E. long. of Washington, 100 ms. E. of R. and 184 from W. C. Westville contains about 30 houses, 4 mercantile stores, 1 tanyard, 3 boot and shoe factories, 1 tailor, 2 black-smiths, 1 saddler, 1 carriage maker, and 1 tavern. The public buildings are a very neat, new C. H., 2 jails, 1 for criminals and the other for debtors, and a clerk's office. These houses are all well built of brick. Westville is a port of entry; there are 2 regular packets which ply between this place and Norfolk weekly, and 1 that runs from it to Baltimore. Population 150, including 3 regular physicians.

*County Courts* are held on the *2d Monday* in every month;—*Quarterly* in *March, May, August* and *Nov'r.*

Judge Semple holds his Circuit Superior Court of Law and Chancery on the Tuesdays after the *1st Mondays in April* and *October.*

North End, P. O. in the W. part of the Co., 91 ms. E. of R. & 175 from W.

. . . . . . . . . . . . . . . . . . . . . . . . . . . . . . . . . . . . . . . . . . . . .

*From* ABSTRACT of School Commissioners' Reports for the year 1832 [p. 78]:

Mathews: No. of school commissioners, 6; No. of common schools attended by poor children, 13; No. of poor children, 90; No. of poor children sent to school, 62; Aggregate number of days attendance of poor children at school, 6,975; Average number of days attendance of each poor child at school, 112; Rate of tuition per diem, 3 cts.; Average amount paid for each poor child, including all expenses, $3.55; Expenditures in 1832 for tuition and all other expenses, $220.29.

## APPENDIX 6

### British Warships in the Chesapeake Bay during the American Revolutionary War[5]

HMS *Apollo**

32 guns, Niger-class frigate, 220 men, Capt. Philemon Pownoll
26 x 12-pounders and 6 x 6-pounders

The HMS *Apollo* was particularly well regarded and was the ship Lt. Gen. John Burgoyne chose to transport him to Quebec to take command of the British army. He seems to have been a personal friend of the *Apollo*'s Capt. Philemon Pownoll, who must have had an excellent reputation as a captain for being given a mission of such importance.

Frigates of the Niger class were known for being excellent sailors, very fast at close-hauled in topgallant gale, 10–11 kts., 13½ kts. with wind abaft the beam, and 12 kts. running. They were remarkably weatherly making only a quarter-point leeway with all sails drawing. They sailed best when deeply laden. They were highly maneuverable, staying quickly without any loss of way and able to wear in four ship lengths. They had a tendency to pitch in a steep head sea but otherwise performed well in heavy weather.

HMS *Augusta**

64 guns, St. Albans–class ship of the line, 500 men, Capt. Francis Reynolds
26 x 24-pounders, 26 x 18-pounders, 10 x 4-pounders, and 2 x 9-pounders.

Built by Thomas Stanton and William Wells, Rotherhithe, England. Dimensions 159 ft., 130 ft. 6 in., 44 ft. 7 in., 18 ft. 10 in., 1,381 33/94 bm. Commissioned May 1763. Sailed for North America on March 28, 1777. Grounded in the Delaware River during the attack on Philadelphia. Fire ignited on board from shore batteries, and the ship was burnt and destroyed on October 23, 1777.

HMS *Brune*

32 guns, captured French frigate, 220 men, Captain Ferguson

---

* Denotes ships in Vice Adm. Richard Lord Howe's fleet of 1777.

26 x 12-pounders, 4 x 6-pounders, and 2 x 6-pounders

Built as a French warship, 1754–March 1756, at Le Havre, France. Dimensions 13 ft. 2 in., 108 ft. 11$\frac{3}{4}$ in., 34 ft. 7$\frac{1}{2}$ in., 10 ft. 7$\frac{1}{2}$ in., 694$\frac{86}{94}$ bm. Four 6-pounders on the quarterdeck and two 6-pounders on the forecastle. Captured on January 30, 1761, by the *Venus and Juno*. She was commissioned in July 1761 and sailed for North America on May 6, 1776. She was sold at Deptford, England, on October 2, 1792.

HMS *Carysfort*

28 guns, Unicorn-class frigate, Capt. _______
24 x 9-pounders

A sixth-rate Coventry-class frigate, built at Sheerness, England, Master Shipwright John Williams, and commissioned in June 1767. Dimensions 118 ft. 4 in., 97 ft. 3$\frac{1}{2}$ in., 33 ft. 8 in., 10 ft. 6 in., 586$\frac{30}{94}$ bm. Draught 7 ft. 6 in./14 ft. Sailed for North America on April 8, 1776, and again in December 1780. She was sold at Deptford, England, on April 28, 1813.

HM Galley *Cornwallis*[*]

5 guns, 40 men, Capt. John Brown
1 x 24-pounder and 4 x 4-pounders

A captured American vessel, commissioned in March 1777. She was fitted for rowing and rigged with one or two masts, with a fore-and-aft sail plan.

HM Sloop *Dispatch*[*]

14 guns, Capt. Christopher Mason
14 x 6-pounders

The *Dispatch* was a small merchant schooner purchased in New York on December 30, 1775. She had a crew of thirty men and carried eight guns. She was captured by the American privateer *Tyrannicide* off the coast of New Jersey on July 14, 1776.

HMS *Eagle*[*]

64 guns, Intrepid-class ship of the line, 522 men, Capt. Henry Duncan and Flagship Vice Adm. Lord Richard Howe
26 x 24-pounders and 26 x 18-pounders

John and William Wells, Rotherhithe, England. Dimensions 159 ft. 8½ in., 131 ft. 3 in., 44 ft. 4 in., 19 ft., 1,372 14/94 bm. Draught 10 ft. 8 in./16 ft. 9½ in. Commissioned in February 1776 as the flagship of Vice Adm. Lord Richard Howe. She sailed for North America on May 11, 1776. She was attacked by the American submersible *Turtle* on September 6, 1776. The *Eagle* was in action against d'Estaing, August 11, 1778. She was broken up at Chatham, England, in October 1812.

HMS *Emerald**

32 guns, Niger-class frigate, 220 men, Capt. Benjamin Caldwell
26 x 12-pounders, 4 x 6-pounders, and 2 x 6-pounders

Built by Hugh Blaydes, Hull, England. Launched on June 8, 1762, and commissioned in May 1762. Length on deck 125 ft., length of keel 103 ft. 4½ in., 35 ft. 2½ in. beam, depth in hold 12 ft. Draught 8 ft. 11 in./13 ft. 10½ in. Tons burden 681 31/94. She was armed with 12-pounders on her upper deck with four 6-pounders on the quarterdeck and two 6-founders on the forecastle. Fitted for foreign service at Chatham, England, October 1775 to March 1776, and recommissioned in November 1775, under Capt. Benjamin Caldwell. She sailed for North America on May 6, 1776. In 1779 entered service in the North Sea. Broken up in 1793 in Deptford, England.

HMS *Fowey*

24 guns, Unicorn-class frigate, 180 men, Capt. ______
22 x 9-pounders

Built by Moody Janverin, Lepe, England. Commissioned in March 1752. Length on deck 113 ft. 2¾ in., 32 ft. 4 in. beam. Served in the Leeward Islands, Newfoundland, North America, on convoy duty, Cuba, Jamaica, South Carolina. Refitted at Sheerness, England, from August 1771 to March 1772, and sailed for North America on May 12, 1772. Served in the Chesapeake under Capt. George Montagu. Captured the 10-gun *Washington* on May 12, 1776. Scuttled and burnt to avoid capture by de Grasse's squadron at Yorktown, October 6, 1781.

HM Sloop *Haerlem**

12 guns, converted merchant ship, 65 men, Capt. John Knight
12 or 14 x 4-pounders

The *Haerlem*, dimensions unknown, was a small vessel purchased in New York on March 31, 1777. She served in Hampton Roads in May 1779 and was captured by the American privateer *Impertinent* off Delaware on July 16, 1779.

HMS *Isis*$^*$

50 guns, Portland-class ship of the line, 350 men, Capt. William Cornwallis
22 x 24-pounders and 22 x 12-pounders

John Henniker and Co., Chatham, England. Dimensions 146 ft., 119 ft. 8¼ in., 40 ft. 7½ in., 17 ft. 6 in., $1{,}050\frac{65}{94}$ bm. Draught 10 ft. 11 in./15 ft. 1 in. Commissioned October 1775. Sailed for North America on March 7, 1776. She served in the Delaware operations and was with Howe's action against d'Estaing, August 11, 1778. Broken up in September 1810 at Deptford, England, after a distinguished service.

HMS *Liverpool*$^*$

28 guns, Unicorn-class frigate, 200 men, Capt. Henry Bellew
24 x 9-pounders

John Gorill and William Pownall, Liverpool, England. Dimensions 118 ft. 4 in., 97 ft. 7¼ in., 33 ft. 8½ in., 10 ft. 6 in., $589\frac{85}{94}$ bm. Commissioned February 1758 and sailed for North America on September 14, 1775, and again on May 9, 1777. She was engaged in the Delaware operations during October 1777. She was wrecked in Jamaica Bay, Long Island, on February 11, 1778.

HMS *Mercury*

20 guns, Gibraltar-class frigate, 160 men, Capt. John M'Cartney
20 x 9-pounders

Built by Barnard and Turner, Harwich Dockyard, England. Dimensions 107 ft. 8 in., 88 ft. 6 in., 30 ft. 4 in., 9 ft. 8 in., $433\frac{16}{94}$ bm. Draught 6 ft. 9 in./13 ft. 3 in. Commissioned in February 1756 and sailed for New York and the West Indies on September 17, 1757. Sailed for North America on May 15, 1774, and was commanded by Capt. James Montagu in 1777. She was wrecked near New York on December 24, 1777.

HMS *Nonsuch*$^*$

64 guns, Intrepid-class ship of the line, 500 men, Capt. Walter Griffith
26 x 24-pounders and 26 x 18-pounders

Israel Pownoll, master shipwright. Dimensions 159 ft. 5 in., 130 ft. 10½ in., 44 ft. 5 in., 19 ft. ½ in., $1{,}372\frac{69}{94}$ bm. Draught 11 ft. 4 in./17 ft. 6 in. She was commissioned in August 1775. Sailed to North America on March 23, 1777, and was with Howe's encounter with d'Estaing. She was broken up at Sheerness, England, in June 1802.

HM Sloop *Otter**

14 guns, Otter-class ship rigged, 125 men, Capt. Mathew Squires
14 x 6-pounders

Designed by Thomas Slade. Classified as a sloop because of the small number of cannon she carried, the *Otter* was rigged as a ship and resembled a small frigate. She was built by Master Shipwright Adam Hayes at Deptford, England, and was commissioned in February 1768. Length on deck 95 ft., beam 27 ft. 2 in., depth of hold 12 ft. 6 in. Sailed for Newfoundland on April 30, 1768. Recommissioned in January 1775 under Matthew Squire and sailed for North America on March 14, 1775. Wrecked near Cape Canaveral, Florida, on August 25, 1778.

HMS *Perseus**

20 guns, Sphinx-class frigate, 160 men, Captain Hunt
20 x 9-pounders

Randall, Gray, and Brent, Rotherhithe, England. Dimensions 108 ft. 1 in., 89 ft. $6\frac{1}{2}$ in., 30 ft. $1\frac{3}{8}$ in., 9 ft. 8 in., $431\frac{88}{94}$ bm. Draught 7 ft. $9\frac{1}{2}$ in./12 ft. 1 in. Commissioned in March 1776. She sailed for North America on July 30, 1776. The *Perseus* took the well-known privateer *America* on October 11, 1779. She was broken up at Sheerness, England, in September 1805.

HMS *Phoenix**

44 guns, Phoenix-class ship of the line, 280 men, Capt. Hyde Parker Jr.
20 x 12-pounders and 20 x 6-pounders

John and Robert Batson, Limehouse, England. Dimensions 140 ft. 9 in., 116 ft. $10\frac{7}{8}$ in., 36 ft. $9\frac{3}{4}$ in., 15 ft. $11\frac{1}{2}$ in., $842\frac{67}{94}$ bm. Draught 17 ft. 6 in./18 ft. 2 in. Commissioned in June 1759. Sailed for North America on September 14, 1775, and was in the New York operations in 1776, also Howe's action with d'Estaing on August 11, 1778. She foundered in a hurricane off Cuba on October 10, 1780, and the entire crew was saved.

HMS *Preston*

50 guns, Establishment-class ship of the line, 367 men, Captain Samuel Uppleby, Commodore Hottham

22 x 24-pounders and 22 x 12-pounders

A fourth-rate, two gun-deck vessel built at Deptford, England, by Master Shipwrights Thomas Fellows, Thomas Slade, and Adam Hayes. Dimensions 143 ft. 3 in., 115 ft. 4 in., 41 ft. 3 in., 16 ft. 3 in., $1{,}043\frac{81}{94}$ bm. Draught 9 ft. 10 in./15 ft. 6 in. She was commissioned in January 1757 and became the flagship of Vice Adm. Samuel Graves. She sailed for North America on April 29, 1774, and returned to England in 1775. She sailed again on May 6, 1776, to New York and then on station in Rhode Island in December 1776 and to the Chesapeake where she served as the flagship for Commodore William Hotham. She was broken up at Woolwich, England, in January 1815.

HMS *Raisonable*[*]

64 guns, Ardent-class ship of the line, 500 men, Capt. Thomas Fitzherbert
26 x 24-pounders and 26 x 18-pounders

Built by Master Shipwright Edward Allin at Chatham, England. Length on deck 160 ft. 1 in., beam 44 ft. 6 in. Draught 12 ft. 1 in./17 ft. 4 in. Commissioned in November 1770. Fitted for sea at Plymouth in February 1777, and sailed for North America on March 23, 1777. Participated with Howe's encounter with d'Estaing on August 11, 1778, and was in Hampton Roads under Capt. Henry Evans during May 1779. Broken up at Sheerness, England, in March 1815.

HMS *Richmond*[*]

32 guns, Richmond-class frigate, 220 men, Capt. John Gidoin
26 x 12-pounders and 4 x 6-pounders

John Buxton, Deptford, England. Dimensions 127 ft. 1½ in., 102 ft. 1 in., 34 ft. 1¾ in., 11 ft. 10 in., $664\frac{16}{94}$ bm. Commissioned in April 1757, sailed for North America on March 13, 1759, later at Quebec. Sailed for North America on September 9, 1776, and was with Howe's encounter with d'Estaing on August 11, 1778. She was at the Battle of the Chesapeake on September 5, 1781. She was taken by the French 74-gun ship *Le Bourgogne* on September 11, 1781. She was burnt at Sardinia on May 19, 1793, to avoid capture by the Spanish navy.

Richmond-class frigates were noted for speed, seakeeping ability, and being remarkably dry in high seas. They had top speeds of 10–11 kts. close-hauled in topgallant gale winds and 12 kts. on a beam reach. They were regarded as being fast and dependable in staying and wearing.

HMS *Roebuck**

44 guns, Roebuck-class ship of the line, 280 men, Capt. Andrew Snape Hamond
20 x 12-pounders and 20 x 6-pounders

The first of twenty vessels built in the Roebuck class noted for characteristics suitable for service in the American war; two gun decks in a relatively shallow draught hull for coastal patrol on the east coast of the United States. Length on deck 140 ft., 37 ft. 10 in. beam. Draught 10 ft. 8½ in./14 ft. ½ in. Built in Chatham, England, under Master Shipwright Joseph Harris. Commissioned in July 1775 under Capt. Andrew Snape Hamond. Sailed for North America on September 4, 1775, and was in the Hudson River, New York, and in Delaware. Was involved with the encounter with d'Estaing on August 11, 1778. Broken up at Sheerness, England, in July 1811.

HMS *St. Albans*

64 guns, St. Albans–class ship of the line, Capt. ______
26 x 24-pounders and 26 x 18-pounders

Built by John Perry and Co. in Blackwall, England, and commissioned in January 1771. Dimensions 159 ft. 3¾ in., 130 ft. 9½ in., 44 ft. 6½ in., 18 ft. 9¾ in., 1,380 23/94 bm. She sailed for North America on April 15, 1777, and was at Sandy Hook, New Jersey, the southern side of the entrance to the New York harbor, on July 22, 1778, and was with Howe's encounter with d'Estaing. She was broken up at Chatham, England, in June 1814.

HM Sloop *Senegal**

14 guns, Beaver-class ship rigged, 125 men, Capt. Anthony James Pye Malloy
14 x 6-pounders

Built by Henry Bird, Rotherhithe, England. Dimensions 97 ft., 80 ft. 8¾ in., 26 ft. 1 in., 12 ft. 5 in., 292 13/94 bm. Commissioned during February 1761. She sailed for North America on October 9, 1767, to Boston. Sailed again on April 16, 1775, and was captured by d'Estaing's fleet on August 11, 1778. She was retaken off Gambia on November 2, 1780. During repairs at Gorée, a small island near Dakar, Senegal, she blew up losing all hands on November 22, 1780.

HMS *Solebay**

28 guns, Mermaid-class frigate, 200 men, Capt. Thomas Symons
24 x 9-pounders

Built by Thomas Airey and Co., Newcastle, England. Dimensions 124 ft., 102 ft. $8\frac{1}{2}$ in, 33 ft. 8 in, 11 ft., $619\frac{4}{94}$ bm. Launched September 9, 1763. Commissioned under Capt. William Hay, sailed for Newfoundland on May 20, 1764. Sailed again for North America on February 12, 1776. Battle of the Chesapeake on September 5, 1781. Wrecked in the Caribbean off Nevis and burned.

HMS *Somerset**

64 guns, Establishment-class ship of the line, 520 men, Capt. George Ourry
26 x 32-pounders and 26 x 18-pounders

Master Shipwright John Ward, Chatham, England. Dimensions 160 ft., 131 ft. 4 in., 45 ft. 4 in., 19 ft. 4 in., $1{,}438\frac{62}{94}$ bm. She was commissioned in December 1748. She sailed for North America on April 22, 1755, and again on October 24, 1774, to Boston and Halifax. She sailed on April 9, 1777, and was with Howe's encounter with d'Estaing on August 11, 1778. She wrecked off Cape Cod on November 2, 1778, with the loss of twenty-one of her crew.

HM Sloop *Swift**

14 guns, Swan-class ship rigged, 125 men, Capt. John Howvorth
14 x 6-pounders

Master Shipwright Edward Hunt, Portsmouth, England. Dimensions 96 ft. 7 in., 79 ft., 26 ft. 10 in., 12 ft. 10 in., $302\frac{53}{94}$ bm. Commissioned in January 1777. Sailed for North America on March 27, 1777, and joined the Delaware operation. She ran aground off Cape Henry while sinking the American privateer *Rattlesnake* on November 22, 1778, and was burnt to avoid capture.

HMS *Thames*

32 guns Richmond-class frigate, 220 men, Capt. Tyringham Howe
26 x 12-pounders and 4 x 6-pounders

It was said of the *Thames*, "The harder it blows she is more weatherly." The *Thames* was built at Buckler's Hard, England, under the direction of Henry Adams and was commissioned in April 1758. She had a length on the lower deck of 127 ft., a 104 ft. $8\frac{1}{2}$ in. keel, a beam of 34 ft. 4 in., a depth in hold of 11 ft. 9 in., and a burden of $656\frac{46}{94}$ tons. Her armament consisted of twenty-six 12-pounders on the upper deck, six 6-pounders on the quarterdeck, and twelve half-pounder swivels. She served off the coasts of France, Portugal, Morocco, and the Falkland Islands and in the Mediterranean and sailed for North America on December 5, 1776, under Capt. Tyringham Howe. She was broken up at Woolwich, England, in September 1803.

## APPENDIX 7

### Galleys of the Virginia State Navy

The following is a composite of information from several sources[6] and contains all that is known about the dates of service of the galleys in the Virginia State Navy.

| | |
|---|---|
| *Lewis* | Capt. Celery Saunders<br>Constructed in Fredericksburg, 1775–1776<br>Service on Rappahannock, inactive 1778–1780, destroyed 1781 |
| *Page* | Capt. James Markham<br>Constructed 1775–1776<br>Service on Chesapeake Bay, inactive 1778, sold 1779 |
| *Norfolk Revenge* | Capt. John Calvert, superintended<br>Construction began February 8, 1776, first cruise July 13, 1776<br>Service in Hampton Roads and Chesapeake Bay, sunk in Nansemond River, May 18, 1778 |
| *Hero* | Capt. George Mutter, Capt. John Barret<br>Construction began March 1776, in service August 19, 1776<br>Service in Hampton Roads and on Eastern Shore, dismantled 1779 |
| *Protector* | Capt. George Goosely, Capt. John Thomas<br>Constructed February 1777, Wicomico<br>Service in Chesapeake Bay, dismantled 1778 |
| *Henry* | Capt. Robert Tompkins<br>Construction began early 1776, Gloucester, in service by September 7, 1776<br>Service in Chesapeake Bay and on Eastern Shore, inactive 1779, Navy Board decided to repair 1779–1780, destroyed Hampton 1780 |
| *Safeguard* | Capt. George Elliot<br>Constructed 1775–1776<br>Service in Potomac and on Eastern Shore, inactive 1778–1781, destroyed 1781 |
| *Accomack* | Capt. William Underhill<br>Construction authorized May 1776 on Muddy Creek<br>Service on Eastern Shore 1778–1779, abandoned 1780 |

| | |
|---|---|
| *Diligence* | Capt. Johannes Watson<br>Construction authorized May 1776 on Muddy Creek<br>Service in Chincoteague Inlet, Eastern Shore, 1778–1779, abandoned 1780 |
| *Manley* | Capt. Edward Travis, Capt. William Saunders<br>Constructed on Mattaponi River[?], keel laid April 1776, in service August 1776<br>Service in Chesapeake Bay and on Eastern Shore, destroyed 1781 |
| *Gloucester* | Capt. Thomas[?] Lilly<br>Construction began August 1776, Pepper Creek, Kingston Parish, Gloucester County<br>Service in James River and then prison ship, destroyed 1781 |
| *Dragon* | Constructed in Fredericksburg, keel laid late autumn 1776<br>First year of service in Rappahannock River spring 1778, surveyed North Channel, Cape Charles, inactive 1780, destroyed 1781 |
| *Tartar* | Capt. Richard Taylor<br>Construction began August 1776 at Frazier's shipyard, Mattaponi River<br>Service in Chesapeake Bay and off the Capes of Virginia, inactive 1780<br>Destroyed April 1781, Chickahominy River Shipyard, by Benedict Arnold |
| *Tempest* | Capt. Celery Saunders<br>Construction began August 1776 at Frazier's shipyard, Mattaponi River<br>Service near Hampton, Virginia, and in the lower Chesapeake Bay, active 1780, destroyed 1781 |

## APPENDIX 8

### Revolutionary War Pension Roll, Mathews County, 1840

| | |
|---|---|
| Thomas Davis | 78 years old |
| Avarilla Owens | 74 |
| George Callis | 78 |
| Johanna Watson | 84 |
| Nancy Morgan | 74 |
| William Degges | 80 |
| Bathsheba Brooks | 75 |
| Mary Minter | 76 |
| Josiah Pugh | 78 |
| Mattias Gayle | 78 |
| Thomas Hall | 75 |
| Dorothy White | 78 |
| William D. White | 78? |
| Elizabeth White | 67 |
| Mary Davis | 86 |
| Hugh Hudgins | 76 |
| Joice Gayle | 79 |

# APPENDIX 9

## Archaeological Survey of Eighteenth- and Nineteenth-Century Hall Family–Owned Land

Beginning in the spring of 2016 and continuing from time to time during 2017 and 2018, an archaeological survey was conducted on a small section of the land originally owned by the Hall family during the eighteenth and nineteenth centuries. DATA Investigations, LLC, Gloucester, Virginia, directed the fieldwork, archaeological testing, and identification and cataloging of artifacts. The final report awaits additional fieldwork; however, the thousands of artifacts that have been found and identified provide more than adequate documentation of domestic usage over a period of at least 110 years, from approximately 1720 to 1830. The variety of items suggests continuous domestic occupation of the survey site. By the end of 2018, the site was one of the most extensively surveyed in Mathews County, and the high quality and great variety of the artifacts offer a highly informative view into eighteenth-century life in the area.

The site is noteworthy for a very large variety of ceramics dominated by delft and followed by creamware, pearl ware, whiteware, redware, and white salt-glazed stoneware. Somewhat expensive commodities at the time, the ceramics suggest a relatively high standard of living among the inhabitants. A large number of hand-wrought nails indicates usage before 1800. A majority of the glass, green wine-bottle glass, was produced in the eighteenth century. A very large number of fragments of handmade bricks, pipe stems, and pipe bowls includes several pipe bowl fragments with maker's marks from Europe. In addition, two half coins, both parts of two Spanish half real coins, were found, one dated 1733 and the other from approximately 1724.

# NOTES

Works consulted, especially for chapters 1–4, include the following:

Billings, Warren M., ed. *The Old Dominion in the Seventeenth Century: A Documentary History of Virginia, 1606–1700*, rev. ed. Chapel Hill, NC: University of North Carolina Press for the Omohundro Institute of Early American History and Culture, Williamsburg, Virginia, 2007.

Bruce, Philip Alexander. *Economic History of Virginia in the Seventeenth Century: An Inquiry into the Material Condition of the People, Based upon Original and Contemporaneous Records*. New York: MacMillan, 1896.

Bruce, Philip Alexander. *Institutional History of Virginia in the Seventeenth Century: An Inquiry into the Religious, Moral, Educational, Legal, Military, and Political Condition of the People Based on Original and Contemporaneous Records*. 2 vols. New York: G. P. Putnam's Sons, 1910.

Carr, Lois Green, Philip D. Morgan, and Jean B. Russo, eds. *Colonial Chesapeake Society*. Chapel Hill, NC: University of North Carolina Press for the Omohundro Institute of Early American History and Culture, Williamsburg, Virginia, 1988.

Chapelle, Howard I. *The History of American Sailing Ships*. New York: W. W. Norton, 1935.

Craven, Wesley Frank. *White, Red, and Black: The Seventeenth-Century Virginian*. New York: W. W. Norton, 1977; originally published 1971.

Deans, Bob. *The River Where America Began: A Journey along the James*. Lanham, MD: Rowman & Littlefield, 2007.

Haile, Edward Wright, ed. *Jamestown Narratives: Eyewitness Accounts of the Virginia Colony: The First Decade: 1607–1617*. Champlain, VA: RoundHouse, 1998.

Haile, Edward Wright. *John Smith in the Chesapeake*. Champlain, VA: RoundHouse, 2008.

Harrison, Fairfax. *Virginia Land Grants: A Study of Conveyancing in Relation to Colonial Politics*. Richmond, VA: Old Dominion Press, 1925.

Horn, James. *Adapting to a New World: English Society in the Seventeenth-Century Chesapeake.* Chapel Hill, NC: University of North Carolina Press for the Omohundro Institute of Early American History and Culture, Williamsburg, Virginia, 1994.

Middleton, Arthur Pierce. *Tobacco Coast: A Maritime History of Chesapeake Bay in the Colonial Era.* Baltimore, MD: Johns Hopkins University Press, 1984; originally published 1953.

Morgan, Edmund S. *American Slavery, American Freedom.* New York: W. W. Norton, 1975.

Murphy, Nathan W. "Origins of Colonial Chesapeake Indentured Servants: American and English Sources." *National Genealogical Society Quarterly* 93, no. 1 (Mar. 2005): 5–24.

*A Perfect Description of Virginia: Being, A Full and True Relation of the Present State of the Plantation, Their Health, Peace, and Plenty. . . .* London, 1649.

Robinson, W. Stitt, Jr. *Mother Earth: Land Grants in Virginia, 1607–1699.* Williamsburg, VA: Virginia 350th Anniversary Celebration Corp, 1957.

Rountree, Helen C., Wayne E. Clark, and Kent Mountford. *John Smith's Chesapeake Voyages, 1607–1609.* Charlottesville, VA: University of Virginia Press, 2008.

Tate, Thad W., and David L. Ammerman, eds. *The Chesapeake in the Seventeenth Century: Essays on Anglo-American Society.* New York: W. W. Norton, 1979.

Whichard, Rogers Dey. *The History of Lower Tidewater Virginia.* New York: Lewis Historical Publishing, 1959.

Wooldridge, William C. *Mapping Virginia: From the Age of Exploration to the Civil War.* Charlottesville, VA: University of Virginia Press, 2012.

**Chapter 1**

1 Middlesex County Deed Book, no. 19, p. 490, and no. 20, p. 215. All of the Middlesex County Deed Books can be found at the Middlesex County Courthouse, Saluda, VA.

2 *A Perfect Description of Virginia: Being, A Full and True Relation of the Present State of the Plantation, Their Health, Peace, and Plenty . . .* (London, 1649), 3–5.

3 Ibid., 5–6.

4 Ibid., 6–8.

5 Ibid., 10.

6 Ibid., 14ff.

7 William Waller Hening, *The Statutes at Large: Being a Collection of All the Laws of Virginia, From the*

*First Session of the Legislature, in the Year 1619* (Richmond, 1809), 2:515.

**Chapter 2**

1 Polly Cary Mason, comp., *Records of Colonial Gloucester County, Virginia: A Collection of Abstracts from Original Documents Concerning the Lands and People of Colonial Gloucester County* (Baltimore, MD: Clearfield, 2003; originally published 1946), 1:35.

**Chapter 3**

1 Polly Cary Mason, comp., *Records of Colonial Gloucester County, Virginia: A Collection of Abstracts from Original Documents Concerning the Lands and People of Colonial Gloucester* County (Baltimore, MD: Clearfield, 2003; originally published 1946), 1:84–85.

2 *A Frenchman in Virginia, Being the Memoirs of a Huguenot Refugee in 1686* (Privately printed, 1923), 99–100.

3 Ibid., 97–98.

4 Ibid., 114–115.

5 Ibid., 107.

6 C. G. Chamberlayne, trans., *The Vestry Book of Kingston Parish, Mathews County, Virginia, 1679–1796* (Richmond, VA: Old Dominion Press, 1929), 2, 3.

7 Ibid., 7.

8 Ibid., 19.

9 Ibid., 15.

10 *Frenchman in Virginia*, 108–109.

11 Ibid., 115.

12 William Waller Hening, *The Statutes at Large: Being a Collection of All the Laws of Virginia, From the First Session of the Legislature, in the Year 1619* (Richmond, 1809), 1:176.

13 Ibid., 1:332.

14 *Frenchman in Virginia*, 111–113.

15 Thomas Ludwell to Lord Berkeley of Stratton, Nov. 4, 1667, in *Virginia Magazine of History and Biography* 19:3 (July 1911): 250–251.

**Chapter 4**

1 Hugh Jones, *The Present State of Virginia* (London, 1724), 43.

2 Robert Beverley, *The History and Present State of Virginia,* in *Four Parts* (London, 1705), book 2:1, 2–3.

3 Ibid., 2:4–5.

4 Ibid., 2:6, 7.

5 Ibid., 2:8, 9.

6 Ibid., 4:53–54.

7 C. G. Chamberlayne, trans., *The Vestry Book of Kingston Parish, Mathews County, Virginia, 1679–1796* (Richmond, VA: Old Dominion Press, 1929), 51.

8 Ibid., 69.

9 C. G. Chamberlayne, trans., *The Vestry Book of Petsworth Parish, Gloucester County, Virginia, 1677–1793* (Richmond, VA: Library Board, 1933), 74–75.

10 Ibid., 85.

11 Ibid., 86.

12 Ibid., 105.

13 Ibid., 273.

14 Ibid., 376.

**Chapter 5**

1 Nell Marion Nugent, *Cavaliers and Pioneers: Abstracts of Virginia Land Patents and Grants, 1623–1666* (Baltimore, MD: Genealogical Publishing Co., 1979), 1:217.

2 Ibid., 244.

3 Ibid., 377.

4 Ibid., 514.

5 Polly Cary Mason, comp., *Records of Colonial Gloucester County, Virginia: A Collection of Abstracts from Original Documents Concerning the Lands and People of Colonial Gloucester County* (Baltimore, MD: Clearfield, 2003; originally published 1946), 1:16.

6 Ibid., 22.

7 Ibid., 71.

8 Ibid., 36.

9 Ibid.

10 Ibid., 64.

11 Ibid., 36.

12 Ibid., 36–37.

13 Ibid., 37.

14 C. G. Chamberlayne, trans., *The Vestry Book of Petsworth Parish, Gloucester County, Virginia, 1677–1793* (Richmond, VA: Library Board, 1933), 37.

15 Ibid., 97.

16 Mason, *Records of Colonial Gloucester County, Virginia,* 186.

17 Chamberlayne, *Vestry Book of Petsworth Parish*, 99, 100, 101.

18 Emma R. Matheny and Helen K. Yates, comps., *Kingston Parish Register, Gloucester and Mathews Counties, 1749–1827* (Richmond, VA, 1963), 59.

19 *Bristol and America: A Record of the First Settlers in the Colonies of North America, 1654–1685* (London: R. Sydney Glover, n.d.), 173.

20 Nugent, *Cavaliers and Pioneers,* 1:4.

**Chapter 6**

1 Robert F. Woodson and Isobel B. Woodson, comps., *Virginia Tithables from Burned Record Counties* (Easley, SC: Southern Historical Press, 1982; originally published 1970), 50.

2 1787 US census, Gloucester County, VA, personal property tax, list B.

3 Thomas Todd patent, Library of Virginia, Richmond.

4 Janice L. Abercrombie and Richard Slatten, comp. and trans., *Virginia Revolutionary Publick Claims* (Athens, GA: Iberian Publishing, 1992), 2:389.

5 Virginia Revolutionary War Public Service Claims, Court Booklet, Library of Virginia, Richmond, p. 28.

**Chapter 7**

The information in the beginning pages of this chapter comes from Ernest McNeill Eller, ed., *Chesapeake Bay in the American Revolution* (Centreville, MD: Tidewater, 1981); Philip Alexander Bruce, *Economic History of Virginia in the Seventeenth Century: An Inquiry into the Material Condition of the People, Based upon Original and Contemporaneous Records* (New York: MacMillan, 1896); Charles B. Cross Jr., *A Navy for Virginia: A Colony's Fleet in the Revolution,* ed. Edward M. Riley (Yorktown, VA: Virginia Independence Bicentennial Commission, 1981); Robert Armistead Stewart, *The History of Virginia's Navy of the Revolution* ([Richmond, VA: Mitchell & Hotchkiss Printers, 1934]); Peter Jennings Wrike, *The Governors' Island: Gwynn's Island, Virginia, during the Revolution* (Richmond, VA: Brandylane, 1993).

1 William Bell Clark, ed., *Naval Documents of the American Revolution* (Washington, DC: Naval History Division, Department of the Navy, 1964), 1:257–259, 261.

2 Purdie's *Virginia Gazette* (Williamsburg), October 13, 1775.

3 John E. Selby, *The Revolution in Virginia, 1775–1783* (Williamsburg, VA: Colonial Williamsburg Foundation, 1988), 81.

4 Ernest McNeill Eller, ed., *Chesapeake Bay in the American Revolution* (Centreville, MD: Tidewater, 1981), xxii.

5 Ibid., 108.

6 As found in ibid.

7 William James Morgan, ed., *Naval Documents of the American Revolution* (Washington, DC: Naval History Division, Department of the Navy, 1970), 5:405.

8 Ibid., 670, 862, 938, 1140.

9 William James Morgan, ed., *Naval Documents of the American Revolution* (Washington, DC: Naval History Division, Department of the Navy, 1972), 6:366.

10 Jack Coggins, *Ships and Seamen of the American Revolution* (Victoria, CAN: Promontory Press, 1969), 152.

11 Morgan, *Naval Documents of the American Revolution*, 6:728, 742.

12 Ibid., 1242.

13 William James Morgan, ed., *Naval Documents of the American Revolution* (Washington, DC: Naval History Division, Department of the Navy, 1976), 7:478.

**Chapter 8**

1 William James Morgan, ed., *Naval Documents of the American Revolution* (Washington, DC: Naval

History Division, Department of the Navy, 1976), 7:1061.

2 Ibid., 1098.

3 William James Morgan, ed., *Naval Documents of the American Revolution* (Washington, DC: Naval History Division, Department of the Navy, 1980), 8:258.

4 Ibid., 267.

5 Ibid., 422.

6 Morgan, *Naval Documents of the American Revolution*, 7:569.

7 William James Morgan, ed., *Naval Documents of the American Revolution* (Washington, DC: Naval Historical Center, Department of the Navy, 1986), 9:198.

8 Charles B. Cross Jr., *A Navy for Virginia: A Colony's Fleet in the Revolution,* ed. Edward M. Riley (Yorktown, VA: Virginia Independence Bicentennial Commission, 1981), 22.

9 William James Morgan, ed., *Naval Documents of the American Revolution,* (Washington, DC: Naval History Division, Department of the Navy, 1972), 6:775.

10 Morgan, *Naval Documents of the American Revolution,* 8:300.

11 Ibid., 487.

12 Morgan, *Naval Documents of the American Revolution,* 9:225.

13 Ibid., 205.

14 Michael J. Crawford, ed., *Naval Documents of the American Revolution* (Washington, DC: Naval History and Heritage Command, Department of the Navy, 2013), 12:26.

15 Morgan, *Naval Documents of the American Revolution,* 9:258.

16 Ibid., 266.

17 Ibid., 339.

18 Ibid., 728.

19 Ibid., 835.

20 Ernest McNeill Eller, ed., *Chesapeake Bay in the American Revolution* (Centreville, MD: Tidewater, 1981), xxvii.

21 Morgan, *Naval Documents of the American Revolution,* 9:749.

22 Ibid., 756.

23 Ibid., 766.

24 Ibid., 856–857.

25 Ibid., 811–812.

26 Ibid., 869.

27 Eller, *Chesapeake Bay in the American Revolution,* xxviii.

28 Morgan, *Naval Documents of the American Revolution,* 9:985.

29 Michael J. Crawford, ed., *Naval Documents of the American Revolution* (Washington, DC: Naval Historical Center, Department of the Navy, 2005), 11:1153, 1154, 1156, 1157, 1159, 1161, 1163, 1164, 1166.

**Chapter 9**

The information in the beginning pages of this chapter comes from Michael J. Crawford, ed.,

*Naval Documents of the American Revolution* (Washington, DC: Naval Historical Center, Department of the Navy, 2005), 11:29, 30, 40, 43, 48, 58, 59, 90, 110, 112, 113, 121, 152, 176, 190, 203, 227.

1 Ibid., 110, 112.

2 Ibid., 112.

3 Ibid., 176.

4 John Frederick Dorman, comp., *Virginia Revolutionary Pension Applications* (Falmouth, VA, 1991), 43:18–19.

5 Crawford, *Naval Documents of the American Revolution*, 11:275.

6 Ibid., 380.

7 Michael J. Crawford, ed., *Naval Documents of the American Revolution* (Washington, DC: Naval History and Heritage Command, Department of the Navy, 2013) 12:92.

8 Ibid., 99.

9 Ibid., 469.

10 Crawford, *Naval Documents of the American Revolution,* 11:1084.

11 Crawford, *Naval Documents of the American Revolution,* 12:1087.

12 Crawford, *Naval Documents of the American Revolution,* 11:1087.

**Chapter 10**

1 Emma R. Matheny and Helen K. Yates, comps., *Kingston Parish Register, Gloucester and Mathews Counties, 1749–1827* (Richmond, VA, 1963), 59.

2 John Frederick Dorman, comp., *Virginia Revolutionary Pension Applications* (Falmouth, VA, 1994), 50:7.

3 Mss 5:5, P3745:1, Virginia Historical Society, Richmond, VA.

4 Michael J. Crawford, ed., *Naval Documents of the American Revolution* (Washington, DC: Naval Historical Center, Department of the Navy, 2005) 11:836.

5 Ibid., 469.

6 Dorman, *Virginia Revolutionary Pension Applications,* 50:7.

7 *Journal of the House of Delegates of the Commonwealth of Virginia; Begun and Held at the Capitol, in the City of Williamsburg. On Monday, the Fourth Day of October, in the Year of Our Lord One Thousand Seven Hundred and Seventy-Nine* (Richmond, VA, 1827), 74.

8 Dorman, *Virginia Revolutionary Pension Applications,* 50:6.

9 John Frederick Dorman, comp., *Virginia Revolutionary Pension Applications* (Washington, DC: 1963), 8:41.

10 William Waller Hening, ed., *The Statutes at Large: Being a Collection of All the Laws of Virginia, From the First Session of the Legislature, in the Year 1619* (Richmond, 1822), 10:55.

11 Dorman, *Virginia Revolutionary Pension Applications,* 50:7.

12 Ibid.

13 Lloyd DeWitt Bockstruck, *Revolutionary War Bounty Land Grants: Awarded by State Governments* (Baltimore, MD: Genealogical Publishing Co., 1996), 485.

**Chapter 11**

1 Ralph D. Paine, *The Ships and Sailors of Old Salem: The Record of a Brilliant Era of American Achievement* (New York: Outing Publishing, 1909), 8.

2 Winthrop L. Marvin, *The American Merchant Marine: Its History and Romance from 1620 to 1902* (New York: Charles Scribner's Sons, 1902), 205.

3 James Duncan Phillips, *Salem in the Eighteenth Century* (Boston: Houghton Mifflin, 1937), 62, 68.

4 Octavius Thorndike Howe, *Beverly Privateers in the American Revolution* (Cambridge, MA: The University Press, 1922), 322.

5 Ibid., 431.

6 *Vital Records of Salem, Massachusetts, to the End of the Year 1849,* vol. 2, *Births* (Salem, MA: Essex Institute, 1918), 117, and *Vital Records of Salem, Massachusetts, to the End of the Year 1849,* vol. 4, *Marriages* (Salem, MA: Essex Institute, 1924), 135.

7 *The Diary of William Bentley, D.D., Pastor of the East Church, Salem, Massachusetts,* vol. 2, *January 1793–December 1802* (Salem, MA: Essex Institute, 1907), 419.

8 *Diary of William Bentley,* 2:463.

9 William Fairfield to Rebecca Fairfield, April 23, 1789, in Paine, *Ships and Sailors of Old Salem,* 315.

10 *Vital Records of Salem, Massachusetts, to the End of the Year 1849,* vol. 5, *Deaths* (Salem, MA: Essex Institute, 1925), 306.

11 A. Frank Hitchings, trans., *Ship Registers of the District of Salem and Beverly, Massachusetts, 1789–1900* (Salem, MA: Essex Institute, 1906), 117.

12 *The Diary of William Bentley, D.D., Pastor of the East Church, Salem, Massachusetts,* vol. 1, *April 1784–December 1792* (Salem, MA: Essex Institute, 1905), 148.

13 Hitchings, *Ship Registers of Salem and Beverly,* 191.

14 The will of Spencer Hall can be found in the Massachusetts Archives, Boston.

15 Trans-Atlantic Slave Trade Database, slavevoyages.org, voyage ID 25361.

16 Trans-Atlantic Slave Trade Database, slavevoyages.org, voyage ID 25302.

17 Governor at Sierra Leone to the Sierra Leone Company, 1795, in Elizabeth Donnan, *Documents Illustrative of the History of the Slave Trade to America,* vol. 3, *New England and the Middle Colonies* (Washington, DC: Carnegie Institution of Washington, 1932), 100.

18 Ibid., 99–100, 99n–100n.

19 *Diary of William Bentley,* 2:77.

20 The court orders, appraisal, inventory, and related documents can be found at the State Library of Massachusetts, Boston.

21 Ibid.

22 Hitchings, *Ship Registers of Salem and Beverly,* 191.

23 Salem Crew Lists, 1799–1879, Collections & Research, Mystic Seaport Museum, research.mysticseaport.org/databases/crew-lists-salem, accessed April 7, 2019.

24 *Vital Records of Salem, Massachusetts, to the End of the Year 1849,* vol. 3, *Marriages* (Salem, MA: Essex Institute, 1924), 459.

25 See "Revolutionary War" and "War of 1812" on American Merchant Marine at War,

USMM.org, last updated August 26, 2018.

26 *The Essex Institute Historical Collections* (Salem, MA, 1901), 37:58, 60.

27 As quoted in Paine, *Ships and Sailors of Old Salem*, 491.

28 Paine, *Ships and Sailors of Old Salem*, 487.

29 *Historical Collections of the Essex Institute* (Salem, MA, 1860), 2:57.

30 Virginia Land Office, Military Certificates, Reel #15, Virginia State Archives, Richmond VA.

**Chapter 12**

1 Testimony in Mathews Courthouse, July 14, 1834, Revolutionary War Pension Records, Pension and Bounty-Land Warrant Legislation and Administration Relating to Participation in the Revolutionary War, National Archives, Washington, DC.

2 John E. Selby, *The Revolution in Virginia, 1775–1783* (Williamsburg, VA: Colonial Williamsburg Foundation, 1988), 224.

3 Mark Edward Lender and James Kirby Martin, "A Traitor's Epiphany: Benedict Arnold in Virginia and His Quest for Reconciliation," *Virginia Magazine of History and Biography* 125, no. 4 (2017): 314.

4 Selby, *Revolution in Virginia*, 305–306.

5 Emma R. Matheny and Helen K. Yates, comps., *Kingston Parish Register, Gloucester and Mathews Counties, 1749–1827* (Richmond, VA, 1963), 9.

6 L. Roane Hunt, *Tax Records of Gloucester County, Virginia, 1782–1791* (Gloucester Genealogical Society of Virginia, 2011), vol. 1.

7 Billups Papers, box 3, folder 8, Earl Gregg Swem Library, College of William & Mary, Williamsburg, VA.

8 Mathews County Land Book, no. 1, p. 102, plat no. 180, Mathews County Clerk's Office, Mathews, VA.

9 Christopher Tompkins Papers, mss 1 T 5996 c 28-37, Virginia Historical Society, Richmond.

10 Indenture between William B. Tompkins and John Patterson, May 2, 1805, Christopher Tompkins Papers, mss 1 T 5996 c, Virginia Historical Society, Richmond.

11 William Hurst, War of 1812, Mathews Co., Virginia Bounty Land Application/Widow's Pension Application, WO 6162, WC 5735, Bounty Land Numbers 3409 80 50 and 6339 80 55, National Archives, Washington, DC.

12 Christopher Tompkins Papers, Virginia Historical Society, Richmond.

13 As quoted in Joan Charles, *Gloucester and Mathews Newspaper Articles, 1737 to 1922* (Gloucester, VA: Gloucester Historical Society of Virginia, 2014), 52.

14 Ship registrations are located in the National Archives, Washington, DC.

15 John Patterson's account books are located at the John D. Rockefeller Jr. Library, Williamsburg, VA.

16 Mathews County Land Book, no. 1, p. 3, Mathews County Clerk's Office, Mathews, VA.

17 The ship registration can be found at the National Archives, Washington, DC.

18 Peter Jennings Wrike, "Mathews County Shipbuilding Patterns 1780–1860" (master's thesis,

Old Dominion University, Norfolk, VA, 1990).

19 Ibid.

20 As printed in the *American Beacon* (Norfolk, VA), June 21, 1820.

21 Christopher Tompkins Papers, Virginia Historical Society, Richmond.

22 Mathews County Land Book, no. 1, p. 139, plat no. 240, Mathews County Clerk's Office, Mathews, VA.

23 Christopher Tompkins Papers, mssl T 5996 c 28-37, Virginia Historical Society, Richmond.

24 Mathews County Land Book, no. 1, p. 52, plat 100, Mathews County Clerk's Office, Mathews, VA.

25 Mathews County Will Book, no. 1, pp. 80, 81, Mathews County Courthouse, Mathews, VA.

26 Joseph Martin, *A New and Comprehensive Gazetteer of Virginia, and the District of Columbia* (Charlottesville, VA, 1835), 227–228.

27 Ibid., 229.

**Chapter 13**

1 Emma R. Matheny and Helen K. Yates, comps., *Kingston Parish Register, Gloucester and Mathews Counties, 1749–1827* (Richmond, VA, 1963), 9.

2 John Frederick Dorman, comp., *Virginia Revolutionary Pension Applications* (Washington, DC, 1990), 41:58–59.

3 Ibid.

**Chapter 14**

1 Mathews County Fee Book, December 1833, p. 111, Mathews County Courthouse, Mathews, VA.

2 Mathews County Fee Book, October 1840, pp. 136, 137, Mathews County Courthouse, Mathews, VA.

3 Middlesex County Deed Book [hereafter MCDB], no. 19, p. 490. All of the Middlesex County Deed Books can be found at the Middlesex County Courthouse, Saluda, VA.

4 MCDB , no. 20, p. 215.

5 Ibid.

6 MCDB, no. 25, p. 165.

7 Middlesex County Will Book, no. 10, p. 214, Middlesex County Courthouse, Saluda, VA.

8 Saunders household, 1850 US census, Mathews County, VA.

9 Ida J. Lee, comp., *Lancaster County, Virginia, Marriage Bonds, 1652–1850* (Baltimore, MD: Genealogical Publishing Co., 1972), 10.

10 1820, 1830, and 1840 US censuses, Middlesex County, VA.

11 MCDB, no. 21, p. 366.

12 Walter C. C. Johnson, ed., *Historic Buildings in Middlesex County, Virginia, 1650–1875* (Charlotte, NC: Delmar Printing, 1978), 282.

13 MCDB, no. 22, p. 1.

14 MCDB, no. 21, p. 10.

15 The tax records can be found in the Middlesex County Circuit Court Clerk's Office, Saluda, VA.

16 MCDB, no. 22, p. 276.

17 Ibid., p. 298.

18 The inventory of Thomas Spencer Hall can be found at the Middlesex County Circuit Court Clerk's Office, Saluda, VA.

19 MCDB, no. 28, p. 112.

20 Middlesex County Marriage Register, p. 276, Middlesex County Courthouse, Saluda, VA.

21 MCDB, no. 26, p. 196.

22 MCDB, no. 24, p. 215.

23 MCDB, no. 25, pp. 165, 166.

24 Middlesex County Will Book, no. 10, p. 214, Middlesex County Courthouse, Saluda, VA.

25 MCDB, no. 26, p. 69.

26 H. A. W. French, comp., *The History of Lower Church, Middlesex County, VA* ([1948?]), 1.

27 Veterans Records, Revolutionary War, Virginia, Sea Service/Mathews County/R40, National Archives, Washington, DC.

28 John Frederick Dorman, comp., *Virginia Revolutionary Pension Applications* (Falmouth, VA, 1994), 50:6.

**Chapter 15**

1 From the 1850 Agricultural Schedule, US Census.

2 From the 1850 Population Schedule, US Census.

3 MCDB, no. 1, pp. 97, 98.

**Appendixes**

1 From Nell Marion Nugent, *Cavaliers and Pioneers: Abstracts of Virginia Land Patents and Grants, 1623–1666* (Baltimore, MD: Genealogical Publishing Co., 1979), vols. 1 and 2; Polly Cary Mason, comp., *Records of Colonial Gloucester County, Virginia: A Collection of Abstracts from Original Documents Concerning the Lands and People of Colonial Gloucester County* (Baltimore, MD: Clearfield, 2003; originally published 1946), 1:84–85; and original patents.

2 From Thomas J. Wertenbaker, *The Planters of Colonial Virginia* (Princeton, NJ: Princeton University Press, 1922).

3 Ibid.

4 Michael J. Crawford, ed., *Naval Documents of the American Revolution* (Washington, DC: Naval Historical Center, Department of the Navy, 2005), 11:225–226.

5 From Rif Winfield, *British Warships in the Age of Sail, 1714–1792: Design, Construction, Careers and Fates* (Barnsley, South Yorkshire, GB: Seaforth Publishing, 2007); Robert Gardiner, *The First Frigates: Nine-Pounder and Twelve-Pounder Frigates, 1748–1815* (London: Conway Maritime Press, 1992); William Bell Clark/William James Morgan/Michael J. Crawford, eds., *Naval Documents of the American Revolution*, vols. 1–10 (Washington, DC: Department of the Navy, 1964–1996); Ernest McNeill Eller, ed., *Chesapeake Bay in the American Revolution* (Centreville, MD: Tidewater Publishers, 1981).

6 Charles B. Cross Jr., *A Navy for Virginia: A Colony's Fleet in the Revolution*, ed. Edward M. Riley (Yorktown, VA: Virginia Independence Bicentennial Commission, 1981), 22; Robert Armistead Stewart, *The History of Virginia's Navy of the Revolution* (Richmond, VA: Mitchell & Hotchkiss, [1934]), 15, 16, 18, 19, 53, 57; William James Morgan, ed. *Naval Documents of the American Revolution* (Washington, DC: Naval History Division, Department of the Navy, 1972), 6:742

# BIBLIOGRAPHY

Allen, John C., Jr. *Uncommon Vernacular: The Early Houses of Jefferson County, West Virginia, 1735–1835.* Morgantown, WV: West Virginia University Press, 2011.

Barbour, Philip L., ed. *The Complete Works of Captain John Smith, 1580–1631.* Vol. 1. Chapel Hill, NC: University of North Carolina Press for the Omohundro Institute of Early American History and Culture, Williamsburg, Virginia, 1986.

Bentley, William. *The Diary of William Bentley, D.D., Pastor of the East Church, Salem, Massachusetts.* 2 vols. Salem, MA: Essex Institute, 1907.

Berkeley, Edmund, and Dorothy Smith Berkeley. *The Reverend John Clayton: A Parson with a Scientific Mind.* Charlottesville, VA: University Press of Virginia, 1965.

Beverley, Robert. *The History and Present State of Virginia, in Four Parts.* London, 1705.

Billings, Warren M., ed. *The Old Dominion in the Seventeenth Century: A Documentary History of Virginia, 1606–1700,* rev. ed. Chapel Hill, NC: University of North Carolina Press for the Omohundro Institute of Early American History and Culture, Williamsburg, Virginia, 2007.

Billings, Warren M., John E. Selby, Thad W. Tate. *Colonial Virginia: A History.* White Plains, NY: KTO Press, 1986.

Bockstruck, Lloyd DeWitt. *Revolutionary War Bounty Land Grants: Awarded by State Governments.* Baltimore, MD: Genealogical Publishing Company, 1996.

Bodie, Charles A., and William H. Siener. *A Guide to Gloucester County, Virginia, Historical Manuscripts, 1651–1865.* Richmond, VA: Archives Division, Virginia State Library, 1976.

Bradley, Dr. Stephen E., Jr. *The 1850 Federal Census, Mathews County, Virginia.* Keysville, VA, 1990.

Bradley, Dr. Stephen E., Jr. *Mathews County, Virginia: Censuses 1810, 1820, 1830, 1840.* [Keysville, VA, 199-?].

Bradley, Dr. Stephen E., Jr. *Mathews County, Virginia: Land and Personal Tax Lists, 1791–1800.* Keysville, VA, 1992.

Bratten, John R. *The* Gondola *Philadelphia and the Battle of Lake Champlain.* College Station: Texas A&M University Press, 2002.

Breen, T. H. *Tobacco Culture: The Mentality of the Great Tidewater Planters on the Eve of Revolution.* Princeton, NJ: Princeton University Press, 1985.

Brewington, M. V. *Chesapeake Bay Sailing Craft.* [Baltimore]: Maryland Historical Society, [1966].

*Bristol and America: A Record of the First Settlers in the Colonies of North America, 1654–1685.* London: R. Sydney Glover, n.d.

Brooks, Catherine C. *Walk with Me: Find How Postal Landmarks Define the Lore, Traditions and Society of Mathews County, Virginia.* West Conshohocken, PA: Infinity Publishing, 2005.

Brown, David A. "'To the Place Where It Began': Seventeenth-Century Settlement Patterns in Abingdon Parish, Gloucester County, Virginia." Master's thesis, University of Massachusetts at Boston, 2000.

Brown, Margie G. *Genealogical Abstracts, Revolutionary War Veterans, Scrip Act, 1852: Abstracted from the Bureau of Land Management, Record Group 49.* Lovettsville, VA: Willow Bend Books, 1997.

Bruce, Philip Alexander. *Economic History of Virginia in the Seventeenth Century: An Inquiry into the Material Condition of the People, Based upon Original and Contemporaneous Records.* New York: MacMillan, 1896.

Brumbaugh, Gaius Marcus. *Revolutionary War Records.* Vol. 1. Baltimore, MD: Genealogical Publishing Company, 1995, 1967.

Burgess, Louis A. *Virginia Soldiers of 1776: Compiled from Documents . . . in the Virginia Land Office.* 3 vols. Baltimore, MD: Genealogical Publishing Company, 2004.

Carr, Lois Green, Philip D. Morgan, and Jean B. Russo, eds. *Colonial Chesapeake Society.* Chapel Hill, NC: University of North Carolina Press for the Omohundro Institute of Early American History and Culture, Williamsburg, Virginia, 1988.

Carson, Cary, and Carl R. Lounsbury, eds. *The Chesapeake House: Architectural Investigation by Colonial Williamsburg.* Williamsburg, VA, and Chapel Hill, NC: Colonial Williamsburg Foundation and University of North Carolina Press, 2013.

Chamberlayne, C. G., trans. *The Vestry Book of Kingston Parish, Mathews County, Virginia, 1679–1796.* Richmond, VA: Old Dominion Press, 1929.

Chamberlayne, C. G., trans. *The Vestry Book of Petsworth Parish, Gloucester County, Virginia, 1677–1793.* Richmond, VA: Library Board, 1933.

Chapelle, Howard I. *The American Sailing Navy: The Ships and Their Development.* New York: W. W. Norton, 1949.

Chapelle, Howard I. *The History of American Sailing Ships.* New York: W. W. Norton, 1935.

Chapelle, Howard I. *The Search for Speed under Sail, 1700–1855.* New York: W. W. Norton, 1967.

Chapelle, Howard Irving. *The Baltimore Clipper: Its Origin and Development.* Salem, MA: Marine Research Society, 1930.

Charles, Joan. *Gloucester and Mathews Newspaper Articles, 1737 to 1922.* Gloucester, VA: Gloucester Historical Society of Virginia, 2014.

Coggins, Jack. *Ships and Seamen of the American Revolution.* Victoria, CAN: Promontory Press, 1969.

Cognets, Louis des, Jr., comp. *English Duplicates of Lost Virginia Records.* Princeton, NJ, 1958.

*Collections of the New-York Historical Society for the Year 1914.* New York: New-York Historical Society, 1916.

Craven, Wesley Frank. *White, Red, and Black: The Seventeenth-Century Virginian.* New York: W. W. Norton, 1977; originally published 1971.

Cross, Charles B., Jr. *A Navy for Virginia: A Colony's Fleet in the Revolution.* Edited by Edward M. Riley. Yorktown, VA: Virginia Independence Bicentennial Commission, 1981.

Deans, Bob. *The River Where America Began: A Journey along the James.* Lanham, MD: Rowman & Littlefield, 2007.

Dixon, Ruth Priest, and Katherine George Eberly, comps. *Index to Seamen's Protection Certificate Applications, Port of Philadelphia 1796–1823, with Supplement 1796–1851.* Baltimore, MD: Clearfield, 1995.

Dorman, John Frederick, comp. *Virginia Revolutionary Pension Applications.* Falmouth, VA, 1958–1995.

Eller, Ernest McNeill, ed. *Chesapeake Bay in the American Revolution.* Centreville, MD: Tidewater, 1981.

Evans, Cerinda W. *Some Notes on Shipbuilding and Shipping in Colonial Virginia.* Williamsburg, VA: Virginia 350th Anniversary Celebration Corporation, 1957.

Falconer, William. *An Universal Dictionary of the Marine.* London, 1769.

Gardiner, Robert. *The First Frigates: Nine-Pounder and Twelve-Pounder Frigates, 1748–1815.* London: Conway Maritime Press, 1992.

Gardiner, Robert. *The Heavy Frigate.* Vol. 1, *1778–1800.* London: Conway Maritime Press, 1994.

Gardiner, Robert. *The Sailing Frigate: A History in Ship Models.* South Yorkshire, ENG: Seaforth Publishing, 2012.

Gleach, Frederic W. *Powhatan's World and Colonial Virginia: A Conflict of Cultures.* Lincoln: University of Nebraska Press. 1997.

Glover, Lorri, and Daniel Blake Smith. *The Shipwreck That Saved Jamestown: The Sea Venture Castaways and the Fate of America.* [Old Saybrook, CT]: Tantor, 2008.

Goodsell, Jane B. *Mathews County, Virginia, Records.* Athens, GA: Iberian, 2000.

Greenhill, Basil. *The Evolution of the Wooden Ship.* Caldwell, NJ: Blackburn Press, 1988.

Haile, Edward Wright, ed. *Jamestown Narratives: Eyewitness Accounts of the Virginia Colony: The First Decade: 1607–1617.* Champlain, VA: RoundHouse, 1998.

Harrison, Fairfax. *Virginia Land Grants: A Study of Conveyancing in Relation to Colonial Politics.* Richmond, VA: Old Dominion Press, 1925.

Hatfield, April Lee. *Atlantic Virginia: Intercolonial Relations in the Seventeenth Century.* Philadelphia: University of Pennsylvania Press, 2004.

Haynie, W. Preston. *Records of Indentured Servants and of Certificates for Land, Northumberland County, Virginia, 1650–1795.* Bowie, MD: Heritage Books, 1996.

Hicks, Robert D. *Voyage to Jamestown: Practical Navigation in the Age of Discovery.* Annapolis, MD: Naval Institute Press, 2011.

Hopkins, William Lindsay. *Virginia Revolutionary War Land Grant Claims, 1783–1850.* Richmond, VA, 1988.

Horn, James. *Adapting to a New World: English Society in the Seventeenth-Century Chesapeake.* Chapel Hill, NC: University of North Carolina Press for the Omohundro Institute of Early American History and Culture, Williamsburg, Virginia, 1994.

Howe, Octavius Thorndike. *Beverly Privateers in the American Revolution.* Cambridge, MA: The University Press, 1922.

Hunt, L. Roane. *Tax Records of Gloucester County, Virginia.* Vol. 1, *1782–1791.* Gloucester County, VA: Gloucester Genealogical Society of Virginia, 2011.

Johnson, Walter C. C., ed. *Historic Buildings in Middlesex County, Virginia, 1650–1875.* Charlotte, NC: Delmar, 1978.

Kimball, Hoke P., and Bruce Henson. *Governor's Houses and State Houses of British Colonial America, 1607–1783: An Historical, Architectural and Archaeological Survey.* Jefferson, NC: McFarland, 2017.

Lavery, Brian. *The Colonial Merchantman* Susan Constant, *1605.* London: Conway Maritime Press, 1988.

Lavery, Brian. *The Ship of the Line.* Vol. 1, *1650–1850.* London: Conway Maritime Press, 1983.

Lavery, Brian. *The Ship of the Line.* Vol. 2, *Design, Construction and Fittings.* London: Conway Maritime Press, 1983.

Lavery, Brian, and Geoff Hunt. *The Frigate Surprise: The Complete Story of the Ship Made Famous in the Novels of Patrick O'Brian.* New York: W. W. Norton, 2008.

Lender, Mark Edward, and James Kirby Martin. "A Traitor's Epiphany: Benedict Arnold in Virginia and His Quest for Reconciliation." *Virginia Magazine of History and Biography* 125, no. 4 (2017): 314–357.

Lewis, Sara E. *Mathews County.* Images of America. Charleston, SC: Arcadia, 2007.

Lutz, Lara L., Martin D. Gallivan, Edwin Randolph Turner, David A. Brown, Thane Harpole, and Danielle Moretti-Langholtz. *Virginia Indians at Werowocomoco.* Richmond: Virginia Department of Historic Resources, 2015.

*Magazine of Virginia Genealogy* 47, no. 2 (May 2009).

Marquardt, Karl Heinz. *Captain Cook's* Endeavour. London: Conway Maritime Press, 1995.

Martin, Joseph. *A New and Comprehensive Gazetteer of Virginia, and the District of Columbia.* Charlottesville, VA, 1835.

Mason, Polly Cary, comp. *Records of Colonial Gloucester County, Virginia: A Collection of Abstracts from Original Documents Concerning the Lands and People of Colonial Gloucester County.* 2 vols. Baltimore, MD: Clearfield, 2003; originally published 1946.

Matheny, Emma R., and Helen K. Yates, comps. *Kingston Parish Register, Gloucester and Mathews Counties, 1749–1827.* Richmond, VA, 1963.

Mathews County Historical Society. *Mathews County Panorama: A Pictorial History of Mathews County, Virginia, 1791–1941.* Mathews, VA: Mathews County Historical Society, 1983.

McCartney, Martha W. *Kingston Parish Register: Mathews, Gloucester and Middlesex Counties, Virginia: Slaves and Slaveholders, 1746–1827.* Baltimore, MD: Genealogical Publishing Company, 2014.

McCartney, Martha W. *Mathews County, Virginia: Lost Landscapes, Untold Stories.* Mathews, VA: Mathews County Historical Society, [2015].

McKay, John, and Ron Coleman. *The 24-Gun Frigate* Pandora, *1779.* London: Conway Maritime Press, 1992.

Middleton, Arthur Pierce. *Tobacco Coast: A Maritime History of Chesapeake Bay in the Colonial Era.* Baltimore, MD: Johns Hopkins University Press, 1984; originally published 1953.

Morgan, Edmund S. *American Slavery, American Freedom.* New York: W. W. Norton, 1975.

Morgan, Edmund S. "Headrights and Head Counts: A Review Article." *Virginia Magazine of History and Biography* 80, no. 3, part 1 (July 1972): 361–371.

*Naval Documents of the American Revolution.* 12 vols. Edited by William Bell Clark, William James Morgan, William Dudley, and Michael J. Crawford. Washington, DC: Naval History

Division/Naval History and Heritage Command, Department of the Navy, 1964–2014. All volumes are available online at history.navy.mil.

Nelson, James L. *George Washington's Secret Navy: How the American Revolution Went to Sea.* New York: McGraw-Hill, 2008.

Nugent, Nell Marion. *Cavaliers and Pioneers: Abstracts of Virginia Land Patents and Grants.* Vol. 1, *1623–1666.* Richmond, VA: Library of Virginia, 1934.

Nugent, Nell Marion. *Cavaliers and Pioneers: Abstracts of Virginia Land Patents and Grants.* Vol. 2, *1666–1695.* Richmond, VA: Virginia State Library, 1977.

Nugent, Nell Marion. *Cavaliers and Pioneers: Abstracts of Virginia Land Patents and Grants.* Vol. 3, *1695–1732.* Richmond, VA: Virginia State Library, 1979.

Paine, Ralph D. *The Ships and Sailors of Old Salem: The Record of a Brilliant Era of American Achievement.* New York: Outing Publishing, 1909.

Phillips, James Duncan. *Salem and the Indies: The Story of the Great Commercial Era of the City.* Boston: Houghton Mifflin, 1947.

Phillips, James Duncan. *Salem in the Eighteenth Century.* Boston: Houghton Mifflin, 1937.

Proulx, Gilles. *Between France and New France: Life Aboard the Tall Sailing Ships.* Toronto, CAN: Dundurn Press 1984.

Robins, Robert W. *The Register of Abingdon Parish, Gloucester County, Virginia, 1677–1780.* Arlington, VA: Honford House, 1981.

Robinson, W. Stitt, Jr. *Mother Earth: Land Grants in Virginia, 1607–1699.* Williamsburg, VA: Virginia 350th Anniversary Celebration Corporation, 1957.

Rountree, Helen C., Wayne E. Clark, and Kent Mountford. *John Smith's Chesapeake Voyages, 1607–1609.* Charlottesville, VA: University of Virginia Press, 2008.

Rutman, Darrett B., and Anita H. Rutman. *A Place in Time: Middlesex County, Virginia, 1650–1750.* New York: W. W. Norton, 1984.

Schreiner-Yantis, Netti, and Florence Love. *The 1787 Census of Virginia.* Vol. 2. Springfield, VA: Genealogical Books in Print, 1987.

Selby, John E. *The Revolution in Virginia, 1775–1783.* Williamsburg, VA: Colonial Williamsburg Foundation, 1988.

Smith, Abbott Emerson. *Colonists in Bondage: White Servitude and Convict Labor in America, 1607–1776.* Chapel Hill, NC: University of North Carolina Press for the Institute of Early American History and Culture, Williamsburg, Virginia, 1947.

Southern, Ed, ed. *The Jamestown Adventure: Accounts of the Virginia Colony, 1605–1614.* Winston-Salem, NC: John F. Blair, 2004.

Stewart, Robert Armistead. *The History of Virginia's Navy of the Revolution.* [Richmond, VA: Mitchell & Hotchkiss Printers, 1934].

Tate, Thad W., and David L. Ammerman, eds. *The Chesapeake in the Seventeenth Century: Essays on Anglo-American Society.* New York: W. W. Norton, 1979.

Tormey, James. *The Virginia Navy in the Revolution: Hampton's Commodore James Barron and His Fleet.* Charleston, SC: History Press, 2016.

Vale, Brian. *A Frigate of King George: Life and Duty on a British Man-of-War, 1807–1829.* London: I. B. Tauris, 2001.

Virginia Genealogical Society. *Some Marriages in the Burned Records Counties of Virginia.* Richmond, VA: Virginia Genealogical Society, 1972.

*Virginia Magazine of History and Biography* 117, no. 2 (2009).

Ward, Roger G. *1815 Directory of Virginia Landowners and Gazetteer.* Vol. 1, *Eastern Region.* Athens, GA: New Papyrus, 2007.

Wertenbaker, Thomas J. *The Planters of Colonial Virginia.* Princeton, NJ: Princeton University Press, 1922.

White, David. *The Frigate Diana.* London: Conway Maritime Press, 1987.

Wilbur, C. Keith. *Home Building and Woodworking in Colonial America.* Guilford, CT: Globe Pequot, 1992.

Willis, Sam. *The Struggle for Sea Power: A Naval History of the American Revolution.* New York: W. W. Norton, 2015.

Wilson, Samuel M. *Virginia Revolutionary Land Bounty Warrants.* Baltimore, MD: Southern Book, 1953.

Winfield, Rif. *British Warships in the Age of Sail, 1714–1792: Design, Construction, Careers and Fates.* Barnsley, South Yorkshire, GB: Seaforth Publishing, 2007.

Woodson, Robert F., and Isobel B. Woodson, comps. *Virginia Tithables from Burned Record Counties.* Easley, SC: Southern Historical Press, 1982; originally published 1970.

Wooldridge, William C. *Mapping Virginia: From the Age of Exploration to the Civil War.* Charlottesville, VA: University of Virginia Press, 2012.

Wrike, Peter Jennings. *The Governors' Island: Gwynn's Island, Virginia, during the Revolution.* Richmond, VA: Brandylane, 1993.

Wrike, Peter Jennings. "Mathews County Shipbuilding Patterns 1780–1860." Master's thesis, Old Dominion University, Norfolk, VA, 1990.

Wyld, Samuel. *The Practical Surveyor.* Edited by David Manthey. Woodbridge, VA: Invisible College Press, 2001. First published 1725, London.

# INDEX

# ABOUT THE AUTHOR

Conrad Mercer Hall is a lifelong resident of Norfolk, Virginia. When Hall was in his early teens, his father bought a small farm on Billups Creek in Mathews County, and for more than forty years his family spent many summers and weekends living in an old house surrounded by fields and woods. He learned something of life in the country by helping neighborhood farmers bring in the hay in early September, tending cows and horses, helping build a barn, and exploring the countryside on horseback along dirt roads. He has vivid memories of old men during the summer sitting on the porch of the Moon post office and general store, smoking their pipes and telling stories, and of the same men gathered around a potbellied stove in winter while Mr. Sadler, the postmaster, greeted each neighbor as they came in for mail and provisions. Many hours were spent in the creek fishing and crabbing in an old wooden rowboat that constantly leaked and exploring Milford Haven and Gwynn's Island at the Hole in the Wall. He recalls the sounds of whip-poor-wills in the evening and the muffled engine in Mr. Morgan's dead rise as he would head down the creek at dawn for a day of fishing in the bay.

Hall earned a BS degree from Virginia Military Institute and served as an artillery officer in the United States Army, including duty with the Eighth Army in the Republic of Korea. He received an MBA from the Darden School of Business at the University of Virginia and has an honorary doctoral degree in humane letters from Old Dominion University. He retired as the CEO of Dominion Enterprises after a forty-year career in the media and information services industries.

In recent years, he has served on the boards of the Children's Hospital of the King's Daughters, the Mariners' Museum, and the VMI Foundation and as a member of the board of visitors of Old Dominion University. He currently serves on the boards of Dollar Tree Stores, Landmark Media Enterprises, the Slover Library Foundation, the Virginia Historical Society, the Colonial Williamsburg Foundation, ACCESS College Foundation, and Norfolk Academy, and he is a member of the board of visitors of Virginia Military Institute.

## *NOTE TAKING*

# *NOTE TAKING*

# NOTE TAKING

# *NOTE TAKING*

# *NOTE TAKING*